ET   33985

W9-CIK-142

UNIVERSITIES
in the
URBAN CRISIS

UNIVERSITIES
in the
URBAN CRISIS

Thomas P. Murphy, Editor

FOREWORD BY MANCUR OLSON

DUNELLEN PUBLISHING COMPANY, INC.
NEW YORK • LONDON

033985

Copyright © 1975 by the Dunellen Publishing Company, Inc.
and Kennikat Press Corp.

All rights reserved. No part of this book may be used or repro-
duced in any manner whatsoever without written permission
except in the case of brief quotations embodied in critical articles and reviews.

International Standard Book Number 0-8046-7081-1
Library of Congress Catalog Card Number 73-89069
Printed in the United States of America.

Distributed by Kennikat Press
90 So. Bayles Ave.
Port Washington, N.Y. 11050

Contents

v

033985

Part our. INTERNAL DYNAMICS AND THE FUTURE OF URBAN HIGHER EDUCATION

Foreword

We can learn a good deal about how many types of institutions respond to changing conditions by asking how a given change affects the needs or wants of the institutions' clients. If, for example, we want to know how corporations or other firms alter their mix outputs when a large part of a nation's population moves from rural to urban areas, we can predict that the increasing urban population's needs for additional stores and houses in the urban areas, or for furniture that will fit into apartments, will bring about a change in what the firms in the economy produce. There is no suggestion here that the process by which firms in the market react to changes in demand is ideal, or necessarily even satisfactory. The point is only that there is some prompt and direct reaction to the changes in customers' wants; the new housing tends to be built in the areas to which people are moving, not in those they are leaving; a larger share of manufacturers' outputs goes to stores in the areas of growing population and a smaller share to those of declining population.

Similarly banal and indisputable observations apply to any governments that we would agree are democratic. If large numbers of black Americans migrate from the rural South to the nation's great central cities, and bring distinct demands for representation and public services with them, it is not surprising that the style of city governments, and the complexion of city councils or on occasion even Mayors, should change. Similarly, if anything should exacerbate racist feelings against Blacks, that too would be likely to have its impact on the character of urban government. Few things could be more absurd than to idealize the governmental process in most American cities, yet the special difficulties of minorities under majority rule, and the legendary venality and ineptness of the governments in many cities, should not obscure the reality that democratic governments cannot continue to ignore substantial changes in the wants of their constituents.

Now let's look at the colleges and universities and ask how they respond to changes in their client's needs. It is not even clear what clients institutions of higher learning are supposed to please, much less how they respond, if at all, to changes in their demands. This is true whether these demands grow out of the process of urbanization or some other change of circumstances. Are the clients state or city governments and their citizenries? Or alumni? Or private donors? Or students? Or federal agencies or foundations providing research grants? In the language of multiple choice exams, the answer might be "all of the above" or perhaps "none of the above," but it could not be correct, for most American institutions of higher learning, to single out any one of the foregoing clients for exclusive consideration. It is this fact, and more importantly the university's limited responses to changes in any or all of its clients' demands, that seems to me largely to explain the university's spastic response to our society's changing urban problems.

I

Consider first the state, city, or other local government as client. By far the largest part of the budgets of the public institutions that educate most of the college students comes from a state or local government, so that, if he who pays the piper really calls the tune, these governments or their citizens would seem to be clients who could demand responsiveness. Yet usually for very good reasons, state colleges and universities are fairly well insulated against at least quick changes in the demands of a state or local political system. Characteristically, a state college or university will be legally under the control of a board of regents or trustees whose members are appointed at different times for long terms, sometimes in conditions which insure that distiguished citizens from the private sector, rather than politicians adept at discussing changes in popular mood, are selected. The arrangement is normally designed to "keep politics out of higher education." I personally support the continuance and probably even the extension of this insulation of higher education from the vicissitudes of partisan politics, but this insulation limits the responsiveness of higher education to the needs that find expression through the democratic process.

It is true that state governments directly control the budgets of state colleges and universities and can thereby exercise some control, whatever the views of the regents. But the state government that reduces the budget of a university system will find that it is forcing families in the state to send their children elsewhere. Since most states have been charging far higher tuition to out-of-state students, or even denying them admission, the state government is not really free to dictate its will to an established university through the appropriation process. A state legislature can typically eliminate a given item or departmental appropriation in a university budget without depriving its citizens of access to higher education, but heavy-handed efforts to control higher education in this way can invite censorship from the American Association of University Professors or occasionally even a possible loss of accreditation. The upshot of all this is that American society has to some degree succeeded in placing higher education "above politics," but that even those of us who think this is a very good thing must concede that the democratic process is not able to insure that the university is responsive to changing needs (nor even capable of holding colleges and universities accountable for the effective and economical performance of their duties).

In some respects, of course, this lack of responsiveness has been desirable. It has made it possible for universities to make the contributions to pure science and high culture that I believe are of surpassing importance. But to say that a lack of responsiveness has brought advantages as well as disadvantages is not to say that the situation is not in need of improvement. There are ways in which it would be possible to get both better pure research and more responsiveness.

II

If the state and local governments are not the clients who can claim ready responses, what about the students? For some private institutions without significant endowments, the students (or their tuition-paying parents) are indeed the clients. And these institutions are, at least, in these depressed days for higher education ,as responsive as could be wished: They have to be responsive to survive.

The public institutions and the well-endowed private institutions must sometimes also respond to student demands, since tuition income, even if only a secondary source of support, cannot be ignored. Still, the aforementioned discrimination against out-of-state students by public institutions, and the accumulated endowments and prestige of the most illustrious private institutions, make it a near certainty that these institutions can get their share of students even if they are not very responsive to student demands. In an educational system in which large numbers of institutions competed on an equal basis, the unresponsive or inefficient institution could lose all its students, but the American system of higher education is set up in such a way that the competition at the undergraduate level is strikingly limited by state boundaries and perhaps also by a parent's loyalties to an *alma mater.*

This lack of competition among institutions is particularly important where students from low income families are concerned. Whereas the student from an upper middle or upper income family can often choose among a variety of high tuition private colleges and is similarly able to afford out-of-state tuition at distant public universities, the student from a poor family must usually choose a nearby public institution whether he likes that institution or not. This particular disadvantage for the student of slender means is a result of the particular method by which our society supports higher education—a method that I think would appear a bit strange were it not so familiar.

Instead of supporting college students whose education is deemed to be in the public interest and who could or would not pay the cost of this education on their own, we mainly support instead certain institutions, namely those that have been "established" by the state or city government. Because these public institutions are substantially subsidized, their tuition charges will normally cover only, say, a fifth or a third of the full cost of the educational services these institutions provide. This means that any student who attends the public institution in his jurisdiction gets a substantial subsidy even if his parents are prosperous and his additional income as a result of the education would be more than sufficient to cover the full cost plus interest of his higher education. Since most of those who read these pages are or have been (as I have) the recipients of such subsidies, or expect probably to benefit from such subsidies when their children enter college (as I do), this subsidy is not likely to provoke much outrage among the middle class.

Yet everyone can on reflection appreciate the weirdness of the distributional impact of this system for supporting higher education on those at the bottom of the income distribution. The poor student without access to a scholarship finds that to enter the state university he must pay a tuition charge which, while only a fraction of the full cost of the instruction he would receive, may be significant in relation to his resources. In addition he must pay some room, board, and/or transportation expenses, and in addition forego the income he could earn if he doesn't try a higher education. If we arbitrarily set the amount of earnings foregone at $3,500 a year, and tuition and room and board costs at $1,500 a year, a four-year degree at a state university could cost a student or his parents $20,000. If this $20,000 can be afforded, but not otherwise, the state gives the student a subsidy which could have a decisive effect on the student's lifetime income. In short, if you already have some resources, you get a substantial public subsidy, whereas if you are too poor to pay the private costs, you get nothing at all. The system has more than a little in common with the practices in pre-revolutionary France by which some prosperous families could use their wealth or position to obtain a noble status that exempted them from taxation.

Some critics may object that there are some other types of programs designed particularly to help the poor and that the middle and upper classes tend to pay, in absolute terms, larger taxes, so the fact that public subsidies to higher education (as well as most donations to private universities) have a regressive effect on the income distribution is not objectionable. Whether public policy ought on balance help low income groups or middle and upper income groups more is a moral or ideological question that is much too broad to go into here. Yet the point remains that, even if public policy on balance should give a greater weight to the interests of middle and upper income groups, the present system of subsidizing higher education would not be close to optimal. Surely it is not wise to use higher education as the mechanism to keep the income distribution from becoming more nearly equal than some would want it to be. That reduces *opportunity* for low income groups, and even most who want inequality of *results* want as much equality of opportunity as is feasible. Moreover, the system of subsidizing those who can finance part of the costs themselves, but not others, could lead to an inefficiently small provision of higher education to those from low income groups, or an inefficiently large provision of education to the upper income groups, or both. It is surely significant that Project Talent data, for example, have shown that even after the positive correlation between social class and IQ is eliminated by comparing groups of equal academic aptitude, young people from low status families have been much less likely than those from high status families to go to college.

Another reason why the subsidized-tuition-but-few-scholarships system should not appeal even to those who oppose egalitarian policies is that it makes universities less responsive to potential students from low income families. These potential students are less likely, for financial reasons among others, to show up at the admissions office, and those that do, because they have few if any viable alternatives, are more nearly captive patrons of the institution they attend. The colleges and universities have accordingly had less incentive to use their most creative talent and their reserves of energy to meet the needs of the disadvantaged student.

Given the attenuated character of the democratic procedures and market forces that might make colleges and universities responsive to what we loosely call the "urban crisis," it is especially important that faculty and administrators go out of their way to think through and develop policies that would make their institutions more useful to a society beset by urban problems. It is particularly for that reason that I believe it is so fortunate that my colleague Thomas Murphy and his co-authors and contributors have written this book. It deals most usefully with an area that has not only been given far too little attention by previous writers, but which (if the foregoing argument is correct) is in danger of continuing neglect. It is in those areas where the institutions do not compel responsiveness that we are most in need of the type of initiative that led to this book.

III

We must now face up honestly to the considerable advantages of the limited responsiveness of our system of higher education. The lack of responsiveness has surely made possible more scientific research, scholarly publication, disciplinary advance, and more exacting academic standards, in any event, at the graduate level. It has done this, in my opinion, because state and local governments, the main source of support for higher education, have very little reason to support basic research and even higher level graduate education. The reason is that the benefits of basic or unpatentable research are diffused throughout the world, so that the individual jurisdiction will get only a small part of the benefit of any discoveries it finances. As Murphy's quotation from Norton Long in the last chapter of this book puts it, universities in this respect "serve the whole world in general and do not serve anyone in particular." If an (unpatentable) cure for some diseases were discovered in a typical state university, the taxpayers in that state who have the disease would be among the beneficiaries. For that reason, as well as the enormously important complementarity between research and teaching, the state will probably be willing to spend something on basic research. Yet, since the state may contain only, say, two percent of the nation's population and income, and only a negligible part of the world's population and income, it will probably get less than one percent of the total benefits of the discoveries it pays for. It won't do to say that the state in turn gets the benefits of discoveries elsewhere: It would have got these whether it spent anything on pure research or not.

Basic research, then, is what in my field of economics is called a "public good," and it has been demonstrated that optimal amounts of such goods will not be supplied by independent jurisdictions acting in their self-interest, if the citizens of each jurisdiction get only a small fraction of the benefit of their expenditure on the good. The validity and applicability of this model have been demonstrated by Bruce Russett and Leon

Sullivan,[1] who found that for the member nations of the Organization of Economic Cooperation and Development, the model's [2] prediction that the smaller nations, who would get a smaller fraction of the benefits of any unpatentable research they financed, systematically spent a smaller *percentage* of their national income on research.[3] Individual students are of course even less likely to want voluntarily to support any pure research beyond that which is necessary to give them up-to-date teaching, through tuition, since the individual student will get only an infinitesimal share of the benefit of any scientific advance he might finance.

If state or local governments and individual students have no incentive to support any pure research beyond that required for good teaching, how can the widespread existence of "publish or perish" policies be explained? Why are there so many complaints that at least the major state universities give too much attention to research and too little to undergraduate teaching? One reason is that the contribution that research makes to good, up-to-date teaching is often not understood, but that is not a sufficient explanation. Another reason is that most university faculties, as I have argued, do not have to be very responsive to the governments (or alumni) who support them, and provide more research than those who pay their salaries would like to buy. Thus, ironically, one problem has *partly* offset another: The unresponsiveness that has limited the universities' contributions to urban problems has *partly* compensated for the fact that state and local governments have an incentive to support only a modest amount of research.

IV

This leaves the problem of responsiveness unsolved; though the unresponsiveness helps solve the problems that arise from the fact that jurisdictions that finance universities are too small to "internalize" the benefits of research, the dis-

1 *International Organization,* XXV, No. 4, 1971.
2 Set out in my *Logic of Collective Action* (Cambridge: Harvard University Press, 1965, 1971) and in Olson and Zeckhauser, "An Economic Theory of Alliances." *Review of Economics and Statistics.* XLVIII (August 1966), 266–279.
3 The R^2 between national income and percent of national output spent on defense was .88.

ciplinary and national or world-wide orientation that is associated with the research does not meet the need for responsiveness to the needs of cities and the potential students they contain. Worse still, to increase responsiveness without making other changes at the same time would endanger our society's main sources of research and high culture. To make universities more directly beholden to the governments that support them, or even the students they train, could merely trade one problem for another.

It would seem that a pair of simultaneous changes is needed. One would be to shift the emphasis in the direction of aid to students, so that prospective students from low income families have equal access to higher education, and to reduce the "tariff" barriers that make it difficult for many students to go to public institutions in other states. Ultimately, this would mean that institutions would obtain more of their resources from tuition, especially tuition payments by subsidized low income students and others with a wider variety of institutions to choose from. This would surely make institutions a bit more responsive to the poor student and the urban crisis; those institutions that remained unresponsive would in any case decline in relation to those that were.

At the same time federal (and ideally even international) sources would have to provide more funding for research, lest the immediate concern for students the foregoing policy would encourage should impair the university's indispensable research function. There would need to be a plurality of national level sources of research funds lest the policies of any one agency limit the variety of approaches to research problems, but it should not be beyond the wit of man to work out pluralistic national level mechanisms for funding research. If universities were more dependent on students for their costs of instruction, and accountable to research agencies for the quality and quantity of research they did, we might get both better teaching and better research. In any event, universities would be paid for what they were *supposed* to do, and by sources which had an interest in how well they did it, and this greater degree of directness and accountability could only be wholesome.

To be sure, the changes just set out are a long way off, if they will ever be attained. Even though the current trend of policy suggests gradual shifts in the direction I recommend, it would be politically naive to suppose that the universities will be given a powerful incentive to be responsive anytime soon, and that if they are it will be without cost to the level of pure science and high culture. In the meanwhile, what we need to do is more of what Tom Murphy and his fellow contributors to the following book have done: supply the initiative and public spirit that will make the universities better citizens of our urban society than they are forced to be.

MANCUR OLSON

Preface

The demands being placed upon the modern urban university are a far cry from the role and pressures previously felt by the traditional private college or the large state university. The constituency of the urban university is different. Not only is there a heavy emphasis on college attendance by students who traditionally would not have been admitted, and many of whom have cultural deprivations, which complicate both their task and that of the university, but also the urban university is expected to relate in some special ways to the urban community in which it is located. This means additional demands in terms of adult education and community service programs.

The elected public officials of the city and state government require much more response from and exert many more pressures on the system than even the stereotyped alumnus of the old university threatening to reduce the size of his annual donation unless the football coach is fired. This should not be surprising. The percentage of students in *public* institutions of higher education has doubled in the last decade. Public appropriations have made this possible, and legislators are being pressured to insist on more accountability from the colleges.

The urban university operates in a whole new ball game. The student body is not only more diverse but also more demanding. Students no longer quietly accept a full diet of large lecture classes taught in some cases by hapless graduate assistants. There are continuous pressures for more involvement in off-campus field experiences and formal internship programs that are closer to the world of action and therefore of more interest to students trying to be "relevant."

What is an urban university? This is a much more difficult question than it might appear to be. Although it is easy to exclude from the definition universities and colleges located in rural areas, it is a mistake to include all those colleges and universities located within the boundaries of a central city: The essence of the urban university is not in its geography but in the way it responds to its urban environment.

Some urban universities are *not* accepting the challenge of urban service programs, adult education programs, open admissions, the university without walls, internships, and student responsibility and participation in deciding what is "relevant." In many cases, the failure of a university in an urban area to become a true urban university may be blamed on the administration. In a far greater percentage of cases, however, the dragging feet belong to faculty members. In most universities the faculty, especially the good faculty, is both underpaid and underworked. A trade-off is reached wherein the faculty members teach a limited number of courses, receive relatively low salaries, and make up the difference with outside consulting work. This explains why few faculty members respond to the call to engage in urban service activities. It also means that when the administration tries to take the lead in organizing new urban academic and research programs, the faculty will frequently drag out the proceedings and delay the new programs as long as possible. Part of this response is simply economic: In days of shrinking budgets, the faculty members located in traditional university departments do not want to see new programs develop, which can only drain scarce resources away from their own departments and out of their own paychecks.

Yet the challenge of the urban universities must be met. A whole new generation of Americans must be given the opportunity for higher education. Urban universities are the only institutions in a position to do this effectively. Poor students who can seldom afford to go away to college need a school in their own city so that they can live at home, ride public transportation, and find part-time employment.

Faculty members will have to change their ways if the urban university is to succeed, but the reward for doing so will be job satisfaction far beyond any currently being experienced. Fortunately, faculty members and administrators do exist who higher education. True, their task will not be an easy one, but want to provide this kind of positive leadership for urban they will never have to worry about being needed.

A variety of factors has accounted for the current crisis in which urban universities find themselves. The temper of the times, the impact of war on college students, the civil rights movement, the women's liberation movement, and the absence of long-standing university-city cooperation have all contributed. So has the migration of middle-class families to the suburbs, which has created economic and racial disparities between the city and its environs.

The federal government is only now becoming involved in significant ways. And although the government lacks a specific federal urban higher education policy, precedents do exist in the form of the Morrill Act and the G.I. Bill. The need is critical not only for money but also for some federally-sponsored research on improved education techniques and innovative ways of educating the youths who are knocking at the doors of urban institutions.

The authors contributing to this book have all had a deep and personal involvement with urban universities as administrators, faculty, and students. Their message and that of the students whose attitudes they often champion should interest all who are concerned about the emerging patterns in urban higher education. It is hoped that this book will fill an existing gap in the literature on this increasingly crucial subject.

In addition to the contributing authors, a project of this scale necessarily involves additional assistance. Special appreciation is expressed, therefore, to my graduate assistants at the University of Maryland—Thomas Chase, Larry Duzor, Sandra R. Huff, Robert Kline, and Michael Krause. Typing and secretarial work related to preparation of the manuscript were performed by Christine M. Hollowej, Rosemary Minni, Willette L. Oliver, Jackie Sanders, Charles M. Stokes, Jr., La Sharn Tucker, Carol Uhler, Gloria W. Waesche, and Evelyn S. Yenias.

Because my chapters were written primarily on Saturdays and Sundays, I need once again to thank my wife, Marcella, and our children—Kevin, Mike, Tom, Dolores, and Danny—for cooperating in making my time available for the purpose.

UNIVERSITIES
in the
URBAN CRISIS

PART ONE

Universities and Government

1

IS THE UNIVERSITY SUPERFLUOUS IN THE URBAN CRISIS?

Samuel C. Jackson

Is the university superfluous in the urban crisis? First, let us consider: Is there really an "urban crisis"? Some university sources seem to think not. They point to a reduction in substandard housing and in the number of officially-defined poor people, and even to a decline in urban travel time. But these relative improvements provide little solace to those hopelessly trapped at the bottom of the economic and housing totem poles, or to the harried commuter who still wastes two precious hours daily traveling to and from his place of employment. Nor do the following facts provide much comfort to the Secretary of the Department of Housing and Urban Development (HUD):

—At least 100,000 housing units have been abandoned in New York City. In the next few years, the federal government may have more than 240,000 subsidized home ownership units in default and with little resale value except at catastrophic levels of loss.

3

—Tangible evidence exists of a widening gap between the rich and the poor. According to economists at the Massachusetts Institute of Technology, the income gap between the poorest one-fifth and the richest one-fifth has nearly doubled during the past 20 years.

—No real lessening is apparent in the polarization of the races in urban regions. The proportion of blacks in the suburbs, 5 percent in 1960, was still only 5 percent in 1970, although the black population of the inner city rose from 16 to 21 percent.

—Urban ghettos still fester with unfulfilled aspirations fanned by hopelessness and frustration.

No one can prove that these and other realities add up to a "crisis," but in my judgment, they do. Perhaps we could agree that, at the very least, there is an urban problem. I am reminded of a definition of "urban problem" suggested by James Kalish in his account of the "flim-flam of the urban-problems industry":

> In short, an urban problem is anything that has happened, could happen, or should happen, in a city, a suburb, or a metropolitan area. In addition, it is sometimes something that hasn't happened, isn't happening, couldn't happen, and shouldn't happen in a city, a suburb, a metropolitan area, or anywhere else. . . .[1]

Members of the "urban-problems industry" view the problems from different perspectives and perhaps differing interests. In order to give some structure to what follows, I consider my vantage point to be that of a federal policy-maker and yours (unless you are an "interested" lay reader) to be that representing three basic functions of a university:

—to educate its student body
—to participate in the affairs of the community
—to perform research

I've probably oversimplified these functions—certainly there are others not covered here—but these are basic.

Educating the Student Body

Although those of us in the federal government who have something to do with funding university research sometimes think that the average professor must spend most of his time in developing research proposals and hunting down grants for them, I would suppose that the basic function of the university is to teach. And the measure of the university's relevance to the urban crisis is whether it equips its students with the tools and desire to effectively help in the crusade for a better environment and an improved community life for all citizens.

It seems to me that the urban university has done rather well in changing its curriculum in response to shifting approaches in treating our urban ills. Thus, beginning in the late fifties, the design and management orientation of the postwar years has been enriched with a heavy dose of the social sciences. Nourished by the social zeal of the war on poverty, it reached a zenith of social responsiveness after the urban and student disorders of the late sixties.

Systems analysis, model building, and computer sciences were added to the educational mix during the sixties, and, if I read the Jay Forresters correctly, may dominate urban education of the near future, with a heavy lacing of environment and ecology. Indeed, the educators may become more concerned about the survival of man than of his cities as such.

Although their footwork seems to be able to keep up with the times, I am not certain whether universities lead in the shifts or merely respond to outside pressures. I do not really know, for example, who can claim credit for stimulating human concerns in the universities that formerly graduated generations of city planners who thought slums were simply expendable impediments to good urban design. I suspect that the awakening social conscience of the college establishment is more the product of recent student disorders than of any self-introspection. Thus, co-ed dorms can be looked upon as merely internal signs of the humanization of the college establishment in response to the changing social values in a youth-oriented society.

And this is essentially a good thing. For too long, college graduates were essentially highly trained technicians with scant understanding of the human elements that are interwoven in any work situation, whether it is running a business or city hall or urban renewal projects.

To continue along this line, two of the basic human causes—or perhaps the effects—of the "urban crisis" come under the headings of *race* and *poverty*. And I doubt that anyone, whether a Ph.D. or not, can understand these elements better than those who have lived under them—blacks, Chicanos, Indians, and the poor of all races. This argues for the universities to provide a suitable education for increasing numbers in these groups, not only because of the morality of equal opportunity in education, but also because education can unlock the dedication, forcefulness, and understanding of the urban people who suffer most from the inequities of discrimination in an urban economy.

I should note at this point that one of the problems we at HUD have been trying to help meet is the pressing need for a greater number of minority urban professionals. In 1969, there were only one black city manager and a handful of black graduate planners. That situation cannot be allowed to continue.

In this connection, it might be pertinent to note that far too many professional urban planners suffer from a basically anticity bias. Their backgrounds are, for the most part, suburban, white, and upper middle class. Their insight into the problems of the inner city is limited and largely theoretical. All of this handicaps the development of plans and programs, which should be geared to the needs and aspirations of people they know little about.

HUD is responding to this situation with two programs. First, we are assisting minority students of urban affairs through the Urban Studies Fellowship Program. This is a program authorized by Congress to provide aid to students enrolled in a full-time course of studies in accredited universities as candidates for master degrees in such fields as urban and regional planning, urban affairs, urban public administration, urban sociology, urban economics, and similar programs oriented to public service careers in urban affairs.

This program is not intended exclusively for minority participation: In 1971, fellowships went to 111 students, of whom 38 percent were minority group members. Fellows receive grants of up to $3,000 for one year of study, plus $500 for each dependent up to a total of two. A cost-of-education allowance covering tuition and fees is paid directly to institutions at which the Fellows are studying.

The second program designed to respond to the need for an educational body of minority professionals is the Comprehensive Planning Assistance Program, known in the trade as the "701 funds"; they are being used to support work-study projects in thirty states and councils of government. Each work-study project calls for a collaborative relationship between a state or local agency that is eligible to receive Planning Assistance funds and one or more universities located in the vicinity of the agency.

Each agency-university consortium is then expected to recruit a predetermined number of minority group students who are to conduct, during the academic year, a full-time academic study program at the university while working part-time (12 to 20 hours a week) at tasks to which they are assigned by the planning agency.

During summer months, the students are occupied full-time with their work assignments. The nature of the assignments, which can be performed either within or outside the agency, is determined jointly by each student, the agency, and the university. Approximately 150 graduate and undergraduate students are currently participating in the program.

A similar work-study program is operating for students of city management in cooperation with the International City Management Association.

Community Affairs

Work-study projects are one way of tying the university and the community together. We often overlook the fact that community involvement was an essential purpose of the earliest universities. In his novel, *The Masters,* C. P. Snow reflects on the role of universities in the Middle Ages:

> The medieval universities came to full existence very quickly . . . the towns which had become small and insignificant in the seventh and eighth centuries, were growing again . . . and there was a need for an educated professional class to cope with affairs that were daily growing more complex.[2]

The heritage of the early American university system, founded in large measure to provide an educated ministry for the church, perhaps progressed too far toward professionalism and away from "peopleism." An exception was the network of land-grant colleges, which has long fulfilled a strong community service function to the rural community.

The urban university, however, has more often than not represented only one-half of the "town and gown" feud and until recent years, elected officials have paid scant attention to the intellectual resources of their educational constituents. Stephen K. Bailey has expressed the common view of the elected decision-makers thus:

> The scholar lives in a strange world, and the decision-maker often treats this world with patronizing contempt —sometimes with fear. I add the "fear" because in one sense all scholars are potentially subversive.[3]

A subversive intent could well have been behind the unholy alliance between urban university administrators and urban renewal directors in pushing the "urban universities" amendment through Congress in the late fifties. This amendment to the urban renewal statute in effect decreased the local share of the cost of a renewal project whenever a nearby university expanded into adjacent lands. Thus, a renewal agency had an incentive to develop projects near colleges and they, in turn, presumed they would benefit by getting renewed land for even more expansion in addition to getting their often blighted surroundings cleared or rehabilitated. Actually, the motives behind this land-grab effort were not so much subversive, if measured by the mood of the times, as they were insensitive to the people living in their community environments.

Prodded by the strife at Columbia over the construction of a gymnasium and by the "people's park" protests at Berkeley, the universities have mended their ways and, I am glad to note, are becoming directly involved in the mini-urban crises on their doorsteps. The university no longer ignores its surroundings, nor does it try to swallow them. Many universities are making their staffs and students available as technical advisers to community groups. Some colleges have become sponsors, even owners, of housing for low-income and moderate-income families.

On April 11, 1968, the U.S. Fair Housing Law was signed, a law which many students and faculty activists helped to bring into being and which needs the continued support of the university community. This law, Title VIII of the Civil Rights Act of 1968, makes it unlawful to discriminate in the sale or rental of housing, the financing of housing, and the provision of brokerage services. In April, 1972, HUD sponsored a campaign to appeal to the American people to support equal housing opportunity. University assistance, especially in fostering stronger state and local fair housing laws, is still needed.

State and local officials may still see some of these university community activities as subversive in that they often undermine authority "to get things done." Volunteer advocacy planners supplied by universities have often led the fight against community-slashing highways; legal aid has helped community groups oppose poorly-planned renewal projects. The requirements of the National Environmental Policy Act will probably provide increased leverage for university-led community actions against capricious decisions by governmental bureaucracies.

Helping citizens fight city hall on certain issues (an essentially negative role) should in no way deter universities from the positive role of helping city hall on other issues. This role is exemplified by the Urban Observatory Program sponsored by HUD. The program was designed to establish a practical working relationship between the university, with all of its training, technical assistance, and research resources, and the city, with all of its problems and needs for study and analysis. The program helps overcome the tendency of academicians to pursue their interests without regard to the needs of the real world and corrects the tendency of city officials to concern themselves with the practical problems of the day without regard to the larger urban crisis. Urban observatories now exist in 10 cities—Albuquerque, Atlanta, Baltimore, Boston, Cleveland, Denver, Kansas City (Kansas and Missouri), Milwaukee, Nashville, and San Diego—with approximately 70 universities acting in consortia with these cities.

A staff secretariat for the observatory program has been established in the National League of Cities. This secretariat has the responsibility for providing technical assistance on local plans and the organization of the observatories. In addition to insuring that the overall research agenda is developed and that meetings are convened, it generally monitors the overall performance of the observatory network.

Research

Turning to the research function of the university, Dr. Martin Jenkins of the American Council on Education has noted (in an address on model city programs):

> The greatest resource of higher education is trained intelligence.
>
> Ask colleges and universities to do those things they can do best—activities which require a high degree of brainpower.[4]

I presume the universities' research activities epitomize their "high degree of brainpower." I think it would be appropriate to quote Walter Lippmann here because he provides a balance to Dr. Jenkins' statement. Lippmann once said:

> Because modern man in his search for truth has turned away from kings, priests, commissars and bureaucrats, he is left, for better or worse, with the professors.[5]

It is difficult for a public official to evaluate the professors in their research role because we sometimes have different interests. We search for practical solutions to immediate crises, whereas the professor tends to be more interested in longer range, more basic concerns and uses research to fill out his current publication demands. For example, the title alone of one of the observatory reports, *Framework for the Measurement of Programmatic Effectiveness,* may look fine in a professional journal, but it will hardly attract the municipal mayor with a daily crisis on his hands.

The HUD official's view of his university research projects may be slightly warped by the knowledge that he must ultimately face his congressional appropriations committee. A budding urban research program was nipped in the early 1950s when the committee began to question the value of such studies as one on "nailing techniques" and other more esoteric subjects. This was followed by more than a decade of lean years when "urban research" were dirty words in the appropriation process. And the research budget remained dry despite occasional cries on the Senate floor that the Department of Agriculture was getting more money to study pigs than the cities were getting to study people. Only in the last few years has the funding of HUD's research activities reached a reasonable level, although it is still short of what you and I might desire.

It is too easy for the bureaucrats and the professors to hurl polemics at each other over our joint research responsibilities. My staff reviews perhaps 75 research proposals annually, and they frequently complain about apparent duplication of existing knowledge—the "re-invent the wheel" problem; the failure to identify hypotheses (these are termed "fishing expeditions"); and the reluctance by the proposers to identify who would use the expected results to affect what decisions. On the professors' part, I'm sure we are sometimes looked upon as the epitome of a narrow-minded, rigid, unimaginative bureaucracy.

Standing above these polemics, however, is a need to join forces to establish some sense of common objectives and strategies in urban research. The major problem seems to be a lack of organization in the urban problems industry, a lack of direction, a lack of interdependence of research and researchers. It would seem to me that there must be a better way to focus our research and development energies on the urban crisis, and we do not need to lose the creativeness of individual research in the process. The urban problems industry is as fragmented as the metropolitan areas that harbor the problems.

Conclusions

In case it has not come through clearly in this discussion, I firmly believe that the universities are far from being superfluous to the urban crisis. They are relevant and becoming even more so. But, as the TV commercial says, I would hope that progress would be the most important product. And I would hope that in the coming years universities would concentrate on:

1. *Providing an increasing supply of educated manpower,*

manpower that is sorely needed to buttress the thin ranks of the professionals in city halls and statehouses. The Bureau of Labor Statistics has estimated that state and local government employment requirements for administrative, technical, and professional workers will number 5.5 million in 1975—or about one-fourth of all such workers in the country. This should be a tremendous challenge to the universities. I would hope, further, that universities will focus more on the educational needs of our minority citizens.

2. *Continuing to improve the university's capacity to spond to the demands of its urban communities,* to demands by activists against injustices, and to demands foı intellectual resources in the official decision-making process. The urban university has a special responsibility to show its commitment to stay in the city and to help maintain it as a vital cultural asset as well as a decent living environment.

3. *And, finally, developing a more organized approach to formulating and implementing the nation's urban research agenda,* a need that will require a joint effort of government and our educational institutions. In this regard, I note that the Council has been considering the establishment of an urban affairs clearinghouse. This is sorely needed as a step toward organizing our research activities.

A giant step forward is needed in seeking a coordinated, organized, and informed attack on the urban crisis. The stakes are too high to permit anything less. In closing, let me quote W. E. B. Du Bois on the relevance of education:

We are training not isolated men but a living group of men—nay, a group within a group. And the final product of our training must be neither a psychologist nor a brickmason, but a man. And to make men, we must have ideals, broad, pure, and inspiring ends of living, not sordid money-getting, not apples of gold. The worker must work for the glory of his handiwork, not simply for pay; the thinker must think for truth, not for fame. And all this is gained only by human strife and longing; by ceaseless training and education; by founding Right

on Righteousness, and Truth on the unhampered search
for Truth; by founding the common school on the university, and the industrial school on the common school;
and weaving thus a system, not a distortion, and bringing a birth, not an abortion.[6]

NOTES

1. James A. Kalish, "Flim-Flam, Double-Talk, and Hustle: The Urban-Problems Industry," *Washington Monthly,* November 1969, p. 7.

2. C. P. Snow, *The Masters* (New York: Scribner's,
1951 , p. 363.

3. Stephen K. Bailey et al., *Research Frontiers in Politics
and Government* (Washington, D.C.: The Brookings Institution, 1955), p. 3.

4. Martin Jenkins, "The Involvement of Colleges and
Universities in Model Cities and Community Development
Programs" (unpublished report for Model Cities, Title I—
Comprehensive Planning Conference, Kansas City, Missouri,
January 27, 1972).

5. William Trombley, "Role of Professors Cited by Lippmann," *Washington Post,* May 9, 1966.

6. W. E. B. Du Bois, *The Souls of Black Folks* (London:
Longmans, Green, 1965), p. 55.

2

THE URBAN OBSERVATORY:
A UNIVERSITY–CITY RESEARCH VENTURE

Thomas P. Murphy and James Zarnowiecki

Our cities have been in transition for decades, but too often we have not been able to measure the depth and the direction of change until damage was done. Thus, ghettos, traffic snarls, fiscal anemia, and environmental pollution have been developing for years. Unfortunately, we have never been able to do more than describe in disjointed fashion the surface manifestations of these changes. Now the combination of problems, if not each one individually, has become critical.

The Need for Systematic Urban Data

Because the science of cities must deal in large measure with human behavior, predicting the urban future is not as methodologically simple as using the telescope to study the heavens. But if it is possible to observe urban phenomena on a large enough scale, and to do so on a systematic basis with truly compatible methods, trends will be detected earlier so that solutions may be devised. The need for impact data and systematic research exists, therefore, in response to the needs of national policy formulation as well as of municipal decision-making. Many national programs intended to ameliorate urban ills have had unanticipated and deleterious side effects because of an inadequate understanding of urban conditions and the potential impact of technological, economic, social, and political phenomena.

In other fields, side effects have been anticipated through research. For example, when President Abraham Lincoln signed the Organic Act of 1862 (the Morrill Act) establishing the Department of Agriculture, the Department was given responsibility for conducting an agricultural research program. Yet a comparable federal stimulus to urban research was not provided until recent years, by which time more than a million acres of rural land were being converted to urban use each year, and when more than two out of every three Americans were living in metropolitan areas.

The Housing Act of 1949 finally provided the Housing and Home Finance Agency (HHFA) with broad authorization to conduct housing research. Under this mandate, an extensive and technologically oriented research program was conducted until 1952 when suspicion in Congress and fear in the building industry that urban research was threatening its economic future led to limitations. Four years later Congress authorized a new HHFA research program whose appropriations averaged $300,000 with a peak of $750,000 in 1966, followed by a leveling off at about $500,000 a year.

Approximately two-thirds of these funds were contracted to the Bureau of the Census for survey data on "volume of sales" and "rentals of new housing" needed for administering current programs. The remainder was used for survey projects to probe areas such as housing conditions for public services, central city functions, and the effects of industrial decentralization on metro-area residential flux. Other programs such as those conducted under Section 701 of the Revised Urban Renewal Act of 1966 provided collateral research and data sources. However, the data produced represented a static collection of fragmented knowledge not adequate for day-to-day use, much less to plan for the needs the future will impose upon the city.

The utility of research also depends, of course, on the availability of trained technical and professional people to employ these tools in an effective manner. Some effort to increase the number of such professionals was made through Title VIII of the Housing Act of 1964. However, the scope and financing were clearly inadequate. Even where sufficient specialists were trained, there was a dearth of able administrators to provide horizontal perspective and complement the vertical specialists. Without that supply of "generalist" personnel at the state and local level, "creative federalism" or the "new federalism" will not work. Only with adequate vision can the planner develop the urban program mix that the future demands.

In the final analysis, new urban technologies had to be developed. Data sources had to be made comparable, standards had to be established, and objectives had to be clarified and documented. Further, the interrelation of physical and social programs required that a successful mating of quantitative and qualitative standards be achieved.

The Urban Observatory Proposal

In 1963, Robert C. Wood, a political scientist at MIT who later became Undersecretary of the Department of Housing and Urban Development, wrote that the study of urban politics lags far behind the study of natural science phenomena in methodology, comprehensiveness, and effect.[1] Wood noted that natural scientists employ field stations, data centers, and observatories working with an agreed-upon set of tools, an accepted field of observation, and a common understanding of the phenomena to be observed. These institutions work together to build a cumulative record. He suggested that this procedure could be applied to urban research and proposed a network of "urban observatories" based upon a working partnership between universities and municipal governments.[2] He urged that they be funded to make possible a common series of investigations under a single research plan. This could provide professionally reliable findings derived from a number of areas, therein subject to analysis and application in other urban centers. Thus a research survey taken in Milwaukee would also be meaningful in San Francisco, Dallas, or Philadelphia if baseline data and comparability were insured.

In proposing the urban observatory idea, Professor Wood voiced several concerns. First, so long as complex problems exist in maintaining and improving the standards of living in our urban areas, these problems will be aggravated daily by governmental officials whose decisions are based on grossly inadequate knowledge, and whose self-confidence is primarily a product of faith or of politics rather than of analysis.

Second, we lack the proper means for evaluating the validity of these decisions. From a research point of view the billions of dollars being spent on programs, such as the social welfare programs, represent a monumental national gamble. There is no basis upon which to justify the prediction that these strategies and programs will correct the social ills at which they are directed. The absence of systematic experiments means that we shall be poorly equipped to modify our strategies in the light of experience.

Next, Wood noted that despite the absence of comprehensive research designs, a great deal of systematic research is conducted on urban problems by scholars in diverse fields such as economics, sociology, psychology, anthropology, and political science. Governmental decision-making and the research related to it, however, exist all too frequently in two separate worlds. He questioned whether society could afford that separation and suggested that one of the great challenges we face is to devise an organizational strategy for interrelating the decisions of governmental officials in urban areas and the research endeavors of relevant scholars.

The urban observatory idea was favorably received by National League of Cities (NLC) president, Mayor Henry W. Maier of Milwaukee.[3] He saw it as offering a continuing program of comparative research to provide information useful for urban decision-makers through the operation of a nationwide network of "urban observatories." Intrigued by the idea, Mayor Maier arranged to discuss it with Wood in Washington in February, 1965. Having moved from academia to the position of Undersecretary of HUD, Wood was now able to take action to implement the concept.

Maier presented the idea to an NLC executive committee meeting on March 30, 1965. Based upon a favorable reaction, urban specialists from eighteen universities were invited to Milwaukee in June, and a panel was organized to discuss a specific problem area in which comparative research would be beneficial. Maier led off with a statement of needs in the field of urban renewal. While endorsing the broad goals of the federal urban renewal program as absolutely necessary, he argued that comparative research on the legal structure of the city and local administrative machinery would be very helpful.

Mayor Jerome G. Cavanagh of Detroit commented that despite all the research being done, numerous questions remained; for example, "How many policemen should a city of our size and characteristics have? How many police departments should a county have? What is the relationship between the number of deaths by fire and fire escape requirements for dwelling units?" Mayor James H. J. Tate of Philadelphia urged that research in urban transportation was needed to stimulate more effective coordination among governmental jurisdictions in our metropolitan areas. Mayor Arthur J. Holland of Trenton, New Jersey, discussed ways in which comparative research could develop an ideal approach for determining both the types and levels of municipal services. Holland also listed municipal government structure as an area where the experiments of cities of similar size and characteristics could be helpful to communities contemplating change. Mayor Ralph S. Locher of Cleveland commented that policy decisions by mayors and city councils are no better than the information upon which those decisions are based. Intuition, a politician's sixth sense, a random sampling of opinion, and other catch-as-catch-can methods frequently result in incorrect analysis.

Mayor John C. Houlihan of Oakland, California, urged that an urban observatory system not be administered by normal university procedures. Its direction, he said, should be based on practical considerations of the greatest benefit to local public officials, with the latter determining the subject of research and with the whole network under the control of the executive committee of the National League of Cities (NLC). Clearly, he was expressing the fears of urban mayors that, left to their own devices, the universities would not produce relevant research.

At the conclusion of the meeting, the following resolution was approved:

> Be it resolved, by the Executive Committee of the National League of Cities and by urban scientists representing universities and colleges from all parts of the United States . . .

1. A concerted, coordinated effort in research and urban
   affairs, involving a guiding of resources, is needed to
   deal more efficiently with the major problems of
   urban areas;

2. A new relationship between urban decision-makers
   and universities is essential to provide the needed
   urban research as a continuing process;

3. An "urban observatory" program is endorsed in principle as an approach to such a new relationship;

4. The National League of Cities should undertake to
   serve as an integrating and stimulating force in developing research programs in cooperation with universities or regional groups of the universities designated as "urban observatories";

5. A steering committee to further these objectives is
   hereby established, to consist of representatives of the
   co-sponsors of this Milwaukee conference and such
   other persons as they might designate, such committee to meet in Washington, D.C., prior to July 1,
   1965, if possible.[4]

Mayor Maier said the Milwaukee meeting was symbolic
of two things: First, that municipal government had reached
an age when it appreciated the value and need for the application of the resources of social science; and second, that within
the academic community there was a growing realization of
both what it can offer to and what it can receive from a closer
alliance with the working levels of government.

The NLC's executive committee established a permanent
standing committee on urban observatories, with Mayor Maier
as chairman. Members of this group met in Washington, D.C.,
on June 28, 1965, with the steering committee authorized by
the Milwaukee Resolution. Besides Mr. Maier, steering com-
mittee members included Professor Robert C. Wood of HUD,
Professor Henry J. Schmandt of the University of Wisconsin–
Milwaukee, Dr. Ralph W. Conan of the Joint Center for Urban
Studies of MIT and Harvard, John E. Bebout of the Urban
Studies Center for Rutgers, and Dr. James G. Coke of the
Office of Community Development at the University of Illinois.
This group determined that the National League of Cities

should establish a permanent secretariat for the proposed net-work of urban observatories with an outstanding scholar as its director. A committee on selection was appointed to choose an initial group of cooperating universities, each working with the local mayor. A committee on finance and procedure was also appointed.

The Demonstration Cities Bill approved by the Senate on August 19, 1966 provided, under Title III, grants for what were called urban information centers. The National League of Cities had supported this proposal because it appeared that these centers could offer an opportunity to get some form of urban observatory under way with partial federal financing. The Senate bill authorized $5 million for the centers in fiscal 1967 and $10 million for fiscal 1968. However, the informa-tion center proposal was eliminated from the bill by the House Committee and was never restored in that form.[5]

Nevertheless, the Department of Housing and Urban De-velopment took several steps to promote research and program coordination on urban problems. A secretariat was established to insure that administrative decisions filtered throughout the agency. To implement the concept of a "metro desk," an urban generalist eventually was placed in every major metropolitan area to assist local governments through the HUD maze.[6] The urban observatory fits into that framework as a program of re-search related to the actual problems city decision-makers encounter.

The urban observatory was never proposed to Congress as a line item. But on July 1, 1968, HUD entered into a con-tract with the National League of Cities to begin the urban observatory program. Funds, derived from the general research and technology appropriation, totaled $2,028,000 to Decem-ber 31, 1971.

The Operational Concept and Criteria
for Selecting Cities

The next step in defining the concept was to hammer out the primary operational objectives. Three major thrusts constitute the prime mission of the urban observatory. The first is pro-viding an improved metropolitan information base, the second is the forging of a new relationship between urban decision-makers and universities, and the third, the establishment of a national network of observatories committed to a common urban-oriented research agenda.

With regard to the development of an improved metropolitan information base, it has been urged that initial observatory planning be based on a union between university and core city. However, the core city is not an island. It can no more analyze its problems and design its course of action if research is limited to its own city limits than it can stop polluted air at those limits. The information and operational base, therefore, must be at least metropolitan in its scope. This calls for cooperation by the metropolitan area local governments. Three broad categories of information are required, it seems, to build a sound metropolitan information base for the urban observatory research program: published information, printed but unpublished information, and basic data concerning urban areas. This information resides in the domain of dozens of disciplines and so is unassembled and unsynthesized..

William N. Cassella, Jr., emphasizes that "an adequate urban research library is one of the most important tools of the researcher."[7] He underscores the frustrations of urban researchers by citing the compilation of a bibliography on metropolitan communities. Researchers in New York City spent over one year going from library to library, consulting source after source in an endeavor to bring together a reasonably comprehensive bibliography. To complete their task, the researchers eventually turned to other cities whose libraries had compiled certain sections of the bibliography. The example is all too familiar.

John G. Kemeny, Robert M. Sano, Gilbert W. King, and William N. Locke have explored the possible nature of "a library for 2000 A.D." The vision is of a library of the future in which all published materials in the United States would be available from any university in the United States through a massive communication and computer system which will become, in effect, the repository of human knowledge.[8] Working from an individual terminal at any point in the United States, each researcher would have access to the entire system. Precedents include the Medical Literature Analysis and Retrieval System (MEDLARS) of the National Library of Medicine at the National Institutes of Health in Bethesda, Maryland, and the Educational Research Information Center (ERIC) established in 1964 by the Office of Education. ERIC is abstracting and indexing education-related papers to assist in information retrieval.[9]

Not only must the urban observatory provide an information base by making available information which has already been produced, it must also consider systematically defining the new information needed. Dick Netzer points out that both public decisions and urban research are virtually crippled by the current lack of data concerning our metropolitan regions.[10] The urban information base is not sufficiently comprehensive, provides incomplete geographic coverage, contains obsolete data and data that is not continuous. And the quality and reliability of much of the available data is questionable.

Netzer proposes development of a metropolitan center to provide statistical information services to a wide variety of individuals and organizations which have regular or occasional need for comprehensive, coherently organized, high quality data on the structure and status of conditions in the region and its components. The center could periodically report on the status of the region, provide statistical development and improvement work, develop a stockpile of information that is easily retrievable, and perform special studies involving quantitative research.

Howard G. Brunsman has outlined encouraging action taken to make the 1970 census more useful to researchers and governmental practitioners.[11] In large part, this was done in response to the new demands that social scientists, researchers, and administrators are making on data collectors. As the potential users become more sophisticated, the system will no doubt be further refined.

To achieve a meaningful urban observatory program will require further definition of the university–urban decision-maker relationship. Urban oriented academics should be involved in the initial planning of a problem definition and data collection system. If the data system reflects research requirements, and is not just data reporting, a clearer understanding of potential demand and information system capabilities will result.

The network idea is the third mechanism to achieve the urban observatories' cooperative action. This is a unique feature of the observatory idea. Although its implementation will be most difficult, its potential rewards are most promising. It is here that cooperation is truly critical. The proposal is that the urban observatories, together, define a set of core problems which would be used as a national agenda for urban research. Through the observatory network, researchers would be encouraged to focus their attention on that agenda. Each observatory would seek to clarify its data requirements, improve its analytical methods, sharpen alternatives, and evaluate the effects of resulting policy decisions on management actions. Obviously, any major university can structure and finance a research operation which will produce high quality results, but the centrifugal effect of the multiple observatory approach cannot be matched by unrelated operations. It would make feasible more systematic analysis than ever before.

One more item which has been discussed is whether the urban observatory should function on a demand-for-service basis. It would seem that university involvement carries with it an obligation to deal with area-wide problems. Further, the university is in a particularly favorable position to bridge the gulf that too frequently exists between independent jurisdictions in metropolitan areas. If metropolitan areas are to assume some order in the explosive years ahead, clearly they need to be vigorously engaged in defining area-wide versus jurisdictional and functional goals, in determining the policy and program alternatives which individual jurisdictions may adopt to achieve those goals, and in evaluating the impact of the choices finally made. The urban observatory could provide staff and suggest alternatives from which political choices could be made by a number of jurisdictions. Because of its university base, it might be able to do this without inviting staff interjurisdictional disputes and without threatening the integrity of local units.

The network can provide a framework for comparative studies involving application of metropolitan research methods to goal setting and policy and program choices. This assignment would give the urban observatory the appearance of an institution with a long-term mission rather than that of a fire-fighting operation. Building a common observatory mission or a common agenda must involve close cooperation between urban observatory personnel who understand research methods and public officials who must anticipate their needs for facts and policy decisions. The mechanics of network operation clearly call for a new specialization and expertise on the part of the urban observatory personnel. The entire network mechanism must be formalized, staffed, and financed. It is here that foundation or additional federal support seems essential. Municipal and university contributions would also be desirable from both a financial and commitment standpoint.

Urban research studies break down into several categories which Frank Steggert has discussed.[12] Theoretical studies attempt to verify the hypotheses which explain some aspect of the functioning systems, while applied or experimental research attempts to verify hypotheses relating ends and means. A second type of studies—developmental—is concerned with the interpretation or application of results of "basic" research to problems and specific situations. A third category of study can be called consensus-building and usually prescribes goals or standards by which the performance of public enterprise may be evaluated.

Developmental studies depend on progress made in basic theoretical and applied research. Consensus-building studies deal with problems identified by political pressures and the concerns of the professions involved. Their prescriptions are based upon assumed ends-means relationships that usually have not been systematically verified.

Wood's proposal suggested than an urban observatory program could concern itself with all three types of studies. Scholars would probably be primarily interested in basic research, or possibly in developmental studies. Most policymakers would probably be more interested in consensus-building studies because they most directly serve their short-run decision-making needs. In many cases, the policy-makers would be unaware of the factual assumptions underlying the prescriptions of consensus-building studies. Yet the degree to which their decisions achieve their objective depends ultimately upon the soundness of such assumptions.

In other words, the problem to be faced in organizing urban observatory programs is fostering a sense of mutual respect and trust among the scholars and political leaders involved. The essence of this trust is the recognition that scholars and practitioners apply quite different criteria of relevance and performance in judging the goals, organization, and operations of such a program. Another condition to keep in mind in planning for the urban observatory program is the importance of the integrated and coordinated information systems, regional and national, and the extremely complex organizational and technical problems to be faced in devising such systems.

A condition of internal political importance in devising organizational strategies for the urban observatory program is to recognize the highly decentralized and individualistic character of scholarly research. University administrators do not tell the scholar what to study or how to proceed. The scholar's choice is dictated primarily by his interest and the mores of his particular discipline, and he will usually resist bureaucratic constraints on his scholarly pursuit.

Frank Steggert, based at Georgia State University, served as coordinator of the first urban observatory national agenda study, a citizen participation survey. In commenting on the necessary institution building in current urban research,[13] Steggert raises several important questions about universities and national urban concerns, suggesting that one pitfall might be that many urban study units exist because they perform a latent function—that of providing partial protection to their parent bodies against any really salient pressures for institutional change. At least some urban study units represent attempts to experiment with structures that may suggest how the local university structure can be adapted to become more urban concerned and involved. These attempts may be tentative and sometimes less conscious than they ought to be so that universities will tend to react and not to lead. Further, the knowledge needed for large-scale university restructuring is not readily available. Similarly, institutions with different tasks and different task environments represent different degrees of concern and involvement.

From a financial standpoint, it has been projected that the urban observatory agency will probably need three basic categories of funds: an annual operating budget to support the staff and facilities of the enterprise, a specific budget allocated for the development of research proposals and designs, and project funding of the approved studies undertaken. At the same time the urban observatory ought to be independently

organized, not just a unit within one of the educational institutions of a metropolitan area.

A position paper on urban observatories could cite the following tasks and functions for an urban observatory:

1. It should serve as a collection point of basic information on urban developments. Since many gaps exist in our basic information about them, cities often know less about their local economies than they konw about the economy of the nation as a whole. Improved comparative data could help a city better realize how it fits into a regional or national economic complex.

2. The observatory should undertake policy-oriented research on selected major issues of direct concern to mayors and others on the firing line. Mayors want to know what is being tried, what is working and what isn't working in the cities, and why.

3. The observatory should set up a comparative study basis for applying new techniques to urban problems.

4. It should make studies available to local officials to help with policy decisions on such things as urban renewal, finance, taxes, and levels of service.

5. The observatory should be staffed by competent urbanists housed in urban study centers, universities, and other professional organizations concerned with urban development.

6. While data collection should be influenced by the immediate and long-range policy concerns of municipal officials, consultation and research should be on a basis which does not restrict the freedom of the scientist.

7. There should be linkage by common agreement of the research network on the types of information to be collected, and inter-communication between the observatories and municipal and federal officials to exchange information of mutual interest.[14]

Organizing the Program

Sir Patrick Geddes, an early twentieth-century British town

planner, in his book *Cities in Evolution,* called for such things as the integration of physical planning with sociology and economics, the syntheses of survey, plan and practice, and local survey and cross-city comparison as basic methodologies for a science of cities. He even mentioned "the outlook tower" which combined the notions of a civic observatory and a civic laboratory. Geddes linked the institutional structures as a correlation of "thought and action, science and practice, sociology and morals."[15]

Other contemporary analysts have emphasized other conceptual and operational facets of the new institution needed—Ralph Taylor, for example, has contended that urban research requires a new institutional technology, a new package of skills, if duplication of present situations is to be avoided.[16] Thomas Davy has pointed out that scholarly research tends to be highly decentralized and individualistic, so that the organizational level and the development of integrated and coordinated information systems involve complex technical and organizational problems requiring even greater institutional developments.[17] It would seem that as universities and cities build up a base for cooperation through the urban observatory, a new institution would come into existence. The major component of the institution building in the urban observatory would be the network-wide common research agenda.

Under the HUD contract, the National League of Cities agreed to survey and analyze relevant local conditions and capabilities and recommend candidate groups in at least six metropolitan areas as well as to provide technical assistance to university and local government officials in developing organizational and administrative arrangements, and in preparing preliminary research programs consistent with overall research agenda. NLC was to develop and submit procedures for coordinating and synthesizing the operations of six candidate observatory groups.

Suggested criteria for selecting the cities to participate included the following:

1. High interest on the part of top governing officials.

2. Evidence of research and data collection efforts by governmental agencies.

3. Interest of good university researchers.

4. Evidence of existing commitment to research on urban problems by the university.

5. Prospective stability of both governmental and university institutional arrangements so that participation would outlast particular individuals.

6. Evidence of collaboration and understanding between officials and academic people.

7. Prospective arrangements for collaborative effort, and commitment that city and intra-institutional funding devices would multiply.

8. Metropolitan dimension—the degree to which research efforts could involve the whole metropolitan region.

9. Willingness of prospective participants to study matters of current policy concern, even in the absence of adequate theoretical base.

10. Interest in and adaptability of existing machinery for Title I programs.

11. Existence and stage of development of "modern city" program.

12. Availability of local contribution to an observatory from governmental or university sources.[18]

The six cities selected first to participate in the urban observatory program were Albuquerque, Atlanta, Baltimore, Kansas City, Milwaukee, and Nashville. Washington, D.C. participation was achieved through the voluntary association of the Washington Center for Metropolitan Studies with the project. Each city received an average grant of $75,000 in the first year. In 1970 four additional cities—Boston, Cleveland, Denver, and San Diego—were added as second round participants in the urban observatory program.

Comprehensive Research Efforts

The urban observatory concept has consistently emphasized the idea of a common research agenda based on the coopera-

tive and collaborative efforts of system members. The pilot
cities therefore attempted to work with the NLC urban observatory staff in delineating an initial common project for the
work year 1969–70. Intensive conference work sessions were
held in which general interest areas were identified: problems
of administrative centralization and decentralization; problems
of evaluation and measurement of public services; and problems attendant on governmental attempts to provide services
to the consumer. After these areas had been identified, the
working group guided by the NLC's project and staff directors
evolved a general research approach.

   One topic emerged as the top priority matter: the question
of citizen participation. Participants became caught up in de-
scribing the increasing efforts to decentralize certain community services, to involve local community groups, and to secure
maximum feasible participation of target populations. Some
were interested in studying participation more broadly, in
investigating the full range of phenomena from active involvement in public affairs to alienation and rejection. Other
researchers focused on attempts to devise measures and indices
of the performance effectiveness of various community services.

   In the end, the parameters of the problem of citizen participation as a common national agenda item included some of
the following guidelines:

   1. To study citizen participation more broadly, citizen
   groups active in public programs would be studied. Such
   groups would be included in the more extended population of selected segments of the citizenry in terms of these
   segments' attitudes and preferences. A study of so large a
   population would require developing relevant measures
   and indices of such attitudes and preferences.

   2. In order to study the more specific issue of involvement of local community groups in local policy-making
   activities, instruments would be developed to assess the
   degree of participation and the perceptions of both
   officials and respective citizens of the quality of involvement. Methodology would include comparative case
   studies which would seek to explain relationships between

certain types of participation and program effects and impacts.

3. To determine further the effectiveness of various community services, new indices could be constructed. Such measures would build from existing planning-programming-budgeting-systems efforts to define specific program goals in terms of quantification of output or results. The research technology anticipated would tend to concentrate on base line data toward developments of social indicators providing information on progress toward community goals.[19]

Anticipated in the agenda was an initial concentration, first on complementary descriptive-analytical case studies, and then on expanding ability to develop more empirical data. Fairly early the group recognized that collaborative research activities require a greater degree of coordination than initially assumed.

The citizen participation study was meant to examine the background, functioning, and adequacy of the structures and arrangements of the broad spectrum of citizen participation groups. This included those required by federal statute, those established by either formal or informal action, and those citizen-initiated groups recognized in the local political process. As part of this study, the groups were classified, the characteristics of the group participants were identified, and efforts to develop hypotheses and predictive models relative to group positions and the likelihood of success were undertaken. In addition, two in-depth case studies in specific areas were carried out. The amount budgeted for the citizen participation study was $442,000 including $80,000 in local matching funds. All ten of the urban observatories participated in the comprehensive citizen participation research project.

Adjunct studies developed as the Albuquerque urban observatory provided technical and research assistance to the Albuquerque Goals Program Committee by collecting information concerning citizen participation in local goal determination. The Atlanta urban observatory developed the case study technique for use in the network study of citizen participation, using the functional areas of housing, transportation, social welfare services, and health services. At the Boston urban observatory a sub-study of the little city halls was undertaken to evaluate the success of this administrative decentralization mechanism. The Kansas City urban observatory developed an initial typology of citizen participation groups and a bibliography of literature in the field of citizen participation. The Nashville urban observatory undertook a special effort to develop and test a survey instrument to determine who participates in citizen groups and to identify the characteristics of participants.

The second national agenda project approved involved a citizen attitude survey. This was a comparative survey of attitudes toward the quality and extent of the municipal performance of local government services such as housing, education, law enforcement, welfare, and city maintenance. The survey instrument and city sample were designed nationally through the NLC secretariat, and field work and analysis were carried out in the early summer and fall of the first action year. All ten cities participated in this study. The total financial investment budgeted for this project was $408,000, including $44,000 in matching money from the local observatories.

The seven-city common research group was expected to define the boundaries and critical concern elements of a study of participation efforts in their respective communities. However, the degree to which network-city studies would analytically complement each other depends on a number of factors, including the simple element of itemizing problems and the experience of working together.

It would be quite unrealistic to expect very much from the early empirical data. However, the cooperating observatories have the potential for moving toward the production of such common information. The need to define and to accomplish a series of compatible community profiles, to establish a common definition of services and citizen groupings, and to create appropriate and common indicators are probably preconditions for generating any meaningful "hard" data.

At the same time a possible over-reliance on the willingness and desire of local observatories to cooperate might run aground on the hard facts of urban-observatory research. The common agenda items are sufficiently important to require the services of a study director with professional credentials. This procedure is now being followed. The research director must build conceptual and theoretical frames of reference to establish a coherent system output. How effectively the individual observatories respond to this will depend in part on the coordinating director's competence, personality, contacts, support, and drives.

Explaining system outcomes at the local level is a problem each observatory will have to confront at some time. The relevance of this "common data" depends in large part on the degree to which the individual observatory has tied its local research projects to the thrust of the common research agenda. Serious problems are also involved in making available the results of such research. For example, the different cities have elections at different times; if general releases are made of research reports, political candidates might seize upon the fact that city "Y" was rated last or next to last in citizen participation or in citizen attitudes and local leadership. This would cause the mayors of the NLC to cool in their support for the urban observatory.

Local Agenda Items

A considerable number of variables, singly or in combination, will determine the local effectiveness level of an individual observatory. The relationship between the municipal government and the local colleges and universities that care constitutes a basis for cooperation and productive relationships between the two. At the same time it must be admitted that, in the experience to date, these were imprecise "starting relationships," even though most of the universities involved in the observatory cities already claimed to be urban-oriented.

Albuquerque attempted several local research agenda items in the first action year. Its first project, an emergency ambulance service study focused on Bernadillo County, resulted in the enactment of a city ambulance ordinance. The ambulance study committee reviewed and revised the initial study, continued research in definitions of quality services, and reviewed final operations of the plan to be recommended to the city commission for adoption. Albuquerque's second project was an analysis of property assessment procedures for municipal improvement. The study assisted the city administration in developing more adequate and equitable assessment procedures for municipal improvement. Third was a water and air pollution abatement and control plan. In its initial phase the study was to concentrate on water pollution control studies in the fields of water supply and waste water disposal. Related problems such as flood control and recreational water resources were considered insofar as they related to the two primary fields of study, which dealt with immediate problems of water supply and disposal as well as questions of water pollution control in the years 1970 to 1980.

Baltimore's local agenda project involved a housing inspection study to develop strategies for using building inspectors equitably and efficiently so as to assure housing standards were being met and that improvement and maintenance of housing was achieved throughout the city. Its second project related to the development and analysis of alternative levels of sanitation services to determine objective and subjective measures of performance of specific sanitation services in a number of city neighborhoods. The third project was a city recreation needs study which assisted city recreation planners in evaluating needs and preferences for different types of recreational activities.

Atlanta attempted to bring together civic leaders, local government officials, and academicians in a series of seminars examining the implications of social change upon the urban community. Special emphasis was given to civil rights, science and technology, urban management systems, and the relationship of the academician to the community. Georgia Tech, Emory University, Atlanta University, the University of Georgia and Georgia State University took part in the seminars. Atlanta also took up the project to study the Development of Model Cities Evaluation System and Conduct of Selected Evaluation Components. Utilizing local Model Cities' funds, observatory staff helped to develop the model cities evaluation system in Atlanta. In addition, Atlanta's observatory carried out a number of major evaluation components, including an attitude survey, institutional studies, project evaluation, and overall program evaluation.

The Boston observatory did a study of the state-local tax and service structure in Massachusetts. The study examined alternatives and made recommendations for service among levels of government within the state and for bringing local needs and financial resources into more realistic alignment. Boston's second local agenda project was a manpower needs study intended to (1) identify current and five-year manpower needs for professional, administrative, technical, sub-professional and other employees, (2) appraise present city staffing patterns and recruitment practices, and (3) make recommendations for improving and upgrading staffing policies and procedures.

Cleveland's analysis of income and spending by the city as well as by other selected jurisdictions proposed to provide current information on the city's sources of finance and the level of goods and services provided by the city compared with similar cities. Additionally, the project was to have an input to revenue projections for the next several years. A second project was an analysis of alternative systems for delivery of services, the purpose of which was to (1) assist city government to develop and incorporate new programs which would provide better delivery of services to city residents, and (2) develop an organization model for Cleveland city government which would reduce duplication of functions and increase responsiveness to the needs of the people.

Denver's first local agenda project was an inventory of problem-solving systems designed to develop a community information system in city government, identifying what was then being done in community problem-solving as an essential element in a comprehensive approach to community development. Four areas—housing, employment, transportation, and economic development—were studied during the first year of the program. The second local agenda project was a data bank on community development resources. The existing data bank was to be extended, with particular emphasis on areas of special interest to the urban observatory. In addition, it would develop the systems necessary for handling that data and establishing linkages with other information systems.

Kansas City's local agenda items centered around several programs of educational and civic leadership development: first, a six-week seminar for school administrators serving low-income areas of Kansas City and for teachers dealing with educationally disadvantaged children; and second, an educational leadership program for community development in the metropolitan area. The project involved both a course to help suburban teachers and administrators become knowledgeable and effective in teaching for good intergroup and interracial relations, and the initiation of cooperation among suburban school districts interested in a planned materials center for improved intergroup and interracial relations.

A third project, designed to increase the ability of local officials to respond to community needs through enhanced managerial and administrative skills, brought together local government officials and citizens to assess current community issues.

Milwaukee developed several projects, one of which provided for an expanded training function for Milwaukee area governments—a pilot for state-wide application. The one-year study is planned to develop a comprehensive career development training program for adoption as an in-service function for Milwaukee area governments. This program would serve as a model for the state.

Nashville's first project assembled a data profile on social change and initiated a pilot study to identify and analyze indicators of social change in education, health, and housing. Its second project was to develop policies for the administration of justice, with emphasis on examining due process concerning temporary detention of juveniles. The points at which juveniles enter, exit, and re-enter the system were identified and the court, probation, police, welfare, and school procedures described.

San Diego's first project was the development of criteria for model cities' evaluation. The project provided immediate research and expert assistance to the city demonstration agency to help in establishing criteria for proposed model cities projects. The second project, an analysis of police recruitment problems and techniques, was to determine whether standards set by the police department were being met by those recruited and whether or not the standards were adequate for the jobs to be performed. Factors such as procedures and opportunities for promotion, salaries, fringe benefits, educational opportunities, and management values and methods were to be reviewed to identify those variables which may produce higher or lower retention rates. Third was a project studying the social service delivery system in the model cities area to determine the manner in which client services are organized and delivered and to provide recommendations for more effective integration of efforts. Besides attempting to arrive at a composite picture of the services provided in this area, special attention was paid to the performance of individual agencies.

One of the criteria in selecting the urban observatory cities was the ability to interrelate Title I programs with urban observatory research. Nine of the ten urban observatory cities had projects under Title I of the Higher Education Act which were related to the urban observatory; only San Diego did not. These projects included community services projects, leadership training programs, planning and citizen participation, principles and techniques of PPBS, consultation in systems installation, training programs for citizen involvement in low-cost housing rehabilitation, programs to improve tenant-management relationships in the housing authorities, marketing assistance to local economic development corporations, neighborhood development systems, and projects on increasing local governments' capability to respond to the community. In addition, Albuquerque attempted a proposal writing workshop which developed into a course for local government units and other interested agencies on design and preparation of grant applications. Atlanta developed a model cities evaluation system and conducted an evaluation of selected model cities components.

Profile of Urban Observatory Cities

Each urban observatory has already written its own unique history. The boards, universities, and researchers have given each city a special flavor. Milwaukee, for instance, has the backing and support of Mayor Maier, who first grasped Wood's idea. Milwaukee has dealt with local and national political realities and with multi-faceted institutional problems, and the university-city venture is making great strides there. Local support for the research-oriented program is being drummed up, and local initiative shows on the city's agenda items. However, the Milwaukee urban observatory expresses concerns about growth at current levels of funding for national agenda items.

Albuquerque's observatory revolves around a five-man

board with excellent response from researchers at the two local universities. Albuquerque was ahead of other cities in laying groundwork for the second-year social indicators project; it also made progress in providing information to other cities about city charter revision and water quality as well as in the success of its citizen participation study. At the same time, Albuquerque has felt theeffects of the philosophical dilemma of emphasizing university research or promoting urban action.

The Atlanta Urban Life Center existed at Georgia State College before the observatory grant; hence urban research was not new there. In the researchers' view the city is not demanding as much as it might from the observatory. This is attributed to different perceptions of the research-versus-action emphasis. The marriage is seen as desirable but objectives are not clear. Local money is available for local projects, but network and information base contacts on the national level and from NLC have not yet been extensive. At the same time, Atlanta academicians and city officials believe the Wood idea's time has come and that further institutionalization is on the way.

The Denver Urban Observatory has met enthusiastic university support even though it was one of the last cities to join the NLC program. City support, too, has been available, but a procedure of clearing projects through the city council has caused extra administrative steps for the city-based director. Other characteristics of the Denver Observatory are the simple five-man board, the interest of university researchers for the third-year social indicators project, round table meetings of 150 public administrators and university faculty, and the director's own experience of twelve years in city hall work. High on the Denver priorities list is the expansion of funds to finance projects. Seventy-five thousand dollars a year is just not enough for a large metropolis research-action-based program.

The Mid-America Urban Observatory (Kansas City) holds a unique position among the ten cities in the urban observatories program. The research projects are derived from the University of Kansas located 40 miles west of the urban area and from University of Missouri at Kansas City. A six-man board representing the two universities, the two Kansas Cities, and the two urban counties in which the cities are located made decisions for a research-action program and directed the program until 1971, when a full-time director was hired. In the third year the Mid-America Urban Observatory will work on a municipal finance program and conclude a special migration study in the Kansas City area. Since the urban observatory straddles the state line between Kansas and Missouri, coordination of funds, cooperation of researchers and of city halls has been a complex job. In April 1971, a new mayor and council were elected in Kansas City, Missouri. The first major vote was on whether to fire the city manager. The mayor, who had this objective, lost on a nine to three vote.

In the metropolis of Boston, the romance of the urban observatory does not exist. With the large institutional empires at MIT and Harvard universities and the equally complex political realities of city hall, the urban observatory is shuttled into the background as a small research project. The Boston Urban Observatory hopes to appeal to the idea-men in city government and to act as a bridge toward action-research. So that there will be no institutionalizing or empire-building at the university level, the lead university in Boston will be transferred every two years. To complicate matters, Boston believes it needs more funds for local projects, better coordination with City Hall, and more communication from the other observatories.

The Nashville Urban Observatory involves six universities, with major emphasis thus far placed on communication between city and university. Nashville has concluded that the average academic is so specialized in his field that he cannot be expected to respond within the time span of decision-making required in city affairs. Other problems are decision-making and the narrow conception by the university people of problems which have large political factors. However, the major task there has been to convince the university man that it makes little difference what the truth is in a situation if indeed the city intends to use that truth as a political reality.

The Nashville board meets once a week in what is mainly an adult educational experience. Research has been initiated through an urban seminar. A major part of this dialogue has been spent in dealing with problem issues at the university level. The dialogue concentrates on pairing researchers with administrators who are at the right levels to do something about urban problems. The mechanics needed for this pairing are dependent upon the education cycle.

On the third-year agenda Nashville sees itself attacking the budgeting process at the state as well as the local level. That entire system has to be investigated as it relates to urban America. At present, many officials involved in budget making are functionally illiterate about the hard issues of money. The director there sees two projects emerging from this need to study municipal finance: first, investigation of the environmental problems—determining which section of the environment demands better use of available money; and second, the people problem—identifying criteria for the evaluation of urban life. This leads into a social indicator project. Three steps are being taken in Nashville to begin the social indicator agenda item—initiating dialogue, sampling needs and criteria, and polling segments of society.

Although the Nashville Urban Observatory seems unconcerned with the comparability agenda items in the observatory network, the observatory's future is bright because of the spirited dialogue, the attitude of cooperation, and the opportunities provided by the six universities.

The Baltimore Urban Observatory has a unique setup. It draws its university cooperation from the Higher Education Council on Urban Affairs (HECUA), which consists of 28 colleges and universities. HECUA existed before the urban observatory and its structural tie benefits the observatory in terms of broad involvement. At the moment there is no lead university. The observatory draws research agenda from only eight of the universities, and the Baltimore Urban Observatory is one of the few which is incorporated. Its director is located at the regional planning center.

In Baltimore a strategy has been worked out which stresses cooperation with department heads. This is done with the knowledge of the mayor's office but is not bottled up there, where a small research program can be lost in the shuffle. The perennial communications gap between universities and city was mentioned in Baltimore interviews. However, researchers are looking ahead to modifying the urban observatory approach. Early contracts were for two year projects, but new ones will be four or five month studies in order to meet the needs of city action-research realistically. This should help reduce the fear of the hidden agenda of policy change in city hall, as well as speed up the research output from the university. The desire to develop research on city problems is high and an optimistic sign for the urban observatory there.

Conversations with the last two urban observatory cities supply the reader with a different perspective of observatory programming. These local agenda items are proposed or planned and demonstrate the possibilities of local programs.

On one hand, Cleveland has initiated two studies in municipal finance. These started as local agenda items but will be expanded in line with the third year national theme. Another local agenda item which has been funded by the Office of Economic Opportunity (OEO) and HUD involves the use of multi-service government centers in the neighborhoods and how they might be better organized. The universities will be used to identify the needs which the multi-service centers are satisfying.

Cleveland has also initiated research on revenue-sharing as a local agenda item. At Case Western Reserve University a study of the differential between the revenue-sharing plan and income already provided to the city through federal programs is being undertaken. Cleveland has also initiated a volunteer program for suburban housewives and college people which is based on research from city hall. This program will provide an information base for citizens who wish to serve the community by providing needed services. In addition, two local summer projects to design recreation areas in Cleveland have been funded by NLC. The projects are intended to be model recreation areas for other densely populated cities. The prototype will document design for the perceived needs of lower income groups. Title I has also funded some first-year projects in Cleveland, including a basic marketing assistance program for a community development corporation and a radio program administered by Case Western Reserve University.

In San Diego the urban observatory has fourteen approved programs for the second year. The projects are funded by a combination of Title I and HUD money. San Diego's citizen participation study sampled brown, black and middle-income white communities. Two police studies were done in San Diego. One involved the recruitment of police officers, and the second researched upward movement within the ranks, a serious police problem. Other social programs involved setting the criteria for model cities evaluations and studying the social service delivery system. In the first year, researchers inventoried the services by users. In the second year, they picked up on the inventory by identifying family-users, and used a group of 50 control families and 50 experimental families for a study of an alternate method of social service deliveries to be operated by the county on a trial basis.

San Diego also undertook a homeownership and home management study. Provisions were made for adult education, including a course in "how to manage a house" which worked with new homeowners and buyers of homes in low-income neighborhoods. Other adult education courses included leadership training funded by Title I, taking leaders from the model cities program and providing special training for them, and a citizen power program, which developed into a political primer, taught in Spanish and English and operated jointly with the League of Women Voters. The question the program addressed was what is the role of city, county, state, and federal government in a citizen's life.

Several spin-off programs have resulted from the basic design of the local agenda projects. The second-year projects will extend the social service delivery system. In addition, an inventory of services provided by retired people for the community will be matched with an inventory of places where volunteer help can be used. Another program has sought state highway commission funds for a drunken driver program. The analysis of 40,000 citations for drunken drivers in three years will be given to judges before sentencing. It is hoped that the study will provide information for judicial discrimination between medical and criminal reasons for aberrant behavior.

The general pattern of university participation outlines varied problems, and several observatories have set up seminars and dialogues to allow researchers and city officials the chance to learn about and discuss them. Further, even though the observatory idea surfaced in academia, university participation in and understanding of action-research has been limited. Constraints on university action have been design of the planned national agenda research, paperwork, time-lag in securing approval, and the inability of researchers and their city counterparts to reach common decisions and convey them in time to help the national office respond to HUD. Several mayors, in addition, have adopted a "wait and see" posture toward the observatory idea which has forced researchers and observatory directors to seek support with the city's idea-men in an attempt to keep directors' exploratory projects alive. The pattern of university involvement hinges very much on the director in each city, and his success depends on his ability to get the political-research-action questions out into the open where they can be placed in perspective by the researcher and the city's representative. In summary, these local agenda items are representative of the information gathering base which the urban observatory is able to provide for city hall. These examples are of practical value to municipal and metropolitan areas which find themselves in the dilemma of over-extended staff and diminished funds.

National Academy Evaluation

In 1971, the National Academy of Public Administration conducted an evaluation of the urban observatory program for the Department of Housing and Urban Development. The academy panel concluded:

    1. Bridges are being built between local government and universities, but the financing, the leadership, and the central organization of the program is inadequate.

    2. The ten observatories have performed unevenly since capabilities and cooperation have diffused.

    3. Little research has been completed and black educational institutions have been under-involved.

    4. Although faculty have been concerned with urban problems, the majority of funds have been devoted to national research. The local research projects have great potential for action, but a number of observatories have run into problems integrating research into the Title I component of the program.[20]

    The panel recommended that the Urban Obeservatory Program be made a permanent part of HUD's research and development activity and that

1. HUD should assume direct responsibility for organizing and administering the program on a continuing basis to provide needed centralization, while continuing to allow flexibility for approximately 50 percent of the funding to be used on local agenda projects.

2. Annual allocations per observatory should be raised to $250,000. (In 1973 HUD cut the original observatory cities to $25,000 as part of a phase-out, while indicating it would fund another set of medium-sized cities.)

3. Each observatory should be organized around a decision-making leadership group from local government and universities, and a scholar group concerned with research.

4. Research should be disseminated not only to the ten observatory cities but also to the nation.

5. Communications between state Title I and observatory principals should be integrated with respect to policy and decision-making.[21]

What Future for the Urban Observatory?

The directors of the urban observatory agree unanimously that more funds are needed for observatory work. They agree that the NLC office staff in Washington is too small to keep up with the comparability studies, the need for more network information, and the heavy load of information based on materials produced by each of the ten observatories. Also, the urban observatories still see themselves as learning to cooperate experientially with the cities. However, problems remain in the institutionalization of observatories as a research-action venture between cities and universities. In some cases, that has already happened; cities have become dependent on the urban observatory and, perhaps even more important, on the men in the urban observatory as key figures in the idea phase, in the fiscal administration, and in the basic research know-how in working with metropolitan problems.

The network idea is slowly taking hold. The greatest trading of information has related to network ideas, agenda ideas, and structure ideas for the urban observatory. Some ad hoc information trading has taken place among cities; for example, ideas on city charter revision have been traded between Albuquerque and Nashville. Washington hopes that a system of quarterly reports will stimulate even more trading of information among the observatories. Communication notwithstanding, most observatory directors feel that it will be five years before there will be any reading of success or failure about the network idea.

Large funding and support questions remain. What will the national office provide in the way of future monies? Some of those questions are about to be answered by the FY 1974 budget. The Administration's apparent plan is to reduce federal funding for the ten existing observatories by one-half and to gradually cut it off while at the same time funding ten new but smaller observatory cities. The assumption is that the original ten should have proven themselves to local funding sources by now.

There are other questions. How can a multi-city-university research-based program trade its information, effect reliable comparability, and share the political realities on the basis of decisions made in the big cities? What is the reality and future of big city research if the social forces of cities are moving faster than sociologists can describe them? How valid is city-university research which places emphasis on impacted urban areas when the danger of the seventies might likely be the waste, crime, and developing service crises of suburbia? Are the university researchers well enough prepared and willing to tackle the suburban problems, the bucolic-urban sprawl living of the seventies, and the metropolitan problems that not only cross municipal and county lines but tend to become a megalopolis stretching hundred of miles?

The urban observatory program is a pilot project which eventually may lead to an even more broadly based and heavily funded research approach. As such, it is serving the purpose of identifying defects in the existing model while educating professors and city hall administrators. However, at this stage it will have only occasional contributions to problem solving.

NOTES

1. Robert C. Wood, "Contributions of Political Science to Urban Form," in Werner Z. Hirsch, ed., *Urban Life and Form* (New York: Holt, Rinehart and Winston, 1963), p. 122.

2. *Ibid.*, p. 123.

3. Henry W. Maier, "An Overview of Urban Observatories," in Steven B. Sweeney and James C. Charlesworth, eds., *Governing Urban Society: New Scientific Approaches* (American Society of Politica and Social Science, May 1967), p. 3.

4. *Ibid.* The resolutions followed the Milwaukee meeting of June 1965 which gathered together mayors and urban specialists. The statement approved at the meeting stated that such a relationship is "essential to provide needed urban research as a continuing process" (p. 6).

5. *Ibid.*, p. 6.

6. Robert Aleshire, "The Metropolitan Desk: A New Technique of Program Teamwork," *Public Administration Review*, June 1966, pp. 87–95.

7. William N. Cassella, Jr., "An Urban Research Library for the New York Metropolitan Region," *Urban Research and Education in the New York Metropolitan Region*, vol. 11 (New York: Regional Plan Association, 1965), chap. 16.

8. John G. Kemeny et al., "A Library for 2000 A.D.," in Martin Greenberger, ed., *Computers and the World of the Future* (Cambridge, Mass.: MIT Press, 1962), pp. 135–161,

9. Lee G. Burchinal and Harold A. Haswell, "How to Put Two and a Half Tons of Research into One Handy Little Box," *American Education,* vol. 2, no. 2 (February 1966), pp. 23–25.

10. Dick Netzer, "A Metropolitan Statistical Center: Purposes and Functions," in *Urban Research and Education in the New York Metropolitan Region*, vol. 11 (New York: Regional Plan Association, 1966).

11. Howard G. Brunsman, "The 1970 Census of Population and Housing: Choices Made and to Be Made," proceedings of the third annual Information Systems Procedures Association (New York: The Association, 1965), pp. 29–37.

12. Frank X. Steggert, "Urban Observatories: An Experiment in Institution Building," speech given at the 1969

The Urban Observatory: A University-City   47
Research Venture

National Conference of the American Society for Public Administration, Miami Beach, Florida, May 19, 1969.

13. *Ibid.*, pp. 2–4.

14. Maier, "Overview of Urban Observatories," pp. 4–6.

15. Patrick Geddes, *Cities in Evolution*, rev. ed. (New York: Howard Fertig, 1949).

16. H. Ralph Taylor, "Defining and Implementing the Urban Observatories Concept," in Sweeney and Charlesworth, eds., *Governing Urban Society*, p. 221.

17. Thomas J. Davy, "Determining Priorities and Developing Basic Research on Urban Problems," in Sweeney and Charlesworth, eds., *Governing Urban Society*, p. 229.

18. Maier, "Overview of Urban Observatories," p. 7.

19. "Work Program 1969–70: Urban Observatory Network," printed memorandum (Washington, D.C.: National League of Cities, May 1969).

20. National Academy of Public Administration, *Evaluation of the Urban Observatory Program*, November 1, 1971, pp. 1–3.

21. *Ibid.*, pp. 3–5.

3

URBAN GOVERNMENTAL MANPOWER

Thomas P. Murphy

A prophetic study by the Municipal Manpower Commission (MMC), which was funded by the Ford Foundation and published in 1962 as *Governmental Manpower for Tomorrow's Cities,* correctly predicted that urbanization of metropolitan areas would continue and outlined some of the emerging urban management manpower problems. Highlighting the need to keep up with change, the report noted that independent civil service systems which had been established to help counteract the power of political bosses in the big cities were now becoming a problem in some urban areas.

Many of these systems were based on the assumption that security was the primary objective to be sought for the employees and therefore put their stress on pensions, job protection, and promotion from within, often to the exclusion of permitting lateral entry into the system. City employee security became very crucial during the depression years. However, as America has become increasingly urbanized and as the scope of government has expanded, many new kinds of positions required for urban management have been created.

Increasingly, for example, urban governments are becoming more involved with computerized traffic engineering, urban renewal, intergovernmental relations, metropolitan planning, management information systems, operations research, environmental affairs, and even grantsmanship. Such positions did not exist in the standard public service functions related to highways, hospitals, housing, police and fire departments, parks, corrections, and public utility systems.

The fact is that local government employment is perhaps the major growth industry in America. However, the various components of local government employment are not growing at the same rate. The Municipal Manpower Commission report concluded that the greatest growth in local government manpower needs would be for administrative, professional, and technical (APT) specialists rather than for manual, clerical, and stenographic personnel.

The report also concluded that many of those in APT positions lacked the proper preparation. For example, "only one in five public safety directors and less than half of all finance directors graduated from college."[1] In addition, "in the case of sanitary engineers employed by the cities, only two department or division heads in 23 cities over 250,000 possess graduate degrees in this field" and "among the nation's 1,500 traffic engineers, only one-third meet the professional standards of the Institute of Traffic Engineers."[2]

The shortage of APT personnel which existed in 1960 was expected to become worse by 1970. The United States Department of Labor predicted that "the demand for professional and technical persons will increase 40 percent, and job opportunities for executives and managers will also open up rapidly."[3] The MMC report concluded "serious national shortages of APT personnel are rapidly intensified by growing demands for such manpower and by the inadequacy of educational programs to meet the present and future needs."[4]

The predictions with regard to manpower shortages turned out to be true. Further, during the 1960s local governments were increasingly called upon to provide more specialized and technical services while the federal government continued to hire a greater proportion of the personnel capable of performing these functions. Once in federal employment, these employees have been used in paperwork jobs rather than in service delivery, which is a state and local function. A great disproportion developed as these federal employees in Washington and regional offices wrote requirements for local government employees to fulfill. The local people often had to choose between meeting the requirements of federal programs and neglecting service delivery or providing services and being threatened with a cutoff of federal funds for failure to comply with the paperwork. There was much waste in these programs, so that in some areas the current need is as much for improved management as it is for more money.

The growth in local government APT positions exceeded all predictions. State and local employment increased 80 percent between 1960 and 1970, totalling 10.1 million in 1970, approximately three times as great as federal employment. In addition, the dollar value of state payrolls increased over 300 percent to $1.6 billion in 1970. The local payroll increased about 250 percent and amounted to $4.2 billion by 1970. Because of suburban growth, urban counties had a higher employment increase in the 1960s than did central cities. The fastest growing functional areas of state and local employment were public welfare, which increased by 119 percent; education, by 69 percent; law enforcement, by 48 percent; and public health and hospitals, by 45 percent. Nevertheless, one of the problems was not so much the number of unfilled positions as the number of positions filled by unqualified persons. This was attributable in large part to working conditions in local government, where salary levels were far below those of federal positions and of those in industry. In addition, the tight civil service systems established for protection purposes were not appropriate for APT positions.

APT manpower also tended to be much more mobile than the service employees formerly covered in city civil service systems. Yet mobility without the opportunity to transfer pension benefits and retirement benefits created a problem for such employees. No such problem existed for federal employees who could transfer all over the country while maintaining their retirement benefits. In addition, the already stifling effects of the independent civil service system were being exaggerated somewhat by the dramatic growth in municipal unions which occurred in the 1960s. Both these forces tended to prevent top management from injecting people into the system who had not entered at the lowest levels and been promoted to the top.

Contrast this picture of the quantity and quality of APT personnel in urban governments with the growth that occurred in the 1960s. Per capita public spending for domestic purposes rose by more than 97 percent, while the gain in per capita defense expenditures was 63 percent and the increase in per capita personal income was 76 percent. However, the governments affected by this tremendous increase—the cities and counties—have had a revenue crisis because of their over-dependence on the property tax. Only a few state governments have taken the initiative to assist their local governments by providing a surtax on the state income tax or by taking on responsibilities for the cost of education or welfare, two of the most rapidly growing cost areas in local government. These economic strains have made it difficult for local governments to offer competitive salaries to APT manpower.

The federal government, especially with the Great Society programs of the 1960s, tried to step into this revenue gap at the local level by providing federal funding for urban programs. However, the mechanism selected was the grant-in-aid system, which involved over 500 separate grant programs and created a management morass at both the federal and local levels. The Nixon Administration proposed a general and several special revenue sharing bills encompassing the functions of many of these separate grant programs so that local governments could set their own priorities. In 1972 Congress failed to act on the special revenue sharing bills proposed by the administration but did enact general revenue sharing legislation.

Compared to the growth in gross national product since World War II, federal taxes amounted to 18.7 percent of GNP in 1946. In 1971 the federal tax take was 19.1 percent. However, during those same years, state and local tax receipts increased from 6.2 percent in 1946 to 14.4 percent in 1971. In the last decade alone, state and local government expenditures have been increasing at an annual rate averaging 9.4 percent. Despite these revenue increases, the cost of providing the services for which local governments are responsible has increased at an even faster rate, and so local government salaries have not kept pace with the federal salary increases.

The effect of the increasing concentration of population in metropolitan areas has been exaggerated by the tendency for low-income, aged, and less educated citizens to concentrate in the central city while the higher income, younger, and better educated citizens have tended to cluster in the nearby suburbs. Metropolitan approaches are necessary to ease the governmental conflict created by these city-suburban disparities.

Given this background, the passage of the general revenue-sharing legislation in 1972 has made the problem even more critical. The Humphrey–Reuss version of the revenue-sharing bill would have required state and local government to meet certain federal criteria for management effectiveness to be able to receive the revenue-sharing funds. The bill finally passed, due to administration pressures, did not have any such requirements. This means that responsibility for managing vast urban programs is now being dropped on the state and local governments, which lack qualified manpower in APT specializations. It might be argued that previously the responsibility was with these governmental units anyway, since the federal government specialists were not directly involved in service delivery and often even tended to tie the hands of local people by their unrealistic paperwork requirements. To the extent that this is true, some of these artificial make-work bureaucratic mechanisms have now been removed for at least a portion of the federal funding, and local government has been given more direct ability to deploy the funds in problem areas it considers most critical. This is certainly progress, but it will be a variable progress depending on the management capability of the various governments to respond.

Serious manpower problems remain, such as the shortage of APT specialists, the loss of over one-third of the top management level of municipal administrators during the 1960s (many of whom were well qualified persons hired during the depression years), and the fact that 11 states still have no formal merit system other than that required by the federal grant programs. In addition, county governments are far behind in terms of setting up merit systems. The problem, then, ranges from the absence of merit systems in some states and county governments to the operation of highly restrictive independent civil service systems in some cities. The need is for something between these two extremes which would make professional, administrative, and technical jobs attractive to quali-

fied personnel yet be adaptable to the kind of mobility necessary for such personnel.

There are other administrative and managerial questions
as well. David Walker, in commenting on personnel trends in
state and local government in the 1960s, described the impact
of increased federal funding for local programs as follows:

> As intergovernmental programs have expanded and be-
> come more intricate and interrelated, the line agency
> (program) specialists have increased their influence
> throughout the system; but the power, professional stand-
> ing and prestige of core management has not been
> strengthened commensurately in most jurisdictions and
> this imbalance is a major factor affecting the position of
> chief executives, the status of comprehensive planning,
> the effectiveness of budgeting, the troubled condition of
> auditing and accounting, the broad problem of adminis-
> trative responsiveness, and the public's cynicism regard-
> ing the capacity of government—all governments—to
> function.[5]

New University Academic Responses

In spelling out actions which it considered necessary to achieve
the management and manpower goals of urban government,
the Municipal Manpower Commission report called for universities to take the following actions:

1. Review and revise graduate and undergraduate programs to emphasize the significance of urbanization in
American society.

2. Emphasize early professional education for APT careers in public service.

3. Seek stronger financial support for fellowships in
urban curricula.

4. Make available career training programs in every major urban center by means of cooperation between state
universities and college and university branches in metropolitan areas.[6]

How have the universities responded to this mandate? A

partial answer to this question is provided by the 1968 survey of political science courses dealing with state and local government, which is reported in Chapter 4. If urban management had to rely only upon the political science departments to develop student interest in state and local government, there would obviously be a problem. Fortunately, the situation may not be quite as critical as indicated by the ACIR report. Especially since the mid-1960s, there has been a dramatic growth in the number of undergraduate and graduate academic programs in public administration, urban studies, and policy sciences.

To the extent that growth in public administration programs has been within political science departments, it is already reflected in the ACIR figures. However, a 1972 survey by the National Association of Schools of Public Affairs and Administration (NASPAA) indicated that about 52 percent of the 125 major graduate and undergraduate programs in public administration in the nation exist independently of the political science department, either as units in social science divisions; as schools of administration, business and public administration, or management; as autonomous programs in centers and institutes; or as professional schools of public affairs and/or public administration.[7] Likewise, the Urban Institute Directory shows that there are 56 graduate and undergraduate academic programs in urban studies, virtually all of which are totally independent of political science departments.[8] It should be added, however, that some political science departments have helped to fulfill their obligation to provide such courses by approving joint faculty appointments to such interdisciplinary urban programs. These faculty often teach courses which deal with some of the subjects covered in the ACIR report.

In addition to providing an alternate source of education of the type required to supply urban governments with appropriate management and APT personnel, the public administration, urban, and policy sciences programs have one distinct advantage over those in political science. Until recently, these programs tended to be primarily at the graduate level and stressed a professional as opposed to an academic focus, especially at the masters level. In this respect, they have had the ability to include specific management courses such as decision-making, human relations, organization and management, budgeting and program evaluation, personnel management, organizational behavior, and logistics management.

An NASPAA survey compared a variety of requirements at the master's and doctoral levels which reflected the professional emphasis. The master's degrees played down thesis and language requirements but emphasized internships, statistics and data processing. Table 3–1 summarives the data.

Table 3–1
PA/A Program Requirements
(N=96)

Program requirements	Master's		Doctorate	
	yes (%)	no (%)	yes (%)	no (%)
Basic statistics	72	28	92	8
Automatic data processing	55	45	64	36
Comprehensive exams	65	35	94	6
Thesis	40	60	97	3
Language	10	90	54	46
Internship	51	49	14	86

SOURCE: National Association of Schools of Public Affairs and Administration, *Public Affairs and Administration Programs,* Washington, D.C., June 1972, p. 108.

In addition, some of these programs have gone further and have included specializations in social service administration, public works management, recreation management, health administration, traffic engineering, transportation management, and urban development. Likewise, the passage of the Federal Law Enforcement Assistance Act led to the growth of a number of institutes of criminology or law enforcement which have provided graduate and undergraduate education to law enforcement personnel. In that same vein, other legislation had earlier provided opportunities for additional training in health-related areas at both the graduate and undergraduate levels.

This professional emphasis seems to be effective in that there is a strong relationship between graduate degrees in public administration and government employment. Table 3–2 gives the distribution of employment of graduates.

Table 3–2
Employers of Degree Graduates

Employers	Percent employed*	N
Federal government	19	49
State government	17	48
City/local government	35	58
Other government	8.6	27
Non-government	8.7	33
Teaching	8	26
Graduate school	9	37

*Due to an unusual distribution of responses, percentages total more than 100% (N.B., median percentages).

SOURCE: National Association of Schools of Public Affairs and Administration, *Public Affairs and Administration Programs,* Washington, D.C., June 1972, p. 110.

As for the magnitude of graduate programs in public affairs/administration, there were a total of 9,915 students in the 125 degree programs in the fall of 1970, and, as shown in Table 3–3, there were over 12,000 such students in the fall of 1971. The table also shows that almost 3,000 degrees were granted in 1970–71, 75 percent of which were at the graduate level.

Table 3–3
Enrollment and Degrees Granted by Degree Program

Types of degrees	Granted 1970–71	Fall 1971 enrollment full-time	part-time	Total fall 1971	Percent change 1970–71
BA-BS	720	3,315	132	3,447	+36
MA (PA)	455	569	1,024	1,593	+20
MPA, etc.	1,675	2,844	3,440	6,284	+22
Ph.D.	68	302	272	574	−16
D.P.A.	23	125	130	255	+11
Totals	2,941	7,155	4,998	12,153	+23

SOURCE: National Association of Schools of Public Affairs and Administration, *Public Affairs and Administration Programs,* Washington, D.C., June 1972, p. 106.

One of the problems related to expansion of the graduate programs in public administration, many of which would concentrate on specializations and approaches essential to the development of urban government manpower, has been the lack of funding. While universities across the country have recognized the need to develop strong professional schools in law, engineering, medicine, business, and education, very few have undertaken to provide a professional school in public administration and public affairs. Presumably, the absence of clear information as to the manpower requirements in this field has contributed to this program vacuum. Another reason is the diversity of such programs. This latter factor is so serious that the National Association of Schools of Public Affairs and Administration has been unable for a number of years to reach agreement on specific standards for member institutions. Further, usable public service manpower projections would require more effective cooperation among the universities, the professional societies, and the national organizations of city, county, and state governments.

Attempts to secure federal funding for academic programs in public administration and public affairs have been largely unsuccessful. After much effort, Congress adopted Title IX of the Higher Education Act in 1968. Titled Education for the Public Service, this legislation authorized substantial developmental assistance for graduate public service education as well as for fellowships in public affairs and administration. However, no appropriation was ever provided for this title. At first Congress was slow to act, and then President Nixon deleted the appropriation request because of his interest in breaking down the categorical grant-in-aid system. The error in this approach was pointed out by Dean Donald Stone, who wrote of the fallacy of assuming that "Title IX is merely a new kind of aid to education to be administered by HEW, rather than viewed as part of executive branch strategy for improving public service."[9]

Later, President Nixon apparently operated on the assumption that the National Foundation for Higher Education Act would be the appropriate place for the purposes of Title IX. Regarding this prospect, Dean Stone responded, "It is unlikely that such an arrangement—even if enacted—would give priority to public service education or be capable of carrying out Executive policy for meeting personnel requirements. An effective strategy requires complementary attention to action-oriented research, a function which the Foundation could not perform."[10]

The rationale presented by the National Association of Schools of Public Affairs and Administration to the President's Task Force on Priorities in Higher Education could be helpful in influencing the eventual decision as to resource allocation for this purpose:

a. The need for administrative capabilities at city, state, and federal levels to plan and implement policies, programs, and services essential to a livable urban-industrial society are obviously enormous. Many national, state, and municipal initiatives of the past ten years have floundered because of the failure to develop the necessary educational and research underpinning to implement these purposes.

b. In responding to national challenges or needs, extraordinary success has been achieved in those fields or areas where the federal government, foundations, and private philanthropy have deliberately created both the required knowledge and personnel for innovative action. We see this vividly in agriculture, aerospace, health, medicine, science, industrial management, and development of public school education.

c. Only miniscule funds are allocated by government and foundations to education and research in public affairs/administration, including such vast and important fields as environmental management, housing, urban renewal, community social planning and action, public works, urban and regional planning, city management, industrial-economic development, state and national administration, administration of international affairs.

d. In contrast, large appropriations, grants, and contracts are available for educational development, training programs, traineeships, fellowships, institutional and individual research, and facilities through the Departments of Agriculture, NASA, AEC, NSF, National Institutes of Health, Office of Education, and Defense for their fields of concern. Foundations have often initiated or

supplemented these purposes. The result is a major imbalance in meeting priority national needs.

e. A further result is the inability of universities to develop a national network of schools and centers of professional education, research, and services covering such
fields as those mentioned in item c. We believe that
education and research interrelating policy and administration to function, substantive technology, and
to the environment in which programs and services are
carried out is extremely urgent to national progress.
Today there is only a handful of such schools and
centers, and these are emaciated for lack of funds.

f. We believe that a rearrangement of educational priorities is called for with an investment in education and
research in these public affairs/administration fields of
several $100 million annually.[11]

The HUD Urban Fellowship Program

The HUD Urban Fellowship Program was one of the first
national programs conceived to provide administrative talent
to the urban public service. In fiscal year 1969, HUD awarded
99 fellowships to students for study at 46 different schools. In
fiscal year 1970, the number of fellowships grew to 107. These
were awarded for study in only 46 departments of 40 different
schools. Although the appropriation for the HUD Urban Fellowship Program was only $500,000 per year, it has had a very
high rate of success in sending administrators into urban public
service. For example, as of 1970 approximately 70 percent of
the then employable Fellows had moved into governmental positions. Also, 18 percent were in related teaching or private
industry positions. Therefore, almost 90 percent of the employ-
ables upon whom information was available had selected occupations in urban-related fields.

The HUD program had been handicapped by recruitment
problems. One way to avoid these problems has been to award
fellowships to particular schools, thereby letting schools themselves select the recipients. This presents problems, however:
should the fellowships be put into the best schools, where presumably the students will receive the best education, or should
they be given to lesser known universities seeking to develop or

expand programs designed to train people for the urban public service?

The latter option obviously has much to commend it; the manpower shortage of the urban public service will ultimately be solved only when more universities have developed programs to produce more graduates for such careers. The grant of fellowships to non-prestige universities would constitute a boost to the development of new programs or a strengthening of small and weak programs. Consequently, such grants could constitute a major investment in the expansion of graduate education for public service careers in the United States.

However, the program is set up so that students are selected and then choose which school they wish to attend. Most students choose the high prestige institutions. In fiscal year 1970, for example, seven schools—Harvard, MIT, Yale, Chicago, The University of California at Berkeley, Columbia, and North Carolina—received 48 of 107 awards granted. Only 10 "non-prestige" universities received fellowships. This is only one illustration of the many problems facing the HUD Urban Fellowship Program in its implementation.

The pattern of geographic distribution poses special problems since state and local government agencies usually follow the practice of recruiting professional help from *local* colleges and universities. Few governments recruit on a national basis, and few job candidates look beyond their immediate region for positions. Therefore, one of the major problems with the HUD fellowship program was that half the states had no university graduate programs in public administration operating within their boundaries and the design of the HUD fellowship Program did not lend itself to creating new programs in universities which did not previously have them.

Furthermore, the HUD Fellowship Advisory Board concluded that in order to have even a *"consequential"* impact upon the needs of the nation, the program itself would have to be doubled in size. Nevertheless, the HUD fellowship program has made an important contribution: it has been a success in sending graduates into urban public service.[12]

The Intergovernmental Personnel Act

The Senate Subcommittee on Intergovernmental Relations, chaired by Senator Edmund S. Muskie, spent several years reviewing manpower needs of state and local governments in terms of their impact on management effectiveness and the success of federal programs. These studies concluded that manpower deficiencies in state and local governments were a major gap in the effectiveness of the federal system. After many hearings, studies, and unsuccessful attempts to secure legislation, the Intergovernmental Personnel Act of 1970 (IPA) was finally passed.[13]

The legislation was based in large part upon the recognition that the categorical aid program had provided mechanisms for strengthening state and local management in specialized fields such as health, law enforcement, and education. The IPA was therefore directed primarily at providing support for general management and staff specialists reporting to general management at the state and local level.

Reflecting its concern with the strengthening of state and local government personnel administration, with special emphasis on improving the recruitment and training functions, administrative responsibility for implementing legislation was assigned to the United States Civil Service Commission. The legislation authorized participation by state and local governments in federal recruitment and examination processes, as well as technical assistance in the field of personnel management. In addition, the legislation helped to consolidate some of the existing federal programs which related to the purposes of the legislation. For example, the Civil Service Commission was designated as the coordinator of personnel management and technical training assistance by all federal agencies.[14] Likewise, the HEW Office of State Merit Systems was transferred to the Commission and incorporated within the Bureau of Intergovernmental Personnel Programs which was established to administer the IPA.

The specific operating areas to be strengthened by the grants authorized under the IPA are personnel improvement, personnel administration, personnel training, and government service fellowships. For example, states and local governments can apply for funds to strengthen their personnel systems, conduct manpower studies, update some of their personnel management functions, carry on special programs for the disadvantaged, and conduct research and demonstration projects related to the purposes of the IPA. The language of the statute is geared toward special consideration for the administrative, professional, and technical people in state and local governments, if those governments are wise enough to use the legislation in those ways. Specific language in the acts precludes the use of training grants for meeting training needs already covered by other grant-in-aid programs. Up to two years of graduate study at universities is permitted by the fellowship provisions and, for the first five years of the program, the federal government will absorb 75 percent of the cost of personnel administration and training grants.

Eighty percent of the funds appropriated must be allocated among the states on the basis of population and employment factors designated in the legislation. In turn, states are required to distribute at least 50 percent of their share to their local governments on a similar basis. The other 20 percent of the appropriation is to be distributed to state and local governments on the basis of competitive proposals submitted to the Civil Service Commission.

The legislation encourages state–local programs in an effort to inspire better coordination and reduce the isolation and fragmentation which now characterizes some of those relationships. There are certain restrictions on when local governments can apply directly for grants. Generally this is not possible if the state has provided an effective state-wide plan after appropriate consultation with the local governments.

One important provision makes it possible for federal agencies to invite state and local people to participate in federal training programs, especially those affecting the APT employees. The impact of this attempt is limited by the fact that federal training programs are not always as good or detailed as would be necessary to meet state and local needs. Exceptions have included the FBI Academy's training programs, which have been used for many years by state and local personnel, and federal training programs such as the Federal Executive Institute at Charlottesville and the regional training centers of the United States Civil Service Commission, which are now open to state and local personnel. Further, training programs of the various civil service regions will be available along with those of the specialized departments and agencies. This should be very helpful to many state and local governments which cannot afford to mount their own training program in some of these subject areas.

Another provision of substantial interest permits interchange of personnel between the federal government and the states, cities, counties, and universities. This could turn out to be very important for, indicated earlier, state and local governments have been unable to compete with federal employees for top specialists and managers. If federalism and decentralization of federal programs is to work, state and local personnel must be upgraded.

However, in situations where there are no state and local personnel to upgrade in the appropriate categories, or where the purposes of that upgrading would be better served by a temporary exchange with a federal employee, this is now possible. Qualified people on federal payrolls can be deployed to state and local governments as well as to universities. There is no requirement that a state employee be exchanged for a federal employee. It is assumed that there will be transfers in both directions, but transfers need not be on a one-for-one basis.

Between May 1971 and July 1972, a total of 283 intergovernmental personnel assignments were initiated. In this period, 149 different organizations, including 38 states, 39 units of local government, 47 universities and 25 federal agencies, participated in the program. Sixty-two state and local personnel were loaned to the federal government and 137 federal employees to state and local governments. The predominant flow with respect to universities was in the other direction, as 52 faculty members were loaned to the federal government and 32 federal employees to universities.[15]

The Department of Agriculture was the federal agency most involved in the university transfers: twelve faculty members were loaned to the Department by twelve different universities, and the Department sent seven of its personnel to work for universities.

Table 3–4 shows how the non-agriculture Department university-federal transfers were distributed. (Not shown is the fact that the National Science Foundation received twenty-two faculty from seventeen universities and sent one staff member to New York University.) The table attempts to highlight the involvement of urban universities and departments in the IPA program. Significantly, the most extensive agency participation after Agriculture was by the Departments of Housing and Urban Development (HUD), Health, Education, and Welfare (HEW), and Labor, and the National Science Foundation (NSF). All except NSF have heavy urban involvement, and NSF has drawn on university faculty for years to fill its key positions. Other urban-oriented agencies participating are the Departments of Transportation and Justice, and the Environmental Protection Agency.

Within higher education, urban university participation was impressive. Of the total assignments to and from universities (exclusive of Agriculture), 58 percent involved institutions in metropolitan areas whose central city had a population in excess of 100,000 in 1970. Interestingly enough, the most prestigious Ivy League universities did not participate at all. There was a tendency for professors assigned to the federal agencies to come from southern cities; on the other hand, federal officials assigned to universities went primarily to schools in California or along the East Coast.

Very few of the largest cities were unrepresented in the exchanges. The only cities having a population over 100,000 which did not participate were Baltimore, Birmingham, Chicago, Cincinnati, Denver, Indianapolis, Milwaukee, Montgomery, and Seattle. However, to have institutions in 35 of the 44 largest cities participating in the program shows considerable balance and urban university participation.

The IPA, then, provides the opportunity for universities to use highly competent federal specialists as teaching faculty or researchers when those needs cannot be met through their traditional hiring mechanisms. At the same time, it creates an easy way of having professors flow to the federal government for specialized assignments. Likewise, the opportunity for state and local personnel to use IPA-funded fellowships to secure graduate degrees and training creates an obligation upon urban universities to be able to offer such training as is needed. In addition, universities will have the opportunity to make major contributions to the training programs established for state and local officials under the IPA.

While the universities are already substantially involved,

Table 3-4

Urban[a] University Participation in IPA Programs

Central city	University	HEW to univ.	Univ. to HEW	HUD to univ.	Univ. to HUD	NASA to univ.	Univ. to NASA	Misc. feds.[b] to univ.	Univ. to misc. feds.[b]
Albuquerque	University of Albuquerque							2	1
Ann Arbor	University of Michigan								1
Atlanta	Georgia State University				1				1
	Spelman College				1				1
Austin	University of Texas							1	
Berkeley	University of California					1			
Boston	Massachusetts Institute of Technology								1
	Suffolk University								
Charlotte	University of North Carolina	1							
Cleveland	Case Western Reserve University								1
Columbia	Benedict College				1				
Columbus	Ohio State University			1	1			1	
Dallas	Southern Methodist University				1				
Dayton	University of Dayton							1	
Detroit	Detroit Institute of Technology								1

Hampton	Hampton Institute	1	
Houston	Texas Southern University	1	
	University of Houston	1	1
Huntsville	University of Alabama		
Los Angeles	University of California	1	
	University of Southern California	1	1
Louisville	University of Louisville	1	
Lubbock	Texas Technical University		1
Miami	University of Miami	1	1
Minneapolis	University of Minnesota		1
Nashville	Fisk University		
	University of Tennessee	1	1
New Orleans	Louisiana State University		
New York	Columbia University	1	
	New York University		
	City University of New York	1	1
Pasadena	California Institute of Technology		3
Philadelphia	University of Pennsylvania	1	1
Rochester	Rochester Institute of Technology	1	
Salt Lake City	University of Utah	1	

City	Institution								Totals
San Jose	San Jose State College								1
	Stanford University						1		
San Francisco	San Francisco State College								1
	University of San Francisco								1
St. Louis	Washington University					1			
Syracuse	Syracuse University								1
Tampa	University of Southern Florida								1
Tucson	University of Arizona							2	
Washington, D.C.	University of Maryland	1							
	Catholic University					1			
	Federal City College						1		
	Howard University			1					
	Washington Technical Institute			1					
	Totals	5	1	3	9	3	1	13	20

aOnly cities with over 100,000 population were included as "urban."
bOthers: NSF, Treasury, DOT, DOD, Justic, EPA, OMB.

SOURCE: U.S. Civil Service Commission Memorandum, "Mobility Assignments Involving Institutions of Higher Education," dated December 5, 1972, with data as of November 30. Additional data were made available by Shirley R. Copeland of the Bureau of Intergovernmental Personnel Programs.

state and local governments have had a higher total of participation, though not nearly as great as is needed. National associations of state and local officials should receive quite a bit of the credit for the passage of this legislation. The United States Conference of Mayors, the National League of Cities, the International City Management Association, the National Governors' Conference, and the Council of State Governments were instrumental in developing the National Training Development Service which was inaugurated on May 1, 1972. NTDS is supported by grants from the Bureau of Intergovernmental Personnel Programs of the United States Civil Service Commission and by the Ford Foundation. One of the prime concerns of this new group was the recruitment and development of minority personnel for positions of administrative responsibility within the nation's cities. Placement, however, was not to be limited strictly to city government; also to be included were federal programs and agencies involved in implementing programs in urban areas throughout the United States.

David Walker, who served on the staff of the Muskie Intergovernmental Relations Subcommittee and later joined ACIR where he performed related studies, has written that

> the Intergovernmental Personnel Act symbolizes the fact that the nation is beginning to become aware of the manpower crisis facing state and local governments. Though its funding is modest ($15 million is requested for FY 1973) and its provisions do not deal with all aspects of the challenge, it can, if properly implemented, go far toward correcting a major problem in our federal system: the imbalance of bureaucratic authority and influence between and among the levels of government and between their core management sector and program specialists. Without this, the promises of any of the New Federalism's proposed fiscal, jurisdictional, and administrative reforms will fall far short of their mark. Devolution will be a detour. Decentralization will be the chaotic design of the program functionaries. And democracy with its promise of a responsible and responsive officialdom will become merely a distant dream.[16]

NOTES

1. Municipal Manpower Commission, *Governmental Manpower for Tomorrow's Cities* (New York: McGraw-Hill, 1962), p. 87.

2. *Ibid.*, p. 56.

3. U.S. Department of Labor, *Manpower: Challenge Of the 1960's* (Washington, D.C.: Government Printing Office, 1960), p. 11.

4. Municipal Manpower Commission, p. 54.

5. David Walker, "The Intergovernmental Personnel Act: Manpower, the Quiet Crisis in Federalism," in Thomas P. Murphy, ed., *Government Management Internships and Executive Development* (Boston: Heath, 1973), p. 249.

6. Municipal Manpower Commission, p. 105.

7. National Association of Schools of Public Affairs and Administration, *Public Affairs and Administration Programs, 1971–72 Survey Report,* Washington, D.C., June 1972, pp. 1, 105.

8. Grace M. Taher, ed., *University Urban Research Centers,* 2d ed. (Washington, D.C.: The Urban Institute, 1971), pp. 1–265.

9. Donald C. Stone, *The Response of Higher Education to the Administrative Needs of the Public Service* (Washington, D.C.: National Association of Schools of Public Affairs and Administration, April 1971), p. 56.

10. *Ibid.*

11. *Ibid.*, pp. 52–53.

12. For a full explanation, see James Banovetz, "The HUD Urban Fellowship Program," in Murphy, ed., *Government Management Internships,* pp. 79–95.

13. *Intergovernmental Personnel Act of 1970,* 84 Stat. 1969. This was S. 11, 91st Congress, signed by the president on January 5, 1971.

14. See Robert E. Hampton, "Partners in Problem Solving: The Essence of the IPA," *Civil Service Journal,* April–June 1971, pp. 1–4.

15. U.S. Civil Service Commission Bureau of Intergovernmental Personnel Programs, "Temporary Intergovernmental Assignments under the Intergovernmental Personnel Act," a report to the President, September 1, 1972.

16. Walker, "Intergovernmental Personnel Act," p. 253.

4

INTERNSHIPS IN URBAN GOVERNMENT

Thomas P. Murphy

One of the most effective options available to universities to help meet the administrative, professional, and technical (APT) manpower needs of cities is the internship. Since governmental internships are at least fifty year old, the internship is perhaps the senior form of off-campus learning. The number and scope of internship programs have been growing measurably for a long time, and the current wave of interest in off-campus learning experiences is contributing an extra push to that growth pattern.

As indicated in Chapter 3, many graduate and undergraduate public administration programs *require* an internship, and others *permit* one. Most of the new urban studies programs have also provided for graduate and undergraduate internships. Further, many of the traditional political science departments have long supported internship programs, although usually with a political rather than a management focus. Departments with public administration programs have generally used both forms simultaneously.

Considering the venerable history of internship programs,

the question arises as to how the urban manpower situation became so serious. If internships may be considered part of the solution now, why have they not been more effective in the past in supplying adequate management manpower? One reason is that internship programs by their nature tend to involve small numbers of students working intensively with a single faculty member—many programs are limited to seniors who qualify for honors, for example. A high proportion of these students have gone to law school after graduation and so never entered the government management manpower pool.

It must be added, however, that internship programs affect a much larger number of students than those directly involved. Experienced professors have noted that interns are able to participate more effectively in classroom discussions because of their experiences, and as they inject some of the raw data from their experiences, they also tend to elevate the level of classroom discussion and enrich the textbook atmosphere which might otherwise prevail. In this respect, the introduction of internship experiences to political science, sociology, and urban studies courses by the interns themselves provides additional leverage not obvious from the small numbers of interns actually involved in a particular program.

Nevertheless, one of the most crucial limitations on expanding the number of such programs is the limited supply of faculty members qualified to serve as internship directors. Bernard Hennessy has written that "the academic world has, as yet, neither the personnel nor the will to provide optimum supervision of participant observation."[1]

The Theory of Internships

Granting their popularity with students and the fact that faculties have permitted, if not promoted, an expansion in the number of intern programs, it is important to review the ways in which internship is relevant to the student's learning program, to the university's educational objectives, and to the advancement of the city's or urban county's governmental function.[2]

Students are less likely to opt for a vocational choice to which they have not been exposed. Nothing makes a career choice so viable as a meaningful, challenging involvement in that profession for some period of time. Such involvement defines the option more clearly, points out career advancement possibilities, creates professional attachments, and stimulates the student's creative energies in that field. Most of all, it offers the student a sense of mission, purpose, and accomplishment —an element missing from the lives of many people in our fast-moving society.

Universities must be concerned with the quality of education their students receive—both in the students' own interest as well as that of the university's reputation. If students are to understand fully how government and politics operate, they must be exposed to more than what is available from textbooks. Internship seminars featuring outside speakers from the world of action who can be questioned are one means of supplying such exposure. However, in terms of its ability to provide the students with an opportunity to "feel" the realities of governmental management and its relationship with policy-making and politics, the internship experience is unique. Further, to the extent that internship sponsors find the program helpful, the university establishes community support useful in its other ventures.

The basis of the internship is that the student becomes a participant-observer in the processes of governmental decision-making and service delivery. By performing work useful to the organization, the intern becomes a member of the team and therefore feels the constituency pressures, develops a better appreciation for the needs of the clientele served, understands the barriers that bureaucracy places in the way of effective government, and learns the difficulty of applying data to justify the establishment of a new program or to evaluate its effectiveness.

On the governmental side, a number of factors motivate an agency to accept interns. Some do so on emotional grounds such as "supporting" the local university; others may participate to show their administrative peers that they are "with it" by working with internship students. The upwardly mobile administrator is generally flattered to be selected by a university as an intern sponsor and is usually willing to trade off what he may perceive as an additional training burden on himself for the enhanced image that it will provide him.

Another motivating factor, especially for city and county

governments that do not offer high salaries, is the opportunity to introduce a bright student to the governmental management system in hopes of later recruiting him. Most interns spend a considerable number of hours at the agency and so can be seen working under a variety of circumstances. This provides a more rational way for employers to evaluate potential employees than does the fifteen-minute interview.

Experienced administrators who have already served as intern supervisors are generally motivated in these ways, but when their prior experiences have been satisfactory, they develop new motives. Some intern sponsors who were skeptical at first about whether the image versus workload trade-off would be worth their time have been very satisfied with the intellectual challenge interns can provide. Interns bring new ideas to their environment and contribute by questioning the reasons for old approaches and policies. Employees who are less perceptive or more security conscious may not be as forthright and evaluative as interns who are on a temporary assignment.

Also, the combination of intern energy, intelligence, and a receptive environment often leads to tangible results of value to the organization. In short, where effective intern experiences have occurred, the internship is looked upon as a fair trade with the student deriving valuable experience and the organization receiving just compensation in one form or another. Whenever this mutual involvement also results in a recruitment, the internship is invariably judged a success by all the parties involved.

Academic Questions

An almost limitless number of questions surround the academic side of internship programs. For example, how much credit should be given and for what kinds of internship experience? Since the best students are not attracted to careers in government after graduation, should the program be limited to only those most academically qualified? What other factors should be taken into account? What should be the criteria for selection? How should time be divided between classroom and work experience? Should the student be permitted to take other courses during the internship, or should the internship be an all-encompassing experience? How should the seminar be used?

Because the questions are potentially limitless, many of the ensuing answers must necessarily be based upon considerations of time and circumstance.

An essential element of the internship experience is the weekly seminar. Generally this is used to provide the students with an opportunity to express to other students as well as to the director what they are learning. In this process the academic director is able to use the effective experiences of one student to inspire the others to greater efforts. Each intern has his antenna up and learns to examine his behavior in comparison with that of the other interns. This can help those who are not receiving good assignments and enables the director to evaluate whether he made a mistake in selecting a particular governmental supervisor as a sponsor. Such seminars can be used to bring together not only students and faculty but also outside resource persons such as city managers and budget and planning directors experienced in urban affairs. This opens up a process of cross-fertilization which provides the student with the broader exposure he needs to evaluate academic theory. Also, some interns find it comforting to learn that professionals in the field are being subjected to the same kinds of frustrations that they are experiencing on the job.

Creating the bridge from the classroom to the administrative world is not an easy task. The internship is, in part, a maturation process, and so the student must realize that the success of the whole endeavor rests largely upon his initiative in seeking out and assuming responsibility. Therefore, the student must think of the internship as an opportunity, for that is essentially what it is—an opportunity to relate everything that he has learned and everything he sees during the internship to his own decisions on career advancement. The seminar can help the intern sift through these thoughts and formulate a position.

Often the seminar series has some kind of unifying theme such as the application of administrative theory. This may be stressed by assigned readings and term papers. It is important, however, that the director not overemphasize the textbook approach. The most important value to be derived is the students' communication of their experiences.

Internship experiences and classroom work gear together very well. As James Banovetz has phrased it:

The internship is an experience in which the participant gains his first exposure to actual job techniques—to paper processing, project execution, and decision-making. Hopefully, too, it is an arena in which classroom concepts can be observed and applied. Classroom work could teach these same skills, but it is more important that the classroom deal with the implications of the techniques and methods used in administrative operations. These implications are insights into administration that a young administrator might learn on the job—or might not. Typically the administrator is so busy coping with the volume of facts, questions, and paper crossing his desk that he has little time to stop and reflect about the implications of what has been happening.

Processes such as decision-making can, in part, be learned in the classroom. Students can be taught how to define the parameters of a problem, identify alternatives, gather pertinent information, assess possible consequences, and make decisions. But, in part at least the process must be learned through actual experience. The internship is the most effective device used to provide actual, monitored experience in the application of administrative processes.[3]

The purpose of internship programs is to provide the student with insights not readily gained in the classroom to reinforce chalkboard wisdom with the meaning only participant-observer experience can bring—in short, to round out the student and provide him with the necessary equipment to make it in the modern administrative jungle. The internship provides the student with an opportunity to work inside the governmental system. The perceptive student can relate his experience to the scholarly theory he has learned. Further, the interns derive satisfaction from serving the needs of the city, rather than simply reading or talking about them. Invariably interns also learn the frustrations of trying to use administrative techniques to bring about change and improve the urban environment, and in doing so, they contribute to its improvement. Doing and thereby learning are the essence of the internship.

However, it is important to stress that the internship is an introductory rather than a finishing experience. Much of the criticism leveled at internships is based on an evaluation of the "urban plunge" experiences connected with urban semester programs which are viewed as containing an internship element. While these programs appear to involve internships, some essential differences must be noted.

First, the introduction to urban experience as part of a general liberal arts degree program *is* often considered by the students and faculty involved to be a temporary immersion in urban affairs. Second, these programs tend to be carried out with a larger group of interns than can be handled effectively by an academic director. They often are nothing more than the physical move of a traditional size class and teacher to the inner city for a semester. Third, the academic director is more likely to be a social critic and observer than a public policy and action-oriented individual. Fourth, because of these other factors, the internship assignments are often very heavily weighted toward social action and social work projects. Fifth, with this combination of people and experiences, even the seminar is unlikely to redeem the program as an internship.

Given this environment, the following critique of urban semester internships by Elden Jacobson and Parker Palmer has much validity:

> Even in the finest of intern possibilities, however, two serious limitations seem to obtain by its very nature, an intern position is based upon what is the case, at a given moment in time, and in a particular governmental or voluntary agency context. Even granting the dubious assumption that such involvement from within illuminates the purpose and decision-making machinery of the particular agency, the student must still determine the degree to which such purposes are worthy of support, or the degree to which his observations are more than idiosyncratic, and hence capable of generalization. Yet, that is to demand of students what academics themselves cannot give; we simply do not know, with precision and understanding, "what is" in scarcely any complex metropolitan area. And the issues become magnified many-fold when we aspire to normative judgments regarding what *ought* in fact to be. Intern programs may, as advertised provide students "maximum opportunity and responsibility to innovate, to pursue their interests while at the same time performing a service to the institution." The more likely, indeed the more rational, expectation, how-

ever, rather compels us to hypothesize that students are
being schooled by the very institutions that account for
much of our present social malaise, and by the very individuals whose own vested interests reside in seeing
"urban" piecemeal—those self-same "city and state
leaders, or experts in various phases of urbanology."

Secondly, and to our minds perhaps more importantly,
intern programs place students in roles vis-a-vis the city
that they are very unlikely to occupy again. "Work as
administrative intern out of school administrator's office,
a city councilman's office, or out of the office of a community organizer," as one program phrases it, has genuine appeal, and in the best of circumstances, affords the
possibility of much substantive insight. But to what purpose? That same urban program, its advocates have in-
sisted, enhances "the adult roles that the students will
shortly be acting out as adults." How's that? In the
mayor's office? In the school administration? Or as a
community organizer? Perhaps so. But that such temporary locations within the fragmented political and social
order of our time do in fact "illumine adult roles" is only
to state the hope, not demonstrate the fact. From the
suburbs they have come, and to the suburbs most liberal
arts college students will most assuredly return, there to
occupy such "adult roles" as dentist, housewife, business-
man, minister, whatever.[4]

Still another problem identified by Jacobson and Palmer
relates to the impact of a "do-gooder" urban semester internship experience:

A further variation on the intern theme derives from
what we have just argued, one having to do with reinforcement of a seldom explicit, though almost always
present, conception of the "adult role" as essentially voluntary. To be an "agent of change," hence, is to relate
personally and immediately to other individuals—
"other," by implication, usually meaning Black or poor
or otherwise "disadvantaged persons." Again, we can
hardly fault the sensitivities from which the voluntary
role emerges. It is indeed the case that, within some
(hardly all) contexts, personal relationships across racial
and economic barriers in fact enhance one's capacity to

see and feel. And it is possible—though contradictory evidence of times appears overwhelming—that such empathetic relationships can and do motivate and direct human action. We ask again, however, to what end? Is "experience" as such adequate? Do programs stressing tutoring, for example, only reinforce a simple, personalistic understanding of ghetto life as one of personal pathology and individual underaccomplishment? Within our own inquiry, involving both students and a wide spectrum of adults, this personalistic attitude prevails above all others, the consequences of which are constantly manifest in activities that stress personal, person-to-person action. The middle-aged, concerned suburbanite continues, to the extent time is available, to tutor, to engage in clothing drives, to transport central city children into the suburbs for summer recreation, to operate "big brother" programs, etc. We do not demean these programs and the sensitivities that motivate them. But we increasingly believe that these *necessary* acts of personal charity and concern are widely perceived as *sufficient* responses to the crucial dilemmas of political, social and economic power that presently undergird societal injustice. Urban programs may in fact heighten personal awareness. They may, contrary to stated intention, simply solidify the voluntary role as the only viable one students see.[5]

The case against urban semester internships is summed up in the evaluation of an internship program reviewed by Jacobson and Palmer. Their impressions after interviewing the interns were that

> not one was genuinely conversant with issues of metropolitan power and with the decision-making machinery that largely governs the shape and quality of urban life, nor was this of any particular interest to them. None could articulate with any clarity the meaning of his urban sojourn for future roles he might live out, whatever those finally become. Indeed, most found this, too, an uninteresting question, predicated on a future orientation they largely rejected. As it were, the dominant image or impression was one of uncertainty and confusion; the urban semester was perceived as an isolated, self-contained experience.[6]

These criticisms of urban semester internships are to some extent true of all urban internships. However, they do not apply with equal force to public administration and urban studies internships whose objective is to develop urban managers, especially those at the master's level. This type of intern is expecting only an introduction, and generally receives it. This type of student is also studying the full range of urban social, economic, political, and service problems and does not expect to change the urban world overnight.

Faculty Internship Directors

In addition to running the seminars, a potential antidote to the "urban plunge" pitfall of internships, other aspects of the faculty director's participation are equally important. Those faculty members who are best qualified have generally been interns themselves and, ideally, have had responsible management experience in state, local, or federal government in addition to appropriate academic credentials. Intern directors with all these qualifications will be in a much better position than others to anticipate the problems of interns adapting to their new environment, to counsel interns so that they may be more useful to their sponsoring organizations, and to help governmental sponsors use interns in the most effective way possible in terms of their learning experience. The intern director who can swap stories with the governmental sponsor about the kinds of assignments interns did for him when he worked in the government has an advantage because many governmental sponsors are reluctant to permit students to work on matters they consider sensitive or complex. However, with a little encouragement and the gradual demonstration by the intern that he or she can be relied upon both for performance and loyalty, these fears can usually be overcome.

In addition to his role in selecting the interns, the academic director also determines the governmental locations where interns will be placed. Both of these kinds of decisions affect the credibility of the intern program. If students are placed in unsuitable places or the governments receive students who are not mature or motivated enough to be effective interns, the program will quickly go downhill. Because of the mystique connected with internships, word of trouble spreads rapidly among both student and governmental grapevines. Even an old program can be killed in a relatively short time by an inexperienced director who is unable to resolve problems which arise between interns and organizations. For example, if an intern is not receiving appropriate assignments, usually because he or she is being used as a clerk instead of a professional trainee, the academic director must be able to counsel the intern on how to change this situation. If that fails, the director must know how to intervene directly with the governmental supervisor. In drastic situations, it may be necessary to move interns—even in the middle of the semester. The academic director must be able to decide when this must take place and do it without creating any lasting damage in the relationship between the intern program and the governmental unit.

The academic director, therefore, cannot effectively discharge the program responsibilities by remaining on the campus; he must make field visits to secure feedback from governmental supervisors. A close rapport between the student and the academic director is essential so that the director will know how the intern is being perceived by the receiving agency, what kinds of assignments he is being asked to perform, and whether the relationship is going to be productive. Frequently, the academic director can point out possibly ignored opportunities such as involvement in regular staff meetings or official hearings. Some of these added touches can make a vital difference in the effectiveness of the internship as a learning experience.

New Directions in City Management Internships

A few years ago some of the most successful internships involved training urban generalists as city managers. Often the participating cities provided six- to twelve-month internships to public administration master's degree students who had completed their academic work. As Fred Fisher has summarized the system:

> These provided a pipeline from a few committed graduate schools to an equally small number of enlightened communities through which dedicated students traveled to

gain exposure to the "real world of public administration."

It was a unique and valuable tutoring system, seasoning
the bright young generalists in the practical world of
urban management, and preparing them for early entry
into the city manager profession. Men like Perry Cook-
ingham, Woodbury Brackett, and Robert Morris became
identified as mentors to be trusted and called upon frequently, to provide the personal capstone touch to a
budding career. They took particular pride in their mission and readily sacrificed privacy and gave long hours of
patient counseling to assure their young proteges a good
start.

These early internships were a bold and noble experiment in the preparation of professional management
talent for our nation's cities. In a sense, they served
to develop an elite corps of professionals woven together
by bonds of loyalty to schools and mentors, reinforced by Christmas newsletters, annual get-togethers at
ICMA conferences, and a good word at the right time
from the academics when their "boys" were under consideration for a new job. It was a system that worked—
and worked well—in the unhurried world of decades
past. It provided a high level of confidence among elected
officials seeking new talent in the market place, reasonably met the needs of a slowly expanding profession, and,
no doubt, developed consternation among competing job
seekers from lesser known schools when they were up
against this cartel of academics and practitioners.[7]

City management internships still exist and are still important. However, as the field of urban management has broadened and some of the old school academic leaders have retired,
new graduate programs concerned with urban management
have grown up, often in urban universities. Paradoxically perhaps, an even more significant factor in their decline has been
the rapid growth of urban America, combined with an ever-
deepening federal involvement in virtually every sphere of
urban life, and the concomitant inability of traditional internship programs to fill the demand for urban administrators
created by that growth.

One of the facts of governmental life is that the largest
cities have generally not used city managers. The requirement

for strong political leadership to hold together a diverse society and help broker its competing demands seems to require that the top position in a major city administration be held by an elected official. In large cities these elected officials work full-time whereas in small cities this is not the case. This factor alone makes it more possible for the elected official to take an active role in management as well as in political decision-making.

However, larger cities have even more need than smaller ones for professional management, and so numerous opportunities exist for professionals to operate within large cities and urban counties. Aided largely by the federal grant programs, which have supported the establishment of many professional jobs outside the often inflexible civil service systems, numerous job opportunities have been created for professional managers in urban government. The narrow focus of the old city manager training programs has not been adequate to deal with this newer, broader approach.

Most professional administrators no longer enter public service with the assumption that they want to be a city manager in a small or medium size city. In fact, many city managers have given up their posts to take key positions in the largest cities as department head, director of the budget, or professional deputy to an elected official. Another major source of generalist urban manpower for large cities and urban counties is the new urban universities and other universities which have urban and public administration programs. However, some functional positions such as the health director and the public works director are still filled with persons having academic backgrounds in health and engineering rather than in public administration or urban studies.

The generalist urban manpower pool, as indicated in Chapter 3, has been growing at a rapid rate. The field of urban management clearly includes many specialists other than city managers. For example, urban counties and major cities with elected chief executives also have a top strata of professional managers, and subordinate administrative, professional, and technical positions are also important. Regional metropolitan governmental organizations and associations, many of which are headed by former city managers, have also expanded rapidly. All these changes led the International City Managers

Association to change its name in 1969 to the International
City Management Association.

Furthermore, another new requirement which has necessitated a much broader and more intensive approach to recruiting urban manpower has been the need to place greater
numbers of minority employees in key positions. Urban migra-
tions which have created black majorities in some cities and
endowed others with large Spanish-speaking populations have
caused intensive reexamination of recruitment procedures. The
intern director, therefore, must pay greater attention to distributive questions such as the race, sex, and age of intern applicants. A large number of minority-oriented special intern programs have emerged to help meet this need.

National Urban Fellows Program

The inner machinations of an urban internship program can,
perhaps, be best illustrated by the National Urban Fellows
Program launched in the summer of 1969 by the National
League of Cities, the U.S. Conference of Mayors, Yale University, and the Ford Foundation, which contributed the financial resources for the program.

The program began with 24 Fellows who demonstrated
potential for urban leadership. Drawn heavily from ethnic
minorities, these Fellows were placed with carefully selected
urban government managers. During an intensive six-week
academic experience at Yale University that involved seminar
participation by key practitioners, academics, and specialists
from urban management, the Fellows participated in small
group sessions which helped to convey new understandings of
theory and reality in urban affairs. The Yale seminars and
workshops were followed by ten-month assignments as special
assistants to elected city and appointed urban executives, city
managers, mayors, and school superintendents. In most cases,
the interns also took graduate courses at local universities, and
three one-week seminars held back at Yale permitted the Fellows to exchange experiences and deal intellectually with some
of the key urban issues.

In selecting its applicants, the program put no primary
emphasis upon professional or technical background. However, the first round of interns exhibited solid experience in gov-

ernmental service, law, the ministry, business, and community development. In 1970, the program expanded both in the *number* of Fellows selected, and in the *range* of ethnic and occupational backgrounds represented. That year 36 Fellows were selected from 265 candidates.

The base of operation and concern in the Urban Fellows Program has been broadened from an "administrative intern to the city manager" approach to a wide array of internship offerings open to all academic disciplines and majors. The job-agency placements of the interns themselves also complement the new academic focus of the program. Although the National Urban Fellows Program is small in numbers, it is especially valuable as an avenue for the advancement of ethnic minorities previously given limited opportunities to penetrate the top echelons of urban management.

The National Urban Corps

The Urban Corps has operated on the philosophy that public service internships should result in helping government to get things done while teaching the student about the realities of urban government and community life. Consequently, its college internship programs have been based upon three principles:

1. It draws upon college students at *any* level of their education and from *any* academic discipline to offer them a significant, career-oriented experience in the public service.

2. It operates through a local Urban Corps office, often staffed by students themselves, which administers the program.

3. And it is offered through the federal "College Work-Study Program," which provides funding to cover (up to) 80 percent of the compensation for students who need money to remain in school.[8]

Because the Urban Corps operates through the federal College Work-Study program, funds for the Corps are distributed by the Bureau of Higher Education of the U.S. Office of Education. Funding for the program involves the Office of

Education's determining the amount of College Work-Study Program (CWSP) funds available to each state according to the allotment formula laid down by Congress. The Office of Education then determines the funds available to the college in each state on the basis of recommendations made by a regional panel which has reviewed the application and the proportion of low-income students attending the institution. Once established, the Urban Corps office receives its funding directly from the university *through* the university's CWSP funds.

As noted earlier, selection for Urban Corps assignments takes place through the College Work-Study Program at the university. Urban Corps policy is to provide higher hourly salaries for interns than for CWSP students employed *on* the campus, the rationale being that Urban Corps internships involve performing a range of more difficult and professional assignments. In addition, the downtown internship results in extra food, clothing, and transportation expenses. Financial arrangements can therefore become quite complicated and may vary widely in Urban Corps programs.

Agencies applying for interns are required to submit a special written "job request" form, completed personally by the prospective supervisor (of that agency) who will be working with the intern. The form must clarify the supervisor's own conception of the nature of the assignment and the type of student needed to fill it. A fundamental operating principle is to insure that staff assignments provide the student with definite and measurable goals, and with leeway for initiative and discretion in carrying them out.

Another unique aspect of the Urban Corps program lies in the fact that most Urban Corps "contract" for the services provided to public agencies by their interns. That is, the responsibilities shared jointly by the institution and the Urban Corps for choosing participating students, their work, and its termination are spelled out in an Urban Corps-College contract. This arrangement provides a feasible mechanism for both the college and the Urban Corps to exercise some semblance of control over a program for which they are mutually responsible.

The Urban Corps placement process has essentially three parts: first is an Urban Corps referral—the local unit matches each student with an assignment based on the written agency request, the student application, and a personal interview; second is the student-supervisor interview—the student and supervisor meet to work out the requirements, activities, and goals of the internship, and, if either the supervisor or the intern is dissatisfied, the student is reassigned; third is the evaluation—the Urban Corps staff visits each student and supervisor at least once a month to smooth out potential differences, transfer students if necessary, and compile information for future program development. The Corps views placement as its most important job, since there is a continual need for a middleman to mediate possible conflicts in student and agency interests.

Most Urban Corps programs evolve around the academic format of a seminar, although this may vary from place to place as the institutional climate dictates. In other words, there is no set pattern with respect to either the types of internship assignments or the academic format used in relating work experience to academic theory.

Although the Urban Corps has drawn its life from Title IV C of the 1965 Higher Education Act, which served to provide needy students with an opportunity for summer and part-time work, the Urban Corps program is by no means a poverty program. Eligibility for the program is a discretionary decision, with school administrators often adopting a liberal interpretation of what constitutes "need."

Leon W. Lindsay wrote an article which gives some meaningful insights on the actual operation of an Urban Corps internship program in the city of Atlanta, Georgia, during the summer of 1969.[9]

As mentioned previously, many traditional city internship programs have been faulted because they allowed only a few graduate students to work with an equally select number of top municipal officials. In dealing with less prestigious internship programs, governments often delegated menial work to these interns, especially if they were minority group students. Atlanta broke this pattern by actively recruiting large numbers of students for important work on matters involving the city and also by involving many non-governmental agencies.

Atlanta interns were gathered from 45 different colleges and universities, 18 of which were in Georgia, and worked in 16 government divisions as well as in 38 private agencies. The

interns served in 53 different job categories such as management, assistant labor relations worker, social worker, dietary
assistant, and teaching assistant. The selection criteria used
favored minority students.

The Atlanta program also demonstrated that the cooperative funding concept is gaining favor in programs that attempt
to address the problems of the public domain. Of the $205,000
necessary to implement the program during 1969, the city of
Atlanta put up $52,000, another $78,000 was provided from
HEW's College Work-Study Program, $40,000 was provided
by the Southern Regional Education Board, and the final
$35,000 came from private business sources within the com-
munity.[10]

The Community Service Learning Program

Federal funds are essential to give permanence to internship
and fellowship programs, particularly those which seek to provide opportunities for minorities. The Education Amendments
of 1972 provide for a Work-Study For Community Service
Learning Program, authorizing $50 million per year to pay
college students for internships in the public or private nonprofit sector.[11]

In February 1972, Senators Edmund Muskie and Edward
Gurney proposed amendments to the Intergovernmental Personnel Act of 1970 to establish permanent funding. These
amendments would provide federal matching funds on a 3–1
ratio to local and state governments for fellowships at their
respective levels.[12]

The Muskie-Gurney Bill calls for 500 state fellowships
(10 per state) modeled after the White House Fellowships and
for 500 federal urban fellowships patterned after those of the
National Urban Fellows Program. This legislation indicates a
concern for current means of *access* to programs which prepare students for future m id- and upper-level government
administration.

The National Center for Public
Service Internships

In addition to this federal legislation, a new program has been
developed with Ford Foundation seed money which will also

promote urban internships. The National Center for Public Service Internships (NCPSI) provides a central organization to disseminate knowledge of programs leading to careers in the top levels of governmental administration and management. NCPSI includes among its priorities: establishing a clearinghouse for information, providing technical assistance, conducting research, and exploring means of financial support for internship programs throughout the United States at all levels of government.

To help broaden access to governmental leadership development opportunities, the Center will compile and disseminate (particularly to minorities and women) a roster of opportunities, objectives, admission requirements, timetables, and benefits of various programs. The Center also hopes to provide public officials, universities, and persons conducting internship programs with access to a broad pool of potential applicants.

The Center was formed with the cooperation of a broad spectrum of national, regional, and local groups concerned with internships. On the governmental side, the International City Management Association and the National League of Cities are represented on the board of directors; also, the National Association of Counties, the National Governors' Conference, the Council of State Governments, and the U.S. Conference of Mayors have given support in a variety of ways. Academic representation is present both through the National Association of Schools of Public Affairs and Administration and the Union for Experimenting Colleges, as well as through various specific college and university internship programs. Other special interests are reflected on the board by members of the Urban Corps and HSPERA, a New York-based Puerto Rican group concerned with internships.

In the words of the chairman of its board of directors, Dr. Robert Sexton, the NCPSI should serve as

> an institutional response to present needs, it should help blend together heretofore divergent forces. By pulling together the resources of academia, government, the public service sector, and the interested public in general, new avenues and new quality should be available in the internship field. The Center will be an advocate for improvement and growth. The Center could produce a network for information exchange and hence vastly ex-

panded service-learning opportunities for those who seek
them. At the same time, research carried out with scholarly thoroughness should improve internships internally,
and answer questions about long-range effectiveness, assessment, and funding. Research will also open new
avenues of funding and ensure the continuance of existing sources. Program model building, for example, could
greatly improve federal legislation and programs; model
design will also be helpful to those drafting legislation on
the state level.[13]

National Association of Schools of
Public Affairs and Administration

The NASPAA (National Association of Schools of Public Affairs and Administration) Urban Administration Fellows Program serves as an excellent example of the typical academic-
ally-oriented internship program. The goals of this program are
double-edged and mutually complementary. On one hand, the
program awards fellowships to minority students to aid them in
completing a master's degree in urban public administration. In
addition, it hopes to provide federal, state, and local governments with highly qualified minority management manpower.
The length of the program may vary from one to two years, depending upon prior experience of the individual Fellow, and
that experience may be counted as "good time" toward the internship aspect of the program, which is the key link in achieving the program's goals.

NASPAA Fellows are provided a quality education in
one of the participating colleges or universities of their choice,
and reinforce formal learning with exposure to the special
skills which only experience can provide. Experience is given
the Fellow through the opportunity to work under the close
supervision of a respected urban administrator. Bonds formed
during this relationship often endure well beyond the life of the
formal program. Thus the NASPAA Urban Administration
Fellows Program incorporates the best aspects of traditional,
city manager programs through its mentors, while serving a
broader purpose than those programs. Thirty-eight fellows
started on master's degrees in public administration in the fall
of 1971 and another sixty in the fall of 1972. To date there
have been only six dropouts.

Miscellaneous Programs

Many other programs nationwide do not rely exclusively upon universities or the federal government for funding or program direction. Examples include the Southern Regional Education Board's Resource Project (initiated in 1967), the Urban Careers Program (initiated jointly by American University and the District of Columbia personnel office in 1969), a statewide program entitled the New Jersey Interns in Community Service, and finally, the year-long full-time program for master's students that has been operated continuously since 1950 by the city of Phoenix, Arizona.

Academically-based fellowship and internship programs are funded by a variety of public and private sources. They include corporations, the Ford and Sloan Foundations, universities, state governments, the Department of Housing and Urban Development, and the Office of Economic Opportunity (OEO). Examples of such programs would be the Stanford Urban Management Program, the ICMA Minorities in Management Program, the Consortium for Graduate Study in Management, the Public Administration Programs of Syracuse University, the Minorities in Urban Planning Programs, as well as the National Association of Schools of Public Affairs and Administration (NASPAA) Urban Administration Fellows Program.

Generally, academic programs feature internship as an essential element and tend to attract younger people whereas experience-based programs most often attract mid-career people. It should be noted also that academic internship programs tend to give minorities greater exposure to potential executive careers in government than do the executive development or mid-career programs.

NOTES

1. Bernard Hennessy, *Political Internships: Theory, Practice, Qualification* (University Park: Pennsylvania State University Press, 1970), p. 115.

2. Thomas P. Murphy, ed., *Government Management Internships and Executive Development* (Lexington: Heath, 1973), pp. 1–23.

3. James Banovetz, "The HUD Urban Fellowship Program," in Murphy, ed., *Government Management Internships,* pp. 89–90.

4. Elden E. Jacobson and Parker J. Palmer, *Urban Curricula and the Liberal Arts College* (Washington, D.C.: Center for Metropolitan Studies—Department of Higher Education, National Council of Churches, 1971), pp. 18–19.

5. *Ibid.,* p. 20.

6. *Ibid.,* p. 22.

7. Fred Fisher, in Murphy, ed., *Government Management Internships,* p. 65.

8. "College Students in Local Government," *Management Information Service,* ICMA, March 1972, pp. 3–4.

9. Leon Y. Lindsay, "Urban Corps Fights for Survival," *Christian Science Monitor,* August 26, 1964.

10. *Ibid.*

11. U.S. Congress, Senate Committee on Labor and Public Welfare, Conference Report No. 92–798, May 22, 1972.

12. U.S. Congress, Senate Bill 2134, 92d Congress. Reprinted in the *Congressional Record* of February 8, 1972, vol. 118, no. 16, p. 51327.

13. Robert Sexton, in Murphy, ed., *Government Management Internships,* p. 270.

PART TWO

Universities and the Community

5

THE UNIVERSITY PUBLIC SERVICE MISSION

George E. Spear

> Celibacy does not suit a university. It must be wed
> with action.
>
> *Alfred North Whitehead*

From 1929, when Whitehead advocated the union of higher
education and action, until the mid-1960s, there was little
romance between the university and the city. Neither showed
an inclination to woo the other, and it seemed that any off-
spring would necessarily be the result of immaculate conception. However, the new-found urban consciousness of the
society, manifested in the Great Society legislation beginning
in 1965, began to encourage new bedfellows, among them the
university and the urban community.

The issue of this union is now being evaluated after the
better part of a decade and, depending on the beholder's eyes,
is seen on the one hand as The Prophet and on the other as
Rosemary's Baby. Fact and truth probably lie somewhere
between these extremes.

The urban consciousness of universities and their faculties has been tied directly to the availability of funds, usually
from federal sources, for projects, demonstrations, and experiments in community and social problem-solving. Title I of
the Higher Education Act of 1965 provided a major stimulus

which has been supplemented by projects supported through
the Office of Economic Opportunity (OEO), the Department
of Housing and Urban Development (HUD), the Civil Rights
Commission, the Law Enforcement Assistance Administration (LEAA), the Department of Labor (DOL), and a spate
of other departments and agencies attempting to implement
the philosophy expressed in the legislation of the past decade.
A total of 143 federal programs which contributed in whole
or in part over $4 billion to extension, continuing education,
and community services activities were identified by the National Advisory Council on Extension and Continuing Education in its sixth annual report.[1]

Lack of experience in applying knowledge to real world
problems, in addition to the inherent reluctance of university
faculties described in Chapter 4, resulted in basic infirmities in
many of the new public service programs. These difficulties
were compounded by an absence of coherence and coordination in federal support. The sheer number of government
departments and agencies involved created a hopeless tangle
of overlapping, competing, and conflicting activities and programs. National priorities, objectives, guidelines and even
philosophies changed almost annually, thereby destroying continuity of effort among compatible programs and the possibility of reliable evaluation of program efforts.

However, the billions of dollars available were sufficient
to call many individual faculty members into the arena and
encouraged massive activity where there was little before.
Whatever was missing in direction and coherence was more
than offset in quantity and diversity. Universities have been,
and indeed continue to be, engaged in a remarkable variety of
service programs, testing social and educational theories at
nearly every level in every institution in society.

Clientele groups include the disadvantaged, the aged,
minority groups, women, the unemployed, public officials,
urban youth, and the adult illiterate. Programs range from
city planning and beginning reading to welding and drug
abuse. Schools of education have sought to improve urban
public schools and schools of law have provided legal services
to the urban poor. No single chapter could provide a comprehensive overview of the service involvements of urban
universities. It may be useful, however, to sketch some of the

variety of programs in progress to provide an appreciation of the diversity of activity and an understanding of how far some institutions have moved from strict adherence to the traditional code of the academy.

One caution should precede any discussion of urban involvement. Since narrow definitions are used by many people concerned with urban problems, to some the words "community" and "urban" refer only to minority people, their neighborhoods and their problems. This poverty of definition has severly restricted the scope of understanding of both the urban dilemma and the means by which universities might impinge upon their social and physical environment. "Urban" should, of course, include reference to the inner city, but it must also refer to the entire metro-complex of city, suburbs, and outer fringes and too all the people and systems which must interface and integrate in order to maintain social viability.

For the sake of organization, program types can be divided into two categories. The first deals with programs which are essentially community-oriented, and the second with programs which focus on the individual. The differences between the two have more to do with concept than content, since it is obvious that both must approach their objectives through people. Community programs often state their goals more generally than do individual programs, which are usually not only better defined but also more easily measured.

Community-Focused University Programs

Representative of the community approach is the Greater Homewood project, established under Title I by Johns Hopkins University in Baltimore, Maryland. Homewood, a predominantly white neighborhood in northern Baltimore, represents much of the heterogeneity found in truly urban places. Over 40,000 people live in the area; there is an ethnic mix, as well as a variety of ages, occupations, and socio-economic levels. Its problems are typically urban, with racial tensions, crowded schools, unsystematic zoning, inadequate traffic control, rising crime, deteriorating business and residential areas, and inadequate health services for the poor among the most serious.

Johns Hopkins University began addressing itself to this

community in 1967. For two years the faculty assisted in developing local leadership, identifying area problems, cataloguing possible resources, and establishing local mechanisms for developing and implementing community action programs. As a result of this effort, a citizen-controlled non-profit organization was incorporated in 1969 to solve the many problems of local concern. Activities included work toward better enforcement of housing, zoning, and health codes; alleviation of traffic problems; development of better schools; encouragement of appropriate businesses and needed social services; and establishment of a master plan for community development. This Johns Hopkins effort gave impetus and leadership to a significant urban community movement that can document measurable effect on, if not necessarily major progress in, specific problem areas.[2]

In Syracuse, New York, the University College established a Thursday Morning Round Table which each week brings together 65 men and women from the community who represent organizations, agencies, and positions which have special public responsibility. The sessions are devoted to discussions of local or area problems and improvement of communications among community leaders. Participants come from government, business, education, and civic organizations, and the Round Table is credited with having served as a launching point for broadly-based community development efforts in the Syracuse area.

In addition, University College semi-annually sponsors a two-day retreat to which 50 to 75 civic leaders are invited for intensive study of a single community problem. Experts of local, state, or national reputation contribute to the examination. Problems addressed in the past have included health care, transportation, law enforcement, public education, housing, and public financing. Through this combination of programming, University College contributes to both on-going and in-depth consideration of community problems with the resources of higher education available to the urban area.[3]

In the Midwest, the Urban Affairs project of Washington University assumed a commitment to establish a partnership with its surrounding community, to work closely with and for the people of the neighborhood. Redevelopment of St. Louis's inner city, part of which is located near the University, has gained a great deal of interest and support from both inhabitants and outsiders, with the result that small plants are being built in the ghetto, housing is being rehabilitated, and once-empty storefronts are opening again with new small businesses.

One St. Louis neighborhood intent on self-reviving efforts is the Yeatman District, where a community corporation is receiving a major assist from Washington University. The University's School of Continuing Education has offered intensive courses in small business management for operating or prospective businessmen in the neighborhood. A conference on environmental problems in the urban ghetto was conducted, and a series of action conferences sought to help inter-neighborhood associations engage in cooperative planning to deal with crime, education, housing, and employment problems. In addition, an architectural skills training program was mounted to support a group of high-school-age youths working with community agencies on site surveys, housing rehabilitation, and building investigations. From these programs a cadre of persons skilled in community planning and development has been established and is a continuing resource for the corporation and the neighborhood.[4]

These community service projects in Baltimore, Syracuse, and St. Louis share the common objective of improving a neighborhood and seeking to influence community response to a variety of problems. Community improvement programs seem to be most attractive to universities, lured apparently by the prospect of creating a better world with massive educational injections. Individual-serving programs seem to present a more tedious route to the utopian state. The fact that the former have been able to demonstrate significantly less success apparently does not dampen institutional enthusiasm.

Characteristically, community service programs begin with substantial involvement of faculty members, and frequently their students, who lend technical assistance to action projects, design and assist with applied research and data gathering efforts, and conduct broad educational courses and conferences. However, the pattern noted in Chapter 9 tends to develop, whereby adult education or service becomes institutionalized as part of the administrative rather than the academic mission of the university.

The Carnegie Commission on Higher Education notes

that an evolution takes place in such efforts, and the role of
the institution becomes "administrative rather than substantive."[5] As the Commission's report states:

> [T]he seekers of the service may look to the college or
> university primarily for financial support for the pro-
> gram, for physical facilities, or for an organizational
> structure within which the program may operate or
> within which it may receive private foundation or govern-
> ment grants. It is particularly this type of involvement
> in service activities that appears to justify the position of
> those within the academic community who urge the uni-
> versity to leave public service to others and to confine
> its own activities to teaching and research.[6]

This finding is reinforced by the conclusion that in cities
where urban universities are engaged in a variety of projects,
there have been demands from the community constituency to:

—encourage large community inputs into training for
community service

—make this training, in part, accountable to the community

—emphasize contact with the real world for more in-
training for urban roles

—blend the professor and the community, decentralizing the training process and encouraging community
people, not academics, to organize field experience.[7]

University Service to Individuals

It is as it works with individuals for their personal development, rather than through community oriented programs, that
the university seems most closely to meet the expressed needs
of the urban representatives. Individual lives require a less
grand design for action, are less complex, more responsive
and susceptible to educational impact, and ultimately are
easier to measure for progress and improvement.

Project 360°, coordinated by the University of Wisconsin
in Madison, is an adult career education program intended
primarily to help the disadvantaged and hard-to-reach adult.

As such it has a broad audience appeal. A fourteen-state consortium plus Canadian institutions cooperate in television, radio, and newspaper dissemination of vocational information. In a non-traditional format the project deals with job finding, interviewing, training, and the use of employment agencies. Also explained is how the adult roles of parent, spouse, friend, consumer, citizen, and autonomous person relate to career opportunity. The program takes into account special local and individual problems related to ethnic, racial, economic, and educational characteristics.[8]

The introduction of such a broad media approach differs from most individual-oriented activities conducted by universities. More characteristic is the program that enrolls the individual in formal course work and provides in addition a variety of supportive services required by his or her economic, social, or educational deficiencies.

The Urban Program in Education (UPE) of the University of Michigan was a five-component effort to attack problems in metropolitan education through individual development. The program experimented with new teaching methods intended to develop more successful and relevant approaches to teaching the poor. Five separate programs were established: New Careers, Experimental Teacher Training, Child Development Consultant, Leadership Training, and Service Components.[9]

New Careers enlisted teacher aides in the Detroit schools and helped them begin work toward ultimate teacher certification while working in paying jobs in public education; it also incorporated community and citizen participation in program planning. Experimental Teacher Training united ten experienced teachers and twenty teacher trainees in a program to learn team teaching and to develop specific skills and insights into the problems of urban education. Twenty Child Development Consultants from teaching and social work backgrounds worked toward making better use of individualized instructional materials and strategies and toward solving non-academic problems that impede the progress of disadvantaged children in school. Leadership Training participants were assigned to make use of their considerable experience to consult, conduct in-service training seminars for urban teachers, and work with central and regional school boards in Detroit's decentralizing school district plan. Under Service Components, the University set up a Fresh Air Camp as a micro-lab to provide a setting for children and educators to develop self-awareness and self-fulfillment. The Community Resource Center, located in the inner city, was established for the benefit of both educators and community patrons with classes, workshops, and seminars as part of the regular fare in addition to self-study opportunities.

The most readily observable value in the UPE was the New Careers component, where the progress of teacher aides toward state certification was apparent in grades and transcripts. In addition, a research study showed that personal attitudes, family cohesiveness, and similar spin-off benefits to the individuals were by-products of the effort.[10] Because impact upon public education in Detroit cannot be similarly documented, the Urban Programs in Education languish with only New Careers and the Community Resource Center surviving. After only three years, many of the people who were central to establishing the program have turned their attention to other matters.

Two programs conducted by the Division for Continuing Education at the University of Missouri–Kansas City concentrate on different objectives, but both single out female populations for study. The first, Teenage Motivation, was begun in 1966 with Office of Economic Opportunity funding to develop both leadership and personal development skills in girls from poverty neighborhoods. High-school-age leadership teams from each of nine neighborhoods were trained and, in turn, recruited groups of their peers to take part in programs dealing with self-concepts, early marriage, career goals, and life patterns. Guest speakers, role playing, and group discussions were used to expand understanding and perception.[11]

Evaluations turned up changes in participants' behavior and dress; increased ability to function in groups; tendencies to seek help with personal problems; increased concern for education and job placement; and more familiarity with the community and its institutions located outside the traditional inner city environment. The project was transferred from the campus to the University of Missouri's area extension center after six years and became part of a new urban youth effort by the Extension Division in its search for innovations to supplement traditional 4-H youth activities.

The second UMKC effort responded to a more recent awareness within the federal bureaucracy concerning opportunities for women employees. A Lunch 'n Learn series of midday seminars featuring speakers and discussions was launched for the Kansas City Regional Office of the Department of Housing and Urban Development (HUD). Clerical personnel participated to expand their awareness and interest in current topics of social consequence. Programs on government, personal psychology, urban sociology, and women's roles were held during the seminars. The favorable response of the women to these sessions resulted in HUD's establishing the model in other regional and area offices and the General Services Administration's contracting for similar programs. Lyceum-like women's programs have less demonstrable value and impact than those that deliver specific skills or recordable degree credit, but they do promote the broad objectives associated with the concept of life-learning stressed increasingly by professional adult educators.[12]

Program Pitfalls

It is not simply by grammatical option that descriptions of projects are usually phrased in the past tense; the reality of most programs' duration is such that present tense descriptions are seldom warranted. Most activities once operative now lie in unmarked graves with the knowledge and experience gained unavailable to anyone other than those who took part in the project.

The problems begin with financing. Title I and related legislation have failed to meet either the needs or expectations of the community by funding projects too often determined by the personal agendas of designated state officials. Faculties have been disenchanted by the intrusion of political motives into program designs and operations, and many have abandoned the streets rather than combat the public purse-holders.

Programs typically have been funded on an annual basis which made the life of each venture precarious and subject to premature termination before its effectiveness could be properly assessed. Funds have usually been delayed by failure of either congressional or state allocating agencies to perform in accordance with announced timetables, and project directors frequently have found themselves called upon to write proposals for the refunding of a project before its initial phase was under way.

Finally, the seed-money concept which prevails in all such service programs calls for institutions to provide a portion of matching funds for every activity. The underlying assumption is that the institution, with an investment in the program, will continue the program after federal money has been withdrawn. This assumption was naive from the outset because it failed to take into account the fact that most programs are experimental and, by their nature—which is extension or adult education—do not represent the core of academic commitment or mission. When a faculty member or department has had to choose between an allocation of resources to traditional or to service programs, traditional missions have won without contest. The availability of federal money did draw widespread interest and participation but failed to provide encouragement to the building of on-going academic support for urban efforts, and the impact, in terms of change on campuses and in departments, has been minimal.

Financial difficulties aside, some basic assumptions about the capacity of urban universities to meet the needs of cities are frail and largely unjustified. The Carnegie Commission on Higher Education stated: "The campus is not prepared to respond to emergency calls for instant action, instant results. The community may expect too much—the campus is only a marginal resource in solving urban problems."[13] The dangers obviously lie with the dimensions of the needs versus the available resources for making university service significant in the urban setting.

The term problem-solving, dear to the hearts of urban and extension program administrators, immediately conjures up visions and expectations for laymen which cannot be fulfilled. Education has always been inclined to make promises not likely to be kept; in the urban arena the difficulties are compounded.

Problem-solving and technical assistance demands are generated in a variety of ways by the urban constituency seeking university faculty to become directly involved with the city or community. Faculty members with the necessary skills are frequently not even on the staff of the institution, however, and those who might help are often preoccupied with their own interests and research. Faculty are most often inclined to view community service as applied research, while community leaders seldom express interest in reseach beyond some low level of data gathering.

Academic reaction to community expectations can be found in the remarks of a college professor, "I am a teacher, a discoverer of new knowledge. We [traditional professors] have no specific contribution to make. We don't even live well in the city. We are more likely to be interested in the history of the sewers of Paris than solid waste management in this city."[14]

The urban constituencies, reports the Organization for Social and Technical Innovation, respond:

> Urban studies centers have not met any real needs and in some cases have exacerbated tensions between community and university by appearing to be a child of the university's bad faith. They are perceived as collected data which they use for their own rather than the city's or community's purposes, as being university-sheltered consulting firms, as being expensive and useless, as imposing themselves instead of coming only when asked —as being in short, empty and foolish gestures. The demand for problem solving and technical assistance is for something different from what universities are now doing.[15]

By contrast, law schools providing legal services for the poor and schools of medicine and dentistry offering health services in the ghetto are usually direct, successful, and appreciated programs that fill obvious personal needs. Programs in education and welfare seldom meet with similar acceptance since they tend to directly challenge the existing programs in fields already crowded with agencies and institutions. Thus conflicting efforts, assumptions, expectations, assessments of needs, and inventories of capabilities between the city and the university impede and discourage university personnel charged with the service mission.

Evaluation

Federal agencies' inability to account for the progress of programs funded under various legislation has become an accepted fact of life in spite of sometimes elaborate efforts to build evaluation into specific activities and the hiring of evaluation teams and firms. If its weakness is forgivable at the federal level, it is not so easily overlooked in the community, and there is even a self-consciousness within universities arising from the uneasy feeling that they are somehow falling short of their own expectations. There is, indeed, a temptation within the academic community to conceptualize social problems globally and thereby to invite evaluations of problem-solving efforts on the basis of global impact and effectiveness.

This problem was illustrated in a meeting of extension administrators called upon to review some outstanding urban program developed by their institution. One spokesman described a neighborhood project in which an abandoned school was converted into a community center, citizens councils were organized, surveys conducted on area needs, and a variety of educational and action programs initiated. While expressing personal commitment to and confidence in the concept and process, he confessed that nearly two years of effort showed little change or improvement in neighborhood conditions. A second administrator, in turn, outlined a special program for teacher aides designed to help them become certified for regular positions in preparation for the day when their jobs would be terminated as federal project funds were exhausted. Seventeen aides received certification and were indeed able to secure permanent employment as a result of their certification. He counted his institution's program a success.

The significance lies in the measures by which effectiveness is reckoned. In the case of the community project, had the lives of selected individuals been used as the basis for evaluation rather than broad neighborhood improvement, the effort would probably have registered some successes. By contrast, had the teacher aide program been measured by impact and improvement in the public school system, it would probably have been recorded as a failure. It seems obvious that some service programs have suffered not so much from poor design or execution as from the measures applied in evaluating their worth.

Recommendations for the Future

There is no question that urban universities must and will continue to involve themselves in public service. Cities and their problems will not go away, nor will the demand of the supporting public that higher education apply itself to the task of helping to ameliorate urban pathology. The only issue is how the university may best assume its role. There are few disciplines that cannot in some manner improve the quality of life if scholars seriously attack the task of application. The potential impact of knowledge must surely be acknowledged if it is dynamic and if it is expanding across broad fronts as in the obvious case of the hard sciences and technology.

This century has offered a variety of social inventions that have contributed significantly to economics, domestic and international politics, government, and education. John Platt, in *Ekistics,* noted among these social advents: Keynesian economics, operations analysis, information and feedback theory, theory of games and economic behavior, operant conditioning and programmed learning, planned programming and budgeting, and non-zero-sum game theory.[16] Among these inventions are a number that made possible the management of a variety of social and political problems. They were the result of men of different disciplines and perspectives joining to address new ways of thinking about problems in the real world.

There is reason to believe that, in truly interdisciplinary efforts, members of university faculties might devise solutions to the problems of their environment. New problems may not be solved by old solutions, but new solutions can be achieved if approached with open minds, creativity, and commitment. A distinction should be made between interdisciplinary and multi-disciplinary efforts. The first suggests focusing the collective knowledge of fields of knowledge, whereas "multi-disciplinary" implies an aggregate, but not necessarily integrated, effort directed toward some common problem or area. The first is the basis of hope for social invention relevant to the problems of a changing society.

If the university is to be of genuine consequence in the urban community, and if the success of its service programs is to be more than modest—a kind word used by the National Advisory Council on Extension and Continuing Education—

the burden must be assumed by the faculty.[17] Service cannot continue largely as administrative doctrine. Administrators must place responsibility with the faculties, demonstrate courage in the allocation of resources to cooperating departments rather than to those refusing participation, and, finally, insist that personal and professional recognition and rewards accrue to those academicians who assume the mission. Such an administrative posture would undoubtedly prove persuasive to many of the reluctant. This approach will contribute to the urban community and, equally important, will enhance the learning process within the institution as professors involve their students in activities and reflect their own new understandings in the classroom. This result would in itself be sufficient reason for university commitment to service involvement.

Commitment without resources is, of course, futile; both institutional and national funding will be required to make university service effective. The institution must also redirect some of its own continuing resources into new and promising programs at the expense of traditional but no longer viable disciplines. These funds alone, however, will never be adequate to the task. The dreams encompassed in legislation such as Title I of the Higher Education of 1965, to recreate the service and impact of Cooperative Extension, will not be realized without federal funding in similar amounts and for similar duration.

Another little recognized factor in the success of Cooperative Extension was the selection of only a few universities in the nation to which all available funds were given. These institutions could build substantial academic resources, undertake research programs, develop new expertise, and create a dissemination/problem-solving system of sufficient size to make noticeable impact. Federal funding for urban problems has been small in dollar amount, spread among as many institutions as possible for political impact, and generally granted for periods of a single year. The result has been small programs usually inadequate to the task, little incentive for universities to build academic resources for service, and termination of programs before a test of effectiveness could be made. If Cooperative Extension is to be the model for urban extension, comparable support and assurances must become part of the national commitment.

The commitment needs to be accompanied by consistent national goals and priorities, stated clearly in order that urban service programs can be designed coherently and toward measurable objectives. The rapidly shifting and generalized goals which have characterized the foundations of program funding in the past encouraged vague concepts upon which vague plans and wandering efforts were established. Granting the danger to innovation, it is nonetheless true that progress is measured not only by distance traveled but also by direction of movement. There is no criticism of the federal direction given to research and its application in the Manhattan Project or in Project Apollo. Social goals are not so easily established, but there is still some national consensus as to certain improvements that woud benefit the human condition.

Once guidelines and goals are clearly established it becomes the burden of the university to choose areas of participation which are within its ability to serve. Careful self-analysis should be conducted, relating continually to the type and magnitude of the tasks to be accomplished. Two temptations persist: first, to embark upon ventures which are unrealistic in terms of the academic and fiscal resources which are available; second, to grasp at any funding opportunity in order to demonstrate involvement even though the central mission of the university is not necessarily compatible. Restraint need not be equated with reluctance, and wisdom can be demonstrated both in knowing what to do and what not to do.

Associated with this wisdom in choosing activities must be considerations of accountability and credibility. Urban service programs need measurable goals, and these are most likely to be found in efforts directed to individual improvement and development. Impact upon the quality of an individual's life is relatively easy to measure and document. Improvement of communities and systems is not only difficult to measure but, perhaps, even impossible to effect. Universities have always measured their worth by the progress they are able to produce within and for the student, one-by-one and rarely on a collective basis. Impact on the world at large has never been an academic goal per se. Development of the individual has been the central focus for higher education, and this is what universities do best by design and by nature. That they should apply similar perspectives to serving the city and its adult population is not only reasonable but also more likely to be successful.

Universities must also develop means by which knowledge and experience gained by one can be disseminated quickly and effectively to others. Once invented, the knowledge of the wheel should become universal. Scholarly journals, extensive bibliographies, and other tedious channels of communication within the academy are inadequate to the task in a rapidly changing society, particularly when so much media technology is readily available. In a world where the report of a boat capsizing in the Sea of Japan is known internationally almost immediately, there is little excuse for the isolation existing among the scholars at work daily at common tasks of major importance to society. National attention should be directed toward this need and resources be made available to the development of the appropriate dissemination systems.

To the university engaged in urban service there is an element of risk, to be sure—risk of failure, of losing credibility, of falling victim between contending clientele or power interests, of discovering that cherished beliefs and traditions have been fallacious and inaccurate. The greater risk, however, lies with the expectation that universities will be allowed to exist at all by a society that has found them inadequate to its existing needs.

NOTES

1. National Advisory Council on Extension and Continuing Education, *Sixth Annual Report of the National Advisory Council on Extension and Continuing Education,* Pursuant to Public Law 89–329, 1971, p. 24.

2. U.S. Department of Health, Education and Welfare, Office of Education, *Program IMPACT Report,* Community Service and Continuing Education, Higher Education Act of 1965—Title I, 1972.

3. Syracuse University, *Memo From Syracuse,* Adult and Continuing Education Report, No. 1, August 1972.

4. *Program IMPACT Report.*

5. Carnegie Commission on Higher Education, *The*

Campus and the City: Minimizing Assets and Reducing Liabilities (New York: McGraw-Hill Book Company, 1972), p. 75.

6. *Ibid.*

'7. U.S. Department of Health, Education and Welfare, Organization for Social and Technical Innovation, *Urban Universities: Rhetoric, Reality, and Conflict,* June 1970, p. 13.

8. Commission on Adult Basic Education, Adult Education Association of the U.S.A., *Newsletter,* vol. 2, Fall 1972.

9. Chauncey D. Moten, "A Study of Perceived Changes in Behavior, Attitudes and Outlooks as Related to Participation in a University-Conducted Four Year New Careers Program," The University of Michigan, August 1972.

10. *Ibid.*

11. Author was consultant to project.

12. Author conducted lectures for project.

13. Carnegie Commission, *Campus and the City,* p. 3.

14. Remarks made in conversation with author's colleague.

15. HEW, *Urban Universities,* p. 20.

16. John Platt, "What We Must Do: A Mobilization of Scientists as in Wartime May Be the Only Way to Solve Our Crisis Problems," *Ekistics,* vol. 28, no. 169 (December 1969) pp. 447–451.

17. *Sixth Annual Report of the National Advisory Council on Extension and Continuing Education.*

6

FREE UNIVERSITIES AND
URBAN HIGHER EDUCATION

Thomas P. Murphy

Student claims that college education is irrelevant are not an invention of the last decade. For at least half a century, candidates for doctorate degrees in social sciences who passed every requirement except the German reading exam have been known to mumble, "What is the purpose of it all?" What is new in the last decade is that students have started to do something tangible about their dissatisfaction. It should not be surprising that students who responded to civil rights crusades, freedom marches, Vietnam and environmental teach-ins, and end-the-war rallies have directed some of this activism toward the curriculum of their college or university.

University higher education curricula constitute a sitting duck in that they are so slow to change. Insecure professors whose courses are required by all majors in their field fight to the last committee meeting to prevent their conversion to electives. The uncomfortable fact is that many professors need captive audiences if they are to have any audiences at all for the ritualistic recitation of their old graduate school class notes. As might be expected, attempted reenactment of classroom scenes created by a Talcott Parsons, a John Galbraith, or a V. O. Key often falls flat.

In a survey of undergraduate curriculum trends from 1957 to 1967, Dressel and De Lisle reported that their sample of 322 undergraduate programs involved very little change. "They reward with scorn the 'tinkering' of faculties, and find 'almost unbelievable' the lack of 'major modifications' in the curriculum. On second thought, they mark the 'vested interests' of 'faculty members and departments' and they are not optimistic about change."[1]

This situation presents both philosophic and pedagogical dilemmas. Students are demanding what they term "relevance" and certainly it is hard to oppose that. There is no reason why social science cources should not use references from current events to illustrate trends and relate to the specific subject matter for the course. Yet anyone who has mingled with the crowd at semester registration and has heard students attempting to advise each other as to which professors to avoid knows how much of a clear and present danger boring teaching is considered to be. The move to mass education with large lecture sections numbering in the hundreds of students has exaggerated the effect of bad teaching. In many cases these large lectures are assigned to the professor with the least seniority to qualify for an upper level seminar. As a consequence, the least experienced faculty member is often given the hardest job—that of meeting three times a week with an audience of 250 intellectual conscripts taking a required course and daring him to make it interesting.

The solution does not necessarily lie in dropping all requirements or in letting students dictate what courses pass the test of relevance and are to be in the curriculum. In fact, student consumer complaints about the quality of teaching have led to widespread adoption of student evaluations of higher-education teaching. In some schools the students even publish course guides which name names and indict professors for their sins of classroom omission and commission while cheering on those who provide a better product.

Even this is not self-correcting, however. Students' evaluations are merely advisory to the faculties of the various departments, especially to their promotion and tenure committees. Often those who are already sitting on the committees and have tenure themselves are on the list of 25 worst professors printed on the back page of the course guide. The result is that a bad rating for a junior professor can be used as a basis for dismissing him, yet a good rating for a junior professor may engender jealousy on the part of those who must decide upon tenure. This is not to suggest that students ought not to have such rating systems. Most open-minded faculty members interested in improving their techniques have long solicited student comments voluntarily and have tried to mend their ways when they thought the students had a valid criticism.

Origin and Philosophy of the Free University Movement

The free university movement, begun in the early 1960s, had its intellectual origin in *The Port Huron Statement* issued in 1962 by Students for a Democratic Society (SDS). The 63-page pamphlet asserted that faculty and students had to "wrest control of the educational process from the administrative bureaucracy. They must import major public issues into the curriculum—research and teaching on problems of war and peace is an outstanding example. They must make debate and controversy, not dull pedantic cant. They must consciously build the base for their assault on the loci of power."[2]

The SDS program then called not only for making changes on the campus in terms of up-dating the curriculum but also for relating these changes to the political process. This approach opened up the whole issue of politicizing the campus, which is of course still a major issue. Although the SDS statement made no specific mention of free universities, the whole approach of linking political and other off-campus movements with student activities and of changing the classroom approach to both content and process was the basis for the free university approach.

The massive movement of college students to Mississippi in the summer of 1964 for the "freedom schools," which combined civil rights and an education crusade, further set the stage by establishing a model for student activity. That same fall the famous sit-ins at the University of California-Berkeley brought the educational process to a halt as students argued for more influence over the nature of the education offered them. In the spring of 1965, after the Johnson landslide victory over Barry Goldwater, a massive American buildup occurred in Vietnam and led to the famous teach-ins on campuses across the nation.

Some analysts of the free university movement consider the Free University of Berkeley (FUB) which was established in December 1964 as the first free university.[3] The movement received major impetus following the SDS convention in the summer of 1965 at which considerable attention was devoted specifically to free universities and their organization. Actually, the movement spread so fast that SDS lost whatever control it may have had. Student dissatisfaction with college education was already widespread, and the free university movement was a natural outlet.

Jane Lichtman, who had the support and sponsorship of the Hazen Foundation and the American Association for Higher Education, traveled across the country in a home truck to visit the free universities after she discovered that they were so uninstitutional that she was unable to derive effective data from the questionnaire approach. According to Lichtman, there were about 150 free universities operating in the spring of 1972, including at least one in every state of the union.[4]

However, Lichtman states that free universities are more likely to evolve slowly than to start during crises. She adds:

> Many develop as student educational activities out of the Dean of Students' Offices. They are characterized by drug seminars, ecology-action programs, birth control counseling, education seminars, election-year political forums, encounter and sensitivity groups, workshops and crafts . . . groups in the arts . . . training in daily needs . . . and sports, such as football, rocketry, frisbee which has been a credit course at one regular university—akido, judo, and penny-pitching. The free university in these instances is a supplement to the classroom, not too different from a university's other student-initiated extracurricular activities.[5]

Free universities fall into three loose groups—those affiliated with the universities, those which are autonomous but rather closely tied to a particular institution, and those which are autonomous but not associated with an institution. The

Lichtman definition for a free university is "a *mechanism* to connect people who want to teach or learn with the resources to meet their needs."[6] Reflecting their origin, few have restrictions on age or background of their students. They tend to use unpaid volunteers to develop and run the courses, charge minimal fees, and do not use grades, diplomas, or degrees. These are the criteria used in compiling the Lichtman Directory; as a result only 110 free universities of the 150 previously cited are included. Seventeen states are unrepresented in the *Directory*.

Some of the most successful free universities are affiliated with traditional universities. Of the 111 in the *Directory*, 69 percent are based on campus, usually under the auspices of the student government association.[7] Table 6–1 indicates the 39 largest programs in terms of student participation, number of courses offered, and budget. Sixty-two of the 111 programs draw their funding exclusively from student activity fees funneled through the student government association, and 15 others draw more than half their funds from this source.

The response to the opportunity to participate in a free university is often surprising. When a group at Dartmouth College started one, their well-advertised venture drew just over 1,000 participants, including one-fifth (585) of the Dartmouth student body, 173 students from Colby Junior College for Girls, 70 faculty members, and 230 residents of the Andover area. This made the Dartmouth Experimental College (DEC) the fourth largest college in New Hampshire. The response was simply too great, and only about half of those who replied were accepted for courses, with 32 faculty members among those rejected. However, the spirit of the venture is reflected in the fact that the dean of Dartmouth College and the director of admissions both applied for courses. The dean of faculty was quoted as saying, "A healthy institution will work very hard to promote this kind of insurgence."[8]

One of the more famous ventures in free universities occurred at San Francisco State College, where an Experimental College (EC) was organized in 1966. In terms of percentage of the total student body, this group never attained the 20 percent figure reached in the early days at Dartmouth, but in 1967 its enrollment soared to about 2,000 which amounted to 15 percent of the total college enrollment.[9]

Table 6–1
Major Free Universities

Name	Year founded	Number of students 1971–72	Average number of courses	Approximate budget	Affiliation and source of budget
ASOSU Experimental College Oregon State University	1969	6,000	165	$11,000	Student govt.
Free University of Penn.	1965	6,000	108	1,700	Student govt.
University for Man Kansas State University	1968	5,000	206	8,030	Student govt.
Free University (N.Y.)	1970	4,800	56	3,750	Student govt. institution
Rochester Institute of Tech. Center for Participant Education Florida State University	1970	4,200	114	10,062	Student govt.
Experimental College University of Conn.	1969	3,000	140	9,300	Student govt.
University of Thought Houston, Texas	1969	3,000	200	1,000	Autonomous donations
Short Courses University of South Carolina	1969	3,000	60	15,000	Student govt.
Experimental College San Diego State Coll. (Calif.)	1967	2,600	56	4,200	Student govt.
Experimental College Cal. State College, Fullerton	1971	2,500	52	2,500	Student govt.
Denver Free University, Colo.	1969	2,500	205	24,000	Autonomous, fees

Major Free Universities

Name	Year founded	Number of students 1971–72	Average number of courses	Approximate budget	Affiliation and source of budget
Experimental College—San Fernando Valley State Coll., Cal.	1970	2,450	50	$ 1,930	Student govt.
Communiversity Univ. of Mo.—Kansas City	1970	2,000	230	6,950	Student govt.
Free University Ga. Institute of Tech.	1969	2,000	80	25,000	Student govt.
Minnesota Free University Minneapolis, Minn.	1967	2,000	237	1,000	Autonomous, fees
Michigan State Perversity Michigan State University	1966	2,000	50	1,200	Student govt. donations
Abenaki Experimental College University of Maine	1970	1,900	191	2,000	Student govt.*
Experimental College University of Cal.—Davis	1966	1,500	30	3,150	Student govt.
Comm-University West Cal. State Coll.—Long Beach	1965	1,200	55	4,200	Student govt.
Free University Penn State Univ.	1970	1,200	100	1,720	Student govt. donations
Free University of Muncie Ball State University, Ind.	1969	1,200	56	1,720	Student govt.

Table 6–1 (Continued)
Major Free Universities

Name	Year founded	Number of students 1971–72	Average number of courses	Approximate budget	Affiliation and source of budget
Community Free School Inc. Boulder, Colo.	1968	1,200	142	$35,000	Autonomous, fees
Kansas Free University Univ. of Kansas—Lawrence	1967	1,150	100	2,400	Student govt.
Free Univ. of Berkeley Berkeley, Cal.	1964	1,000	200	12,000	Autonomous, fees
Experimental College Cal. State Coll.—Los Angeles	1968	1,000	80	2,430	Student govt.
Oshkosh University of Wisconsin	1970	1,000	40	2,500	Student govt.
Amistad Univ. of New Mexico	1968	1,000	32	2,100	Student govt.
Free University Temple University (Pa.)	1968	900	50	1,000	Student govt. donations
Baltimore Free University, Md.	1968	800	100	2,500	Autonomous, fees and donations
Alternate University Univ. of Illinois	1969	700	54	4,600	Student govt.
Nebraska Free Univ. Univ. of Nebraska	1967	600	N/A	2,100	Student govt.

Table 6–1 (Continued)
Major Free Universities

Name	Year founded	Number of students 1971–72	Average number of courses	Approximate budget	Affiliation and source of budget
Washington Area Free Univ. Washington, D.C.	1969	550	60	$ 2,700	Autonomous donations
U.C.L.A. Experimental College Los Angeles, Cal.	1966	500	63	2,000	Student govt.
Entropy San Francisco, Cal.	1970	500	100	9,650	Autonomous, fees
Experimental College Univ. of South Alabama	1969	400	40	3,600	Student govt.
Experimental College San Jose State College, Cal.	1966	400	25	4,000	Student govt.
Free University of San Diego, Cal.	1970	250	52	1,500	Autonomous, fees
Alternative Education Sacramento State Coll., Cal.	1970	120	N/A	1,400	Student govt.
Dartmouth Experimental Coll. Dartmouth College, N.H.	1967	N/A	N/A	N/A	Student govt.

*Affiliation only, no funds provided.

SOURCE: Jane Lichtman, *Free University Directory*, (Washington, D.C.: American Association of Higher Education, 1972).

One of the unique features of the Experimental College (EC) at San Francisco State was the existence of a 60-member faculty that was paid subsistence wages. "Money was important to the Experimental College because their idea of organized and committed staff called for salaries. The staff was paid from $50 to $150 per month for teaching or office work."[10] As it happened, some in the EC were also leaders of the student association. James Nixon, a founder of the EC, was president of the Associated Students which provided $6,000 out of its budget of $412,000 raised through a mandatory student activity fee. The total EC budget exceeded $21,000, with the rest of the money derived from foundations and other fund raising ventures. The EC staff worked full-time at the tasks of running an academic program.[11]

The EC catalog declared, that from a philosophical standpoint,

> The idea is that students ought to take responsibility for their own education. The assertion is that you can start learning anywhere, as long as you really care about the problem you tackle and how you tackle it. The method is one which asks you to learn how you learn, so you can set the highest conceptual standards of accomplishment for yourself. The assumption is that you are capable of making an open ended contract with yourself to do some learning and capable of playing a major role in evaluating your own performance. The claim is that if people, students, faculty, and administrators work with each other in these ways, the finest quality education will occur.[12]

In terms of goals, free universities have four common features. First, they aim to create a new environment for learning. In a reaction to the large lecture classes becoming more common at major univresities, the free university has provided a seminar environment providing an opportunity for expression and for feedback from fellow students. Nevertheless, the academic content of such sessions may be lower than desired since the free university is rarely in a position to require extensive reading lists. Furthermore, the opportunity to express opinions may amount to a pooling of ignorance.

Second, there is an emphasis on improving the relationship between the faculty and students by making participating faculty members more available to students. In these non-structured situations faculty need not be dominant figures. This can contribute to the students' learning how to take more responsibility for their own education and understanding that education does not mean having a professor inject facts into the students.

A third element involves efforts to make education available to all kinds of people. Some of the free universities have attracted a fair number of people over thirty from the community. This happened at Dartmouth and also in many cities where the community is more diverse than that of a college town such as Hanover. Sometimes people from neighboring military bases have come as students or even faculty; this has led to some interesting confrontations and some surprising accommodations. Contributing factors to the diversity are often the loneliness of people looking for someone to talk to or the frustrations of older people looking for the opportunity to talk to young people as a means of understanding their own children.

A fourth characteristic is the stress on learning about more relevant subjects. A review of the course offerings in most free universities immediately points up the more contemporary nature of the free univerity courses and their preoccupation with contemporary events. They are also more likely than traditional programs to take advantage of the overstatement techniques of advertising. In reality, some of them are not nearly so shocking as their titles would suggest.

The very existence of the free universities and their courses is a critical commentary on the ability of the traditional universities to perform effectively. The involvement of the over-thirty folks in the free university suggests that universities are also failing in their adult education responsibilities. College administrators are often as dissatisfied as students are with faculty-centered learning in a departmental context. This is reflected in the great desire of administrators to work with foundation and government projects offering greater flexibility of operation and fewer barriers to hiring specialized people needed for the project.

Operation and Curriculum

As would be expected, the curriculum of a free university is extremely broad. Most programs issue open invitations to virtually anyone to organize a course which is then offered through the group's catalog. The catalog may be a slick printed brochure or something run off on a mimeograph machine.

In some situations the course coordinator actually writes a syllabus and constructs a reading list. Often the coordinator does nothing more than propose a subject and convene the group to work out its own procedures. Generally, outside speakers are invited only with the consent of the group. There is much reason to leave the course somewhat unstructured since it is intended to serve the needs of those who indicated an interest and there is no way to know what these interests will be until the first meeting of the course.

The courses that develop in the free environment seem to fall into four major categories. Political causes are likely to dominate the total number of offerings. However, they generally eschew the traditional political science approach and instead take on a problem orientation which involves applying student values to some problem in society. Frequently this results in castigating the traditional governmental institutions which are supposed to be dealing with that problem. The next most popular category seems to be what might be called counter-culture courses dealing with occult, philosophic and religious questions, modern music and arts, and the application of social psychology to the new life styles. A third major category consists of self-improvement courses that, with the exception of some psychology offerings, are unlikely to be in college curricula. The fourth category might be labeled "community involvement." Here again the focus is on a problem, but it may go beyond studying the social problem to include an action project to alleviate whatever difficulties are perceived. Virtually all programs have examples representing the first three categories, while some other programs have explicitly stressed the educational element to the exclusion of action projects.

There are numerous other distinguishing characteristics. In terms of faculty, for example, some of the free universities, such as the one at Ohio State, have used only official faculty from the traditional school on a moonlighting basis. Others have relied heavily or even exclusively on non-professional teachers, a format reflecting the views of those questioning the value of course credit. Groups heavily influenced by SDS, such as the Free University of Pennsylvania, generally thumb their noses at the prospect and, in fact, probably would have some difficulty receiving credit approval. But even groups such as the more sedate one at Dartmouth have just not desired the entanglement and limitations that would come with credited courses. On the other hand, in its first year, twenty-two of EC's courses were approved for credit by San Francisco State College, and approximately one-sixth of the students registered in all the courses received official credit.[13] Numerous other free university students were able to take courses which were credited toward degrees at the traditional colleges.

The Communiversity program in Kansas City, Missouri, is a good example of a free university.[14] It made its first start in 1968 but after two semesters died for lack of leadership and funding. In 1970, the candidate for president of the All Student Association (ASA) at the University of Missouri-Kansas City ran on a platform of beginning a "student university." After his election, he succeeded in sponsoring the allocation of $5,800 from the ASA for operating expenses of the program; it has continued to be funded by the students' association, although in 1972 there was a move to cut that support in half on the basis that up to 60 percent of participants in the courses were from the community rather than the student body. Action was postponed after a plea from the director that the program's original two objectives—providing education different from that of the classroom and providing a forum for community and university people to interact—had been achieved and that any attempt to change the percentage of funding provided by the student association would result in losing student control of the program.[15] That is, any outside source would be likely to put more pressures on the program or to change its direction.

Success of the program is illustrated by the data in Table 6–2, which shows a continuous increase in the number of courses offered, the number of registrants for courses, and the total number of individuals involved. Similar growth has been experienced by the summer session, which had 60 courses in 1971 and 87 in 1972. By 1972, the budget had climbed to

$10,000 a year, approximately half of which was used for the salary of a full-time director and the rest for printing, supplies, communications, and travel.

The program does not involve any student fees and makes extensive use of university facilities. Because no credit is given for courses there are no grades. Teachers are called conveners in an effort to break down the traditional student–faculty relationship and insure that students become more involved in formulating their own education.

Table 6–2
Enrollments in Communiversity

	Courses offered	Course registrations	Approximate number of enrollees
Fall 1970	40	600	400
Spring 1971	80	1,400	800
Fall 1971	90	1,700	1,000
Spring 1972	120	2,100	1,200
Fall 1972	150	2,700	1,600
Spring 1973	135	3,000	1,900

SOURCE: Alice Lawler, Director, Communiversity UMKC, "History of the Program," 1972, and letter from Alice Lawler, February 10, 1973 and March 6, 1973.

An interesting aspect of this particular university is one of its sub-units, the peoples' law school run by the Kansas City chapter of the National Lawyers Guild. Courses were offered in the fall of 1972 on the following subjects: Laws and Politics of Grand Juries, Constitutional Challenges to Urban Existence, Drug Law, Researching the Law, Police Misconduct and Citizens' Rights and Remedies, Juveniles and the Law, Municipal Court Law, Tenants' Rights, How to Get Unemployment Compensation, Consumer Awareness, and Women and the Law.

These course titles had action overtones and, when added to the clearly action-oriented projects, constituted a reasonably heavy emphasis for a supposedly conservative midwest university. The action projects included: In the Footsteps of Ralph Nader—Environmental Action (Cleaning Up the Missouri River), the Citizens' Lobby for Penal Reform, Consumer

Lobby, Crisis Intervention–Suicide Prevention, and Telephone Reassurance Service for Live-Alones.

The political courses had titles such as Current Events and the New Media, Politics and Literature, the Kansas City Committee to Defeat Nixon, Campaign Issues of 1972, the Relevancy of Socialism, and Why Bother to Vote. This selection is proportionately smaller than that available in the free universities associated with eastern or western universities.

In the self-improvement category the fall catalog offered: Jazz Ensemble, All about Harp, International Folk Dance, Beginning Folk Guitar, Theater for the Hell of it, Folk Music Workshop, Taking the Mystery out of Investing, Communication through Photography, You Are What You Eat, Drawing and Painting, English Refresher Course, Reducing Your Income Tax, Beginning Chess, Macrobiotic Cooking, Pottery, Crocheting, Leathercraft, Table Tennis, Modeling, and Conversational English for International Students.

In the occult and counter-culture category, there was a course on draft counseling, four courses on yoga, four on astrology, and one titled God-Realization by Soul Travel. There was also a full schedule on religion including Mormonism, Introduction to the Bible, the Parables, Hassidism, Conflict among Jews, How Odd of God to Choose the Jews, American Catholic Experience, Buddhism, and Religious Rap, which was convened by a panel of five campus clergymen.

A special series of courses limited to women offered subjects such as Women's Rap Group, How to Present Yourself on the Job Market, Basic Readings in Women's Liberation, Women's Studies Planning Groups, Nutrition, Basic Auto Care for Women, Auto Maintenance for Women, Feminine Exercises, and Arts and Crafts for Women. How to Fight Fairly and Effectively in Marriage, a course convened by the Episcopal chaplain, was open to both women and men.

Five courses dealt with human relations and sensitivity training, two with foreign languages, and only two with science —Geology and Kansas City, and Chemistry: Participational Research. Other courses used nationally were Ecobike, the Comics as Art, and Let's Disarm the Campus Police.

A reflection of the urban nature of the university can be seen in courses titled Kansas City Racial Crisis, Practical Problems in Mass Transportation, the Inner City, Urban Problem-

Solving Processes, Ecology in Kansas City, Geology and Kansas City, and some of the law courses such as Tenants' Rights and Constitutional Challenges to Urban Existence.

Such courses differ from regular campus courses as well as from adult education courses. Interestingly enough, if the courses were to be evaluated in terms of potential credit, the group that seems most qualified would be the urban courses, athough politics, literature, music, and language courses might also qualify. The emphasis is on bringing people together and exchanging opinions and knowledge. The courses are an extension of the university and yet they differ from even non-credit adult education courses in that they do not involve payment and there is less stress on the instructor. It is not hard to see why the community would be interested in and less reluctant to participate in these courses than in adult education courses which are more formal and are generally held in traditional facilities. The Communiversity has no such constraints. The course in Auto Maintenance for Women, for example, was scheduled to meet at "the fourth level of the multi-level parking lot at 50th and Cherry Street."

Urban Free Universities

What special meaning does the free university movement have for urban universities? Certainly the problems of relevant education and the relationship of the university to the community are more intense in urban areas. The frustration of government attempts to deal with community problems provides an opportunity for universities to be of service. The fact that the university and the city share the same terrain and the same constituency gives them some common bonds to be developed. Because the city tends to attract the economically disadvantaged, urban universities have a greater responsibility to respond.

How about the free university and its impact on urban areas? Table 6–3 involves an analysis of the cities in the United States with a population of 500,000 and above and the level of activity of the free university movement in those cities. As can be seen from the table, 22 of the 27 cities falling into this category currently have active free university movements. Many other movements have faded away, in part because the local urban university responded to the challenges, thereby co-opting the program of the free university.

Nevertheless, it would appear that free universities are more likely to be established in urban academic settings than in non-urban ones. If they are to succeed in their attempt to integrate the students who by traditional standards are academically marginal, urban universities will have to be in the forefront of educational innovation. The substantial involvement of urban universities in the free university movement is encouraging. The open admissions program discussed in other chapters is further evidence of the need and effort of urban universities to respond.

In the sense that establishing a free university is a means of students showing dissatisfaction with the administration in a peaceful way, this serves as a very important escape valve. The greatest impetus for the establishment of the early free universities came from the civil rights and Vietnam issues. In more recent years it was the Kent State University shootings and the Cambodian invasion of 1970 which triggered the movement.

The prevalence of interdisciplinary courses in the free university movement reflects some of the same causal factors affecting the growth of urban studies programs. Many black studies, urban studies, and, in more recent years, environmental studies programs have started in free universities, which are more flexible and so more conducive to problem-oriented students. The free university models, then, may speed up the rate of change in urban universities where it is needed most. In this respect urban free universities may have greater impact than those operating in non-urban areas.

Evaluation and Prognosis

Evaluating the free university movement is difficult. Obviously its continued existence suggests strongly that traditional education has failed to provide some of the intellectual needs of students. It is also instructive that while many free universities have been started by radical elements, most of them have been taken over by dissatisfied traditionalists or non-radicals. One positive spin-off of the movement has been that students, faculty, and administrators had to come to grips with questions

Table 6-3
Central Cities and Free Universities

Largest central cities	Population (in thousands)	No. of free univ.	Names of largest free universities
New York	7,895	2	Emmaus
Chicago	3,367	1	Alternate University
			Univ. of Ill.—Chicago
Los Angeles	2,816	3	Experimental College
			California State College
Philadelphia	1,949	3	Free University of Pa.
			Univ. of Pennsylvania
Detroit	1,511	2	Free University
			Wayne State University
Houston	1,233	1	University of Thought
Baltimore	906	1	Baltimore Free University
Dallas	844	1	Free University
			Southern Methodist University
Cleveland	751	1	Free University
			John Carroll University
Indianapolis	745	1	Free University
			Bethlehem Lutheran Church
Minneapolis	717	2	Minnesota Free University

Largest central cities	Population (in thousands)	No. of free univ.	Names of largest free universities
San Francisco	716	3	Experimental College
			Entropy
San Diego	697	1	San Diego State College
San Antonio	654	1	Universidad De Los Barrios
Boston	641	3	Beacon Hill Free School
Memphis	624	0	
St. Louis	622	0	
New Orleans	593	1	Free University of New Orleans
Phoenix	582	0	
Columbus	540	1	Ohio State Free University
Washington	538	3	Washington Area Free University
Seattle	531	1	Seattle Free University*
Jacksonville	529	0	
Pittsburgh	520	0	
Denver	515	1	Community Free University
Kansas City	507	1	Communiversity
			University of Mo.—Kansas City
Atlanta	497	2	Free University
			Georgia Institute of Technology

*Activities suspended as of 1973.
SOURCE: Jane Lichtman, *Free University Directory*, American Association of Higher Education, 1972, pp. 1–44.

such as how learning occurs, what makes an effective teacher, and what constitutes a stimulating learning environment. The answers have shown that these questions are harder than they look and also that the apparent intransigence of the traditional institution is due in part to a lack of knowledge of *how* to improve things.

Surely the free university has the ultimate evaluation mechanism. Since no one is required to do anything, courses that are not found useful are soon dropped. Often courses die after a few meetings for lack of an audience. The official program, therefore, has much to learn from evaluating those courses which not only survive but continue to grow.

Frederick Rudolf has chronicled the student societies that grew up in the nineteenth century to enliven schools bogged down with fundamentalist and narrow religious approaches. Rudolf says, "What is remarkably instructive about what they did is how much more effective they were than the would-be reformers in the ranks of the presidents and professors."[16]

Lauter and Howe point out that "the logic of free universities leads directly to the breakdown of the university as a trainer and a channeler of elites. The logic leads directly to open admissions and to self-determination by students of the content and quality of their education."[17]

Perhaps the eventual fate of free universities will resemble that of third parties in the political realm, which have been successful only when the traditional parties were ignoring some major issue. Historically, when these third parties gained a substantial following at the polls, the major parties preempted their support by adopting similar stands on the issues. Few third parties have been sufficiently broad-based to continue after losing control over their prime issue.

Somewhat the same thing is happening with respect to the free university in that the existence of a parallel educational experience and model alongside the traditional one has led to much reexamination on the campus. Many universities which would have been more slow to do so have been adopting work-study programs, independent study courses, student-proposed majors, and interdisciplinary programs which permit more flexibility. At the same time, these institutions are reducing the number of required courses and making it easier for faculty to offer experimental courses on a one-time basis without going through the whole bureaucratic mechanism of curriculum committees to do so.

A national vice president of Students for a Democratic Society (SDS), Carl Davidson, wrote a paper in 1967 titled "Multiversity: Crucible of the New Working Class" in which he said this about free universities:

> At best they had no effect. But it is far more likely they had the effect of strengthening the existing system. How? First of all, the best of our people left the campus, enabling the existing university to function more smoothly, since the troublemakers were gone. Secondly they gave the liberal administrators the rhetoric, the analysis, and sometimes the manpower to co-opt their programs and establish elitist forms of "experimental" colleges inside of, although quarantined from, the existing educational system.[18]

Lauter and Howe state that by 1967 SDS was no longer supporting the establishment of free universities. By 1968 the free university movement was dedicated to educational reform and was becoming increasingly legitimate. For example, the National Student Association received a Ford Foundation grant of $305,000 to use on educational reform projects.[19]

A new wave of free universities followed the broadened philosophy of the movement and produced educational reform in two interlocking ways: "by channeling the energies of students into constructive study programs, administrators could at the same time fill in those ever present gaps in the curriculum. Thus, the administration at the University of Iowa initiated a free university, making funds available to a student-faculty steering committee and arranging for some course credit."[20]

One effect of the new changes was a reduction in the number of political courses and in the number of community projects. The new tone was away from a crusade for change in education and toward emphasis on new educational experiences in an intellectual environment. In a sense these new courses have been a way of providing some relief from large lecture courses.

Lauter and Howe conclude that "setting a good example on the campus ('blackmailing the institution with quality') has not worked. Habit, self-interest, and power dominate the university as they do the wider society, in spite of rebellions, confrontations, or riots. The faculty and administration are in charge and they intend to keep things that way."[21] Nevertheless, the movement succeeded in spreading the idea of a student-centered curriculum and in causing university administrators and faculty to question their elitist assumptions and the way they relate to the community.

Some institutions will surely proceed to activate reform. Just as certainly, some other institutions will become entwined in their own bureaucracy or will never get beyond the stage of talking about the reforms. Those who fall into the latter category are likely to hear further from their student constituency, because the free university movement will not just blow away; it has provided an alternative model to which administrators and faculty must respond, even if it must be at their own pace.

Meanwhile, advocates of expanded education opportunities who are not overly concerned with credits and formalism have already moved on to a new frontier—using individuals in a particular community as a source of education. Variously referred to as guerrilla universities, free learning exchanges, and neighborhood resource materials, these programs will use retired persons, administrators, housewives, and any of the traditional teachers available as volunteers to bring more learning into neighborhoods in work-based learning centers.[22] They will aim not only at teaching but at teaching related to local problems and action targets similar to those which have proven of interest to the free universities. It would appear that bureaucracy-free education is here to stay and that the formal urban university may never catch up with its constituency.

NOTES

1. Paul Lauter and Florence Howe, *The Conspiracy of the Young* (New York: World, 1970), p. 125.

2. Students for a Democratic Society, *The Port Huron Statement*, August 1962.

3. Jane Lichtman, "Free Universities" in Dychman W. Vermilye, ed., *The Expanded Campus* (San Francisco, Jossey-Bass, 1972), p. 149.

4. *Ibid.*, p. 150.

5. *Ibid.*, pp. 152–53.

6. Jane Lichtman, *Free University Directory* (Washington, D.C., American Association for Higher Education, 1972), p. 1.

7. *Ibid.*, p. 3.

8. Ralph Keyes, "The Free Universities," *Nation,* October 2, 1967, p. 294.

9. Paul Lauter and Florence Howe, "What Happened to the Free University," *Saturday Review,* June 20, 1970, p. 81.

10. Lauter and Howe, *Conspiracy of the Young,* p. 94.

11. *Ibid.*

12. Experimental College at San Francisco State College, "Catalog of Courses, Fall 1966."

13. Lauter and Howe, *Conspiracy of the Young,* p. 94.

14. UMKC Communiversity, *Communiversity, Fall '72,* the course catalog.

15. The Communiversity is run by a director selected by the Communiversity advisory board, which according to Article III of the charter, is composed of "four students—the President of the All Student Association plus three students appointed by the President of the All Student Association and approved by the All Student Association; three faculty members appointed by the Chancellor; and one administrator appointed by the Dean of Students."

16. Frederick Rudolf, quoted by Keyes in "Free Universities," p. 299.

17. Lauter and Howe, "What Happened to the Free University," p. 82.

18. *Ibid.*, p. 93.

19. *Ibid.*

20. *Ibid.*

21. *Ibid.*, p. 94.

22. See Ivan Illich, *Deschooling Society* (New York: Harper & Row, 1971), and Jane Lichtman, "Free Universities," pp. 158–59.

7

THE UNIVERSITY AS AN URBAN NEIGHBOR

M. Gordon Seyffert

With the signing of the armistice and the coming of prosperity in the 1920s, Americans found themselves worrying, probably for the first time, about the future of their cities. Political reform had been in the air for several decades prior to that time, and the council-manager form of government had been proposed two decades or so before as a means of securing business-like governmental operation. Now it was time to consider such imponderables as the development of the motor car and urban street systems, construction of public water and sewer utilities, and acquisition of urban park lands and public centers. Most of the major westward migration had ceased, and it was not until later that urban migration of the racial minorities would begin. It became natural in those days of fleeting prosperity to begin to identify with cities. Perhaps, as the landscape architects had suggested, there could indeed be such a thing as the "city beautiful." Perhaps the city was now worthy of an investment, worthy of becoming a source of pleasure and a place of attachment.

The universities, meanwhile, had not been standing still.

Originated as a promising source of scholarship centuries ago,
they were initially founded in this country as a spawning
ground for the professions and became the source of doctors,
attorneys, clergy, and educators. As the population moved
westward, so did the concept of the university. The Morrill Act
of 1862 set up the land-grant colleges and agricultural experiment stations which built many public universities and paved
the way for their success. Having successfully applied scientific findings within agriculture, the parallel movement of
public universities into research relating to general industry
was a natural direction to take. Those few universities and
colleges then located within the central cities were often muni-
cipally sponsored, such as the University of Cincinnati and
City College of New York. These institutions served to produce
locally educated talent where other sources of education were
not suitably accommodating. But until very recent times, community service apart from the provision of trained manpower
was not very much within the vocabulary of the metropolitan
supported university. Cities had suffered from their historical
American interpretation as hand-maidens of commerce and
could not be taken seriously as a topic of concern in their own
right until after they had, for the most part, fully developed.

Thus in a sense both the city and university are relatively
recent institutions in America. It can be argued that the
current haphazard adjustment of town-gown relations in urban
settings is a function of the delayed development of those institutions. It is ironic that while universities have been desperately
competing to establish clientele and funding sources on a national scale in support of their scholarship and research functions, they have simultaneously come under fire locally for
being too remote and too complex to be responsive to community needs. And, as if to add insult to injury, the very
scholarship and career education opportunities that have given
countless urban dwellers a chance to become affluent are now
used as passports to the suburbs by the sons and daughters of
many urban neighborhoods seeking to be protected from the
"ruthless" university trying to expand its territory under the
cover of urban renewal.

Ironies such as these make it difficult for university administrators to comprehend what is expected of them. Being as defensive as other mortal souls, they have—many of them—

sought to ignore what they did not understand in the hope that it would go away. However, community resistance to an urban university has often hardened as the university came to be seen as more successful and, by implication, more expansionist and threatening to the neighborhood. Although it is frequently overlooked, university–community relations would be much simpler for all concerned were it not for the fact that both the university and the city experiencing substantially the same pressure to develop new relevance in mass society. Higher education received a tremendous boost after sputnik, while President Johnson's war on poverty kindled pressures to rebuild urban foundations with similar immediacy. A review of the current situation reveals that few authorities have given comprehensive attention to the problem of carving out a new concept suitable for future decades.

The Trials of Being an Institutional Neighbor

While university administrators think of themselves as professionals concerned for the future of the neighborhoods they serve, residents—especially those with low incomes living in decaying housing—may take a more critical view of the administrator's role and motivations. It is commonplace for residents to express fear and suspicion of the purposes of university expansion projects since they are often unsure of their own relationship to the university. They usually express at least some fear of losing their homes, often because of their knowledge of unsavory urban renewal programs in other areas. In a more general way, however, residents are frequently afraid of losing "their neighborhood." Physical changes often beget social changes which long-time residents deem undesirable. Congestion, overcrowding, and noise are already evident by the time most urban universities feel the need to originate community-oriented services or physical expansion of the campus. Thus the resident feels imposed upon when the university—the source of the discomfort—presents itself as the proper midwife for the birth of community-centered planning and service programs.

Part of the difficulty may center around a general hostility directed toward all agents of authority. Aside from whatever powers of eminent domain the university may be privileged to enjoy (and this power is certainly a stumbling block to community trust), many neighborhoods view universities as elements of the community power structure. "Power structure," to an urban neighborhood, is often synonymous with "politician," even though the latter is frequently a person who may feel obliged to take an arbitrary stand against the university if it will protect him from the wrath of an angry electorate. But mass psychology does not allow for such distinctions, so that residents may take a simplistic view of actual relationships within the total community so long as all persons of authority may accurately be described as external to the neighborhood. When, by contrast, community leadership springs from the neighborhood, few problems arise. This happier circumstance is probably due at least as much to familiarity with the decision process used by the neighbor-representative as to the skill of indigenous leadership in protecting local interests.

A related problem arises when the university is inaccurately perceived as being in league with the governmental bureaucracy at city hall. This problem may be especially acute if a neighborhood is being simultaneously besieged by municipal housing inspectors, utility employees, social caseworkers, health professionals, and students or community organizers from the urban university. From the viewpoint of many unsophisticated residents, all that is known is that many different persons enter the neighborhood in search of information about its history, physical condition, residents, and their life styles. In his confusion, the resident makes rash associations which are often unfair.

A description of neighborhood suspicion of community organizers in India might apply just as well to some areas of the United States:

> Many of the area residents looked upon the organizers'
> daily visits and their questioning not only as strange but
> also as threatening, and many rumors spread. Some be-
> lieved the visits were actually of a political nature; others
> were certain that the odd questions asked about such
> things as the sizes of families, the occupations of the resi-
> dents, and the lengths of residence in the area were for
> the purpose of raising rents, moving the people to new
> housing colonies, increasing taxes, rationing food, or
> restricting the numbers of their children. . . .[1]

Those who recall the furor that arises every ten years over the content of questions asked by the U.S. Bureau of the Census concerning housing conditions and bathroom facilities can understand the scope of the issue of community rights to privacy. Many persons in central city areas feel less privileged than those they encounter working for institutions. Feeling insecure, they often become ashamed to admit their problems even if they consider the outsiders sincere in their efforts to render assistance. And the resident may argue that since outsiders appear to have much in common with local status quo business operators (who may indeed live elsewhere), then why should residents expect to be any less exploited by university programs which serve broader interests than by companies who send their revenues out of the neighborhood? Without an adequate foundation of trust constructed through years of conscientious town-gown contact, attempts to allay suspicion can be frustrating.

Solutions do exist, however, given the time and resources to combat the problem, plus the commitment to face it. A prominent example of university-neighborhood collaboration in the United States is the Hyde Park-Kenwood experience of the University of Chicago. Following World War II it became evident to administrators that the university would have to take a hand in addressing problems of neighborhood deterioration and overcrowding inasmuch as undergraduate enrollment and faculty strength were beginning to reflect dissatisfaction with the school's physical environment. University sources have since reported that the quality of local housing had declined in the decade following the war to the point that faculty leaving the University during this period showed strong inclination to cite "the decline in the caliber of Hyde Park as a source of disaffection."[2]

Unlike some other institutions, however, the University of Chicago had long been involved in the neighborhood through real estate activities on behalf of faculty and through support of a number of community organizations devoted to community conservation.[3] University personnel were not strangers to their environment, nor were university policies alien to the affected areas. That the university could have at least a quasi-legitimate role to play in community affairs was important to its eventual ability to grant itself the primary role in achieving orderly planning for community renewal. This occurred even though the university's original commitment to residential segregation placed it initially at loggerheads with strong citizen interest in the possibilities of interracial living.

Faced with a need to halt the deterioration of its environment and isolated by its past policies from existing citizen groups, the university decided in 1952 to build from scratch an organization concerned with conservation and rehabilitation. This was the genesis of the South East Chicago Commission. The occasion for its formation came indirectly from a series of law enforcement and crime prevention problems confronting the neighborhood, but the initial thrust was in the direction of rehabilitation and conservation of housing. At the same time, Chicago and a civic association concerned essentially with planning became interested in the Hyde Park-Kenwood area as an example of the kind of residential community that might be preserved through conservation and renewal. With regard to this parallel development, it has been observed that the close connection of university personnel with "downtown" renewal elements at this particular time indicates how informal actions taken by university personnel may facilitate more formal actions taken by the institution itself.[4] The informal actions of faculty, insofar as they relate to the community as well as to the metropolitan leadership, serve to build upon the all-important visibility of the university at the neighborhood level—and in terms the neighborhood may find at once more understandable and less threatening.[5]

While not all of its objectives were achieved, the South East Chicago Commission sought to view community problems in a manner sufficiently broad to permit university and non-university goals to coalesce into a unified agenda. According to Rossi and Dentler, the Commission sought "to obtain proper police protection in the area; to work out a program of action that culminated in the urban renewal plan for the community; to encourage residential stability and community identification among the upper-middle-class residents; and to build support among leadership groups in the area and in the city as a whole for a program of amelioration of neighborhood conditions."[6]

It is especially interesting to note that some of the failures of the organization (e.g., public relations) are ascribed not to the organization itself but to the individuals associated with it.

One may speculate that much of the failure of colleges and universities in dealing with community problems may be due to intellectual naiveté and inexperience in dealing face-to-face with the public. Hopefully, then, as universities learn from their past mistakes, they will become more sensitive to community feelings and reactions.

As a postscript, it is interesting to note that while the University of Chicago was able to help create a South East Chicago Commission for the benefit of one adjoining neighborhood, it was unable to avoid a massive confrontation with another of its own neighborhoods. The Woodlawn Community south of Midway became the site of radical organizer Saul Alinsky's most famous community development operation: Alinsky successfully defied the university by building a workable community organization in a transient neighborhood to oppose a "South Campus" expansion proposed by the university. The difference apparently was that whereas in Hyde Park-Kenwood a community plan was developed to satisfy participants representing all points of view, the Woodlawn area was substantially overlooked as a source of partnership because of its less substantial nature as a neighborhood and (as a consequence?) because of fewer faculty contracts with the neighborhood.

Nevertheless, residents of any community will have strong feelings about the future of their environment, and in this case it took the forming of The Woodlawn Organization (TWO) to demonstrate to the university the power of citizen participation. To the north, a separate Hyde Park-Kenwood Community Conference had been able to assist the university's South East Chicago Commission in areas such as citizen contact, and thus to avoid a stalemate between competing interests. In general, it may be said that the amount of cooperation received in a given neighborhood is directly proportional to the amount of attention which the university gives to broad community goals and the ways in which they may be advanced through joint participation.

By the same token, it may be said that the success of university goals will be inversely proportional to the amount of ignorance about neighborhood attitude toward university policies. The first step to successful community relations is mutual understanding. Only after both sides are talking can the administrator formulate a strategy for future university action which directly or indirectly impinges upon the neighborhood. Naturally such a strategy is limited by the constraints of the educational goals and policies which are in effect at the time. Upon reflection, however, the administrator's discussions with neighborhood residents may prove to be a worthwhile test of even these lofty guidelines.

Managing Neighborhood Relations

A number of tactics can promote a strategy of university-neighborhood collaboration; they are limited only by the extent of the administrator's imagination and the commitment of his institution. As has been implied throughout this chapter, the first move is a declaration of will to listen to any reasonable complaint, suggestion, or statement registered by residents of the neighborhood. This can best be accomplished with the help of a bona fide community organization which has taken an interest in community planning. Such an organization should be looked upon by the university as valuable resource for communication, just as the university would like to be thought of by the community as an indispensable source of continuing education guidance.

The Hyde Park-Kenwood Community Conference was a substantial factor in the communications process existing between the University of Chicago and its northern neighbors, as has been pointed out. Ideally, a university should attempt to locate that community organization which best serves communication with a given audience, and coordinate between audiences as necessary after proper "grass roots" contact has been established. This is because most communities are made up of many "publics," no one of which can speak for all of the community. As long as university responsibility for community relations and coordination is centralized in one identifiable office, no confusion need ensue.

As a part of the listening function of the university, membership in these community organizations should be encouraged by the president's office to provide visibility to the neighborhood and alert the university to local developments. Especially where membership entails a fee, faculty and staff participation may be particularly appreciated as a contribution to the costs of maintaining the local organization. University reimbursement of these fees would encourage memberships and at the same time provide a large measure of goodwill at small cost.

Another reimbursement, which may be warranted in cases of high dedication and meritorious service, is granting released time to a faculty member able to assist the organization's development. This practice may be especially warranted from the university's standpoint if the activity in question may stimulate direct benefits to the institution in other than community relations categories. If, for example, it appears that contracts with local industrialists and government officials might stimulate contracts for services with university research outlets, then it clearly pays the institution to support of person-to-person contacts which may produce such results as a by-product. In addition, some types of contacts may provide national publicity for research work and community services, which can enhance a school's reputation in important fields. The urban observatories discussed in chapter 2 provide one ready example of such activity.

The university must also maintain contact with city hall, particularly if neighborhood or storefront centers are used to maintain the city's own ties with urban subregions. Contact with the city will usually relate to matters of institutional planning and its ramifications for city planning. Often universities, hospitals, research, and other institutions will join together in making available to the city planners estimates of their total capital budgeting program. Given the need of most institutions for expansion of facilities as well as programs, checking with the city may be crucial to the optimum use of resources by financially pressed institutions. Through urban renewal and other programs, the city is in a position to provide extra funds for supporting purposes such as streets, utilities, and open space. But beyond the physical advantages, the city may also be in a position through its own contact with neighborhoods to explain and defend the overall need of the university for room to grow. As a rule of thumb, it may be said that the greater the number of contacts the university maintains, the greater the chance that university goals will be understood and dealt with in a responsible manner.

In order to reach this level of understanding, the university will have to get its own house in order. As it tries to relate to municipal officials and neighborhood leaders, it must move with a unified voice in expressing objectives. This may be difficult to do. The point has been made that a university has often found itself supporting opposing policies at the same time. One way this can happen is for the university to take a public stand in favor of neighborhood preservation (since nobody likes decay) while simultaneously failing to deal with neighborhood qualms about institutional expansion. The institution does this in full realization that fear depreciates the value of residential and commercial property, making it easier to buy and cheaper to finance when the time comes (as it usually does) for the institution to expand its borders into the community. The disadvantage of such a conflicting set of motives is that when they are discovered, the resulting uproar tends to create a great deal more ill will than is healthy for either neighborhood or institution. The effect may be to spur citizens to active resistance of a plan for the neighborhood, however logical and proper it may appear to the planners.

Other pitfalls are sometimes created by the students, who may antagonize the local townspeople to the extent that lack of control over its student body results in a black mark for the university. The question of whether or not to call in local police during campus riots was a particularly vexing question in this regard. Many urban institutions felt a strong loyalty to the traditions of academic independence in disciplinary matters while at the same time recognizing the validity of community fears of unleashed campus violence that could spread into surrounding private property. The surest way to avoid such dilemmas is for the university to plan in advance and to enable local leaders to participate in the planning.

One of the major decisions a university can make in furthering its community relations arises from its tax-exempt status. While it is true that universities are presently undergoing a financial crisis, the same may be said of most major cities. A knowledge of trends in land use during the past half-century quickly illustrates the problem now presented by the proliferation of tax-exempt educational properties. In the earlier years of this century, before the advent of urban society as we know it today, much urban land was devoted to wholesaling and warehousing operations and to industrial sites which have now moved beyond the central city. At that time railroads constituted a major portion of the transportation network and were a major source of tax income for cities. Now the central cities are sliced up by major tax-free highways and freeways containing huge rights-of-way and cloverleafs. Open space and semi-public uses also siphon off considerable potential revenue for the cities.

Universities can help pull their load as major population centers and traffic generators through voluntary contributions in lieu of taxes or with mutual city-university dollar participation in vital urban renewal programs. A good compromise may be to pay taxes on those activities that are primarily non-academic in nature. A policy guideline is provided by President Asa S. Knowles of Northeastern University:

> The nonprofit and tax-exempt status of educational institutions is a frequent cause of strained relations between the college and the metropolitan community. This is particularly true when universities own and operate bookstores, cafeterias, dormitories, parking facilities, faculty housing, and such other services and facilities as might seem to be in competition with local businessmen. Frequently the public, and sometimes even the students themselves, challenge the nonprofit nature of operations when prices are competitive with those of local merchants. It often becomes necessary to explain that any excess of income over expenses realized from some of these operations helps to defray the costs of basic educational programs, such as the doctorate, which are administered at great expense to the institution. Profit in one area off-sets a deficit in another, with a total nonprofit operation being the end result.
>
> When questions are raised relative to the taxation of the above-mentioned enterprises, various solutions are employed. In some cases, institutions pay taxes on all but their academic operations, i.e., parking and housing facilities. Some institutions, on the other hand, elect to devise a formula for the payment of a contribution to the city in lieu of taxes.[7]

Hopefully, if such "taxes" are paid, the university will be in a position to capitalize on this by making the fact known. As a further step, the city and university together could plan

for improvements which might upgrade both the neighborhood
and the valuation of its property. The institutional purpose
would be to increase the neighborhood tax base, but the property owners would at the same time benefit from the public
improvements.

Some complaint may be heard from persons on a fixed income or small shopowners who are not intending to sell their
property and thus do not expect to reap that benefit. But this
problem can be partially offset if the university is in a position
to hire neighborhood residents for service jobs and to do business locally. In the first case, the neighborhood may be a good
source of minority employees who, although probably requiring some skills training or on-the-job training, may offer better
stability and loyalty as university employees than others who
may have to commute to their jobs and who do not have the
same identification with the neighborhood. In the second case,
expansion of physical facilities may be just the opportunity
needed to foster goodwill with local businessmen.

Knowles outlines the case for fully utilizing the economic
weight of the institution:

> The presence of a college or university offers the com-
> munity more economic advantages than disadvantages in
> the long run. Colleges are big business, and a great deal
> of revenue is poured into the tills of local merchants
> through the supplies and services ancillary to college
> operations. In addition to outright purchases, it is becom-
> ing increasingly common for local businesses to be
> awarded many of the concession rights relative to the
> operation of such enterprises as university housing, food
> services, etc.[8]

If this creative use of purchasing power is further extended to include the stimulation of minority business (especially if done through the offices of a neighborhood business
organization), then clearly the university has met several local
needs at once in its effort to promote good neighborhood relations. As a final suggestion, using local banks in declining
neighborhoods for university accounts may, if the bankers can
be persuaded to increase rehabilitation loans, create the capital
necessary for both citizens and businessmen to adequately
finance neighborhood preservation.

No stone should be left unturned in the effort to build a better environment for the university. The university has a duty to seek out the optimum solution and promote its discussion. Julian Levi, of Southeast Chicago Commission fame, provides some good advice:

> The boards of trustees and the traditions of most universities suggest that the institution is very often a center of great persuasive power. No institution about to engage in a program which involves public discussion ought to shrink from the exercise of the power of persuasion which it has.

> One of the functions of American higher education is to find the facts, to talk about them, to educate and persuade. The public forum, whether it is the hearing before the city council, or the planning commission, or the public reply to the unfair attack is an appropriate place for the institutional mission of education and persuasion to be practiced.[9]

There are other remedies for university inattention to neighborhood relations, many of them less complex than the suggestions outlined above. Most of them relate to the use of physical facilities by local residents. Athletic facilities such as swimming pools and playing fields are often desirable supplements to public facilities. Residents of the area may be wrong in *assuming* that a university owes them the use of these facilities, but for the sake of good relations it is best to remember that most adults feel very strongly about their children's opportunities and that providing access to athletic resources may be one of the cheapest ways of maintaining a cooperative image before the public.

Classrooms, eating facilities, meeting rooms and even expensive television and radio facilities may be desired by community groups for both public and private use, and while it may be necessary to formally schedule such uses, it should be apparent to the university administrator that such groups would be more accessible to the university under such circumstances than if the university were forced to seek contact with them. Particularly if educational or cultural activities are the basis of the group's interest, the university will do well to examine how it can contribute "community" facilities.

The Impact of University Expansion

It is always amazing to discover how little is known within
any given city about the precise impacts of major institutions
upon the local economy. Census figures abound, of course, and
various business indicators exist which may provide the urban
economist with a fairly accurate view of the city economy. But
within the ranks of institutional planners and decision-makers,
it often appears that a myopic view of physical development has
allowed the larger meaning of a university's presence to go un-
noticed. Like most city planners, university planners are
schooled in the technical aspects of growth and find their greatest demands to be in the area of designing for maximum effectiveness and least cost major capital improvements which, by
definition, will have a long-term impact upon the growth patterns of a city or university.

In planning such developments for universities, the major
considerations will be those related to the projected use of the
facilities and their interrelations with existing *physical* structures. University planners examine most closely (1) the projected future levels of student, faculty, administrative, and
service personnel; (2) the distribution of functions and uses
among existing campus facilities; (3) the nature of future
standards and goals for campus development; and (4) the relation of campus development to existing and future non-university land uses—including property ownership, traffic ar-
teries, and public usage development.

What so often is overlooked in planning for a new classroom building, auditorium, or parking facility are the non-
physical effects of campus development. These effects are both
economic and social in nature, the first being understood in
many cases, the second rarely at all. Knowledge of the economic impact is important, in this case, not so much for what
it says or does not say about the viability of university physical
expansion programs, but rather for what it may indicate about
the larger social scheme. In many towns outside urban areas,
it is well known that the university is *the* major influence upon
the flavor of neighborhood life, simply because of the sheer
numbers involved. In metropolitan areas, this impact is much
less visible but may be equally substantial.

Consider some statistics cited in a 1963 conference sponsored by the American Council on Education:

Economic advantages to institutional uses for land are shown in some figures for the University of Pennsylvania. It has a total payroll of $25 million a year; it draws to Philadelphia out-of-town students who spend an estimated $15 million a year; it lends its facilities for conventions and meetings to some 20,000 annual visitors; it pays the city nearly $500,000 a year in taxes on wages and real estate investment and spends another $500,000 on utilities and insurance alone.

In the Boston Metropolitan Area institutional employment is the third largest, accounting for estimated payrolls of more than $250 million per year. In the next decade, about one quarter of a billion dollars will be spent by institutions in this area for construction.

In Cleveland four of the 28 institutions involved in the University Circle urban renewal project have an annual payroll of more than $28 million.[10]

In addition to direct employment and spending, the above-mentioned institutions also encourage knowledge-related industries that expand rapidly, are pollutant-free, add significantly to the tax coffers of local government, and attract professional, managerial, and scientific employees who influence the educational and cultural development of the city. In conjunction with university populations, the addition of such industries may have a sizable impact upon both the economics and the social organization of a community and its neighborhoods.

But there are negative effects also, many with both economic and social aspects. As a first consideration, the very existence of the university effectively blocks any competing use of the land. Nothing can be done about this, of course, but it may be helpful to consider what the community might desire for the site. A little imagination in projecting the desires of the neighborhood is an essential step in preparing the administrator to understand and deal successfully with campus neighbors.

Along more down-to-earth lines, the administrator will surely find that even if the campus cannot be made to disappear, certain pressures the campus places upon the neighborhood can often be removed or alleviated. For example, the pressures of students and younger faculty looking for inexpensive housing is a factor in the decline of neighborhood housing standards. If adequate facilities do not exist on campus to serve present enrollments, then students are forced to seek housing within walking or close driving distance of campus. Retired persons or absentee landlords seeking additional income subdivide their buildings to make room for students, even if the original density of the neighborhood had not included plans for multi-family housing. The addition of extra people of any kind may make the neighborhood less desirable for families and, as a consequence, housing values in the area may decline.

Should the new residents be considered "different" or "undesirable," the reaction to the changing character of the neighborhood will take on social as well as economic tones, and the tendency to deterioration will be all the stronger. Furthermore, if the well-meaning university has been advertising expansion of its campus without designating the areas to be encompassed, homeowner maintenance will also decline as a consequence of local investment uncertainty. As rooming houses are serviced by increasing numbers of commercial services and as traffic levels and on-street parking become strained, old-time residents come to view the presence of the university as an unstabilizing influence upon the community.

This is usually the existing state of university-community relations at the time most university administrations have begun to attack university image problems with a concerted strategy. By this time easy solutions have disappeared. The neighborhood is wary of the university as a result of past indifference and transgressions, and the decayed state of neighborhood structures has by now indicated a need for "renewal" activity in place of less drastic rehabilitation measures. And because major surgery is indicated, more perceptive residents will soon realize that the neighborhood is due for yet another transition in character, which will doubtless force a new adjustment to change.

Over the past decade it has become commonplace to associate changes in institutional/community character with the urban renewal programs of the federal government. In the sense that so many dollars and so many people are involved in such programs, the close association is perhaps not unexpected. However, in light of the critical problems which result from such programs, university administrations should take an active part in the urban renewal planning and not assume that government programs will do the university's dirty work. The institution may be left, after the present administrators have passed from the scene, with the unsavory task of explaining the failures of the urban renewal program and its implementation.

This subject is worthy of some discussion. One sore spot with urban renewal is sure to be the manner in which relocation of long-time residents is carried out, and it appears that the "establishment" always loses on this issue. The early history of urban renewal was characterized by the belief that relocation would take place without effort if suitable housing existed within the city. This assumption was wrong, for planners had underestimated the extent of community ties among slum dwellers and the reluctance of residents to break ties with friends and neighbors for the sole benefit of receiving better housing. Thus it has been that low-income residents everywhere have quickly become angered when asked to leave the immediate area. The federal government, unfortunately, has come to be viewed as somewhat partial to sweeping programs. But in Europe, where the sophistication of relocation programs has reached the point that mass temporary housing is sometimes constructed within easy distance of the project area, residents are still found to be so attached to existing environments that, once removed to these temporary sites, they soon grow to like the temporary quarters well enough that they would gladly stay to avoid another move. Given this tenacity, then, officials must be prepared for a difficult and trying period of community relations if urban renewal is indicated as the only hope for neighborhood housing.

But in addition to the immediate difficulties officials must also be prepared to weather the headaches of program failure. Martin Anderson, author of the well-known book *The Federal Bulldozer,* charged that even the tax returns expected to result from urban renewal could not be seen to materialize after program completion. Beyond this indictment, however, Anderson and other observers have argued that urban renewal does not necessarily provide better living conditions for the poor or stem the spread of urban blight. While an illusion of change may be evident within the immediate project area, the nature of housing-related problems is so complex as to be overwhelming, in that the urban renewal project may cause other destructive pressures within the neighborhood. The university may be able to assist the city in determining the nature of the housing system and may thus perform a valuable service to the community, but the administrators of the university should never underestimate the time and effort involved in providing backup services to an urban renewal project. Specialized organizations created on behalf of the university and other institutions and groups have been the vehicle for coordination in most of the better urban renewal endeavors.

The source of university and hospital participation in the urban renewal program was the enactment of Section 112 of the National Housing Act of 1959, as amended in 1961. The advantage of the amendment to universities is that it provides an incentive for the city to select urban renewal project sites near the institution. This is achieved through the provision for so-called in-kind matching of the cost of university expansion projects against federal dollars, so that the city participation in the matching grant program is of a non-cash nature. The hitch is that any such projects undertaken with the aid of non-municipal expenditures must be located close to the physical improvements which constitute the non-cash matching portion of the grant. The rationale is that the expansion of non-municipal facilities will still have a beneficial economic effect locally, and may thus be viewed as contributing to the overall success of urban renewal.

The use of this arrangement as outlined in a recent report of the Carnegie Commission on Higher Education has been spectacular at the very least:

> This section provides that for every dollar spent by an educational institution or its "non-profit agent . . . for acquisition of land, buildings, or structures within, adjacent to or in the immediate vicinity of, an urban-renewal project, for demolition . . . for relocation of occupants and for rehabilitation of buildings," the city may receive $2 to $3 of federal urban-renewal assistance. The land and the buildings acquired must be used for educational purposes. This section led to joint action by urban universities and city governments in renewal efforts. By June 1967, the date of the latest published Department of Housing and Urban Development Survey, 115 projects utilizing Section 112 credits with a total area of 12,000

acres and almost $500 million in federal grants had been approved.[11]

The Carnegie Report goes on to mention that other "community development" projects may be expected to result from Title VII of the Housing and Urban Development Act of 1970, which provides for federal government guarantees of obligations issued by developers of "large-scale, long-term, comprehensive" projects.

    The danger lies in the possibility that universities and other institutions undertaking such projects as urban renewal and community development may become sidetracked from their moral obligations as educational or service resources in their desire to save their investment in plant and equipment. As William L. Slayton, then Commissioner of the Urban Renewal Administration in HHFA, wrote in 1964:

> There is a great danger with Section 112 that it may be considered by the universities solely as an advantageous mechanism for the expansion of their campuses. To the extent that this is true, we are in danger of creating an unfortunate image of the urban renewal program and a difficult situation for both the locality and the university.[12]

    The Carnegie Commission comes down particularly hard on this question in 1972, almost a decade after Mr. Slayton's comments:

> Some universities have gone beyond the usual pattern of funding for urban renewal and have themselves become, in a sense, developers, using endowment funds for rehabilitation and construction not only for university housing but also for low and moderate income housing for their immediate environs. During a period when many institutions are questioning the wisdom of serving as landlord to students and faculty, we wonder whether it is sound policy to become landlord or developer to those who are not members of the university. It is one thing to act as a major participant, catalyst, or facilitator in the planning and implementation of urban-renewal programs; it is quite another to invest scarce university resources on any large scale basis as a general developer.[13]

Besides the possibility of overextension of resources—financial or otherwise—the role of the university as landlord or developer seems likely to place the university in a position of alienating as many local residents as it mollifies. Imagine, as an example, the effect upon relations with the community should tenants on university property have to be evicted for any reason! Most institutions seem to care little about how such things are done so long as the offending party is removed from the premises. Certainly a back-handed manner of dealing with residents would eventually place the university at a disadvantage.

This is not to say, however, that a development strategy encompassing non-university individuals and businesses is inappropriate for an urban university. Such a strategy is probably to be recommended inasmuch as it is now becoming recognized that the areas of interaction between city and university are vital neighborhoods in themselves and ought to be taken seriously by the planners as primary and not secondary zones of activity. Where the university developers have erred is in allowing development to overshadow education as the rationale for the university's urban existence. Misuse of scarce funding is certainly one important ramification, but such a misrepresentation has even larger implications when viewed as a misuse of nonmonetary resources of the city, of which educational resources comprise one part.

In this view, development, whether for direct educational purposes or not, should serve to enhance the university's role as an educational resource of the city. Development may well serves this purpose if it promotes uses, services, and activities which make university resources more accessible to the city of which it is a part. Often this happens as universities abandon their sequestered image as bastions of academic tradition in favor of an open, aggressive image as a leader in community, regional, and national advancement. As a consequence of this altered approach to educational purpose, campuses begin to shift from low-rise country settings to more intensive, high-rise structures which encourage diverse uses of valuable real property. This, as Warren Rovetch has indicated

> means breaking out of the fortress concept, rejecting the
> physical boundaries that represent the university as a

closed system. It means extending fingers of the university beyond its present boundaries wherever land is available and useful for university purposes, thus extending the points of contact of the university with the city. It means maximizing front footage to maximize meaningful contact.[14]

Conclusion

In the past the strong inclination of administrators and planners to visualize educational activities and "urban" activities as being naturally separate has led to few attempts to relate the two. Because of the early development patterns of American universities, it is still hard for some to forsake traditional rural or urban enclave stereotypes. What we are now beginning to observe in some quarters is the discovery that educational functions can survive, even flourish, in an active and diverse urban climate and at the same time increase their usefulness to urban neighbors. This is a process which can be visually documented.

Educational Facilities Laboratories, Inc., a nonprofit corporation established by the Ford Foundation to help schools and colleges with their physical problems, has written in this vein:

> The dawning commitment of urban colleges and universities to a new role in their communities has physical ramifications. Here and there, institutions are beginning to throw outposts into the city. In a number of instances, community services and facilities are to be found within the campus. The boundaries between campus and community are beginning to blur. A pioneering handful of institutions have accepted the need for a total physical commitment to the community. These institutions are beginning to plan neighborhoods rather than campuses.[15]

This approach offers some hope of avoiding the insular mentality in planning campus expansions. The problem is still complex, however. Even a new university such as Cleveland State, which has a large percentage of black students, is open to charges of having insufficient interest in its slum neighborhood where the Hough riots took place in the 1960s.

The Educational Facilities Laboratories report concludes:

It is fair to say that, despite the encouraging signs cited in this report, none of our urban colleges and universities has yet produced and implemented an effective physical plan to meet the realities of institutional life in today's cities. There have been many protestations of good will, many statements of intent, and a few elaborate and expensive planning studies. But nowhere have we created the new, organic urban campus and, at the moment, nowhere has a college or university made a firm commitment to do so.[16]

Probably this is a bit harsh, inasmuch as the giant step which the report describes must be made in the context of other pressing urban demands. Perhaps if the United States were fortunate enough at some point to reap a "fiscal dividend" of the sort promised during the 1960s, we could hold urban universities strictly responsible for their potentials. For the present it will prove difficult to hold their attention.

It took almost a century and a half for Americans to "discover" the city, and roughly 50 years for us to realize that universities were, or could be, a vital part of the city. We are impatient to make use of our knowledge, to make that "firm commitment." We can do it successfully if we plan for it successfully; stopgap measures will not take us where we want to go, but only soothe the pains of the present. The university will truly be an urban neighbor when it comes to share in the values and dreams of its surrounding community.

NOTES

1. Marshall B. Clinard, *Slums and Community Development: Experiments in Self-Help* (New York: Free Press, 1966), p. 287.

2. Peter H. Rossi and Robert A. Dentler, *The Politics of Urban Renewal: The Chicago Findings* (New York: Free Press, 1962), p. 67.

3. Harvey Perloff, *The University of Chicago and the Surrounding Community* (Chicago: University of Chicago Press, 1953) as reported in Rossi and Dentler, *Politics of Urban Renewal*, p. 69. See Julia Abrahamson, *A Neighborhood Finds Itself* (New York: Harper & Brothers, 1959) for a history of the Hyde Park-Kenwood community conference.

4. Rossi and Dentler, *Politics of Urban Renewal,* p. 77.

5. Columbia University's problems with the Morningside Heights neighborhood stemmed in part from the fact that so few faculty and staff lived in the area or had contact with it.

6. Rossi and Dentler, *Politics of Urban Renewal,* p. 79.

7. Asa S. Knowles, *Handbook of College and University Administration—General* (New York: McGraw-Hill, 1970), pp. 5-34–5-35.

8. *Ibid.,* p. 5–36.

9. Julian Levi, "Ground Space for the University," in Charles G. Dobbins, ed., *The University, the City, and Urban Renewal* (Washington, D.C.: American Council on Education, 1964), p. 13.

10. llWiiam L. Slayton, "The University, the City, and Urban Renewal," in Dobbins, ed., *University, City, and Urban Renewal,* p. 5.

11. Carnegie Commission on Higher Education, *The Campus and the City: Maximizing Assets and Reducing Liabilities* (New York: McGraw-Hill, 1972), p. 82.

12. Slayton, "University, City, and Urban Renewal," p. 6.

13. Carnegie Commission, *Campus and City,* p. 83.

14. Educational Facilities Laboratories, *Campus in the City, 1968,* p. 15.

15. *Ibid.,* p. 10.

16. *Ibid.,* p. 16.

8

MANCHESTER'S URBAN UNIVER-CITY

Peter Spang Goodrich

A glimpse of the future is suggested by examining the experience of Europe's largest urban campus, the Manchester Education Precinct. This project is a development of the Victoria University of Manchester and the Corporation (city) of Manchester in cooperation with other institutions and authorities. One of the largest and most important educational institutions in the United Kingdom, the University of Manchester has been situated at its present location just a mile and a half from Piccadilly, the city center, since 1873. The university lays claim to a long tradition of being a good community neighbor and is doing some of the things American experts have warned higher education not to do.

A Heritage of Univer-City Cooperation

Historical factors were especially important in shaping the relationship which developed. Mancunians, as the citizens of Manchester are called, desired to establish a university as early as 1640. While both Oxford and Cambridge wished university education to continue to be predicated upon Anglican religious beliefs and convictions, Manchester was dedicated to a non-comformist ideal of training young men regardless of religious conviction for professional and commercial life.[1] The present University of Manchester traces its roots to 1851, five years after the death of John Owens, a leading merchant, who bequeathed £96,654 to establish Owens College. City linkages were firmly established by Owens. All the trustees were "highly respected and prominent city men of varied religion and politics. [Owens] also made it a condition of the trust that every trustee must reside within fifty miles of Manchester or be replaced."[2]

Success for the college and ultimately the University of Manchester lay in breaking new ground—emphasizing applied scientific subjects better suited to the education of the citizens of industrial Manchester. During the fiftieth anniversary celebration in 1901, the Duke of Devonshire contended that Owens College would probably have failed if it had literally followed Owens' directives. Owens' idea was "to provide in this great centre of industry higher education in such branches of learning and sciences *as are usually taught in English Universities.*"[3] At that time, however, higher education was dominated by the classics, literature, and philosophy.

Oxford and Cambridge, by placing their emphasis on the arts and classics, tended to concentrate on the leisure class and ignored education for the professions and occupations of life. Manchester sought to fill this void. With the possible exception of the University College in London, no other college could serve as a model for the University of Manchester. Founded on the "first conscious union of town and gown in English history, the meeting of scholar and merchant on common ground and with common aims," Owens College became the "pioneer of the twelve other University Colleges since established in the centres of utilitarian energies and commercial ideals, which leaven their surroundings with scholarly influences, and derive, in turn, material support for them."[4]

"Relevance" has always been a primary concern at Manchester. From the earliest years, Owens College was molded to the ideals of the city; the strengths of the college logically became economic thinking and engineering theory, both vital to the industry and commerce of the city. For example, William Stanley Jevons, appointed to the chair of economics in 1866, revolutionized economic thought by his final utility theory of value in *Theory of Political Economy,* which also subtly justified Manchester's social and business practices. When the chair of engineering was established in 1868, most of the city's great engineering firms ardently gave their support. By placing this applied science into the academic curriculum, the vital contact between the academic and commercial community was reinforced. Plainly, the work of the first professor of engineering, Osborne Reynolds, in the fields of lubrication, river movements, and mechanical heat equivalents was crucial to the interests of Lancashire heavy industry.[5]

"Pure" scientific research by men such as John Dalton and James Joule endowed science with two of the three basic foundations of mechanics—the law of conservation of chemical elements and the laws for conservation of heat. The third law of mechanics was Sir Isaac Newton's law of the conservation of momentum.[6] These successes made Manchester prestigious as a center for both learning and practical applications. As a result, growing Owens College was able to attract a strong faculty, and at an early stage the Manchester district came to appreciate the role that academia could play in its development. Conversely, Owens College realized the stimulation that district thinkers could provide for it.

In 1880, Owens College was made a university, but of a different form than that desired by Mancunians. It became the federal Victoria University with Owens College as the only constituent college. University College, Liverpool, and Yorkshire College, Leeds, were acquired in 1884 and 1887 as additional colleges under Victoria University.[7] This federal structure temporarily muted the city-university character that contributed to the development of Owens College and was to be central to the development of the Victoria University of Manchester.

After 1900, awareness of the growing close association between not only commercial interests in Manchester but also the city government of Manchester and the university, led to the call for the separation of the three constituent colleges and the formation of an independent, autonomous University of Manchester. In 1902 Samuel Alexander, professor of philosophy, argued that the development of the university required a sense of the crucial organic interplay between the university and its urban district, and that academic work should be viewed as something which must not be remote from its surroundings, but must become a form of citizenship by taking an active interest in people's needs.[8]

Once Manchester University became autonomous in 1903, academic expansion along the lines suggested by Professor Alexander commenced. Commerce and theology faculties were immediately added to the existing faculties of arts, law, medicine, music, and science. Characteristic of the Manchester ideal, Professor H. B. Charlton notes these two balanced "the claims of the moment and the consciousness of eternity. . . ."[9] From the standpoint of city-university cooperation, however, the establishment of the faculty of technology in 1905 marked a significant milestone in urban relations. The city council and the university became constitutionally linked in determining and controlling certain courses of study. The four paragraphs which follow briefly summarize the sequence of events.

Historically, the city had been involved in technical education since 1827 when the Mechanics' Institute was formed to show workers the principles of their trade and to correlate mechanical jobs, manual arts, and scientific principles for greater efficiency. The Institute was changed in 1883 to a Technical School teaching bleaching, chemistry, dyeing, engineering, printing, spinning, and weaving. In 1892 the city assumed control of the school and expanded it into a Technological Clolege under thecontrol of a city official, the director and secretary of technical instruction.

The technical school realized that its primary function should be the *application* of theoretical training,[10] and a joint committee was established in 1894 to coordinate the city and college educational programs. Owens College agreed to limit evening classes to subjects which were not being taught by city or district institutions. Duplication of daytime courses remained. In 1896, the college formally recognized courses at the technical school, and by 1900 the joint committee resolved that the Manchester Municipal School of Technology had primary responsibility for applied science and Owens College had primary responsibility for theory.

At this time, the university's superior attitude was diminished by the fact that the caliber of students attending both institutions was equivalent. Thus, in 1901, the city felt justified in taking the tactical steps required to give technology equal status once the college received its anticipated autonomy. This was accomplished by withdrawing funds from the college and urging that cooperation cease between the city and the college. In addition, new quarters were built and the technical school was renamed the Manchester Municipal School of Technology.[11] Combined, these three factors—equal students, fund withdrawal, and new buildings—all encouraged the university to grant equality in 1903 when autonomy was granted.

Technical school department heads were recognized as professors and granted chairs in the university senate. Other staff members of the technical school were accorded equal status with university teaching staff. The most important factor in this recognition is that "all this was done in the full knowledge that the authority which finally determined the actions of the Technical School staff who had now become integral members of the University was not the University Council and Senate, but the *Manchester City Council*."[12]

This cooperative venture was made possible due to the roots of Owens College in the civic community of Manchester. It has proved a brilliant success, measured by the respect and admiration that the University of Manchester Institute of Science and Technology (UMIST) enjoys today, and has rendered other joint university-city cooperative projects possible.

The Manchester Education Precinct

This heritage paved the way for development of the most recent example of the Manchester tradition of the university as a community neighbor. The project to develop the largest campus in Europe, the Manchester Education Precinct, is in the spirit of the "Redbrick" British civic universities which draw their strength and support from the cities which they occupy. For this, the universities express gratitude and attempt to become an integral part of, and not just an adornment to, city life.

By 1873, the college had been established in its present location on Oxford Road just a mile and a half from Piccadilly, the city center.[13] There it occupied a set of "impressive Victorian Monuments," befitting its official title of "The Victoria University of Manchester," which formed the nucleus of the rapidly expanding university.[14] Impressive as these buildings were, however, their surroundings were so haphazard and derelict that their impact and unifying influence on the neighborhood was lost until recently. After World War II the situation was acute. In the university area, many of the buildings—the most closely-packed terraced housing imaginable—were simultaneously decaying.[15] Although some were habitable, most, being built at the same time in the nineteenth century, were deteriorating at the same rate. The one-square-mile city center near Piccadilly was old, but its streets had been widened and it had been rebuilt. Immediately surrounding this, however, was a slum belt about one-half to two miles wide which contained the tightly crammed houses, factories, and warehouses built before 1890.[16] Since the university occupied a portion of this concentric slum belt radiating from the city center, the 1956 Ministry of Housing policy to attack this urgent problem throughout Britain meant that the area around the university would benefit from the national redevelopment policy.

There was an awareness among the national planners that comprehensive, long-range plans would be beneficial, both aesthetically and economically. After World War II, the rebuilding of the City of London from the devastation of Hitler's blitz in 1940 had proceeded haphazardly due to lack of funds. Although individually the skyscrapers erected were often well designed and were crucial to the financial function of the city, architects, planners, and citizens were well aware that the haphazard growth had resulted in an incoherent jumble. St. Paul's Cathedral, Sir Christopher Wren's masterpiece, was itself wedged in on all sides. To a large extent its dramatic effect had been destroyed.[17] By the 1960s, the British realized that had London been modernized coherently from an overall plan, many of the resulting urban problems—ecology, function, and transportation—might have been averted.

At this time, there was also rethinking in the Department of Education on the future role of British universities. *The*

Robbins Report of 1964, the first comprehensive survey of higher education in Britain, summarized this thinking in a precise, concrete way and provided a blueprint for the future.[18] Since Manchester was one of the largest and most important universities in the United Kingdom, its expansion was supported at Whitehall. Thus, housing and educational policy in the national government created an atmosphere conducive to the development of the Manchester Education Precinct.

Prior to the 1960s, there had been no "system" of higher education in Britain, only a "pattern." Since the universities became "pensioners of the state" during the higher education boom, they lost much of their financial independence and were encouraged to take more concern for public interests to include technology and training. The basic principle was that "courses of higher education should be available for all those who are qualified by ability and attainment to pursue them and who wish to do so."[19] To fulfill this goal, the 216,000 places in 1962–63 would need to be expanded to 558,000 in 1980–81.

In line with this expansion rate, the number of students at the University of Manchester was to expand from 6,642 in 1965 to 13,730 in 1984. The total population at the University, UMIST, and the City Colleges was to rise from 17,772 in 1965 to 37,070 in 1984.[20] The problem for the city and the university became how best to resolve this need for expanded higher education.

With land near to the central city more expensive and congested than in suburban Cheshire to the south, Manchester University had a choice to make regarding its expansion as part of the national plan. Should it move its campus twenty miles south to the quiet, more serene, more spacious and beautiful Cheshire countryside?[21] Or should it remain closely linked to the city in contrast to the trend to build the new British universities on 200-acre suburban sites? The decision, in view of the strong city-university ties, was undoubtedly a foregone conclusion. Manchester University belonged in and to Manchester. It did not wish to become isolated, remote from "real" life, but agreed with the thesis of R. G. Jobling that

> An effective university should be part of the local community, contributing as well as receiving. Universities

should not be planned in such isolation that they risk
becoming closed communities. "Green fields" universities limited their value.[22]

Thus, Manchester had no doubt that it would stay
within the city. Yet the plan adopted was unique in many ways.
First, the Manchester Education Precinct, to be the largest
urban campus in Europe on completion, was the result of
joint action by the corporation of Manchester, the University
of Manchester, the University of Manchester Institute of
Science and Technology, and the United Manchester Hospitals
in response to Whitehall's redevelopment and education policies. These four bodies, with the responsibility for developing
the precinct as part of the overall city redevelopment plan,
formed a joint committee to work out a long-range, integrated
program. Despite the fact that each of these bodies has its
own planning section, the overall scheme, it was decided,
should be allocated to a firm of private consultants. After
considering a half-dozen Manchester firms, the planning consultants chosen were the chartered architects Hugh Wilson
and Lewis Womersley.[23]

Second, it is noteworthy that the plan was known as the
Manchester Education Precinct rather than the University
Precinct. The precinct encompassed nearly all the higher education facilities of Manchester within a 280-acre area that
measured 1.25 miles by .33 miles. The goal was "to achieve
a comprehensive approach to Higher Education to meet the
needs of a wide range of students with each contributing to
the whole and in turn being enriched by the broad spectrum
of studies and activities to be found there. The concept of creating a Precinct . . . is a bold one and a site so close to the
City centre lends itself to the possibility of a significant fusion
of town and gown."[24]

Third, although the plan recognized the inherent difficulties in teaching academic subjects in a noisy, busy, thriving
city and thus proposed "sound screens" in the form of large
buildings, car-parks, and walls on the boundaries of the precinct, there was a desire to integrate Mancunians in the activities of the precinct and encourage the residents of neighboring
communities to use the many public facilities and resources.
The word "precinct" denotes, of course, an enclosure, but

the planners and the committee never intended that the precinct should be isolated from its surroundings. By planning the facilities within the area in a comprehensive manner, it was possible to provide for the city's needs in the overall plan. Specifically, the blueprint provided for a shopping center to serve not only the precinct occupants, but also the neighboring residents of Hulme and Brunswick. Elsewhere throughout the precinct, professional offices, public houses, and restaurants open to the public would be established.

Two policies were inherent in the concept of the site. Meeting rooms, theaters, and halls were to be made available to the public for city purposes and the entire length of Oxford Road, running north-south through the center of the precinct, was set aside for communal, public, or joint-user buildings.[25] Second, students were encouraged to use the city facilities outside the precinct. Their proximity to the city center made it easy for students to take advantage of entertainment, cinemas, theaters, Free Trade Hall (home of the world-famous Hallé orchestra), and the City Central Library.

In fact, a student survey showed that the Central Library—"the largest municipal library in the country, with a reading-room second in size to that of the British Museum"[26] —received nearly as much usage as the University and Institute libraries, clearly demonstrating the interdependence of city and university facilities in Manchester higher education.[27]

The fourth point of this unique plan was that by developing the precinct from a single, unified plan, the expenditures on housing and highways and the growth of the University, the City Colleges, the Institute, and the Hospital have been coordinated so that money spent would achieve its best value. "To spend money on new individual buildings, however finely conceived, scattered about a city may certainly create local improvements, but where a concentration of capital outlay is possible, as in the Precinct, a whole segment of the city can be renewed and made more efficient and pleasing." Such a plan avoids duplicating facilities and provides cost savings by "using standard building components, modular coordination, industrialized building processes and the provision of common services"[28] for the average outlay of £3.5 million throughout the precinct redevelopment.

Fifth, the citizens of Manchester have the advantage of

having this large educational center right on their doorstep. A wide variety of lectures, films, concerts, and conferences of interest to the general public are being held within the precinct. The University Theater presents plays with a wide general appeal, foregoing avant-garde and esoteric productions of more limited appeal. In the heart of the precinct, the new Northern College of Music will attract a wider public and need a range of specialty shops to serve its needs. These shops, to be located in the adjoining Precinct Centre, will also draw patrons from all over the Manchester area.

Ultimately, the physical placement of the City Education Committee's buildings on a site adjacent both to the University and the Institute may be the cornerstone for integrating town and gown.[29] These buildings include the Adult Education College, the Regional College of Art, and the John Dalton College of Technology. This closeness has the social advantage of sharing residential, dining, and Union facilities. Moreover, the proposed Indoor Sports Centre should provide physical recreation for all precinct students, spectator sports for all Mancunians, and training for the international caliber athletes of the region. Next to this planned sports centre, the BBC is building its Manchester studios and a Regional Computer Centre is being developed.

Sixth, the university took the idea of integrating with the community even further. Without a focal point, the precinct could easily become a large but amorphous campus. The university, therefore, made a brave academic decision to enter into a commercial venture which, if successful, would provide a practical, psychological rallying point for the new campus. It chose to build the Precinct Centre which included shops, offices, restaurants, a pub, and student residences all in one structure. In an architectural appraisal of the Precinct Centre, David Gosling noted that

> It is unusual to find a British university in the role of commercial developer. This is a pity because a university campus should always be thought of as a total urban complex, not just a mixture of teaching buildings and residential buildings.[30]

Although the Precinct Centre is located at the intersection of the two principal routes through the precinct—Oxford Road and the boundary between the City Colleges and Student Quarter areas—it has not yet fulfilled the dream of becoming the key building in the precinct. It must be emphasized, how-ever, that the Manchester Education Precinct development plan is a long-range plan which may run into the twenty-first century before completion. As late as 1969, the area around the university was said to "resemble Berlin in 1945."[31] Today, the Precinct Centre is bounded on the north and east by demolition and construction work. But the outlines of the Education Precinct are beginning to fill out; for the time being, the widespread depopulation and disruption has severely af-fected the present short-term prospects for the Precinct Centre as a viable commercial enterprise.

In clearing out the tightly-packed terraced houses, the redevelopers have temporarily left the precinct a ghost town after the last classes are finished in the evening. Students ap-plying to the university are forewarned of the housing shortage in the vicinity. For the short term, then, it is not surprising that the Precinct Centre is isolated from the surrounding neighborhoods of Hulme and Brunswick. As the potential uni-versity core, it has not yet replaced the Union as the center of activity. This is most probably due to the phasing of the development. Once the turmoil of construction surrounding the Precinct Centre has ceased, this modern, attractive, red-brick building should live up to its expectations as a commer-cial enterprise. If that is the case, the university contemplates erecting another such shopping center in the southern part of the precinct. Once upper-level walkways join the Precinct Centre to the whole precinct instead of just the Business School, Computer Centre, and Mathematics Building, it should replace the Union as the rendezvous for University, Institute, and City College students.

In implementing the Manchester Education Precinct, planners for the city, the university, and the consultants agree that the overall format and concepts have thus far been closely adhered to.[32] The development of this much land so close to a city center has been made possible by the joint efforts of the city and the university, the educational and redevelopment programs of the government at Whitehall, and the procedures for land clearance in the British system.

Dislocation Procedures

Once the government at Whitehall had decided to clear the slum areas in 1956 and the Manchester Corporation had followed suit and declared the entire precinct a clearance area, home owners were liable to compulsory purchase orders on their homes no matter what the condition of any particular dwelling. If a house was considered, by the medical authorities, to be unfit for habitation (as most of the houses were), it was labeled a "pink" area by the city planners. As was often the case, however, a single house on a block might be in very good shape. In considering the overall redevelopment plans, the city planning officer recognized that it would be necessary to purchase these adjacent areas, called "grey" lands, which themselves might not be unfit in order to set aside an area of suitable shape and size adequate for redevelopment.[33] Because of the comprehensiveness of the Manchester Education Precinct, all properties within it were labeled either "pink" or "grey."

An estimated 5,000 homes were torn down without any appreciable public outcry. It was generally agreed among inhabitants of the area that most of the homes were, in fact, unfit for human habitation. Just after World War II, it had been estimated that only 55 percent of the homes in Manchester had baths;[34] presumably, the vast majority of the 45 percent bathless homes lay within the slum belt. People were ready, therefore, to suffer the temporary inconvenience of rehousing because their new housing would have the basic amenities and be an improvement.

Still, this rehousing often meant that many neighborhoods—slums though they might be—were uprooted and spread throughout greater Manchester. The poor were the main dwellers in this jumble of housing and industry. Narrow streets, terraced houses, and crude factories gave the area a stifling congestion. Nonetheless, without proper procedures and fair treatment for the people, the redevelopment could have encountered major snags in uprooting so many people and demolishing so many flats, often packed at a density of forty to the acre.[35] After all, many people would have to pay increased rents, travel greater distances to work, make new friends, and send their children to new schools. Could it be that the reason for the lack of protest was the prevalent notion of British deference to authority? It was tempting to believe so in this case,[36] but a visit to the city housing office clarified matters on that score.[37]

Any tenant issued a compulsory purchase order immediately received top priority on the Corporation Council housing list. Indeed, "applicants living in houses deemed as unfit in a confirmed Clearance Area," such as the Education Precinct, received preference over "applicants living in conditions of serious overcrowding and recommended by the Medical Officer of Health for priority on medical grounds."[38] In general, these council houses were far superior to the precinct dwellings. In addition, no one was evicted from his house until suitable accommodation was found for him. Consideration was given to the tenant's stated preference of locality and type of housing.[39] Tenants were normally rehoused between three months to a year after the compulsory purchase order had been confirmed. No home was demolished until the tenants had been offered at least three suitable council residences.

Although the entire precinct has been declared a clearance area, certain properties, such as well-maintained shops along Oxford Road, have not been demolished since they are in good repair, serve the community, and are not presently required to carry out the overall plan. For its part, the university, considering the one-year rehousing time-lag, does not ask the Corporation to issue the required compulsory purchase orders until it actually needs a particular site or area for new construction. If a particular site becomes vacant within the university or the corporation (because of economy) desires to demolish certain properties before the university is ready to build on the site, the university implements a very worthwhile suggestion incorporated into the planning document. Therein, Wilson and Womersley suggest that all such cleared land should be "grubbed up, top soil spread and the areas sown with grass."[40] While some of these areas remain open spaces, others will later be building sites. Yet this landscaping creates a very pleasant effect by minimizing the transient nature and turmoil of the redevelopment program with its ever-present demolition and construction cycle. Further, this policy proves practical since some of these sites can be used as nurseries to plant trees and shrubs to be transferred later to completed buildings in other parts of the precinct.

Summary and Conclusions

The development of the Manchester Education Precinct marks yet another progressive, innovative chapter in the history of Manchester University's role as a community neighbor. In the early years, Owens College benefited from a receptive, though small, group of influential commercial businessmen and citizens. In turn, the growth of the college brought prestige for the city. Thus, the city's desire to fill the need for practical technical education at the turn of the century in an economical manner resulted in a formal, coequal partnership with the university which has continued to the present.

This strong, mutually favorable link encouraged both the university and the city to take advantage of national policies to solve pressing redevelopment and educational problems in postwar Britain. The net result has been the Manchester Education Precinct. While it is still too early to see if the precinct will develop as planned and result in an increased interaction between Mancunians and the university, and among all the elements of higher education included within the precinct, it would seem encouraging that in the first five years of the project, the plan has been scrupulously followed. So far, the Manchester Education Precinct is a well-conceived plan that has a great chance for creating a sense of community and identity for the student through careful planning of the education facilities and their relation to the city. The Victorian University of Manchester has derived a modern solution to the problem of relevance. But it has not done so alone. Speaking for the Corporation of Manchester, a city planner emphasized the determination that "the precinct would not become an educational enclave but a center to be used by all people of the city."[41] The lesson to be highlighted here is that the four authorities acting together gained far more than they could have individually.

Perhaps this example will be emulated in other cities. It must be noted that the fundamental factor in Manchester University's successful community role relates to the fact that the university knows the character and priorities of its city.

For another urban university to slavishly imitate the Manchester plan would be foolhardy unless the values and structure of that city were essentially similar. Still, the concept of joint cooperation between government and university authorities should be copied. Once each recognizes that their roles must be complementary rather than competitive, the development of one will become the goal of the other. This can only benefit both institutions, as well as the people they serve.

NOTES

1. A. C. Magian, *An Outline of The History of Owens College* (Manchester, Eng.: Pontefract, 1931), p. 5.

2. H. B. Charlton, *Portrait of a University, 1851–1951: To Commemorate The Centenary of Manchester University* (Manchester, Eng.: Manchester University Press, 1951), p. 9.

3. The Duke of Devonshire, President of Owens College, "The President's Speech," in *Record of the Jubilee Celebrations at Owens College Manchester,* for the Committee of the Owens College Union Magazine (Manchester, Eng.: Sherratt and Hughes, 1902), p. 2.

4. Josephine Laidler and A. R. Skemp, "Historical Sketch of the Owens College, 1851–1902," in *Record of the Jubilee Celebrations at Owens College Manchester,* for the Committee of the Owens College Union Magazine (Manchester, Eng.: Sherratt and Hughes, 1902), p. 2.

5. Charlton, *Portrait of a University,* pp 63–64.

.6 Peter Montague, "Civil and Mechanical Engineering," in John Knapp, Michael Swanton, and F. R. Jevons, eds., *University Perspectives* (Manchester, Eng.: Manchester University Press, and New York: Barnes and Noble, 1970), p. 141.

7. Mark Pattison, "On Education", a speech given before the Social Science Congress, October 13, 1876, quoted in Charlton, *Portrait of a University,* p. 138.

8. Samuel Alexander, quoted in Charlton, *Portrait of a University,* p. 138.

9. Charlton, *Portrait of a University,* p. 111.

10. *Ibid.,* pp. 114–115.

11. *Ibid.,* p. 115.

12. *Ibid.,* p. 117. (Emphasis added.)

13. Charlton, *Portrait fo a University,* p. 138.

1b. David Gosling, "Appraisal: Precinct Centre, Manchester," *The Architects' Journal,* 49 (December 6, 1972), p. 1309; and University of Manchester, *Calendar: 1972–1973* (Manchester, Eng.: Manchester University Press, 1972) p. 15. Note, however, that this official title is rarely used. The university, even in its official publications, chooses to be known as a city university. Also, Franklin Medhurst and J. Parry Lewis, *Urban Decay: An Analysis and a Policy* (London: Macmillan, 1969), p. 162.

15. Medhurst and Lewis, *Urban Decay,* p. 58.

16. Robert E. Dickinson, *The City Region in Western Europe* (London: Routledge and Kegan Paul, 1967), p. 228.

17. Valerie Singleton. "Blue Peter Special Assignment: The City of London," BBC-1 Television, January 21, 1973.

18. Jean Floud, "The Robbins Report and the Reform of Higher Education in Britain," in George Z. Bereday and Joseph A. Lauwerys, eds., *The World Yearbook of Education 1967: Educational Planning* (London: Evans, 1967), p. 87.

19. *Ibid.,* pp. 87–90.

20. Population includes full- and part-time students, academic, and other staff. See Hugh Wilson and Lewis Womersley, *Manchester Education Precinct: Final Report of the Planning Consultants, 1967* (Manchester, Eng.: Manchester University Press, 1967), p. 80. The university student enrollment for selected years is as follows: 1851–52, 62 students; 1881–82, 619 students; 1901–02, 706 students; 1921–22, 1,678 students; 1949–50, 4,068 students; 1965, 6,642 students; 1984 estimate, 13,730 students. See Charlton, *Portrait of a University,* pp. 164–167, and Wilson and Womersley, *Manchester Education Precinct,* p. 80.

21. A site near Jodrell Bank, where the University Department of Radio-Astronomy conducts research using the world's largest fully steerable radio telescope—the 250-foot Mark I, may have been feasible, among other options.

22. R. G. Jobling, "The Location and Siting of a New University," *Universites Quarterly,* 24 (Spring 1970), p. 127.

23. See Wilson and Womersley, *op. cit.,* and Wilson and Womersley, *The Manchester Education Precinct: Interim Report of the Planning Consultants, 1964* (Manchester, Eng.: Foster, 1964). Hereinafter the first (1967) report shall be referred to as *Final;* the second, *Interim.*

24. Wilson and Womersley, *Final*, p. 7.

25. *Ibid.*, p. 30.

26. Stuart A. Rossiter, ed., *The Blue Guides: England* (London: Ernest Benn, 1972), p. 530.

27. Wilson and Womersley, *Final*, p. 112.

28. *Ibid.*, pp. 7–8.

29. *Ibid.*, p. 8.

30. Gosling, "Appraisal," p. 47.

31. J. P. Powell, "The Universities of the Midlands and West," in Peter H. Mann and Ronald P. Dorg, eds., *British Universities Annual, 1969* (London: The Association of University Teachers, 1969), p. 24.

32. During January 1973, the author held personal interviews with Ms. V. J. Wales, a senior planning officer of the Manchester Corporation, and Mr. A. S. Wear of the University Planning Office. In addition, he interviewed, by telephone, Professor D. G. Robinson, University Town and Country Planning Department, and Mr. W. Armstrong, a partner of Wilson and Womersley, the planning consultants.

33. City of Manchester, *Rehousing and You* (Manchester, Eng.: Stationery Department, Town Hall, n.d.), pp. 5–6.

34. Lady Shena Simon of Wythenshawe, "Manchester," in *Great Cities of the World: Their Government, Politics, and Planning,* ed. William A. Robson (London: George Allen and Unwin, Ltd., 1954), p. 326.

35. Dickinson, *City Region,* p. 228.

36. The convincing writings of Dennis Kavanagh, lecturer in government, University of Manchester, prevented the author from jumping to this conclusion. Kavanagh generally asserts that the deference stereotype of the British may be overstated. See recent issues of *Goevrnment and Opposition* for his comments.

37. The author interviewed Ms. C. Shuttleworth, housing advisor for the Manchester Corporation, in the Housing Aid Center, Town Hall, Manchester, on January 16, 1973.

38. See Reg. 6, "Selection of Tenants for Council Houses," City of Manchester, Housing Department, Town Hall, 1973.

39. City of Manchester, *Rehousing,* p. 11.

40. Wilson and Womersley, *Final,* p. 72.

41. Robert Maund, City Planning Officer, the Corporation of Manchester, quoted in the *Manchester Guardian,*
November 9, 1967.

PART THREE

Universities and Students

9

THE UNIVERSITY AND ADULT EDUCATION

George E. Spear

Two difficulties beset any discussion of adult education in the urban university: first, adult educators have never been able to arrive at a satisfying definition of their field; and second, according to certain definitions, the United States has no urban universities as yet.

Adult education, to its various practitioners, ranges from literacy training for the disadvantaged to post-professional upgrading of skills, and from the much-maligned basket-weaving to environmental control courses. Adding further to the confusion is the fact that adult education may be organized and labeled as continuing education, extension, community education, community service, problem-solving, and even institutional citizenship. Its students may be adults or minors who have taken on roles commonly regarded as adult. At the same time, it seldom means education for "perennial students."

The dilemma is obvious when the situation calls for relating so amorphous a definition to so elusive a concept as that of urban university. Dr. Harvey S. Perloff, Dean of the

School of Architecture and Urban Planning, University of California at Los Angeles, points out that as recently as a decade ago there were no urban economists, anthropologists, or political scientists being graduated by U.S. universities.[1] In its study of the universities and the urban crisis, the U.S. Office of Education and its Organization for Social and Technical Information discovered that none of the institutions selected for study "qualified as an urban university if by that we mean an institution peculiarly responsive to its urban context, with all that implies about the makeup of its student body, its preparation of students for urban roles, its service to its immediate city."[2]

Nevertheless, some universities in urban areas do respond in varying measures to the demands and needs of their community and a non-traditional student body in ways which set them apart from the ivory tower and Ivy League stereotypes. That their response has been inadequate and belated is scarcely debatable—the question here is with the future.

To resolve the problem for the purpose of this discussion, adult higher education will also be referred to as continuing education and/or extension because these are the terms most commonly used by universities. Universities will be defined as urban if they are located in urban areas.

Foundations of Adult Education

If adult education has a short and perhaps undistinguished geneology, historians are able to document both interest and activity by American universities dating from the early 1800s. Most activities centered around public lectures and were directed essentially to the well or moderately educated. Public libraries and private enterprise dominated the field through the 1880s with university interest developing suddenly in the 1890s.

The first truly urban institution to move formally into adult education was the University of Chicago under President William Rainey Harper, who organized extension and gave it full university status in 1892, thereby setting a precedent. For all its apparent vigor, university extension seemed doomed. C. Hartley Grattan notes five major problems plaguing the field by 1900: the limited number of faculty capable of dealing with adult audiences; lack of money; faculty preoccupation with regular campus responsibilities; competitive administrative priorities; and competition of less expensive education activities.[3]

University extension as a field did survive and was shortly to prosper under provisions of the Smith-Lever Act of 1914 which established the Cooperative Agricultural Extension Service, a venture uniting state land-grant universities, and federal, state, and county government with private farm organizations in an attempt to bring scientific knowledge and practices to the American farmer. Generally, Cooperative Extension is hailed as the world's grandest and most successful experience in adult education, and to it is attributed much of the credit for the United States' outstanding achievements in agricultural production. The teaching of university-generated knowledge and associated research was indeed accomplished with a high level of performance, enthusiasm, and dedication by extension field workers.

Yet its benefits are now being questioned by critics who suggest that, as with the Crusades, as many Christians as infidels may have been slaughtered along the way. Recent studies suggest that Cooperative Extension has ultimately served the few large producers to the detriment and demise of many small farmers who could not adjust economically to the new demands and opportunities.

However accurate these criticisms, the studies are significant to those who would enhance adult education. First, they tested and proved the viability of large-scale extension organization and effort. Beyond that, they demonstrated solutions to the basic problems currently faced by urban extension.

Adult education in the early 1970s can list as major impediments those same five factors cited by Grattan. Cooperative Extension placed full-time teachers of adult education in the field across every state, supported them adequately, subsidized backup research and teaching faculty in university departments, and delivered a combination of education and technical assistance largely without charge to rural farm families.

The United States saw the balance of employment move from agriculture to non-agriculture in the 1920s, signaling the beginning of its urban era. However, the past half century has seen no attention comparable to Cooperative Extension devoted to the problems and educational needs of urban dwellers. Urban adult education, during most of this period, was characterized by offering traditional degree or college programs at non-traditional times and places, by evening colleges catering to the part-time student, and university resident branches operating at remote sites.

Evening colleges, which are an urban phenomenon, began with the founding of Cleveland College of Western Reserve University in 1925. Special units such as this addressed themselves to the needs of urban communities large enough to have a significant population of people who worked full-time and could devote only part-time to advancing their education. The evening college made it possible to fulfill requirements for a degree on a part-time basis. However, such colleges depended upon part-time faculty, the quality of their programs was suspect, and they were never accorded the status associated with full-time, traditional programs.

Urban Adult Education

True urban adult education or extension, if it has any history at all, can count only those years beginning with the mid-1960s and the enactment of the Great Society legislation which encouraged for the first time social experimentation on a nationwide scale. It coincided logically with the sudden urban self-awareness in society, a glossy view of education's potential, and the resulting federal funding.

Central to the early involvement of universities was passage of Title I of the Higher Education Act of 1965, which was intended to bring university resources to bear upon the problems of the urban community. The record and legend of the Cooperative Extension Service gave rise to the hope that what had so effectively improved life in rural America could have similar impact upon the growing problems and apparant decline of the quality of life in the nation's cities.

Clearly, Title I failed to meet expectations, but its indictment should be accompanied by an acknowledgment that it was never given reasonable opportunity to succeed. No more than $10 million annually has been allocated to it to be divided among the fifty states, the District of Columbia,

Guam, Puerto Rico, and the Virgin Islands. Small sums available for small projects, subject to termination annually, did not give adequate time or support for most efforts to reach fruition, nor did they encourage universities and their faculties to build strong resource bases for community problem-solving. It should be noted also that the task of urban extension is to deal essentially with complex social variables rather than with the simple technological transfer task of agricultural extension. The realities of Title I then are in no way to be equated with those of Cooperative Extension, and genuine comparisons still cannot be tested.

Regardless of impact, the importance of Title I is in bringing to the fore in higher education the need for addressing the problems of urban society and providing educational services to new groups in the community. The reference to adult education is both explicit and implicit. Nevertheless, Title I monies were sought out by most academic departments as well as by continuing education administrators.

An Administrative Philosophy and New Forces

Acceptance of the public service of extension responsibilities is nearly universal among university administrators. Few address themselves to the major issues and forces shaping higher education today without emphasizing the public service role of higher education. Their words affirm a moral responsibility to the society and the community, and their pragmatism acknowledges that the society and community will not long tolerate the elitist aloofness enjoyed by universities in former days.

However, the really critical problem of institutional commitment remains unresolved. Acceptance of the extension or service mission has always been a part of the administrative philosophy of the American university, but never a part of its academic philosophy. It has been the administrator's creed, not the faculty's. While institutional statements of responsibility always contain reference to service or extension along with teaching and research, the translation of philosophy into commitment, and responsibility into action, has rarely taken place.

Universities' academic resources have remained generally inaccessible to those programs and activities outside the traditional on-campus degree and research programs. The status of extension or adult education programs has been marginal at best and considered to be of a quality beneath the dignity and reputation of the true scholar and educator. It is reasonable to assume that this attitude held by a majority of the faculty remains unchanged in spite of growing pressures on every hand.

New forces are at work and evidence mounts that higher adult education is about to enjoy its finest hour. These forces, generated both within and outside the university, are creating pressures that require changes of attitude and practice, an abandonment of unilaterally determined institutional goals, and an unprecedented responsiveness to the outside world.

Two of these broad societal forces seem to conflict. On the one hand, the exponential increase of knowledge and resulting obsolescence of current information bring a critical demand by growing numbers of people for continuing education. Career updating and personal growth and development are required not only for upward mobility but simply for keeping pace with occupational requirements.

It might be noted that in revolutionary and developing societies adult education becomes a priority activity, because the circumstances of violent or rapid change must be accommodated by persons currently functioning in the institutions and systems. Leaders in emerging societies recognize that they cannot defer such education until a generation of children has been schooled and socialized into the new systems of the altered society.

An analogous situation thus pertains in any contemporary technological society where accelerating change requires the adaptation of presently productive citizens. Education for change cannot be deferred until succeeding generations.

A counter force is the growing skepticism of traditional education in general and higher education in particular by a public grown weary of unkept promises. Public education has failed to adequately teach basic skills, and higher education has demonstrated little relevance to productivity or even capability outside certain professional areas. School district voters, state legislatures, and private contributors increasingly withhold financial support as evidence of this collective disenchantment. A 1972 Harris poll, reported in *The Chronicle* in

December 1972, indicated that only 33 percent of the American public had "a great deal of confidence" in educators, a decline from 37 percent in 1971 and 61 percent in 1966.[4]

The contending pressures of increased need for education and disenchantment with educators suggest a possible stalemate. However, the forces are brought together because it is not education as such that is under indictment but rather its traditional forms. The result is increased demand for education but in new forms with new or redesigned subject matter, offered in flexible time frames, utilizing a variety of teaching and study methods; and, of primary importance, education with clearly defined and measurable objectives, relevant to the needs of the individual.

Adult education, at this point, emerges as a response to the problem. Extension or continuing education divisions of the university have espoused the philosophy and pioneered the practice of non-traditional education since their inception. Most universities have already established mechanisms via these extension units for involvement in the community and for meeting the diversity of non-traditional needs of the adult urban population. Programs and projects addressed to teachers in the inner city, literacy and job training programs for mothers on welfare, seminars for city and other local government officials, leadership and motivation training for teenagers, health and legal services for the poor, local neighborhood action organizations—all are part of an almost inexhaustive list that represents involvement of the urban university with its community.

A Question of Organization

The major problem occurs, however, in creating a non-traditional, community orientation for the university. Almost invariably, institutions have difficulty in separating conceptually and administratively their urban programs from university extension. Recognizing rightly that society's expectations extend beyond the production of college graduates, institutions are establishing new programs, centers, offices, and institutes labeled urban. The difficulty arises inherently since urban programs also emphasize involvement and service in the community—which is by definition the adult education function of the institution. As long as the urban programs are confined to on-campus degree-related courses for the education of urban specialists or generalists the problem is minimal.

There is little evidence that the dilemma will be quickly resolved because the dichotomy is basic. Adult education divisions have been organized apart from the mainstream of institutional concern, staffed with administrators, established without a faculty of their own, dedicated to activities viewed as marginal in quality, and looked upon with disdain by most traditional academicians.

It is both curious and important to note that urban programs in universities represent faculty acceptance of the principles of adult education, and, indeed, the urban thrust of most universities incorporates both the philosophy and practice of adult education. The faculties that have rejected and continue to reject extension operations are now developing new structures to provide an identical function, utilizing the concepts and processes first established and tested by extension. It is largely from faculty acceptance and involvement that a proliferation of non-traditional degrees, non-degree credit, and non-credit programs and activities has been generated for the urban community.

Non-traditional degree programs are a national preoccupation among colleges and universities. The National University Extension Association (NUEA) reported in 1972 that external or non-traditional degree programs were being announced at the rate of more than one a week.[5] Typically these have been traditional degree programs in which progress might be achieved in part by non-traditional means such as credit by testing, credit for work or life experience, independent study, and acceptance of non-credit educational experiences. The emphasis is on education for the out-of-school youth and adult. This practice approaches the treasured concept of adult educators—that of life-long learning. Occasional skepticism is expressed concerning the value of such programs to a significant number of people, but the pace of development proceeds unabated.

While credit and degree programs are taking on new trappings, the much-maligned non-credit programs are being awarded a new legitimacy by the introduction of the Continuing Education Unit (CEU), a system of recording student participation in non-credit classes and programs. By definition one CEU equals ten hours of participation in a formal non-credit educational activity. No testing, grading, or other evaluation is implied, but a permanent record is kept by the sponsoring institution.

The CEU was developed cooperatively by a group of thirty-three educational, business, professional, labor, and governmental organizations and associations to satisfy an increasing need for validating professional continuing education, often a legal requirement for continued licensure in certain states. In 1971, the CEU was adopted by the Southern Association of Schools and Colleges, making mandatory the granting and recording of CEUs for students in non-credit activities by member institutions. Thus, the place in higher education of non-credit classes is seemingly secure, along with acceptance of responsibility to the adult student.

The effect of liberalized traditional credit programs and the new legitimacy of non-credit activities is demonstrated clearly in emerging programs such as the professional development degree. This program, offered by such respected state universities as Wisconsin, Michigan, and Nebraska, is designed to give to the narrowly trained professional or technician advanced education in subjects not covered in his basic degree program but necessary to his career advancement. Directed primarily toward the engineer at present, professional development degrees encourage both professional and intellectual growth. Within the program's framework, the individual may take basic refresher courses, courses related to new knowledge in his field, or completely unrelated studies that contribute to his personal interests or development. Logically, the professional development degree has application to all professions and vocational roles.

The unique characteristic of this degree is not its subject matter, however, but rather its acceptance and accreditation for degree purposes of both traditional credit and non-credit (CEU) educational experiences. The gap between continuing education and traditional programs narrows, but the march goes forward under new banners and behind new leaders.

A new leadership for extension now emerges from a program base or from the academic (rather than the administrative) representatives of higher education. This is perhaps the most significant factor in projecting the future of higher adult education. Traditionally the field has primarily enjoyed the advocacy of university administrators. The National University Extension Association (NUEA), higher education's representative national body, was from 1915 until 1970 an organization of institutions represented by administrators. Professional or individual memberships were instituted in 1970, but the character of the association was not altered significantly.

The structure of the NUEA organization itself emphasizes extension as a delivery system bringing a university's courses and faculties to a clientele outside the regularly matriculated student body. NUEA's structure is organized around methods of education such as conferences, short courses, independent study, evening colleges, media, and around certain groups such as women, business, industry, and labor. Missing has been organizational recognition of program areas and of the substantive content related to adult and community needs and, thereby, a real acknowledgment of the faculty and its role in extension activities.

Some recognition of the new movement in higher education was evidenced by the organization's "view of the future" committee in 1972, which suggested in its report that the traditional approach would not be adequate for the 1980s. While still preoccupied with delivery, new concerns for program and content emerged in the report. George B. Strother, vice chancellor, University of Wisconsin–Extension, warned fellow delegates at an NUEA regional meeting that "extension as a process is unsaleable but it is viable as a set of principles."[6] Strother's remark points up the central factor in the current change higher adult education is undergoing.

Extension as a set of principles is gaining rapid acceptance among increasing numbers of faculties. Not so curiously, they, in fact, continue to reject and bypass the administration-dominated and process-oriented structures for continuing education within the institutions.

The new leadership moves higher adult education to the base required to make it an integral part of a university's function. Classroom teaching and research have been central to that function because they have been the responsibility of and accepted by the faculties. As adult education is similarly accepted it becomes centrally important to real change. Administrative advocacy alone provides it only marginal status.

It is via the new urban consciousness that higher adult education garners faculty attention and acceptance because the concept of urban is related directly to existing social conditions. Traditionally higher education has been attached to a concept of universality existing, in fact, apart from the immediate concerns of any given point in time. Conversely, urban universities are by definition related to and involved in the immediate community and recognize and accept a service role to persons and institutions beyond their traditional regard for students and programs. It is an implicit, if not explicit, commitment to adult education.

Again, it must be noted that the new leadership has not as a rule sought out the universities' continuing education divisions as the means for implementing urban programs. Rather, the urban institute, office of urban affairs, center for public affairs, or urban university department has been created in most institutions as the vehicle for addressing the urban environment. Descriptions of the activities of the new urban centers read much like those of the extension division but with the significant addition of a relationship to the ongoing academic program of the institution.

Urban-designated units promote on-job-training, applied research, programs for community leaders, problem-solving, certificate programs for urban-related skills, experimental courses, non-credit conferences and institutes—all of which are extension-like activities. The difference lies in the relationship between these programs and the ongoing education of students in the regular departmental degree programs —building urban consciousness and expertise of graduates while enjoying the involvement and endorsement of the faculties.

If expansion of this new commitment has a major barrier other than the ivory-tower syndrome, it is financing. Urban adult education over the years has been dependent upon the fees paid by students. This tainted it with entrepreneurship and underlay the disdain faculties expressed. Social problem-solving by contrast fails to provide a constituency either able or inclined to support instruction in this fashion. This helps explain the success of the free university movement discussed in chapter 6. As long as such efforts are financed by federal, state, or local agencies, or by volunteer arrangements, the taint is removed and the academician is lured into the real world by the opportunity either for personal gain or the chance to experiment and test social theories or sometimes by both.

While universities are criticized for subsidizing the education of the young and giving little support to the adult student, realities of financing through state legislatures and private contributions preclude significant assistance to adult education. The burden must eventually fall upon the federal government either through direct funding or the return of earmarked funds to states and local governments. Some support may be achieved by reallocation of funds currently being used by institutions for adult education purposes; these become available, however, only when structural or organizational changes are effected.

Structure, Faculties, and Advocacy

Some educators suggest that higher adult education must ultimately have a faculty of its own, a philosophy pursued by the University of Wisconsin–Extension. This view has at least two basic weaknesses. The first is the unlikely prospect that most institutions could finance a second faculty in the foreseeable future. The second is that the genuine integration of adult education with the mission of higher education and urban commitment can be accomplished only when the entire university faculty has accepted and accommodated the service function.

New structures are required to bring together traditional extension organization and emerging urban program units that overlap and duplicate both administration and function. Not only does efficiency suffer but the resulting lack of communication and coordination renders all such efforts less effective. This recognizes that too few resources are available under the best of circumstances in all major universities. Further, the reward system under which individual faculty members progress will never give full credit for adult education activities or urban involvement until such activities are recognized as peer functions with classroom teaching and research.

Further, this poses a critical question of organization. The machinery required for non-traditional or service programs is not generally present in most institutions except as part of the continuing education division. That unit serves not only as advocate for adult education but also usually as the clearing-house for community communications for the entire institution. In addition it can promote audience attendance, arrange facilities, equipment, and materials, register students, collect fees, and arrange necessary financing.

No individual school or faculty is prepared to perform these functions regardless of its willingness to assume responsibility for the adult education function. There is a fear among most adult education and extension administrators that their advocacy role will never be filled adequately by a faculty that will most certainly have to choose between the allocation of resources for traditional departmental needs and support for service activities.

Such fears probably are not unfounded, and a search for organizational or structural models is going on in many universities. While extension administrators may be expected to defend their vested interests in the existing structure in the same manner faculties have defended their traditional domains, it is becoming increasingly apparent that reorganizational efforts must be made in most institutions.

One model, with only limited credentials at present, suggests an assistant dean for extension be located within each academic school, with administrative responsibility for the adult continuing education program. Such an administrator would have budget authority with funds to marshal portions of faculty teaching loads as appropriate to the school's annual continuing education program. The extension activity of the school would be a part of that school's regular annual budget request, and the dean would be ultimately accountable for his school's performance in the service area. Mechanical and logistical support could be supplied to the extension programs of all schools by a central services unit staffed by non-academic personnel.

This structure places both advocacy and responsibility for extension with the academic school and faculty, provides a basis for evaluation of performance, opens the way for extension activities to be included in the faculty reward system, and suggests a scheme for providing the required mechanical

services. Most significantly for urban universities, it overcomes
the divisiveness and duplication that now attend the separate
organization of extension divisions and urban centers and
institutions.

One further item bears particular note—extension has
stood in actuality as a barrier to the ultimate service role of
the university. With the service function vested in a separate
administrative unit, the faculties of universities have never
been truly responsible for extension activities.

Likewise, the development of urban centers, offices, and
institutes in universities has added the trappings of urban-
orientation, but again without basic responsibility being carried by the regular faculty. They have been shields behind
which most faculty members could take shelter from the real
world and continue the myth of universal education. The few
committed faculty members who have been interested have
carried the responsibility for and suffered the intolerance of
their peers.

Until and unless adult education and all other urban
activities are woven into the entire fabric of the university, they
will remain peripheral, and urban universities will serve only
the marginal interests of a society that is demanding full involvement and response.

Expectations Are too Great

Caution is urged upon all advocates of any adult education or urban thrust by higher education. It is increasingly
unrealistic to expect of higher education performance in the
urban setting comparable to that of Cooperative Extension
in rural areas. The point is made in the Sixth Annual Report
of the National Advisory Council on Extension and Continuing Education:

> The problems of urban America are different in scope
> from the problems of rural America on which the Coop-
> erative Extension Service has had a large and successful
> impact. The sheer magnitude of urban problems is
> what weakens the will of those who would most want to
> move and change the world.[7]

Concentration of people and problems in urban areas,

and the complex jurisdictions and authorities make urban problems institutionalized in a way unlike those in rural areas. The report concludes:

> Frustration with the intractability of urban problems has led to disappointment with current approaches and a search for better solutions. At the root of this search is the need to develop within universities an organized capacity for urban extension. Until this is done, the value of unversity involvement is diminished because the community does not exist. Yet providing this link will entail a massive joint effort on the part of universities, cities and the federal government, an effort far beyond that foreseen by any current federal urban program of continuing education.[8]

Hazel Small underscored a related issue in *Adult Leadership:*

> Today the assumption that effective educational programs to treat social problems such as illiteracy or economic dependency will vastly improve the quality of life of the country or within a single selected community is incorrect. While on the one hand it is true that individual members of a community may realize a measure of increased self-esteem and may have more options available to them for pursuing activities that enhance the quality of their individual lives (the evidence accumulates that improving the quality of their individual lives is the rationale upon which education and teacher training proposals are successfully funded), it is equally true that significant educational achievements per se not only have not improved the quality of life for the community but may indeed have contributed to the totality of social problems apparent.[9]

The basic problem seems to have two facets: first is the complexity of urban needs and the limited resources of the universities; second, and perhaps more important, is the measurement of effectiveness. Small programs conducted with limited funds, personnel, and time cannot be expected to bring sweeping change to the urban community. The best hope of all university effort might be to effect some change and improvement in the lives and functions of certain easily identified individuals. Community-wide benefits will require community-wide resources which universities do not command.

The future of adult education in universities is likely to be tied to its record of performance in the urban community, and the quality of that performance will, to a large extent, depend upon the measures that are applied. It is important, even critical, that university urban adult education programs be conceived realistically with reference to the magnitude of the problems faced, the available resources that can be marshalled, and the susceptibility of those problems to modification or solution by educational intervention. It may well be that, in the final analysis, the urban university stands in much greater need of its community than the urban community of the university; that in the symbiotic relationship, the university will be the better nurtured.

NOTES

1. Harvey S. Perloff, "University Urban Programs: An Overview," *Corporate Role with University and Community*, National Association of Manufacturers, Spring 1972, pp. 6–8.

2. U.S. Department of Health, Education and Welfare, *Urban Universities: Rhetoric, Reality, and Conflict* (Washington, D.C.: Government Printing Office, 1970), p. 10.

3. C. Hartley Grattan, *In Quest of Knowledge: A Historical Perspective on Adult Education* (New York: Association Press, 1955).

4. *The Chronicle of Higher Education*, vol. 7, no. 11, December 4, 1972.

5. *National University Extension Association Newsletter*, vol. 4, no. 26, December 31, 1971.

6. George B. Strother, in speech given at meeting of Region 4, National University Extension Association, Ann Arbor, Michigan, October 1972.

7. National Advisory Council on Extension and Continuing Education, *Sixth Annual Report of the National Advisory Council on Extension and Continuing Education*, Pursuant to Public Law 89–329, 1971, p. 33.

8. *Ibid.*

9. Hazel C. Small, "Special Programs As Research," *Adult Leadership*, vol. 7, no. 6 (December 1972), p. 191.

10

FREE-ACCESS COLLEGES: WHERE THEY ARE AND WHOM THEY SERVE[*]

Warren W. Willingham

We are clearly beyond the time when concern about college admissions was restricted to professional educators. With growing and justified impatience, minority and poor Americans want to know why it takes so long to accomplish a semblance of representativeness in the student body of higher education. The silent and sometimes strident majority worries about the influx of large numbers of poor students—Who will pay? Who will be thus excluded? How will the quality of education be affected? Accordingly, the question of "open admissions" and the accessibility of higher education has become the subject of intense public debate.

The debate has not typically included systematic consideration of the extent to which higher institutions are presently accessible and to whom. This report provides new information on the question. It is based upon a national demographic analysis of those people who live within commuting distance of an inexpensive and nonselective higher institution. The results

*Reprinted, with permission, from *College Board Review,* Summer 1970, no. 76, pp. 6–14, College Entrance Examination Board, New York, 1970.

constitute a very limited though revealing status report on the accessibility of higher education near the end of the 1960s.

The nature of access to higher education has been changed fundamentally by several developments of major significance during the past decade. Extensive federal funding has supported a quantum leap in the rate of college attendance. (The ratio of college freshmen to high school graduates is now .70.) The civil rights movement and the student rebellion have brought into serious question the academic values that underlie restrictive admissions and discipline-oriented curriculums. Accelerating public expectation now demands that equal opportunity for relevant education beyond high school is a right—not a privilege. The assumption of public responsibility in order to meet these public interests is reflected in the rapid development of state planning and coordination. Greatly expanded research and technology are becoming integral parts of the whole process of planning and monitoring access to higher education. These trends have changed the nature of higher education in three ways.

First, they reflect a marked shift from a scholastic to a societal view of the admissions process. The former implies restrictive admissions, traditional curriculums, and close attention to academic standards and preparation.[1] Historically, college has been for those who could afford to go and who had the inclination to study or sit through what was offered. A 1970 interpretation of the societal view of college admissions does not, strictly speaking, involve admissions at all but rather assumes a predictable and continuous relationship between a student and his local college. It emphasizes periodic enrollment to develop and maintain the individual's intellectual awareness, his career skills, and his value to the community.

Second, proximity has become a key element in the accessibility of higher education. The most important considerations are related to the demonstrated connection between proximity and probability of attending college.[2] It is reasonably assumed that a marginal student is more likely to attend a nearby college where he can live at home, work part-time, and attend classes under conditions that only commuting status permits. Furthermore, a substantially larger responsibility for continuing education will make it important for colleges to be located where these people live and work.

Third, these social changes have created a new level of commitment and accountability which require public demonstration that opportunity is equal and education is relevant. This means a great deal more than social bookkeeping, but the process has to start there. While it is obviously true that accessible education is not equivalent to genuine opportunity, it is nonetheless worthwhile knowing the extent to which higher education is not even accessible.

Method of the Study

From the foregoing considerations, accessible higher education must have at least three characteristics. It must be relatively inexpensive so that cost does not arbitrarily exclude those who cannot pay or are unwilling to burden an uncertain future with a long-term debt. It must be willing to admit (and educate appropriately) the majority of high school graduates if that is what universal opportunity is to mean. And it must exist in such proximity that neither geographical nor psychological distance constitute a major barrier.

In order to incorporate these three characteristics into a study of the accessibility of higher education, each college in the country was rated on a five-point scale based jointly upon tuition and selectivity. For the purposes of this analysis the two lowest levels were designated "free-access" colleges. Of some 2,600 colleges, 789 or about three in ten were free-access as of fall 1968. In practical terms this means that they charged no more than $400 in annual tuition, and at least one-third of their freshman class ranked in the bottom half at high school graduation. This criterion of selectivity was chosen because a number of institutions are ostensibly open-door but *de facto* selective.

Of those colleges that were not free-access, 500 were special purpose or heavily religious. The remaining 1,300 or so institutions were inaccessible in roughly equal measure due to cost or selectivity—but more often both. Free-access higher education, as here defined, is almost exclusively public; it constitutes 60 percent of the public and 1 percent of the private sector. Accessible higher education is also very heavily represented by two-year colleges that constitute three-quarters of the total free-access group. Three out of ten public senior institutions are free-access; the same proportion holds for their branches.

The 789 free-access colleges were plotted on detailed maps with commuting perimeters around each. In consideration of results of prior studies and various rules of thumb used by state planning agencies, a one-way commuting guideline of 45 minutes was used in this study. This time interval was translated into commuting radii that ranged from 2½ miles in the larger cities to 25 miles in small towns or rural areas.

The National Picture

Free-access higher education is represented schematically on the national map shown on pages 00 and 00. The map includes the names of all metropolitan areas with a population greater than one million, and a location symbol for each of the other 200 metropolitan areas of the country. Each of the 789 free-access colleges appears as a commuting area with a diameter appropriate for the population density of its location. These commuting areas were not extended across state boundaries on the supposition that such colleges are not typically accessible to out-of-state students—either because of higher tuition or a natural institutional preference for state residents.

It turns out that slightly more than two-fifths of the population lives within these commuting areas. In a sense it is remarkable that the country has developed accessible higher education to this extent. On the other hand it is sobering to realize that the educational opportunity of three-fifths of the population is inhibited by the simple fact that they do not happen to live near an accessible college. This is one of the less complicated indices of how far the country has to go in equalizing educational opportunity.

It should be clear that the absolute level of this and other estimates reported here is fallible in the sense that different definitions of accessibility will yield different estimates of the population covered. For example, if the tuition limit for a free-access college were set at $600 rather than at $400, the national proportion of population covered would be 46 percent rather than 42 percent. The primary value of these estimates is the fact that they are more or less comparable from one area to another and thus provide a specialized sort of benchmark. In the following sections we use this benchmark characteristic to explore various types of discrepancies in the accessibility of higher education throughout the country.

Inequities Among Communities

There are systematic differences in the proportion of people living near free-access colleges in different types of communities. As Table 10–1 shows, a small metropolitan area is the most favorable location for a poor, marginal student to find accessible higher education. Moving from sparsely to heavily populated areas, the proportion of people having ready access to college first increases—24 percent in rural areas to 63 percent in the small metropolitan areas—and then decreases to 38 percent in the major cities.

Even though it may be unfair, it is nonetheless largely unavoidable that students in sparsely populated areas are less likely to live near an accessible college. On the other hand the orderly differences in accessibility among different sized metropolitan areas make little sense. It is true that the more populous metropolitan areas are more likely to have free-access colleges—half of the small metropolitan areas have an accessible college, whereas four out of five of the largest do. But the number of accessible colleges doesn't compensate for the large number of people in the more populous areas. Metropolitan areas of one-half million or more are frequently shortchanged when it comes to accessible higher education.

From the traditional pattern of the city as the seat of learning, one might assume that college is more available in the central city than in the urban fringe of the major metropolitan areas. Across the nation this is generally not true. Considering that median family income is about one quarter higher in the fringe than in the city,[3] it can be argued that free-access colleges should be overrepresented in the heart of the metropolitan area. Equally important, however, are the marked variations that occur among the major cities.

Of the 29 metropolitan areas that have a population of more than one million, Atlanta, Boston, Buffalo, Cincinnati, Detroit, and Paterson-Clifton-Passaic did not have one free-access college located within their city limits as of fall 1968. In eight additional metropolitan areas, less than one-third of the central city population lives within commuting distance of a free-access college. In another nine metropolitan areas, less than a third of the fringe population is covered. Since any one of these conditions must be regarded as a serious urban problem, it is reasonable to conclude that 23 of the 29 largest cities of the country have a major deficiency in the accessibility of higher education. Equally disturbing is the number of metropolitan areas that have no free-access college at all. As of 1968, the Census Bureau defined 228 Standard Metropolitan Statistical Areas, most of which had a population of 100,000 or greater. In 102 of these metropolitan areas the principal city has no free-access colleges.

Racial Imbalances

Across the country a slightly larger proportion (47 percent) of blacks live within commuting distance of a free-access college than is true of whites. At first thought this seems inconsistent with the fact that rural areas and large central cities are less likely to have accessible colleges and these areas are where most blacks are generally presumed to live. In actual fact, blacks are almost proportionally represented in communities of all sizes with an important exception—there are more blacks in the central core and fewer in the outer fringes of the largest cities. As Table 10–1 indicates, blacks are somewhat more likely than whites to live near a free-access college in all types of communities except the fringes of the largest cities (where they are least numerous).

Mexican-Americans (in the five southwestern states) and Puerto Ricans (in New York City and Chicago) are also somewhat more likely to live near an accessible college than are whites. This was a fairly consistent finding in the various areas where demographic data for these groups were examined.

While it is also true that the overall analysis indicated no marked regional variations in the percentage of blacks living near free-access colleges, there are obviously some very important exceptions and qualifications. First, there are states and metropolitan areas where these generalizations do not hold. In California, Maryland, Massachusetts, Nebraska, and New York, substantially fewer blacks than whites live near accessible institutions. The same is true of Atlanta, Boston, Buffalo, and Los Angeles. On the other hand, there are states and metropolitan areas where blacks are much more likely than whites to live within commuting distance of a free-access college. The best statewide examples are Missouri, New Jersey, and Pennsylvania; a similar trend exists in Kansas City, Milwaukee, and Newark. Another general exception to the data on minority groups cited in Table 10–1 is the problem of discrimination. Of course, discrimination is another form of selectivity that can make an institution inaccessible just as surely as cost or academic requirements can. It would have been useful to include discrimination in this analysis as a form of selectivity were it not for the impossible task of deciding which colleges discriminate against which students to what extent. Through much of the country one must simply introduce a subjective "correction" for the obvious fact that much of higher education is, for many reasons, less accessible to blacks and other sociocultural minorities than to middle-class whites. The situation in the deep South, however, is even more complicated by a long tradition of formally segregated institutions, including many that serve blacks almost exclusively.

Since the predominantly black colleges of the South cannot be construed as free-access for whites, it is possible to partially correct the estimates of white populations covered by accessible institutions in the southern states. This can be done simply by excluding the predominantly Negro free-access institutions and repeating the estimates. In most states the difference is not very noticeable. This is because relatively few colleges are involved. Among all recognized colleges that are more than 85+ percent black[4] or listed by McGrath[5] as predominantly Negro, only one in five can be classified here as free-access. Excluding the Negro institutions reduces the percentage of whites covered in the South from 50 percent to 47 percent.

This correction clearly underestimates the effect of segregation upon accessibility in the South because it does not reflect the limited access of blacks. It seems doubtful that it is possible to make realistic and defensible estimates of the proportion of blacks living within commuting distance of an accessible institution in some of the southern states. It is clear from available statistics that blacks do not have ready access to many public higher institutions.[6] On the other hand, many of the predominantly white free-access colleges do serve substantial num-

bers of blacks—obviously estimates for blacks could not be
based upon the Negro colleges alone. It would appear that the
only safe working assumption is that the various estimates for
minority populations included here are generally inflated and,
in some areas, substantially so.

Table 10–1

Percentage of Different Populations Within Commuting Distance of a Free-Access College in the United States

Area	Total population (millions)	Percent within commuting distance			
		White	Black	Mexican-American[b]	All U.S.
Metropolitan areas (SMSA)[a]:					
1,000,000+					
central cities	32.6	36	42	42	38
fringe	33.2	37	31	68	37
500,000 to 1,000,000	20.0	36	46	66	38
250,000 to 500,000	16.0	47	61	37	48
50,000 to 250,000	16.2	62	70	56	63
Counties not in SMSA's:					
over 20,000	45.0	48	52	42	48
under 20,000	16.2	24	27	13	24
All United States	179.3	42	47	47	42

[a]Standard Metropolitan Statistical Area.

[b]Mexican-American in five southwestern states; also includes Puerto Ricans
in New York City and Chicago.

The Regions Vary

The accessibility of higher education varies markedly among
the four main census regions of the country but not always in
expected ways. The Northeast, for example, has never been a
region known for accessible colleges. Private education has
been dominant to such an extent that some states—particularly
New York and more recently Pennsylvania—have purposefully
allocated substantial student aid resources in order to use the
private sector for public purposes. Furthermore, the Northeast
has been slow to develop the egalitarian interpretations of
higher education represented by the community college and
comprehensive post-secondary educational opportunity.

Despite these facts the Northeast is only slightly below the national average with respect to the proportion of people living within commuting distance of a free-access college. As Table 10–2 indicates, this region falls behind the South and West only in metropolitan areas of one-half million or more people. However, such areas contain two-thirds of the population in the Northeast. In addition to its urban problem, the Northeast has frequently not developed and supported its free-access institutions—public higher education in the region often receives niggardly appropriations.[7]

The Midwest is the surprise of the four regions. Traditionally, it has assumed a view of higher education in contrast to that of the Northeast. Its state institutions, long a source of national pride, have been identified historically with inexpensive, nonselective admissions. The data of Table 10–2 seem inconsistent with this tradition. The proportion of people living near an accessible college is substantially lower in the Midwest than in other regions. It is lower in each type of community except the largest and the smallest. The coverage of free-access colleges in midwestern cities of one-half to one million population is extremely low, although the largest cities hold their own

Table 10–2

Percentage of Population Within Commuting Distance of a Free-Acress College in Different Types of Communities for Each Region

Area	*Northeast*	*Midwest*	*South*	*West*
Metropolitan areas (SMSA)[c]:				
1,000,000+				
central cities	29	44	38	44
fringe	27	30	38	62
500,000 to 1,000,000	38	12	53	55
250,000 to 500,000	49	39	53	48
50,000 to 250,000	71	47	71	61
Metropolitan areas (SMSA):				
over 20,000	51	35	55	50
under 20,000	24	23	28	17
Overall percentage for				
each region	38	33	50	51

with cities of other regions. The principal reason that the largest cities appear better off than the Midwest generally is the existence of the community college systems of Chicago and St. Louis. These systems serve a great many people and seem attributable to unusual leadership—they are not typical of the region. Of all moderately large metropolitan areas in the country without any free-access colleges, more than half are located in the Midwest. Thus, there seem to be special (and outstanding) exceptions to the general finding that the midwestern region provides accessible higher education to a smaller proportion than the rest of the country. Of course, local conditions vary and most states have peculiar characteristics that make any generalization conditional.

It should be recognized further than many state universities have nonselective colleges or divisions. Also, a number of public institutions are officially open to any high school graduate in the state but enroll most of their students from the upper half of the high school class. Both of these circumstances may be more common in the Midwest than in other regions. In neither case are such institutions classified here as free-access because the definition depends not upon whether *some* less apt students are admitted, but whether the total institution is likely to be regarded by prospective students as truly accessible. The best generally available measure of that accessibility would seem to be the proportion of lower-half high school graduates actually on the campus.

The situation in the South is interesting for several reasons. Despite very limited resources and a decentralized population, the region has managed to place free-access colleges within almost as large a proportion of its people as is true in the wealthier and more centralized West. This has come about through the use of widely different models; the comprehensive junior colleges of Florida, the technical education centers of South Carolina, the open-door senior institutions of Louisiana, and the university two-year system of Kentucky are good examples of the diversity.

Concerning the accessibility of higher education, the southern region has two large problems—too well-known to belabor and too critical to dismiss. Racial segregation of institutions will necessarily hinder educational opportunity as long as it drains attention and resources from the development of

relevant educational opportunity for high school graduates.
And it is the limited resources and opportunities that constitute
a second difficult problem. In spite of considerable progress in
making higher education available to their youth, some southern states still have a very low rate of college attendance.

Roughly half of the population in the western United
States lives near an accessible institution. This proportion is
somewhat lower than one might have expected, considering
that one westerner out of two lives in California, the state
known for accessible higher education. The proportions indicated for different types of communities in Table 10–2 are not
unusual except in the case of central cities versus the fringe of
major metropolitan areas in the West.

In a region usually associated with statewide planning of
higher education facilities, it is ironic to find that suburban
areas are better provided with free-access colleges than are the
central cities. This result is largely attributable to imbalances
that exist in the three major metropolitan areas of California
—Los Angeles, San Francisco, and San Diego. In each, residents of the fringe areas are much more likely to live near a
free-access college than are residents of the central city. This
condition, not typical of the country, may relate to the tendency
in California to locate junior colleges where fairly large tracts
of land are available. Of course, one can argue that the commuting radii should be larger in these cities because of the
emphasis upon personal transportation on expressways, but it
seems doubtful that this consideration changes the general
result described.

It is important to recognize, however, one other important
characteristic of the West. Individual free-access colleges in this
region are highly developed. They typically offer comprehensive programs, provide an array of community services, and
attract large numbers of students. In this sense free-access
higher education is particularly well-developed in the West as
compared to the Northeast. The extent of geographic variation
is indicated by the percentage of new freshmen in each region
who are enrolled in a free-access college. That comparison
runs: Northeast, 22 percent; Midwest, 34 percent; South, 50
percent; and West, 71 percent.

A complementary way of looking at the accessibility of
higher education is to examine who is *not* served. There are

Table 10–3

**Number of Whites and Minorities Not Living Within
Commuting Distance of a Free-Access College in
Different Communities in Each Region
(in millions)**

Whites:	Northeast	Midwest	South	West	Total for U.S.
large metropolitan areas	15.3	10.4	4.6	5.4	35.7
medium metropolitan areas	5.7	9.0	6.1	3.2	24.0
other counties	4.4	12.8	10.7	3.8	31.7
Minorities*:					
large metropolitan areas	2.2	1.5	1.2	.8	5.6
medium metropolitan areas	.1	.6	1.6	.3	2.7
other counties	—	.2	3.4	.3	4.0
Total for U.S.	27.7	34.5	27.6	13.9	103.8

*Blacks, Mexican-Americans, and Puerto Ricans.

two main questions: What kinds of people do not live near an accessible institution? And what sort of locations are not covered? It is these interpretations of the data that lead most easily to implications concerning the need for new institutions or new arrangements. Data based upon individual states are the most useful for practical purposes, but space limitation restricts us here to summary information that does provide a useful national perspective.

Table 10–3 summarizes the nature of the total population which does not live near a free-access college. The largest group of people not living near a free-access college is easily the whites in the large metropolitan areas of the Northeast. Other very large groups of people not having ready access to higher education are whites in the nonmetropolitan areas of the South and whites in each of the three demographic divisions of the Midwest. All other categories of whites plus blacks in the rural South account for smaller but still substantial numbers of people not living in proximity to accessible colleges.

With respect to location, there are several states that are far below the norm in the availability of accessible colleges. For example, there are 14 states in which less than one-third of the population is covered. Preceding paragraphs contain several references to the numerous urban areas which are either deficient or lacking in free-access colleges. This circumstance has an important bearing upon the strategy of improving accessibility—first, because accessibility is deficient in urban areas generally, and also because the congested areas are where additional colleges can most efficiently cover large numbers of people.

Location of New Colleges

Unfortunately, there is little sign that recent emphasis upon expanding educational opportunity has had much effect upon the overall efficiency of college location. In the fall of 1968 a large number of new free-access colleges opened (76 in fact). These colleges increased the proportion of the nation's population living near such a college from 38 to 42 percent. On the average these new colleges each serve some 100,000 people. This is essentially the same average number of people living within commuting distance of those free-access colleges in existence prior to 1968.

As a matter of theoretical interest, these new colleges were plotted in 76 hypothetical locations throughout the country where they could cover the maximum number of people. The results were not surprising; those 76 colleges in ideal locations could have covered an average of 300,000 people and raised the national proportion so covered by 14 percent instead of the 4 percent increase that actually resulted. Putting it another way, 28 states added one or more free-access colleges in 1968; in only 8 of those states was any college opened in the general location where it could serve efficiently the most people.

Naturally, the location of a college is determined by a number of factors, many of which may be quite valid and have little to do with accessibility. The data do illustrate, however, that estimates of the number of colleges that might be required to achieve various goals with respect to educational opportunity are subject to considerable uncertainty. Furthermore, the various forces that determine college location are not likely to result in new institutions always being placed in convenient commuting locations.

These comments provide a useful introduction to Table 10–4, which estimates the resources required to increase the proportion of the population within commuting distance of a

Table 10–4

Estimate of Additional Colleges Required to Put Specified Percentages of the Population for Each Region Within Commuting Distance of a Free-Access College

Region	Present free-access colleges	Additional free-access colleges required to cover*: 50%	60%	70%	80%	90%
Northeast	92	20	14	21	32	56
Midwest	193	56	41	43	80	138
South	312	20	33	65	103	153
West	192	16	13	45	37	63
Total for U.S.	789	112	101	174	252	410

*These figures refer to additional colleges required and should be added to find the total required at any percentage level for any region.

free-access college. Entries in this table show the present number of free-access colleges in each region and the number of colleges (new or redefined) that would be required to increase the percentage of population covered to various levels in all states in the region (for example, 16 additional colleges would increase the percentage to 50 percent for each state in the West). A systematic qualification is the assumption that no state would add a college that did not cover at least 25,000 people within its commuting area.

These data in Table 10–4 were developed by plotting hypothetical new free-access colleges in optimal locations in each of the 50 states and estimating the populations so covered. It is evident that accessibility could be greatly improved in the Northeast with a limited number of colleges. This is also true in the West, but the gross population involved there is much smaller. The South and Midwest have a large and widely distributed population. A high degree of coverage in these regions would require more than twice as many additional colleges as in the West or Northeast.

Roughly speaking, this analysis indicates that some 375 additional colleges in optimal locations would put two-thirds of the population of most states near an accessible institution. Considering that locations cannot be expected to be optimal, it would appear from recent experience cited above that the 550 new colleges recommended by the Carnegie Commission[8] would have the approximate effect of raising the national proportion of population covered from 4 in 10 to 7 in 10. It should be emphasized, however, that this rough estimate assumes that the 550 colleges would be opened immediately. In the 5 to 10 years that might be required to develop that many institutions, the accessibility of existing colleges would likely erode to an unknown extent due to urbanization, increasing costs, and selectivity.

In some areas it may be quite unrealistic to consider a new college as the only or even the preferred answer to a lack of accessible higher education. For political, educational, or financial reasons, it may be more reasonable to change the admissions characteristics and fees of an existing college. It should be recognized, however, that some senior institutions have little interest in serving the free-access function and will do so only under considerable pressure—and even then perhaps halfheartedly. In any event the foregoing discussion assumes that state planning groups consider local conditions and weigh the advantages of new institutions versus alterations in existing ones.

Many distinguished groups—notably the Eisenhower Commission in 1969[9] and the Carnegie Commission[10] a decade later —have recommended a national goal of providing higher education within commuting distance of most of the population. The data of this study amply illustrate how far we have to go in meeting that goal. It is important to say again that the definitions used here can give only the most general indications of accessibility. A good part of the intent of this study is to urge closer local attention to the real conditions of access to college. Furthermore, living near an accessible college does not guarantee access to genuine opportunity, a useful education, or an enriching experience. The data do, however, provide clear indications of some serious problems, and they bear upon educational strategy.

There are many geographic imbalances in the availability of higher education, but the inadequate coverage of major urban areas is a general case so serious as to require special emphasis. Considering the urban problems of physical decay, deprived populations of minority/poor, and the constricting lack of individual alternatives, the addition of inadequate educational opportunity in many cities is best described as repressive.

There is no doubt that the country needs far more community institutions than it presently has, but in many states the development of existing colleges is just as urgent a problem if not more so. There are very many colleges with quite small enrollments and a narrow view of their responsibility to the world around them. In any community which as a free-access college, a primary question is whether that college has been supported and developed sufficiently to actually provide relevant opportunity to a significant proportion of the local population. Over the long range, it seems entirely likely that community service and continuing education represent even greater developmental needs of local institutions.

But perhaps the root problem of access to higher education in the 1970s is how to expand equal and relevant opportunity as rapidly as possible without slipping into one or both of the alternate chasms—stifling individual choice or crippling higher institutions. There must be quality institutions with sufficient autonomy to develop the advanced academic disciplines and to meet local needs as the college and its community see them. There must also be mechanisms which guarantee that students retain control over their decisions so that utilization of talent does not mean exploitation of the individual and more steps to a mechanistic society.

NOTES

1. Frank H. Bowles, "Observationsand Comments," in Earl J. McGrath, ed., *Universal Higher Education* (New York: McGraw-Hill, 1966).

2. Wilbur L. Bashaw, "The Effect of Community Junior Colleges on the Proportion of the Local Population Who Seek

Higher Education," *Journal of Educational Research,* 58 (1965), pp. 327–29. Also, Leonard V. Koos, "How to Democratize the Junior College Level," *School Review,* 5 (1944a), pp. 271–84. Also, Leland L. Medsler and James W. Trent, *The Influence of Different Types of Public Higher Institutions on College Attendance from Varying Socioeconomic and Ability Levels* (Berkeley, Cal.: Center for Research and Development in Higher Education, 1965).

3. U.S. Bureau of the Census, *Income in 1967 of Families in the United States,* CPR Series P-60, no. 59 (Washington, D.C.: Government Printing Office, 1969).

4. "Negro Enrollments This Year on the Nation's Campuses," *Chronicle of Higher Education,* 3, no. 16 (1969), p. 3.

5. Earl J. McGrath, *The Predominantly Negro Colleges and Universities in Transition* (New York: Columbia University Press, 1965).

6. John Egerton, *State Universities and Black Americans* (Atlanta, Ga.: Southern Education Foundation, 1969).

7. "What States Spend Per Capita," *Chronicle of Higher Education,* 4, no. 5 (1969), p. 1.

8. Carnegie Commission on Higher Education, *Quality and Equality: New Levels of Federal Responsibility for Higher Education* (New York: McGraw-Hill, 1968).

9. Eisenhower Commission, *Goals for Americans: The Report of the President's Commission on National Goals* (Englewood Cliffs, N.J.: Prentice-Hall, 1960).

10. Carnegie Commission on Higher Education, *A Chance to Learn: An Action Agenda for Equal Opportunity in Higher Education* (New York: McGraw-Hill, 1970).

11

HIGHER EDUCATION FOR ALL?

The Case of Open Admissions*

Martin Mayer

Access to education has been one of the most durable issues in the political life of this century, and not just in the United States. Lunacharsky's expansion of the Russian secondary schools persuaded visitors that the Soviet future would work; Jean Zay's democratization of French schooling was the most admired (and the most feared) accomplishment of the Léon Blum government in the 1930s. In England in the 1960s, the left wing of the Labor party went along with Harold Wilson's imposition of charges on prescription drugs in return for the establishment of Open University, a television-based, degree-granting extension program. African political life has been torn apart by the debate between those who wish to expend scarce resources on universities for the benefit of a numerically small leadership and those who wish to use the money to build a broad system of secondary schools (in most regions of Africa the "elitists" have won).

Like so much else that has occurred across the oceans in the twentieth century, these issues were first raised in America during the nineteenth. Indeed, by the time the Educational

*Reprinted from *Commentary,* by permission; copyright © 1973 by the American Jewish Committee. The article appeared in the February 1973 issue, pp. 37–47.

Policies Commission of the National Education Association published its "Cardinal Principles" in 1918, the idea if not the reality of universal secondary education had been completely established everywhere in the United States outside the South. Moreover, many of the publicly funded land-grant colleges were already required by their state's constitution (not just by law) to accept all applications from graduates of the state's high schools.

Few of the extensions of American education were egalitarian in original intent. The founding fathers sought not to eliminate either distinction or aristocracy, but to rest the recognition of distinction on merit rather than on birth. Proposing a system of twenty fee-supported secondary schools for Virginia, Thomas Jefferson urged that each take one scholarship boy from each elementary school in its area—and keep the best individual in the group through the entire program. "By this means," he wrote, "twenty of the best geniuses will be raked from the rubbish annually. . . ." Subsequent expansion, especially of higher education with the federal land-grant subsidy, was argued for in large part on grounds of utility: the presumed role of universities in promoting agricultural and mechanical arts. No surplus of applications was foreseen; numbers, it was thought, would be held down by the loss of income necessarily suffered when a boy went to college rather than to work. Only unusual ambition, or perhaps unusual talent, would lead to attendance at college, and a kind of osmosis would draw through higher education those who would most benefit from it.

In fact, of course, social propellants intruded almost from the start. Because attendance at college involved the sacrifice of income, sending a boy to college became a significant example of what Veblen called "conspicuous consumption," affirming the position of the family. And in turn, university alumni (not necessarily graduates), if only because they were drawn mostly from families of income and influence, came increasingly to dominate the leadership positions of society. This is not to deny the hunger for learning that could drive a Sam Johnson to Oxford or a Felix Frankfurter to New York's City College —but City College at the turn of the century was a no-elective, post-primary school that took students from eighth grade and set them forth with a B.A. five hard years later.

After World War I, the notion that going to college was the way to get ahead in the world took hold in the United States, and then reality came to match belief. An increasingly professionalized society demanded academic preparation rather than apprenticeship from entrants to the professions (even in teaching, where post-secondary training was once considered more than enough); and an increasingly bureaucratized business world established educational requirements for entry to the managerial levels of enterprise (even in retailing, where everyone admitted that a talent for selling was a wholly independent trait). What S. M. Miller has called "credentialism" became a guiding principle in wide areas of economic activity, accepted by both employer and job applicant. In 1971, according to a study by the American Council on Education, 85 percent of black freshmen and 78 percent of "the non-blacks" said they were going to college "to get a better job."

The other side of this coin, of course, was that those who did not pick up tangible evidence of higher education lost their chance to become part of the nation's professional and managerial cadre. What had started as an educational ladder, one of several routes upward for the mobile, became a set of educational barriers, hurdles that had to be cleared on the *only* way ahead. The demand for college places far exceeded the supply, and except in a few states access to university became subject to some form of competitive examination.

In New York City, up until the late 1960s selection to the free, tax-supported City University (which enrolled about 140,000 students in 1969) was made according to high-school grades, supposedly uniform across all the city's schools. In 1920, a graduate with a 72 average would have gained entry to City College, recently promoted to post-secondary status; by the late 1960s, most of the four-year colleges in the city system were requiring an 82 average, which in effect meant the top 40 percent of the city's high-school graduates (or the top sixth of the age group, academically, because three-fifths of the city's adolescents do not complete an academic program in an academic high school). For entrance to the city's two-year junior colleges (locally called "Community Colleges," though none in fact drew from a geographically restricted area), requirements were generally much lower: a 70 average, which was earned by almost 90 percent of all graduates from the high schools.

Thus, though neither a "general" high-school diploma nor a vocational diploma granted automatic entrance to any college, City University was deep in the social-mobility business long before the day of Open Admissions; at all times in its history, 90-odd percent of its entering freshmen were from homes where neither parent had attended college. The fact is, however, that these entering freshmen were not themselves representative of the high-school population as a whole. The "general" program in the high schools was heavily black (and Puerto Rican), and in both high-school grades and in competitive exams, black students consistently ranked lower than white students. With increasing frequency since the 1940s, educators and social reformers have been drawing baleful correlations between the preponderance of whites in the universities and in the seats of the mighty. At one level, promoters of the black cause began to demand greater opportunities for blacks to move up the educational ladder; at another level, spokesmen began to insist that educational barriers, especially competitive examinations of any kind, be removed from the forward march of the black young.

At first these pressures concentrated on improvement of secondary education: New York's much advertised Higher Horizons project of the 1930s was started by a junior-high-school principal who had discovered that only about 4 percent of the graduates of his school went on to college. Programs like Higher Horizons produced a steady but fairly slow expansion in the number of blacks proceeding to college. In 1964, the Economic Opportunity Act made the recruitment of blacks a prime goal of the poverty program, and New York funded its first College Discovery venture. The federal government dropped the other shoe in 1965 in promulgating the Higher Education Act, and a year later the state funded the Search for Education, Elevation, and Knowledge (SEEK) program, by which students from poor neighborhoods who were not otherwise eligible for regular admission to the City University four-year colleges were accepted into, and paid to attend, special programs run more or less by the colleges and designed to remedy deficiencies in skills and attitudes.

In 1969, nevertheless, a New York City school system

that was more than half black and Puerto Rican in student composition was still feeding into a four-year college system that was less than one-tenth black and Puerto Rican. Economic conditions in the city, coupled with the immense demographic bulge of the age-classes born shortly after World War II, meant that a majority of "minority" college-age New Yorkers not in college were unemployed. Especially where the colleges were located in slums, pressure to do something for the young people of the neighborhood had become very strong.

At this time the Board of Higher Education, the controlling body of City University (appointed by the mayor), began a number of studies looking toward the day when the university would undertake to accept *all* graduates of the city's high schools, regardless of their performance in high school or their achievement in examinations. In general, the evidence turned up by these studies was discouraging: the centerpiece, an examination of the high-school senior class by Vice-Chancellor Robert Birnbaum, produced a well-documented opinion that virtually every New York City high-school graduate reasonably ready for an ordinary college program was already going to college. Nevertheless, both Mayor Lindsay and City University Chancellor Albert Bowker felt a political need to affirm the eventual establishment of an Open Admissions program, to take effect some time in the mid-1970s—a date far enough in the future to ensure that their successors rather than they themselves would be stuck with the problem.

The model originally in mind was the California state system, with its three tiers of higher education: the universities, which accept the top 12 percent of each high-school graduating class; separate four-year colleges, which take the balance of the top half; and the two-year junior colleges, which take the rest (plus some nongraduates of high schools). Among the drawbacks of this arrangement is the heavy concentration of blacks and Chicanos in California's junior colleges (a concentration that tends to get heavier as progress is made in desegregating the high schools: the top half of an all-black school is, of course, all black, while the top half of the high-school graduating class nationwide, as measured by standardized tests, is only about 3 percent black). Such imbalances have consequences: the Black Panther party started at predominantly black Merritt Junior College a few miles down the road from what was an almost entirely white University of California at Berkeley. In New York, the planners had to consider also the fate of the students at the city's four selective-entrance college preparatory high schools. Most of the students who ranked in the bottom 10 percent of the graduating class at the Bronx High School of Science, for example, were better prepared for college than most of the students in the top 10 percent of some of the other high schools.

Moreover, if one assumed—as one had to assume—that the great majority of newcomers taken into the four-year colleges under any new program could not routinely handle college work, it was necessary to devise means of helping them catch up. Sensibly, Bowker took an interest in secondary education, and tried to arrange to have five public high schools put under the wing of City University, to experiment with new programs. Some work was already being done, through a program called "College Discovery Prong II," in which university professors and students were working with about 1,500 high-school students selected in the ninth grade for their *unlikelihood* of proceeding to college. The city-wide Council Against Poverty had sabotaged this project in a fit of pique against the school system, withdrawing the $5 weekly grant the students had been paid in the first years of the experiment, and the Board of Education was being unhelpful, but the students were coming along much better than would have been anticipated from their ninth-grade academic and psychological test scores. Given actual control of some schools, the university might, just possibly, have been able to bring greater numbers of "disadvantaged" students up to the minimum levels of skill required for college.

But the Board of Education was unwilling to turn over control of any school (it still is), and in 1969 circumstance outran planning. In May, a small group of black students, abetted and probably led by militants from the neighborhood, "seized" the South Campus of City College on the western edge of Harlem. They chained the gates closed and themselves to the gates, vowing to remain in adverse possession until the Board of Higher Education met the five "demands" of the "movement." The most important of these demands entailed a vast increase in the still small number of black and Spanish-speaking students at a college located in an exclusively black and Puerto Rican section of the city.

Confronted with a court order, the demonstrators disappeared, but the situation they had dramatized did not.* "It was not only the blacks," says Frederick L. Burkhardt, president of the American Council of Learned Societies, who was then president of the Board of Higher Education. "It was the eight-thousand-dollar-a-year whites, saying, 'We pay our taxes. We want to go to college, and we have the right to go to college.' It was a demand that was irresistible." City University Vice-Chancellor Seymour Hyman, an alumnus of City College's student body and professorate, remembers a slightly different scenario: "I got a call from Al Bowker—he was at a meeting somewhere and couldn't leave it, and there had been a report over the radio that the Great Hall of City College had been set on fire. I went up there, and I saw the smoke pouring from the windows. We had a meeting that night, and I was telling people about what I felt when I saw that smoke coming out of that building, and the only question in my mind was, How can we save City College? And the only answer was, Hell, let everybody in. . . ."

The compromise was worked out by Robert Birnbaum, a tall, elegant young man whose manner is closer to that of the Ivy League than to that of the City University. Allen Ballard, then head of the SEEK program at City—black, a former student of Merle Fainsod's at Harvard—was fighting for a compensatory approach and a quota for "Third World" students (at least half of all entrants to City College). Others, politically more aware, were urging an expansion of SEEK, a sheltered college-within-a-college, rather than a quota system that would exclude "qualified" whites for the benefit of "unqualified" blacks. Birnbaum suggested that every high-school graduate

*The president of City College was then Buell Gallagher, and among his early concessions was the closing of the North Campus, where engineering students had continued to attend classes. It did not occur to Gallagher that his sympathy for those chained to his gates gave him no authority to continue spending public money on his faculty and staff (at a rate of $40 million or so a year) while prohibiting them from performing any publicly useful functions. The then city comptroller, Mario Procaccino, went to court for an injunction to force the Board of Higher Education to keep City College open and in business. This action later won him the Democratic mayoralty nomination, and won the rest of New York four more years of John V. Lindsay.

be admitted to some branch of City University, even if his high-school work had been in a non-academic program, but also that everyone who would previously have qualified for one of the four-year colleges be guaranteed his place, and that the freshman classes at these colleges be expanded drastically to secure a better ethnic mix.

The formula Birnbaum worked out, which has been operative starting with the high-school graduating class of June 1970, was complicated and in the end not as effective as he and the Board had hoped. Each graduating senior from the city's high schools lists in rank order the colleges he would like to attend. For each college, the computer takes the first choices, up to the numbers accepted in 1969 (or half the total for the next year, if that figure is larger), simply by running down the grade levels. This produces a cutoff grade by college, and by program within the college if the programs admit separately (as engineering and nursing do, for example). In 1972, the cutoff grade for entry to Queens College (the highest) was 85; the cutoff grade for entry to City College was 77.5. The rest of the class is filled with students who did not achieve the cutoff grade but did achieve a rank in the graduating class of their own high school matching the citywide percentage of students who *did* achieve the cutoff grade. Thus, 23 percent of the city's graduating seniors in 1972 averaged 85 or better, so anyone in the top 23 percent of his own high-school class, regardless of his grades, was acceptable at Queens College. Sixty percent of the city's graduating seniors averaged 77.5 or better, so anyone in the top 60 percent of his graduating class was taken at City College—if City was his first choice or if he had failed to get in at his first choice and City was his second choice.

In general, the community colleges take what is left, though some students who could go to four-year colleges choose to attend a community college nearer their homes (transfer from community college to senior college is now automatic if a community-college graduate wishes to continue, so a student may feel he has nothing to lose by starting off in the neighborhood); and a few of the programs at the community colleges (nursing at New York City Community College in Brooklyn, for example) are so popular that their entrance requirements are higher than those of City College.

Birnbaum's scheme required that the entering classes at all

the four-year colleges be substantially expanded—doubled, potentially. And if the high-school grades meant what they seemed to mean, new courses and programs would have to be developed to give the newcomers any chance at all. What the City College protesters had demanded, after all, was not access to higher education but possession of diplomas; they were not willing to accept what they called the "revolving door" approach of the Midwest land-grant colleges, where a third to a half of each entering class is flunked out before the end of the freshman year.

The man charged with finding or inventing and determining the cost of these programs was David Newton, dean of Baruch College, a former City College psychology professor and a tough-minded believer in his job. He is now vice-chancellor in charge of personnel for City University, and has been handling management's end of the interminable contract negotiations with the faculty union. ("As a reward for distinguished service in setting up the Open Admissions program and starting York College in Queens," he says, "I have been sent to Vietnam.") In retrospect, Newton is less than proud of the performance of his committee: "We were given less than a year, and one of the initial cues was that we weren't properly funded. And the sense of commitment and dedication I had expected from my colleagues was nowhere to be found." But in any event, there was not much Newton and his committee could order people to do: they had no power. Each of the 18 colleges in City University is essentially autonomous, appointing its own faculty, offering its own courses, allocating the money it receives from headquarters according to its own perception of budgetary needs (except that everyone must live by the city-wide union contract). Each was to make its own decisions as to the severity of the problems represented by Open Admissions and devise its own programs accordingly. All Newton's committee could do was recommend an allocation of an extra $400 per student for special services (over and above the $1,700 per student that was in 1969–70 the standard budget formula), and suggest a reading of the literature of remediation (none of which is much good). "The only thing I regret," Newton says, "is our failure to spend money to research and develop new educational techniques and curricula."

"You had a faculty asked all of a sudden to do something they didn't know anything about," says Chancellor Robert Kibbee, who arrived from Pittsburgh in 1971 to find Open Admissions in existence. "Even those who thought they knew couldn't conceive how badly many of these kids were prepared. Nobody knew really what he was doing. The combination of compassion and disbelief—and people who thought it was a lousy idea—meant that the first year, and [grudgingly] the second year, were a hell of a mess. It takes a lot of time to recover from a start like that."

In 1969, City University admitted a freshman class of just under 19,000; in 1970, the total was just under 35,000. At the time, a City University press release trumpeted the "fact" that the 1969 proportions had shown only 14 percent black and Puerto Rican, while the 1970 entrants were 33 percent black and Puerto Rican; subsequent investigation showed that the 1969 proportion had actually been 19.7 percent, and the 1970 proportion was only 26.2 percent. Of the increase of 16,000 in the number of freshman, "others" made up 10,000; and today's visitor to remedial courses at Hunter and Baruch will find them overwhelmingly white (less so at City and, this year, at Brooklyn). All high-school seniors applying to City University in 1970 were asked to take standardized tests for diagnostic purposes. The results showed that there were a few hundred Open Admissions students who did not in fact need remedial work in English or math—and no fewer than 6,000 regularly admitted students who *did*. (An effort was made to keep the scores on this test secret, but the figures leaked to the *Times*, and since then, to avoid similar publicity, each college has been told to administer its own test, the results of which are not collated at headquarters.) It is a sobering thought that in 1970 one-quarter of the entrants to City University who had earned grades of 80 or better in the city's high schools scored below the national average for twelfth graders on a standardized reading test.

At some colleges, efforts were made to handle the influx of unprepared students by tutoring alone. Weaker freshmen were counseled to take fewer than the usual number of courses, and urged to try music-appreciation or sociology rather than chemistry or modern language; in addition, "buddies" were assigned from the ranks of upper-classmen to offer help on an unstructured basis. At most colleges, some special remedial courses in English and math were organized. Typically, these courses did not in the first year carry college credit; but today they do, almost everywhere in the City University system (job-oriented New York City Community College and Baruch College, once the business-school division of City College, are notable exceptions).

The decision to give college credit for what is often junior-high-school work has most often been taken strictly as a result of pressure from desperately unhappy (one remedial teacher at Baruch says "demoralized") students who feel they are being asked to suffer and sweat "for nothing." But there have also been practical reasons. Hostos Community College in the Bronx, for example, has a twelve-hour-a-week "Libra" program (remedial English, black or Puerto Rican history, performing arts, and social science) for students whose reading scores fall below tenth-grade level on entrance to college. Its "unique feature," says Zane Rodriguez, the young chairman of the Hostos English Department, "is the credit-bearing remediation concept. The students can earn nine credits the first semester for the twelve hours. The Veterans' Administration, Model Cities, and the union all require that students take twelve hours and earn nine credits to be eligible for benefits. Libra keeps them eligible."

At City College, the argument has been that the college's requirement of 128 credits for graduation is the highest in the city, and the awarding of credits for remedial courses is merely a way to bring City into line with its sister schools. At LaGuardia Community College, president Joseph Shenker takes the position that "the remedial program is part of the regular curriculum and we give credit for everything." Hunter gives only one (rather than three) credits for the lowest-level reading course; only two for the upper-level reading course. But Queens, like LaGuardia, has decided that a course is a course, and its 40 freshman who entered in 1972 with high-school grade averages below 76 (out of an entering class of 2,600) will receive a full semester's credit for a program of Reading 1; Remedial English 01; Contemporary Civilization on a low reading level; and a fourth course of their own choosing (something in the art or music field is recommended).

Two of the new community colleges—Hostos, opened in

1970, and LaGuardia, opened in 1971—are operated on original principles designed in large part to help Open Admissions students, defined for community-college purposes as students whose grade average in high school is under 75 or whose preparation is in non-academic secondary programs. Such students constitute the majority of entrants at both of these colleges.

LaGuardia, located in a converted Sperry Rand factory in Long Island City, describes itself as "the first co-op community college." Its academic year is divided into four quarers, and students must commit themselves for all four (teachers work three quarters). An entering freshman takes two quarters as a full-time student, and in his third quarter the college finds him a nine-to-five job, most frequently in a retail store, a city office, a bank, or an insurance company. The public schools also hire some students, and this fall ten LaGuardia students were in Puerto Rico working as teacher aides. The employer's reports on his work at the job become part of the student's academic record; LaGuardia keeps up with his progress through visits to the job site by a liaison staff and a "practicum," a two-hour evening seminar that meets six times during the student's quarter on the job. Attendance at the "practicum" is compulsory.

In his fourth quarter, the student returns to school full-time; and in his second year he alternates quarters at school with quarters on the job (with a new "practicum" each time). Another LaGuardia innovation is an intensive week at the beginning of each academic quarter during which the student devotes full time to the study of a single urban topic, combining instruction and field observation in an *ad hoc* mix.

The current academic year is LaGuardia's second. Out of 550 students who started just after Labor Day in 1971, 400 were still matriculated when the current year began, but attrition in the students' fifth quarter (their second on a job) seems to have been higher than the college wants to admit. Students get unhappy at the department stores, where they are often used as stock boys and girls, and at the banks, where they typically start as teller trainees. Yet the job program, in the opinion of Harry Heinemann, the dean of the cooperative education division at LaGuardia, has educational advantages for both the students and the college quite apart from the money the students earn. "For our students, an educational experience means sitting on a chair and the teacher gives assignments— that's learning. Then there's the real world, which is different. We're giving them the idea that you learn from experiences on a job. Meanwhile, we can adjust our programs to the jobs available. . . ."

It would take much more time than I could spend at LaGuardia to form even a vague opinion about the chances for success of so new a program; the one "practicum" I attended was an infuriating disaster. About 70 percent of the staff at LaGuardia are experienced college teachers; the rest come from high schools. Remediation involves course work plus "study labs" with standard remedial materials. On one level at least, the cooperative program has been a measurable success —jobs were in fact found for everybody the first two times around. This spring, however, LaGuardia will need no fewer than 650 thirteen-week jobs for its students, and may not be able to find them. Shenker crosses his bridges one at a time.

Hostos represents an intellectually more radical venture than LaGuardia in adapting higher education to special needs. City University headquarters speaks of it as a college using programmed instruction and computer-assisted instruction as major elements, but in fact students are using neither programs nor computers. President Candido de Leon, a man in his late forties but much younger in appearance, developed the basic Hostos approach while working at the Board of Higher Education. (De Leon did not start the college himself; he was called back from sabbatical to rescue it after a disastrous first year.) The approach seeks to determine "performance objectives" for groups of brief "modules" which taken together constitute a course. Each module ends in a "milestone," an examination the student takes when he or she feels ready for it, at a separate testing center. Some of the descriptions of these courses, as they appear in the catalogue, are pretty sorry stuff: Sociology 1231, for example, carrying three credits—"The student will be able to define *or recognize* [emphasis added] terms related to social mobility, role, status, race prejudice, and factors leading to social change." And the tests given are nearly all teacher-tests administered when the teacher thinks the class should be ready—in standard academic style.

Hostos is located in a wretchedly crowded former factory

loft in the Bronx; nearly 90 percent of its students are Open Admissions students by the under-75 grade-level definition. They are older on the average than students at most of the colleges. Many are primarily Spanish-speaking, and 70 of the college's 150 courses are offered in Spanish as well as in English. "The first-year students," de Leon says wearily, "were given the impression they could complete the entire program in Spanish. That was not my idea—they must have an intensive English program in case they wish to transfer; to tell them anything else would be irresponsible." The career emphasis at Hostos is on health services; de Leon is still appalled by his predecessor's notion that people could work effectively in responsible jobs in New York City hospitals without a good reading knowledge of English.

Probably because of de Leon, there are people of unusual distinction on the Hostos faculty. Among the mathematics professors is Mariano Garcia, a smiling white-haired man who was chairman of the mathematics department at the University of Puerto Rico, has written a Spanish-English math dictionary, and teaches in both languages. Lois Lamdrin, who supervises the English end of Hostos's Libra program, taught at Pittsburgh's Carnegie-Mellon before she came to New York. "When I started," she says, "I had all the white liberal biases about what these students could achieve if given complete freedom. We all lost those." Quite apart from questions of "performance objectives," which still bedevil all those in the non-science and non-vocational areas at Hostos, work in English is now pretty thoroughly structured, with assignments like writing descriptions of photographs supplied by the instructor, and vocabulary lessons like one relating to the five senses.

Most of what happens at Hostos is clearly not college work, but some of it is. Students in a recorder class (learning musical staff notation for college credit!) are carrying books which include *Four Ibsen Plays*, Bone's *Freshman Calculus*, and Broom and Selznick's *Principles of Sociology*. Almost inevitably, the college can show one really spectacular success: a Puerto Rican girl who got through the two-year program in one year, then went on to Queens College and got through her last two years of college in one year, and now is back at Hostos teaching while doing graduate work. Equally inevitably, the records are littered with failure; and the great majority of those who graduate are simply not ready for the third year of a senior college, to which they gain automatic entrance on presentation of the Hostos degree. Still, I for one will remember the hush that fell on Mariano Garcia's math class as he came to something his class found difficult but Professor Garcia said they had to know.

At Baruch, some of the remedial work in English is tied directly to course work in other subjects. (Similar procedures are apparently employed at Bronx Community College.) The remedial teachers, mostly former high-school (and junior-high) teachers, are separate from the rest of the faculty; most of the professors have taken the position that the Open Admissions students will have to get through the same courses everybody else gets through. ("Their expectations of what college freshmen should be able to do are way high," says one of the remedial teachers, forgetting that these expectations derive from experience with regularly admitted students; one of the strengths, and dangers, of good remedial teachers is that they become strong partisans of their students.) So the remedial staff, now isolated in a freshmen-only annex where a high school used to be, schemes and works to get the Open Admissions students through the courses.

The device used is a "study lab," which gathers together as many as possible of the students with reading problems who are taking a given course. The teacher goes over the textbook for this course with groups of perhaps a dozen students, outlining the ideas and reinforcing the vocabulary, sometimes helping with papers and with the spotting of items likely to be on future exams. Many Baruch professors are less than enthusiastic about this procedure—"They're afraid you're touching their subject matter," says Stephen Urkowitz, an earnest young man who started in the Baruch remedial staff part-time while working toward his Ph.D. in English literature, and has chosen to identify with the remedial teachers rather than with the English Department. Still, the fact is that Baruch Open Admissions students in some numbers are getting through the same courses that the best of the regularly admitted students are taking, and this is not happening at many colleges in City University.

Dean Ballard, who should know, says that "the best programs in English are kind of uniform." Last spring, more than

600 teachers working in English remediation at City University met at the Hotel Commodore for a two-day weekend conference which presumably should have spread the word about any original or especially successful program. Hunter has gone in for a "sector analysis" approach, derived from linguistics, for the teaching of writing skills; Brooklyn College is reputed to have a "bidialectal" program for black students whose spoken English diverges drastically from standard English.* But so far there have been no breakthroughs, no techniques

---

*A visit to this Ford-funded operation was entirely unproductive. Its operators first wanted me to understand that the *Times* had made a lot of unnecessary trouble for them by saying that they stressed the validity of Black English, when really what they were stressing was "giving the students standard English rhetorical style, to help them pass courses."

"Of course. What do you give the students to do?"

"We're adapting an English-as-a-second-language approach."

"Fine. What do the students do?"

"The students who tend to have the problems are those who have been turned off by the cultural identifications of standard English. The way we have taught them in the past has not taken account of what they come into the classroom with."

"Yes. But what do you then ask them to do?"

"You look at what the student brings with him. You have to get rid of those attitudes he has, that he's been making random errors. You make the student aware, get him to see that when he makes this mistake it's nothing to be ashamed of. His language is in conflict with the standard language."

"All right. What do you do to make him aware?"

"What we do is focus on the dialect grammar, systematically. Where the grammars conflict and where they don't conflict. Opens up a whole new world for them—they're not intimidated by the English class again. And we're doing this with these students at a time when they're becoming very conscious of their own identity. That adds tremendously to their motivation to learn."

"Sure. What materials do you use?"

"We're developing our own book."

"May I see some of it?"

"No. We've had too many bad experiences with people coming in and picking up our ideas and using them to get foundation grants of their own."

"May I sit in on a class?"

"No. I don't want to talk to you any more. You're patronizing and hostile. . . ."

"[departing] . . . If you have something you are doing with these students that is genuinely helpful to them, you have an obligation to trumpet it to the world, not hide it."

Then, with that mixture of rage and despair unique to this problem: "We'll trumpet it when we've got it. *You can't trumpet something that doesn't exist yet.*"

This project is now in its third year, and the people running it are intelligent. What is to be done?

that can be transferred down to the high schools, and the New York City high schools continue to deteriorate.

The failures of both student and program are often distressing to watch. Nearly three months into the academic year, a group at Hunter was offered a lecture in how to use the library, essentially an introduction to the arcana of the Dewey decimal system, which is part of the fifth-grade curriculum. The librarian asked how many of the class of fifteen had used the library yet, and was rewarded by one rather tentatively raised hand, by a girl who said that she hadn't actually *used* it, but she worked at the library part-time. With the arrival of the first Open Admissions transfers from community colleges to the four-year colleges, professors in upper-level courses are meeting utterly intractable problems of sheer bewilderment in their students. "They've been getting As," said one, "and they're devastated when I have to give them Ds. Now what I do is show them an A paper, and they're honest about it: they say, 'I just can't do *that*.' But I'm not sure what good it does them." At City College, where the administration has forbidden the imposition of prerequisites, a larger than usual proportion of the faculty has been making contact with truly hopeless students, and has not the vaguest notion what they are supposed to do about it.

Vice-Chancellor Hyman speaks approvingly of "compensatory courses," intermediate between remedial and regular: "English 1, say, meets six times instead of three times a week, and for twice the time and effort the student gets the usual three credits." Tom Carroll, assistant dean of the faculty at the New York City Community College, warns against this approach on the basis of advice from California, where he visited junior-college faculty who had been living with Open Admissions for a long time. "They all told me," he says, "that if you attach a remedial course to a regular course the whole course becomes remedial." What can be said for certain is that the most publicized (and interesting) such venture, Chemistry 5-6-7 at City College, can claim only very mixed results.

Chem 5 is the brainchild of Abraham Mazur, who has been at City for more than forty years, as a student and then as a professor, and who was chairman of the chemistry department when Open Admissions came about. Mazur's thesis was that Open Admissions students would be able to master the normal two-term first-year chemistry course if given three terms to do so, and that they would want to take such a course even though they could get only two-thirds credit for each semester's work. "Even the kid who was the worst prepared in high school," Mazur says, "who did badly and knew it, has the same ambition as the Jewish middle-class kid: he wants to be a doctor." The second part of the argument has proved entirely correct: enrollment in the first semester of Chem 5 has been high every term. But the first part is wrong: the students are in much worse shape, especially in mathematics, than Mazur had imagined. "I have identified kids," he says sadly, "who don't know that 373 over 273 is greater than one."

Of the 73 students who enrolled in the first semester in Chem 5, only four survived to enter the third semester—which is where college-level work begins. "By the spring of 1971," Mazur recalls, "it was clear we were facing a disaster." At a time when City College was removing *all* prerequisites to courses in the humanities and social sciences, Mazur arranged with the math department for an elementary algebra and remedial arithmetic course that would henceforward be a prerequisite for students in Chem 5. By 1972–73, City College was giving full credit for each of the three semesters of Mazur's course (i.e., instead of working three semesters for two semesters' credit, the unprepared student now gets nine credits for —ideally—the same work that earns the prepared student only six credits). Mazur also convinced the nursing department that the first two semesters of his course should be enough to meet nurses' requirements in chemistry, and enrollment in Chem 5 mounted to 190 in fall 1972. But in the third semester of the course there were still only 17 students, from an entry of 120 two terms before. And the first semester, which is all that most students enrolling in the course actually complete, is described by Mazur as "junior-high-school general science." It is in fact a little better than that—Boyle's Law, which I watched being taught to a rather unreceptive class, is not in most junior-high programs—but it isn't much better.

Ivo Duchacek's course on Political Ideas and Issues, offered only to Open Admissions students at City, is probably more demanding. Duchacek is a white-haired Czech refugee whose scholarly concern has been with the fate of his motherland, and he is not teaching for the purpose of radicalizing his students. (He is also not teaching the course for gain: he has donated it to City College, over and above his normal load.) Two English instructors work with him on the problems of 27 students: they attend his classes and he attends theirs. All students are asked to read brief excerpts from material of some significance (mostly modern). The assignments are imaginative: in one, for example, Duchacek presents paragraphs by Fanon, Mao, Chiang, and Touré, and asks his students to write two sentences—"just two"—answering the question, "What anxiety is common to all these men?" Of the current group of 27 students, Duchacek feels he may have some chance with 22: "I'm really pleased with them—the only thing is, their English is awful." There were 70-odd in a similar class last year, and Duchacek reports that when he took over Professor Hans J. Morgenthau's work for a month this fall he found five former Open Admissions remedial students in Morgenthau's European theory course. "I watched them carefully and listened to their questions, and no doubt about it, they are 'in.' "

Elsewhere, courses with names like Political or Urban Ideas and Issues are likely to be taught by instructors who feel humble before their illiterate Third World students, to whom they believe will fall the honor of making the revolution. Some of these courses lie below junior-high level: Hunter's first course in urban studies, for instance, sends students out on field trips to make color slides they will later screen for the class (rock music playing on a cassette as they go, to make the presentation multimedia). This is fourth-grade show-and-tell. "The course culminates," said one of its young teachers, "in change strategies—the whole idea of change." Even this stuff has its defenders. "Rhetoric," says Hans Spiegel, who set up the course, "is the first important rung up the abstraction ladder." But college is late in the game for a first step toward abstraction.

As for black-studies courses, many of these are doubtless "revolutionary" in tone; neither time nor patience permitted an investigation, and anyway, access is usually by invitation only. At both City and Hunter, and perhaps elsewhere, there is pressure to permit black and Spanish-speaking students to take all or nearly all their courses in a black-studies or Puerto Rican-studies department. This is not the place to hash over once again the pros and cons of such departments: clearly, there is a need for a black perspective in all social and historical studies; equally clearly, black-studies departments often become shelters for untalented students, and in education as in the economy, protective tariffs typically lead to overpriced and shoddy goods.

In an article in *City Almanac* last summer, Joe L. Rempson of Bronx Community College projected "attrition rates" of 60 to 70 percent for Open Admissions students in the senior colleges, 70 to 80 percent for Open Admissions students in the junior colleges. Rempson considered these figures "astonishing"—and indeed they are, though not in the sense Rempson intended; for the evidence of their previous schoolwork would have argued that virtually *none* of these students could handle a full program of higher education without kinds and degrees of help beyond what CUNY has provided. Until the fall of 1972, when Manhattan and Queensborough Community Colleges wielded a small ax, no Open Admissions students were flunked out anywhere in the City University system, and the 50 percent or so who left during the first two years did so on their own.

A substantial proportion of those who leave the colleges do so for economic reasons: many are from fearfully poor families, and find $1.40 a day in carfare a heavy burden to carry. But there is no question among either supporters or opponents of Open Admissions that a considerable majority of the survivors are doing badly. They are mostly dull students, and they sit as dull students will in a class, wrapped in an invisible blanket that protects them from all the things they do not dare. For what the observation is worth, the black and Puerto Rican students seem on the average more alert: the counselors' typical statement that "test scores do not really predict performance for black students" is not just propaganda for the cause. Still, most of the black and Puerto Rican students accepted under Open Admissions are doing badly, too.

What constitutes "success" for the Open Admissions venture is an impossible question to answer. When the doors first opened to the freshmen of 1970, Vice-Chancellor Timothy S. Healy told *Time* magazine that if "20 percent of these kids get a degree, that's 20 percent above zero." Recently Mrs. Jacqueline Wexler, president of Hunter College, commented that "if we can move 25 percent of these kids it would be the greatest thing in the history of New York." No one (except, unfortunately, the students themselves) expects Open Admissions entrants to complete their degree work in four years: conventionally admitted freshmen at City University, and their peers in the country's other urban colleges, average little short of three years for an A.A., six years for an A.B. The final figures are thus a long time away. And it should be remembered that the 75 percent who do not complete the course are not necessarily losers. "The *institution* may want them to get a degree," says Harry Heinemann of the cooperative education program at LaGuardia Community, "but if they take thirty hours and that gets them a job they like, they haven't failed—they've succeeded."

On the other hand, what defines *failure* for Open Admissions is an easy question to answer: it is a decline in the respect accorded to a diploma from a branch of City University. "If we move 60 percent of these kids through social promotion," says Mrs. Wexler, using an elementary-school term of art, "it will be a disaster for the city. Unless the city can be got to see that, we will be doing a terrible disservice."

City headquarters has begun judging the colleges by the numbers of credits Open Admission students receive—and the students themselves, of course, have been learning from the grapevine about teachers who pass everybody. With the elimination of all degree requirements other than numbers and the removal of prerequisites from all courses at places like City College, the chance to collect empty credits has been multiplied, and so has the chance to collect empty diplomas. The losers will be not only the regular students, but also that fraction of the Open Admissions students who in fact complete a valid college program at what Vice-Chancellor Hyman calls "some level of acceptability." Marvin Schick, a former Hunter political-science professor who is liaison between the mayor's office and CUNY, points out that "many state universities, including some famous ones, were giving diplomas for very low qualities of work for years, and the country was none the worse for it." But the fact is that high-school diplomas are being given today in New York for work below anything that would be considered acceptable outside big cities, and it is hard to see why City University will not follow the same path.

The pressures City University must resist are not just political. Open Admissions has turned most of the campuses into enclosures crowded to the limits of endurance. Four-year colleges in the state university system outside the city average about 205 "gross square feet" per student, excluding residential space; City University four-year colleges in fall 1971 averaged 86 "gross square feet" per student. (The opening of new buildings at CCNY and Brooklyn improved this figure to 97 GSF in 1972, but better than that it will not be in this decade.) It is not uncommon to see students sitting on the floor in the hallways, getting some work done between classes; at Hunter College during class breaks the elevators are as jammed as a rush-hour subway car. The atmosphere is uncivilized, denying all those values beyond course work which a college is supposed to inculcate.

One of the greatest threats to the quality of the diplomas may come from the growth of a central City University bureaucracy that will, like all bureaucracies, seek neat answers to difficult questions. Already some of the resemblances to the Board of Education are startling and frightening. (When I called and told the secretary of a vice-chancellor that I was writing an article about Open Admissions and wished to see her boss, she said sweetly, "You want his permission to write the article?") A central task force is now at work on the problem of continuing racial imbalance among the campuses, and it will probably recommend a "comprehensive school" solution, with everyone to take the first two years at two-year colleges. "That," says Mrs. Wexler, "would *really* be the destruction of the city." But it may happen.

Though the numbers of able students entering the city colleges have not dropped seriously, the proportion of able students a professor encounters during his day is down considerably; and at some of the branches, notably City College, it seems possible that the tipping point has been passed. This is a grievous worry. "The performance of a given staff," says City's Abraham Mazur, "will depend on the presence of a certain number of really good students. It's happened to me—I put out more, I'm more creative, when I have really good students. We felt the difference here when the cutoff dropped from 85 to 82 back in the 1950s, and now . . . If it weren't for the Chinese we'd be in trouble already."

Yet when all one's outrage at these attitudes has been expended, it remains true that what is most objectionable in the promotion of Open Admissions is merely a natural outgrowth of the abuse of educational credentials by employers and, indeed, by the public at large. The students at LaGuardia Community College are entirely right in their argument that one does not need a college education to be a bank teller, but as the supply of college graduates increases, the banks will certainly begin to demand an A.B. from all candidates for such positions. When there was a shortage of engineers in this country, employers happily imported English "engineers" who had been through a year or two of post-secondary training—but they would not hire Americans with less than a B.S. The nursing profession has now succeeded in imposing an A.B. prerequisite on future nurses in New York State. Many of our best airline captains are alumni of high school and the World War II air force, but now neither the airlines nor the air force will accept for pilot training anyone who does not have a bachelor's degree. One can easily foresee a future in which policemen, factory foremen, barbers, morticians, apartment-house janitors, TV repairmen will be required to show possession of a baccalaureate.

Despite many gloomy forecasts, America need never worry about a large class of unemployed college graduates: the system is rigged so that demand must grow to meet the available supply. What will happen to the colleges in the process is visible in the current plight of the high schools. But higher education today is intellectually defenseless against the insistence on ever-expanding enrollments, and ever-easier degrees. "The American university," Reck Niebuhr of Temple once said, "has failed to *conceptualize* its manpower function." And in the meanwhile it has become saddled with a function it cannot perform.

There are more false gods here than one can shake a stick at. Education is inherently a promoter of inequality. The musically talented and the tone deaf play the fiddle equally well in a community where there is no violin teacher; once instruction begins, a gap develops. Very nearly the only operational truth ever demonstrated in education is that something

must be worth doing if the results of the work show some improvement for everybody and a widening of the gap between
the best and the poorest. The better the training the more
salient the revealed differences in natural ability; only academicians who live in the literature of their subject rather than
in their experience could even imagine education as a promoter of equality. More strikingly for individuals than for
groups (as Christopher Jencks has so wearisomely pointed
out), education can open opportunities that would be closed
in its absence. But its necessary social function in a complex
modern society must be to raise the general floor under performance and understanding, not to reduce the distance between the floor and the ceiling.

Though I know many brilliant people I would not care
to have as my doctor or my lawyer or my children's teacher, it
is undoubtedly true that a unidimensional measure of academic
excellence can be used to set a special, higher floor for many
occupations and professions. The ardently egalitarian researchers of the American Council on Education are fundamentally
unconvincing: one can dismiss them with the curse that they
should cross the river on a bridge designed by an engineer from
an engineering school where students were admitted by lottery;
and that their injuries should then be treated by a doctor from
a medical school where students were admitted by lottery; and
that their heirs' malpractice suit should then be tried by a
lawyer from a law school where students were admitted by
lottery. The problems even of affluent America are not primarily distributive—it still makes an immense, perhaps even
a growing, difference who does how well a large number of
highly skilled and difficult jobs. But that number is already
much smaller than the number of college-trained workers,
and it is surely appropriate to wonder what social function is
served by maintaining high "standards" for credentials that
then grant exclusive access to jobs that can be done just as
well by people who have not achieved such standards.

The Open Admissions students deserve better than that:
despite all the media images, they are in overwhelming proportion grave, earnest, desperately hardworking, and insecure.
It is not their fault that they must make their rites of passage
to adulthood in a society that values not education itself—let
alone learning—but the institutional evidence that education

has occurred. They are not very bright, most of them, but their perception of their social situation is correct.

No doubt college does civilize some who were merely acculturated by elementary and secondary education. Higher education for those who wish to understand better and enjoy more profoundly should always be "open," voluntary on both sides. But these are not the drives that can (or will) fill City University (or combine to finance it at a rate of nearly half a million dollars a year). What is beating at all the universities —but especially at CUNY—is involuntary education on the tertiary level, the forced prolongation of an outworn adolescence for purposes that are quite separate from the civilizing Idea of a university.

12

UNIVERSITY WITHOUT WALLS

James Zarnowiecki and Thomas P. Murphy

The university without walls movement has stimulated references to the genesis of the classical university structure of the Middle Ages. The Bolognese and Parisian centers of learning placed heavy emphasis on the learning of the streets, the need for individual tutoring by well-known professors and magisters, and the usefulness of what one learned from making a living in society.

Philosophers and theologians plied their trade in the courts of Salamanca and Rome not because those classes were opportunities for leisure conversation and speculation, but because man was wrestling with reality in philosophical and theological terms. Those who *used* philosophy daily could explain the mysterious workings of the geocentric world; and he who took God seriously enough to structure reality in that geocentric world was thought of as a master—one who could live in the moral and legal constraints of the Middle Ages.

Galileo was the heretic not because he challenged a belief central to Rome, but because he challenged how man had structured his knowledge of the universe and how man claimed a position at the "know-center" of the planets. If Galileo could prove his theory, it was thought he might destroy the theological fabric of western knowledge. He might also change the organizational structure of the university faculties and put someone out of a job.

Even medieval scientists were impeccably practical. Note the cranial charts to tell us about man's varying humors; the attempt of metallurgists to do something valuable—like make gold from rock; the necessity for man to explain his universe in terms of herbs, brews, chemicals, and witches.

The university was organized for one purpose—to help man *do* something practical in the universe. In today's terms we would call that the development of a career or a skill useful to society. Though not generating the rebuilding of gigantic medieval structures and hallowed halls, the new thrust of open schools and universities is causing an examination of the basic learning principles and objectives that gave rise to the university as we know it today.

Along with the growing demand for accountability, man finds himself in some cultural situations that closely resemble those of the Middle Ages and Renaissance. In the midst of a communications revolution, man once again finds himself in a knowledge explosion paralleled only by that following the creation of the written word and the invention of the printing press. Whereas the press forced a horizontal and paginal thought process on the medieval mind, the computer and the television have molded man into an instantaneous and multidimensional humanoid with thought powers far beyond his physical capabilities.

Instant communications have also catapulted man centuries back into the village. In a McLuhanesque sense, each of us possesses the power to transcend space and time in an attempt to re-create almost tribal relationships in the midst of the technological age. Man seems simultaneously caught in an ever-increasing technological suicide net while enamored of an expanding control of mind and matter. Five years ago, for instance, a sense of the American Civil War was available only in the vivid verbal descriptions of Bruce Catton; suddenly, the fratricidal century-old battles are re-created in our living rooms, in living color, by Alistair Cooke. For historians, Antietam, Vicksburg, the Boston Tea Party, and Henry VIII are available; for armchair sports enthusiasts, Sapporo, Munich, and the Super Bowl. Each one of us knows intimately places we have never visited. This is a strange mix of events, but one with which medieval man would be familiar: events too mysterious to measure yet too significant to ignore. Knowledge is queen and man pretends to court her as he masters all that is known and unknown.

The Challenge of the University

All of these events converge on the academic community of the university. Students question not only their position in the academic community but also the ability of the university to deal with basic principles of learning. For whatever reasons, the doctor or magister became the guiding influence of the medieval students who were most eager to matriculate. And for whatever reasons, during the evolution of the university to the present day, the professor has become more and more impersonal, more and more removed from his students, more and more a fixture of the institution rather than a catalyst for learning.

A second frustrating experience for the student is the inability of the institution to meet his or her specific needs. For what seems to have been an eternity, courses have been divided into semester and trimester periods with eighteen-week grading sections and fifty-minute classes. Learning what one needs to know depends more on the ability of the university to schedule than on the willingness of the student to learn or his need to master the information. Dictated by schedule alone, professors have been forced to assign work beyond the classroom, which, if not largely ignored, seems to have evolved as a pitifully redundant mechanism for learning.

A third difficulty is that for the majority of students in the university system learning-by-doing is not even an alternative. The pure sciences have consistently prepared students with laboratory experiences, but not until very recently were labs considered part of the general learning curriculum in most other subject areas. Today, at any given hour, an observer will note that nine out of ten classes in the senior high school, college classroom, and graduate school are undergoing that excruciating lecture-torment, which has caused varieties of

cerebral and physical anguish over the years. It has been suggested that this results in millions of dollars worth of wood-
carving, graffiti, and other damage to "learning" institutions.
Despite what any building custodian might consider excellent
evidence of student unrest, boredom, and discontent, we have
continued to re-create generations including large numbers of
proficient woodcarvers, chronic truants, clandestine poets, and
most recently, drug addicts.

These deficiencies have given rise to a school of authors
who have proposed everything from de-schooling the entire
society to creating total schools without any failure. At the
same time, credential organizations and administrator associations charged with educating hundreds of thousands of students
in the nation's public schools have repeatedly challenged those
doom-prophets to produce a better system to educate the
masses. The alternative school proposals are sporadic, poorly
financed, short-term, and in some cases, social rather than educational answers. Until recently few experimenting school districts have been able to continue their efforts with the help of
community support.

We need only look at the recent unemployment figures to
discover what the college graduate attains at the end of four,
six, or ten years of university work. The effort put into philosophy, English, history, and journalism classes has failed to
provide job preparation. Further, the student has wasted valuable time which could have been spent in some skill training.
While he has devoted four years to liberal arts or the humanities, many of his contemporaries have developed a salable
skill, a profession, something that has immediate return. The
argument does not simply center around the humanities versus
the professions or the liberal as opposed to the practical arts.
Most of us who have landed somewhere in the education profession have been forced to face the fact that our formal education did not prepare us for what we are doing, that we had to
seek avenues of new training, counseling, and skill development. How can we evaluate the twenty weeks of forty-five-
minute classes of History 101? Most students find that a few
historical novels give the salient facts and are much more interesting and painless.

Thus the question of accountability enters the academic
picture. The thousands of student dollars and hours spent have

little or no relation to the manner or extent to which the faculty, the university, or the student has been held accountable. We can say that the sheepskin cost Y dollars and the student entered the labor market at X dollars. But how much did History 101 cost? What was the return? What is an A worth?

True, knowledge can never be measured in terms of dollars. Yet at the same time, our much-touted educational system places a premium on the *cost* of the education, and in fact the "better" the school and the more prestigious the diploma, the higher the tuition and costs. What responsibility has the student previously had to evaluate any of the costs of his education, the quality of the faculty or the environment, or the learning techniques used? A visitor on this planet would enjoy seeing the exodus of senior high-school students on spring weekends as they travel, parents' checks in hand, to institutions of higher learning, presumably to make an educated guess about the relative quality of education available.

The University Response

As indicated in the chapters on free universities and open admissions, embattled administrators have tried to make education more relevant to a more diverse and expanding student body while at the same time contending with rising costs, shrinking appropriations, and increasingly reluctant donors. The results have already been satisfactory, and so the free university has flourished, open admissions has been a continuing debate, and students with means, mobility, and motivation have been attracted to universities without walls.

In many respects the university without walls is intended to be as flexible as the free university in its ability to utilize community resources for learning. Classes may be held off campus as well as on, and heavy use may be made of nontraditional faculty with some special skill to contribute. Serious attention is paid to the educational value of experience-based learning as well as to student input to the learning design. The difference between the free university and the university without walls is that the former usually operates without credit and is essentially supplementary education, whereas the latter is a fully accredited degree process covering the student's whole program.

Given the greater degree of legitimacy involved, the university without walls operates within the context of the traditional university, not as an adjunct to it. Yet unstructured learning and student responsibility for program definition do not fit the needs or the desires of every student. Therefore, many university without walls programs are not labeled as such but rather exist as options open to students at traditional universities.

For example, in 1973 the University of Maryland approved two new degrees for undergraduates, a bachelor of general studies and a bachelor of independent studies. The general studies degree frees the student from the lock-step requirements imposed by many departments for their majors and allows the student to develop a smorgasbord program, which meets his ideal of rationality, subject only to approval by an advisor. Though the independent studies degree does much the same thing, it also stresses field learning, independent study, and internship experiences.

This flexibility is welcomed by the students but has some drawbacks when compared with the broader university without walls concept. For example, some employers may have difficulty evaluating the applicability of a B.A. in independent studies to their qualifications requirements. A university without walls student might be able to take a similar program yet still major in a traditional department and receive a traditional degree. In that respect the nontraditional degree from a traditional university may be suboptimizing when compared with a flexible degree program at a university without walls—assuming that university itself has some acceptance and reputation among employers.

Another problem is that students with a university without walls or a nontraditional degree may find it difficult to gain admission to a traditional graduate program. Such a student may be considered unprepared because of the often ambiguous content of courses taken on an independent study or a field-experience basis. Although these questions are usually resolvable, graduate schools with a good supply of traditional degree applicants may not be motivated to do the extra work necessary to qualify the exceptional applicants.

A related problem concerns the granting of credit and grade point averages. Schools such as Antioch that were universities or colleges without walls long before the invention of the term, do not provide grade point calculations for their graduates. Students from such schools must therefore rely heavily on Graduate Record Examinations to establish statistical base lines for competitive admission to graduate schools. This could work for or against a particular student but is almost uniformly viewed as an inconcenience by graduate admissions officers.

The obvious answer to some of these problems is the development of graduate programs in the university without walls format; this is occurring at the masters degree level. Antioch's Graduate School of Education has evolved a new program. Beginning with only eleven students on two campus sites in 1964 (Yellow Springs, Ohio and Putney, Vermont), the program highlights the same points: student-evolved curricula, independent study, and practical experience. The program now enrolls more than five hundred students involved in educational change patterns in half a dozen urban and rural centers, with minority students constituting at least two-thirds of the total. In education, the Bank Street College of Education and, in humanistic psychology, Sonoma State and West Georgia College have exciting programs similar in scope and intent.

Campus-Free College

An organization with a substantial board of trustees, which is attempting to be both a graduate and undergraduate university without walls and even without a campus, is the Campus-Free College (CFC). The board includes the provost of Massachusetts state colleges, a distinguished professor of urban affairs and planning at Hunter College in New York, the 1972–73 president of the American Association of Higher Education, and the director of the Center for Research and Development in Higher Education at the University of California at Berkeley. The full-time director spent twenty years in teaching and was president of Franconia College.[1]

The CFC is organized as a nonprofit educational institution incorporated in the Distict of Columbia. Formed in 1971, it advertises itself as "a continent-wide, independent, nonresidential college, new in concept but traditional in its desire to help students learn useful values, skills, and knowledge."[2] The reference to continent is justified by the fact that it operates in "one hundred and ten cities, in thirty-four states in the U.S., Canada, Mexico, Iran, and Australia."[3]

The structure of the organization involves not only the board of trustees, but also an academic council composed of a small number of program advisors (which meets monthly to review and approve programs submitted by students, pass on credit for academic work, and provide advice both to students and other program advisors), the program advisors who work directly with the students, and a small central administrative staff located in Boston.

The college intends to provide education to persons of varying ages, objectives, backgrounds, budgets, and learning schedules. As a nonresidential college, it owns no facilities; rather, the resource people attached to the CFC provide their own facilities and communicate directly with their students, generally by mail. It is advertised that this will result in a significant lowering of educational cost while at the same time connecting highly motivated students with proven teachers and practicing professionals.

This description of the organization raises certain questions which the materials try to answer by listing what the CFC is *not*. Significant items in the list include the following:

1. A correspondence school

2. An "alternative" college for a few special-interest groups

3. A "free school" in the sense of no requirements, no costs, and no evaluation

4. An "establishment" or "antiestablishment" college

5. A college with "something for everyone"

6. A college that believes every student should do, or become, or learn, the same things, or in the same ways, or in the same order[4]

The academic services of CFC are made available through approximately 200 "experienced academic and professional 'program advisors,' who work personally with students to help them plan college-level study programs and find high-quality learning resources. These may include private study with tutors or other professionals, classes at local colleges or universities, on-the-job learning, workshops, seminars or other short projects and independent study."[5]

Full-time credit students must pay a *quarterly* college fee of $250; noncredit students pay $160. However, the college fees cover only the program advisor fee and an administrative fee—only a portion of the student's total expense. In addition to college fees there are instructional costs, "which are paid directly to the instructor, tutor, program, or institution providing your learning experiences. The Campus-Free College does not set instructional expenses and is not responsible for them."[6] This is not cheaper than traditional education, but it certainly is more flexible.

The CFC has applied to the District of Columbia for authority to grant degrees: the associate, the bachelor, and the masters of arts and of science, as well as specialized degrees such as the bachelor and master of fine arts. Its manual also indicates an intention to provide students with degree opportunities through CFC affiliation with colleges and universities having degree authority. However, these authorities have not yet been worked out, and it is not clear that any CFC students have yet been able to apply any credits to any degree at a degree-granting institution.

The CFC literature includes the following statements intended to indicate why a student should become involved with or needs CFC rather than a traditional institution:
where. We believe CFC can and is improving on some

> We recognize good teaching and learning go on every-
> features of the conventional colleges; but we believe
> that, for some students, such institutions are still the
> best choice. No one has a monopoly on good education,
> but we do believe that many people are finding it difficult
> to use the structures, schedules and facilities of other
> kinds of colleges; for them CFC may be a good choice.[7]

In the spring of 1973, CFC had fifty students, and only four colleges (Armstrong, Hampshire, McGill, and the University of Massachusetts-Amherst) had agreed to accept its credits for transfer. However, if the CFC can work out its legitimacy problems and attract paying students it will be an interesting experiment providing another challenge to traditional education.

The Union Graduate School
Doctorate Program

A better picture of the problems related to the doctoral world can be attained by considering the program of the Union Graduate School (UGS) of the Union for Experimenting Colleges and Universities, now in its third year of operation after a long period of gestation. The Union grew out of a felt need shared by twelve institutions willing to experiment as early as 1964, and it has now grown to include twenty-five schools.[8] These institutions had found it increasingly difficult to woo their own faculty members into developing an independent program.

From 1964 to 1969, Judson Jerome of Antioch, Goodwin Watson of Columbia, Sam Baskin of Antioch, the president of UGS , and a score of others contributed to developing a proposal to found a Ph.D. program with both theoretical and action components; in fact, this program rests solidly on the philosophical foundations laid by Rousseau, Froebel, Dewey, and the phenomenologists. Founded in 1969, the UGS became operational in January 1970, when requirements of the program were set with students who agreed to meet for a colloquium in Denver. Students have thus far fulfilled residential requirements in Colorado, Ohio, Florida, New York, and California and are literally pursuing independent work from Honolulu to Nairobi, and from Saskatoon to St. Thomas. They average thirty-five years of age and cover a universe of occupations.

Students in the program include many college professors, one former college president, corporation presidents, and practitioners from the fields of psychotherapy, organizational development, social work, and community change. A colloquium assembling such persons in one location becomes a mind-blowing experience for students, consultants, and faculty members. Not only is the diversity of backgrounds extraordinary, but fellow students are the key resource persons.

Some of the conceptual and operational aspects and problems related to the evolution of the venture will provide more food for thought:

—Application is encouraged for those who cannot get the advanced training they require in more conventional programs;

—Admission depends upon high intelligence and demonstrated capacity for self-direction and disciplined effort toward self-chosen objectives;

—Students are encouraged to use the world as their own classroom, developing workable plans and then implementing them by drawing upon resources both within and outside academic institutions, fitting means to needs. Each program is tailor-made, with the student and faculty together selecting advisors, evolving a learning contract with a committee comprised of a minimum of two adjunct professors (specialists in their fields), two UGS peers, and a UGS core faculty member;

—Each student's program consists of a study component (what he wants to learn) an experimental component (an internship, broadly defined), and a "project demonstrating excellence";

—Since a student either passes or drops out, there are no credits, grades, or points; a cumulative record consisting of log materials, papers, and anything he and his committee deem relevant, becomes the basis of evaluation;

—A "project demonstrating excellence" (the "thesis" or "dissertation" terminology is eschewed) may take any number of forms and is limited only by the imagination and daring of the student and/or his committee. He may publish a book or a number of scholarly articles, design and implement a project of significant social change, or create poetry, painting, sculpture, musical composition, dances, films, or other art forms.[9]

In short, the Union approach is a program synthesizing thought and action, the affective and cognitive, the conceptual and perceptual. It aims to transcend empiricism while recognizing the value of pragmatic method. It revolves around the belief that fact is a function of the method used to derive it, and hence must be judged by the internal logic and/or criticism of that methodology. It is a praxis approach to learning; the thrust is both transdisciplinary and interdisciplinary.

The student starts with a colloquium designed not only to broaden his personal awareness as he meets a wide array of other highly motivated and experienced people, but also to challenge his fundamental assumptions. The colloquium tests his ability to do independent work without the warm arms of the protecting institution and is an opportunity to expose his prospective program to peer feedback, especially from those outside his field. He experiences the tension of peer criticism, learns to criticize, and gets a chance to become involved in a learning community. The student also learns how to construct a functional committee; and, as he becomes acquainted with the material and human resources at his command, he is encouraged to take risks which he may never have considered feasible.

Much of the success of the project demonstrating excellence and of the concluding "terminar" depends on the faculty chosen by the student. As Roy Fairfield has pointed out, it is important to have faculty who are "more cosmopolitan than provincial, more open than closed, more learned than ignorant, more sensitive than indifferent to human need, more sympathetic and attentive to interdisciplinary approaches and not highly specialized in a narrow field, and more rather than less familiar with group processes."[10]

Accessibility for human support—without creating dependency relationships—is a sine qua non of faculty involvement. A feeling for the process can be derived from part of one of Fairfield's unpublished working papers:

> ... there are hurdles and/or requirements, such as the evolving of a program, including study plans, internship and project ... such as a certification session, which cannot be held until there is consensus among the committee that it should be held ... as "keepers of the process," core faculty have a special responsibility to UGS students, encouraging them to choose effective, committed and creative committee members rather than persons who will simply scratch their backs or be in too much

accord; . . . as "keepers of the process" too, during certification sessions core faculty must be sensitive to the
kind of "contract" which students and committee members are evolving for a student's tenure in the program,
sensitive to and responsible for putting it into writing for
the student's protection (however, attending to the inclusion of flexibility clauses which permit maximum
creativity) . . . *any* member of a student's committee
may have to be a "slower" of the process as well as a
facilitator of learning if he or she sees that a student is
trying to slide through, is hell-bent to finish regardless of
consequences and the implications for the next person
and the total UGS processes. . . .[11]

Perhaps the largest part of learning in the graduate school
is moving from rhetoric to risk. At one time or another each
student in the Union program has had to face the conclusion
that what he or she was learning is totally irrelevant to real
life. It is relatively easy to mouth pious platitudes for the oral
examinations, and even easier to follow the graphs in one's
thesis and interpret the data so that all emotion is out of the
"objective" study. However, it is very difficult to align oneself
so closely, to become such a part of what one is doing, that the
student is ready to take on any professor or fellow student who
challenges the thesis or objectives of the project. The questions
get down not merely to "What am I doing?" but to "Who am
I?" and range from doubting the ability to know to defining the
values that guide the very existence of the individual. And why
should this not be so? Learning is really life.

Union sets as its purpose finding a means to have the
student help himself, driving him to the very center where all
this mix of emotional and intellectual ferment begins, and
helping him face the consequences of his actions as he faces
the real task of learning. The final consequences of the process
are said to be much more joyful. The student who masters the
process is able to feel a sense of power in being able to make
his own decisions. He dares to force himself into other areas of
self-expression and life style, to think the unthinkable, and to
defy the brainwashers who have attempted to define the world
for him.

Union Graduate School does not have the only doctoral
level programs in the university without walls movement.

Walden University advertises that it is "less interested in research activities leading to an exploitation of minutiae than it
is concerned with the addition of meaningful information useful in developing concepts and practical implementation of
ideas of importance."[12] Walden offers programs leading both
to the Ed.D. and Ph.D. in education and features a summer
program of residency plus off-campus independent study under
able specialists; it is national in scope and action-oriented in
thrust. The newly initiated off-campus Ed.P. program at Nova
University also broadens the learning contexts for school administrators wishing to gain insight into independent learning
with self-determined student programs.

Accrediting and Experimental Doctoral
Programs

Accrediting is a complex process. Elements of accreditation include the library facilities, the faculty degrees, the number of
administrators, and the academic strengths of the institution.
However, the quality of learning and the decision-making ability of the student within the institution are not among the
criteria used. Further, accrediting associations have been slow
to admit that life-experience and nonacademic training are elements of learning. As in the open school experience at the
secondary level, colleges and universities are stymied by restrictions which prevent the local glassblower, guitarist, architect,
or even doctor and lawyer from becoming a real part of the
curriculum. The Parkway Project in Philadelphia and Metro
in Chicago have been paralyzed by the rules that govern the use
of certain types of faculty in their schools without walls.

Universities without walls question not only the traditional curricula but also the basis of accrediting decisions.
Their proponents point out that only in a few professions is
accrediting meaningful. For example, even in these days of enlightened public administration, there are very few administra-
trators in colleges and universities who have been trained as
such. Likewise, most professors were accredited in their discipline and not as teachers. Seeing accreditation as a security
blanket, many nontraditional educators argue that some accrediting programs are too circumscribed and learning too individual. At the same time, the procedures of university and

college faculties perpetuate some of the myths of quality learning. Seniority, tenure, publish or perish, committee service, activity in academic associations, and convention often carry more weight in determining which faculty are assigned to which courses than the ability to interest students in taking responsibility for their education.

If learning is central, why worry about the degree at all? The degree problem tempts critics to raise the issue of double standard in the university without walls movement. If the movement is viable, it really need not grant a degree. If, as it claims, degree programs can be layer upon layer of sham, why create yet another attempt and perhaps just another layer? Part of the answer is built into the Archimedean retort, "Give me a place to stand and I will move the world." One needs credentials to live in the world, and society needs credentials, in part to protect itself.

Another part of the answer might be that the student *really* deserves the degree because several things happen to the student in such degree programs that do not happen in others. While doing everything expected in traditional doctoral programs, the university without walls student is responsible for his own experiences, his own learning, and his own faculty. The student decides how and when he is to learn and for how long. Perhaps the best answer then is that the student basically awards himself the degree he is seeking.

When does the student receive his degree? Generally, the candidate has contracted a certain project of excellence at an official certification meeting, fulfilled the goals of that project with the help of a committee, reviewed the work with his committee and the coordinating faculty member, and then held a "terminar" as an ending ceremony to the process. This is the point at which the student is eligible for the degree. However, the student sees early in the first colloquium that learning is a never-ending process and that a person does not become a Ph.D. on any one day.

Nevertheless, degrees are an essential means through which the accrediting associations and the state governments can exercise their quality control responsibilities in the interests of the profession and of society. The university without walls format is vulnerable to abuse by cynical degree-held operations, and both society and students need to be protected against these charlatans. On the other hand, traditionalists should not be permitted to use these legitimate fears to block the accrediting of experience-based programs which are conscientious in their application of high standards. The Union Graduate School is under consideration for accreditation, and the guidelines developed in that precedent-setting arrangement will be useful as other university without walls programs develop.

Implications for the Future

What will be the new trends for the universities without walls? The present institutions must realize that their days of non-productivity and self-denial are numbered. As they intend to educate the students who are now in the public open schools or the small private secondary schools without walls, they may be in for some surprises. Those schools are developing learning communities, students and teachers who are cataloguing life experiences. In doing so they make use of community resources and talents, travel in vans or in groups, and decide in community what should be the nature and the process of *this* learning community. They use peer learning as the basis for all their procedures. Unless the universities, large and small, face and adapt these processes, the young learner who is in tune with himself may well decide that these institutions are not even worth protesting against.

The days of the ivory tower professor seem to be coming to a close. Not only is there increasing demand for relevance, but a concurrent drop in citizen satisfaction with and confidence in university faculties. Gallup polls in recent years have documented this decline.

The facts with regard to financial support seem clear. As costs increase, the percentage of students in private institutions of higher education is steadily dropping, and state institutions are being called upon to do more. It is precisely these state institutions that must be responsive to public opinion. A few endowed private institution are isolated from the cries for relevance, but public institutions are not—and neither are the increasing numbers of private institutions receiving public funds and subsidies.

Attacks on the tradition of tenure for professors are also

increasing. Again the state legislatures are the battlefield. Pressures on appropriations have helped to convince university administrators that they must be more responsive, and threats to tenure will eventually have the same effect on the faculties.

The future is likely to include more rather than less experimentation in higher education. University without walls programs will play a major role in developing new models of education at all levels. At the federal level, the new National Institute of Education (NIE), which is discussed in Chapter 17, would do well to fund a series of educational models built on career education concepts and offering some measurable results. Not only will this type of research fit into the prescription for production-oriented research, which the Institute seems mandated to support, but it will also be beneficial for the overall thrust of the university community. Such experiments should be small, restricted to faculty who have already taught in environments such as the university without walls, and required to develop a learning community and the ability for the student to make decisions. Above all, these centers should become training and placement institutions available throughout the citizen's lifetime.

Further, NIE must begin to fund experimental universities for minority groups, not only to prepare them for acculturation or assimilation, but also as service institutions to help individuals and groups who desire training in law, medicine, religion, and languages, and other areas which will further the goals of that minority community. The same emphasis should be placed on programs for individuals particularly suited to teach and preserve the culture of minority groups.

These are some of the questions that the universities without walls should be addressing. The Union Graduate School, with its growth to three hundred students of every ethnic and geographic representation, is just a beginning. So are the open elementary schools, the street academies at the secondary level, the bachelor of independent studies degrees, the Campus-Free College, and other efforts to "free up" the educational establishment.

NOTES

1. Campus-Free College, *Operations Manual*, July 1972, p. 40.

2. Campus-Free College, *Resources Directory*, April 1972, p. 1.

3. *Operations Manual*, p. 4.

4. *Ibid.*, p. 5.

5. *Resources Directory*, p. 1.

6. *Operations Manual*, p. 25.

.7. *Ibid., p.* 37.

8. Members of the Union are University of Massachusetts, University of Minnesota, Morgan State College, New College at Sarasota, Northeastern Illinois University, University of the Pacific, Pitzer, University of Redlands (Johnston College), Antioch, Bard, Roger Williams, Shaw, Skidmore, Friends World College, University of South Carolina, Goddard, Chicago State University, Franconia, University of Alabama (New College), Hofstra University, Loretto Heights, Staten Island Community College, Stephens, Westminster, and University of Wisconsin at Green Bay.

9. Union for Experimenting Colleges and Universities, *University Without Walls,* February 1972, pp. 10–34.

10. Roy P. Fairfield, "Quality Control and/or Health in Union Graduate School," unpublished working paper, 1971.

11. *Ibid.*

12. Walden University, *Bulletin,* p. 13.

13

URBAN TEACHING TRAINING

Daniel U. Levine

Because we are a predominantly urban nation, almost any teacher preparation program not specifically oriented toward rural schools could be classified "urban teacher training." The great majority of existing programs, after all, are preparing teachers who will live in urban areas and teach students from urban communities. How then could some programs be considered "urban" and others "nonurban"?

Rather than attempting to make sharp distinctions between urban and nonurban training programs, therefore, this chapter will attempt to identify the elements of a good teacher training program in general and then to describe several special programs that exemplify some or all of these elements and that are aimed specifically at preparing teachers for big city schools.* This procedure is justified because current thinking about teacher education in general has been influenced substantially by problems that relate particularly to urban education.

*This chapter also will bypass other terminological issues such as whether teacher "training" is different from teacher "education" and whether a university is "urban" if it is located in a city but not avowedly oriented toward "urban" affairs.

For example, the challenge of teaching economically disadvantaged pupils and the manifestations of alienation (protest, drug abuse), which have become so marked among high school students, have underlined the inadequacy of traditional programs and stimulated awareness of a need for new approaches. Even though this awareness is largely verbal in many teacher training institutions, some have begun to modify their practices in accordance with the demands their graduates face when they obtain positions in difficult schools.

Like any other training activity, a teacher education program implicitly or explicitly is based on a particular conception or philosophy of what one hopes ultimately to achieve. If teachers are trained to use primarily rote methods of instruction, whoever is in charge of the training has decided either consciously or unknowingly that this is how trainees should teach when they enter the classroom. If trainees are not prepared to handle discipline problems in their classrooms, whoever designed the training program—assuming it was systematically planned in the first place—must have assumed that this function was not an important training objective.

From this point of view, teacher training should reflect contemporary thinking and research on the process and objectives of education. Stated differently, teachers should be prepared to function in accordance with up-to-date conceptions and knowledge of instruction and learning. It is beyond the scope of this chapter to undertake a detailed review of recent research on this complex topic, but it is necessary to begin with several principles and generalizations that illustrate the kinds of skills and understanding teachers should acquire if they are to function successfully in urban classrooms.

Effective Education and Successful
Teacher Training

Among the most encouraging developments in educational research in the past ten or fifteen years have been the tendency to move away from simplistic notions of teaching and learning and an increased understanding of the complex instructional and situational variables that result in effective education. Of course, the ideas of many educators and lay "authorities" still derive essentially from simpleminded propositions such as "leave the kids alone and their instinctive learning needs will guide them properly," or "the teacher's job is to tell students what they should learn and the student's job is to learn it." Fortunately, such philosophies are gradually being displaced by more defensible points of view, even though books that expound them sometimes have considerable influence.

From the perspective of designing teacher training programs, some of the important propositions established by research are as follows:

1. All students do not learn in the same manner, and a student may learn best with one method at one time and with a different method at another time. For example, some students appear to learn most efficiently through methods that emphasize auditory presentation and others, with visual media. One student will have reading handicaps, which can and must be corrected, and the student next to him may require help on study skills and library research techniques. A student may benefit most at one point in time from a lecture, and at another, he may benefit most if he seeks out appropriate material for himself and works out his own conclusions and interpretations.

One particularly important aspect of the learning environment, which must be adapted to fit the characteristics of individual pupils, involves the degree of structure that should be provided in planning and carrying out instructional activities.[1] For some years now, competent scholars such as David E. Hunt have been reporting research indicating that some students tend to perform better in structured settings, whereas others do better in nonstructured settings. Moreover, Hunt and his colleagues have shown that students' levels of readiness for nonstructured learning environments can be identified easily and that these environments can be suited to each learner.[2] This is but one example of the way in which differences in personality, level of readiness, and preferred style of learning should be taken into account in planning instructional activities in the public schools.

2. As a corollary to the first point, different types of subject matter are best communicated by different modes of pre-

sentation. In some cases, for example, subject matter should be structured using an inductive approach, building toward an ultimate generalization; in other cases, a deductive approach starting with a basic principle is desirable. Subjects such as mathematics may require greater explication by an instructor or textbook than an art course concerned with eliciting students' reactions and feelings. Rules concerning the standard presentation of all types of subject matter are no more attainable than a panacea to cure every conceivable illness or a policy to govern all the contingencies of a military campaign.

3. Many situational variables may need consideration in choosing a particular instructional strategy to use with a given student or group of students at a specified point in time. For example, a student who has recently failed at a series of tasks should not be asked to carry out an assignment he may find difficult until his confidence has been restored. At the same time, care should be taken that his assignments do not remain so simple that he is not challenged to develop his abilities further. The level of stress a student experiences in a particular situation, the value he places on mastering a specific assignment, the degree to which he is inclined on a given day to pursue a particular subject, the influence of his classmates on his perceptions in a small group, and countless other variables can have a major affect on his reactions and performance, and consequently, should influence the teacher's choice of strategies to help him learn.

Much of the research related to these themes has been summarized by Robert S. Soar in a paper on "Teacher-Pupil Interaction" prepared as part of a reexamination and reassessment of "progressive" education sponsored by the Association for Supervision and Curriculum Development. After examining a number of studies in which various investigators reported "discrepant findings," Soar concluded that

> The larger view of the research of the past decade appears to be one in which the major trends furnish clear support for the principles of progressive education. In general, these trends indicate that growth-producing classrooms have a number of characteristics—they are low in criticism of pupils; pupil ideas are praised, accepted, and used by the teacher; and there is a minimum of restric-

tive direction and control by the teacher. . . . Involvement of the teacher in higher level thinking activities . . . tends to be accompanied by a similar increase in the level of the thinking activities of pupils. . . .

The findings of the research [also] demonstrate that too much freedom (indirectness) and too little criticism do result in decreased pupil achievement gain, and apparently in increased anxiety as well . . . within the range of freedom which is most useful, the teacher should vary the amount provided: creating more structure and direction for simple learning tasks, but more freedom for the complex abstract tasks.[3]

4. Like anyone else, teachers must have actual experience in using a skill or they will likely be unwilling or unable to incorporate it in their behavioral repertoire. Although it may satisfy a trainer's conscience to know that his trainees have read a good deal on topics such as how to teach word-attack skills to first graders or how to use questions in leading discussions, teachers are human and tend to use methods they feel comfortable with in the classroom. That is, they tend to teach as they were taught and to limit themselves to skills that they have practiced enough so that they do not appear hesitant or uninformed in front of their students. Teachers who lack experience with differing approaches to an activity will probably fall back on an approach they have already utilized.

This problem is becoming more pronounced as the job of teacher becomes increasingly dehumanized. More and more, the role of the teacher being defined as "facilitator" of learning, in part because it emphasizes guiding students' activities and assignments using multimedia learning systems that allow for individualization of instruction. But teachers cannot perform adequately as managers of learning systems unless they are skilled in using such systems.

5. Teachers especially need practice in classroom management techniques. Classroom management skills sometimes are downgraded in discussions of goals and problems in the public schools—but seldom by anyone who has spent a good deal of time in classrooms. It is extremely important to know how to develop students' love of learning and their sense of self-worth, but it is equally important to be able to establish a classroom atmosphere that allows these goals to be pursued. Classroom experience is required for the skillful presentation of subject matter, for the diagnosis of students' learning problems, and, to a greater extent, for classroom management. Lacking such experience, teacher trainees gain little from a college teacher-training program no matter how competent the instructors or how well designed the curriculum.

6. *Teachers must be familiar with the home and neighborhood environment in which their pupils grow up and live.* Most training programs provide future teachers with ample opportunity to read about the ways in which social background influences pupil behavior and achievement, but reading is not an adequate substitute for personal familiarity with the environment. For several reasons, which need not be spelled out here, future teachers in particular require direct experience in and knowledge of the environment of the inner city, if they are to work effectively in urban schools with high proportions of students from low-status families. Without such knowledge, teachers may make a multitude of mistakes that possibly could be avoided if they understand the problems and pressures that make learning difficult in the inner city. Experience itself may be of little value, of course, unless it is shaped by interpretations gleaned from books, discussions, and expert observers, but that does not make it any less a prerequisite for most future teachers.

Although this discussion has touched on only a few generalizations about teaching and learning that have implications for urban teacher training programs, enough has probably been said to indicate that traditional programs are sadly out of touch with requirements for teaching in the schools.

In traditional programs, future teachers take a few introductory courses in the foundations of education, and, perhaps, make occasional field trips to public schools, and/or have occasional contact with children in the classroom or in some other setting. Then, they take "methods" courses in general pedagogy and their specialties, while serving for a semester or at most a year as a practice teacher under the guidance of a master teacher and university supervisor. Finally, they complete general education and subject-field requirements as specified in state government regulations and receive a certificate of eligibility. That, basically, is all—a trainee presumably has now mastered all the skills and acquired the wide range of practical experience needed to teach effectively!

What kind of training program is required to impart to teachers the skills and sophistication implied in the preceding analysis? This question can be approached from at least two directions. First, one can outline a training sequence that allows for the development of appropriate skills and understandings in a carefully planned schedule. Second, one can describe some of the necessary skills and attitudes and illustrate the kinds of experiences required to develop them, without trying in a chapter of this length to treat the topic comprehensively.

Outline of a Superior Teacher Training Program

The following description of a teacher training program considers primarily the professional experiences and assumes that general requirements (e.g., philosophy, history, literature) and subject-area specialization (e.g., content in high school social studies, elementary school mathematics) remain at least at their current levels of coverage.[4] It also assumes that

—Subject-matter studies will be most useful for the future teacher if they are spaced throughout the training program lumped at the beginning so that trainees can think intelligently about how to teach material they are learning.

—Whenever possible, it is desirable to integrate various parts of the program rather than to maintain an academic distinction among courses. For example, a trainee should be exposed to educational psychology and sociology and draw on them in carrying out a project instead of attending completely separate classes.

—The training experience should be cumulative in the sense that a trainee begins with observation but moves gradually and steadily into supervised teaching and then into a full-time, paid internship.

The outline of a program that might accomplish these purposes is described below. Only general features are included because each teacher training institution is a little different, and too detailed a program could not be made to fit many local situations.

Freshman and Sophomore Years

The student would take most of his work in the liberal arts and sciences, with some exposure to a specialized field such as history or mathematics. Which students are interested in careers as teachers would be determined, and candidates who are unsuited to the field would be screened out. If possible, those who wish to become teachers would take an introductory education course including extended observation in a public school classroom.

Junior Year

Students would continue work in the liberal arts, those who did not take the introductory course would now fulfill this requirement, and all would move on to an assignment as a teacher's aide. Part of this assignment should be served in a middle-status school and part in a low-income (i.e., inner city) school, and it should include learning experiences in the local communities.

During the semester he serves as an aide, the future teacher would begin to take course work in the foundations of education. In addition to the studies in educational psychology, sociology, history, and philosophy, course work here would also emphasize fundamental material relating anthropology and urban sociology to education. Unlike the usual situation, where future teachers view much or most of their foundation studies as meaningless "mickey mouse" work, this part of the training program is judged relevant and important because the trainee now would have sufficient classroom experience to make use of what he learns on the campus.

Senior Year

The major component at this stage would be a "professional" semester devoted *entirely* to satisfying the practice teaching requirement for certification and to completing foundations and educational methods courses. However, these courses would not be given as distinct entities but would instead be woven into seminars taught jointly by a team including the student's practice teaching supervisor. Emphasis in the semester would be on practical application of theory to actual classroom situations. If possible, classes would be held in a field location rather than on the college campus.

Fifth Year

After receiving his bachelor's degree and teaching certificate, the student would serve in a supervised, paid internship in a school. This assignment might well be reimbursed at four-fifths pay, allowing the trainee an opportunity to continue seminars and courses with other interns as part of a special program for credit toward a master's degree.

The five-year program outlined above could possibly be compressed into the standard four-year period now considered the norm for teacher training, but only if candidates were screened and selected by the beginning of the sophomore year. However, unless special circumstances dictate otherwise, a five-year sequence is both reasonable and feasible. For one thing, four years is generally not enough time to prepare for a professional position, if general and academic preparation must be accomplished at the same time. Second, teachers no longer are in short supply in most subjects; as a result, school districts together with training institutions should insist that new teachers meet higher qualifications. Third, a large proportion of undergraduates attending universities in urban areas already take more than four years to complete their degrees; from this point of view, it is not unreasonable to require a fifth-year internship in teacher education.

Characteristics of a Superior Training Program

Several principles vital to the success of a teacher education program alluded to in the preceding sections will now be made explicit. The following list is far from exhaustive; it is intended mainly to identify critical considerations in designing superior programs for training urban teachers.

1. Most of the staff members should constitute a discrete group directly responsible for the quality of training. The usual pattern in training teachers is to draw instructors from a large faculty representing a number of specialties and disciplines such as instructional methods, curriculum content, educational psychology, and the philosophy of education. Courses are given according to a schedule that generally allots the same amount of time to each subject—as if this were equally appropriate for each trainee throughout the training period.

This pattern is a proven failure in preparing professionals who can make effective use of training curricula and experiences in teaching. Teacher educators may not talk much publicly about the quality of training in the United States today, but it would be hard to find an outstanding educator who believes that current practices do more than turn out barely adequate teachers.

One trouble with this pattern is that staff members do not work closely with trainees to integrate the theoretical and practical components. In addition, the fragmentation of the curricula violates every rule we know about effective instruction. At the same time, trainers feel they will be evaluated on the basis of other activities such as publishing, which many are inclined to do anyway. And worse still, no staff member can be held accountable for results so long as inputs come independently from so many sources. It is hard to see how programs can be conducted successfully unless a staff team is given primary responsibility for the quality of training.

2. *Much, if not most, of the training should take place in real or simulated public school classrooms rather than in traditional college classrooms.* This principle is offered with little comment because it has become almost a truism among teacher educators and has been stressed repeatedly by law observers such as James Conant as well as in innovative programs sponsored by the federal government, foundations, and other sources. Unfortunately, the principle is still honored much more often in the breach than in practice.

One should not interpret a stress on field-oriented training as minimizing the necessity of theory or as negating the importance of strong academic training in preparing professionals. To give clinical experience its rightful place in teacher education, after all, is only to draw an analogy between education and other professions, such as medicine, in which knowledge that trainees are unable to translate into practice is as useful as an automobile without an engine.

3. Teacher training programs should be jointly planned and governed—at least to some degree—by personnel from public schools as well as from the university. For some years now newly trained teachers employed in big city schools have quickly been stripped of their enthusiasm for teaching and determination to affect the lives of the children with whom they work. It is a shattering experience to find out that what has been learned in a two-year teacher training program has not equipped one to function even passably well in a real class-room. The reaction of new teachers may range anywhere from despair to a nervous breakdown and from formal resignation to a mean-spirited acceptance of the status quo.

Teachers who have not been prepared to handle the problems of urban education face the prospect of a lifetime career in work that is not only enormously difficult physically but, ultimately, emotionally unsatisfying as well. If there is any truth to the rhetoric of some establishment critics that children are being "murdered" in big city classrooms, it is equally true that their teachers are being ravaged and destroyed. This "slaughter of the innocents" is particularly acute in the inner city school. It will continue as long as we maintain the wall of separation that presently exists between teacher training insti-tutions and the public schools. As long as teachers are trained entirely in the universities, school officials will tend to blame the universities and do little to change the schools. As long as trainers are isolated from the public schools, they can blame the schools for teachers' inadequacies that result from the train-ing program.

Joint planning and governance do not necessarily mean that universities give up control of their programs. Much of the planning can be shared informally, and school officials can participate in decisions about the shape and scope of a training program without violating the professional prerogatives of university faculty. It is true that there is much potential for increasing overt conflict when training programs are governed multilaterally, but it is unlikely that urban teacher training will improve unless authority is wrenched to some degree from the unilateral clutch of the university.

Content of a Superior Training Program

To attempt to describe all the skills and understanding necessary to a superior teacher preparation sequence would require
more space than is available here. Fortunately, nothing so complete is required for the purposes of this chapter; only a few
basic generalizations need be stated to illustrate the directions
in which teacher training should move in order to produce
effective teachers for urban schools.

First, the teacher should develop a variety of competencies
in order to function successfully in a modern classroom. For
example, Smith and his colleagues on a task force of the
National Institute for Advanced Study in Teaching Disadvantaged Youth have identified the "minimal abilities which a
program of teacher education should develop" as follows:

1. perform stimulant operations (question, structure,
   probe)
2. manipulate the different kinds of knowledge
3. perform reinforcement operations
4. negotiate interpersonal relations
5. diagnose student needs and learning difficulties
6. communicate and empathize with students, parents,
   and others
7. perform in and with large groups
8. utilize technological equipment
9. evaluate student achievement
10. judge appropriateness of instructional materials.[5]

This list is very general. Each ability specified above would
have to be broken down into many components if one is serious
about having trainees master the role in practice. Considering
the types of behaviors that may be required just to function as
a communicator of concepts, for example, Smith lists the following "modes of input":

1. cites one or more characteristics of the referent class
2. cites a set of characteristics sufficient to identify
   something as an instance of the class
3. cites a class of which the referent is a subclass
4. describes a referent

5. compares the referent to something else
6. tells what the referent is not
7. tells the opposite of the referent
8. tells the difference between the referent and something else
9. notes the similarities or differences between two or more instances of the referent class
10. cites an instance o fthe referent
11. cites something that is not an instance of the referent
12. tells how an instance may be produced, or
13. gives evidence that a suggested instance is in fact an instance.[6]

After identifying the necessary skills and understanding, one must consider what is required to produce them in a group of trainees. Here, too, Smith provides a brief but useful summary of the steps involved. He points out that the "training process must include the following eelments":

1. establishment of the practice situation
2. specification of the behavior
3. performance of the specified behavior
4. feedback of information about the performance
5. modification of the performance in the light of feedback
6. continuation of performance-feedback-correction-practice schedule until desirable skillfulness is achieved.[7]

It should be obvious that we are now discussing a carefully planned and supervised sequence of activities, which includes detailed specification of goals and careful recording and evaluation of performance. Furthermore, a wide variety of materials and equipment specially selected and/or prepared for each training task must be available and utilized properly if a program is to proceed on anything but a hit-or-miss basis and thus develop more than a very limited number of skills and understandings. One does not prepare a successful teacher by telling him what good teaching is, by having him master a text on instructional methods, or even by requiring him to observe a hundred outstanding practiioners. Effective teachers can be trained in quantity (i.e. apart from the occasional "natural" who requires relatively little preparation) only if the training program ensures step-by-step development and mastery of the skills.

In addition to the technical skills and understanding, which constitute the nucleus of the professional role, teacher training programs must also make provisions for a variety of other goals and prerequisites. As one example, consider the personal understanding and strengths a person must possess or acquire in order to function effectively in a public school. Whatever an individual's profession, a certain amount of self-confidence and emotional security is required before he can make decisions based on knowledge and experience; the person who doubts his basic adequacy often fumbles around so much that he cannot reach even the first stage of professional competence. This problem is particularly severe in teaching because new teachers are usually acutely aware of their significance in the lives of the young and because the teacher usually has nowhere to retreat when he perceives that his performance is inadequate.

What we are talking about is the mental health of the teacher, and the training institution's obligations to this neglected but vital aspect of successful teaching. Francis F. Fuller and her colleagues at the University of Texas probably have done more than any other group to show what can be done in making provisions "for the personal growth and therapy" of prospective teachers by identifying the following "stages," which future teachers typically go through, and the ways in which seminars, psychological services, and other components can be built into a training program aimed at the successful negotiation of each stage:

Stage one: Where do I stand?
Stage two: How adequate am I?
Stage three: Why do they [the children] do that?
Stage four: How do you think I'm doing?
Stage five: How are they [the children] doing?
Stage six: Who am I?[8]

At this point, it is appropriate to mention some of the recent trends in superior teacher education programs:

1. Establishment of teacher training centers operated jointly by school districts, institutions of higher learning, and, in some cases, teachers' organizations and public representa-

tives. Although still in its infancy, this movement is growing and may become a significant force for improving the training of urban teachers. The U.S. Office of Education has provided much money to help establish such centers during the past few years, and nearly 100 of them are already in existence or planned. Because their structure, governance, and membership varies widely from location to location, it is not yet possible to identify one or two best models for their organization and administration. Most likely these centers will concentrate on in-service training, but some may have an important role in preservice and internship-level training as well.[9]

2. *"Packaging" of materials to develop specific teaching skills.* Much effort is being invested in the development, testing, and dissemination of packages of materials that can be used in developing various skills as part of preservice and in-service teacher training programs. For example, the Far West Laboratory for Educational Research and Development (primarily sponsored by the federal government) has developed videotaped "minicourses," which provide trainees with step-by-step instruction and practice in the use of specific skills such as individualizing instruction in mathematics and handling interracial discussions in the classroom. (Packaged materials for training sessions developed by the Laboratory are now available through commercial and nonprofit sources.) In addition, publishing companies also have developed their own sets of materials, some of them—like Science Research Associates' Simulated Inner City Classroom—intended particularly for future inner city teachers. Many of the packaged materials already available provide an excellent foundation for parts of a training program for inner city teachers.

3. *Introduction of competency-based training approach*—Related to the movement toward packaged materials is the recent effort at a number of institutions to develop so-called "competency-based" or "performance-based" teacher education programs. In a competency-based approach, traditional curricula and instructional methods are replaced partly or entirely by learning activities closely related to behavioral objectives. After the desired behaviors are specified, self-paced packages of assignments and materials are prepared, and students work with the packages until they can demonstrate proficiency in meeting a specified standard of performance.[10] This

approach has great potential for overcoming many of the deficiencies of traditional programs, but the difficult task of setting it up and making it work has begun on a significant scale only in the past few years.[11]

4. *Development of training exercises for building skill in coping with day-to-day problems in urban classrooms.* As mentioned above, one of the most important deficiencies in traditional programs is their failure to prepare teachers to cope with the problems they encounter in urban classrooms, particularly in the inner city. Accordingly, several institutions have been developing exercises and assignments to help trainees master the skills and understanding needed to function effectively in difficult urban school settings. Many exercises of this type employ videotape, tape recorders, role playing, and other techniques to simulate situations and problems trainees will encounter. Probably the most outstanding work in this regard has been accomplished in the Syracuse University Urban Teacher Preparation Program, where exercises have been developed to help future teachers gain both the *strength* and *sensitivity* that together are vital prerequisites for successful performance in inner city schools. It is likely that more colleges and universities will develop and/or utilize such exercises as they begin (or are forced) to accept their responsibility for training effective urban teachers.

Exemplary Programs

The remainder of this chapter provides brief descriptions of two special teacher training programs that exemplify some of the characteristics identified in the preceding sections and are aimed specifically at preparing teachers for inner city schools (i.e., schools serving predominantly low-income neighborhoods in big cities). Although the number of future teachers now being trained in such programs is only a fraction of the number who will eventually teach in big city schools, the programs are significant because they demonstrate how improvements can be made in the training of urban teachers in general and those of inner city schools in particular. No attempt has been made to survey and assess *all* the programs that might have been included here, and no claim is made that those mentioned necessarily are the best. They do constitute, however, a reasonably representative sample of the kinds of programs that have high potential for improving the quality of urban education through improvements in the preservice training of teachers.

Urban Education Teacher Training Program—
University of Connecticut

The University of Connecticut initiated an urban education teacher training program in 1968 in conjunction with the boards of education in New Haven and Hamden. The basic elements in the program are as follows:

1. staff assigned full-time to the program
2. living in the urban environment for one full semester
3. student-teaching in the city in which the students live
4. community-oriented seminars
5. on-location methods courses in specific educational areas
6. community involvement on the part of the student teachers
7. "articulate members" of the community included in in the staff with full faculty status
8. concentration on community study and participation in the first part of the semester, shifting to a concentration on classroom activities during the last part.

It is difficult to evaluate training programs like the Connecticut urban education semester because criteria are difficult to devise and apply. For example, there is much disagreement about the specific attitudes and behaviors that programs should try to develop with future inner city teachers: The criteria chosen by one evaluator may be opposite to those selected by another. More important, trainees usually go into ongoing schools after they graduate, and it is impossible to separate the effects of the new institution from those of the training program.

However, there is one measure that most evaluators do find acceptable: Graduates of traditional programs generally have not felt competent to teach in the inner city; thus, producing graduates who are willing to accept and can retain a position in inner city schools is often a big step forward. (Of course, problems related to selectivity in entering the program usually complicate evaluation.)

In this regard, the Urban Education Teacher Training Program (and others like it) have had generally favorable results. Following the first year, for example, more than 50 percent of the trainees obtained employment in inner city schools, and a large proportion of the remainder reported that they wanted to teach in the inner city but were unable to find positions there.[12]

Cooperative Urban Teacher Education (CUTE)

The CUTE program was started in Kansas City in 1967 by Grant Clothier of the Mid-continent Regional Educational Laboratory (McREL). Co-sponsored by McREL, the public school districts in Kansas City, Missouri, and Kansas City, Kansas, and—over most of its early history—approximately twenty regional colleges and universities, the CUTE program has the following characteristics:

1. a 16-week, full-time professional training semester in the inner city, with the middle eight weeks devoted primarily to student teaching

2. a staff including an educational sociologist and inner city instructional specialists who work full-time on the program

3. emphasis on learning about inner city families and communities, often including "immersion" experiences such as a "survival weekend" with only five or ten dollars for food and shelter, or "live-in" experiences in the homes of low-status families[13]

4. a regular seminar, usually conducted by a psychotherapist, devoted to analyzing and understanding trainees' personal perceptions about teaching in the inner city

5. substantial integration of educational foundations, sources, and materials (e.g., psychology, philosophy, sociology) and pedagogical methods in a context emphasizing their applicability to actual classroom problems

6. use of modern training approaches such as microteaching (a technique in which videotape equipment is used for recording and analyzing short simulated lessons)

and interaction analysis (a classroom observation technique that enables trainees to portray and analyze the student-teacher interactions in their own or other classrooms).

Information collected on trainees who have participated in CUTE generally has been encouraging. For example, questionnaire data obtained from 22 first- and second-cycle graduates (1967–68) who had been teaching for one year (mostly in the inner city) showed that:

—Twenty said they would volunteer for CUTE if they had to start their teaching training programs over again.

—Fifteen of 17 who responded to the appropriate item said they felt they were "doing a better job than teachers of equal experience . . . who were not in the CUTE program."

—Twenty agreed with the statement "I felt I better understood the pupils after the CUTE program."

—Twenty agreed with the assertion "All those who plan to teach in the inner-city should take a program similar to CUTE."

—All 21 who responded to the item "The teaching techniques I learned in the CUTE program have been helpful" agreed with the statement.

—Not one respondent agreed with the assertion "The regular university program would have been just as helpful as the CUTE program."

By no stretch of the imagination could these data be construed as proof that even a single CUTE graduate is a successful inner city teacher or that CUTE provides better training for inner city teaching than programs at most colleges and universities. But to anyone familiar with the extremely negative opinions new inner city teachers commonly express concerning the adequacy of their preparation, such responses are highly encouraging.

In 1969, CUTE programs similar to the parent model were started in Wichita, Kansas, and Oklahoma City, Oklahoma, and in 1972, the program was enlarged again to include eight additional cities throughout the country. (The program at each location is sponsored and administered locally, with some supporting services and assistance from McREL.)

The establishment of CUTE and similar programs elsewhere definitely marks a step forward in preparing teachers for inner city schools, but it should not be viewed as a fully adequate response to the problems to which it is addressed. In particular, the one-semester training period is too short to allow for true mastery of the skills and understanding required to function successfully in urban schools. Thus, CUTE director Clothier summed up its achievements and limitations as follows in a newsletter circulated to members and friends of McREL:

> CUTE has real potential, but we've got to be realistic. Education alone can't solve the urban problem; it can only play a part. Second, there's a limited amount of change that can take place in students participating in our 16-week program. Obviously, at the present stage we're producing so few teachers that, in terms of the magnitude of the problem, we're making a relatively small impact. What we have done is show that teacher education institutions can cooperate to prepare teachers who seem to have positive attitudes toward teaching in the inner city and who apparently possess some skills that help them relate better to inner-city children.

Undergraduate Urban Teacher Education
Program—Buffalo

The State University College in Buffalo is one of the few institutions that had provided more than a single semester of training as part of a program geared to preparing teachers for urban schools. The college's Undergraduate Urban Teacher Education Program is a three-semester sequence beginning in the first part of junior year.

According to a description of the program's first year of operation in 1970–71, the first semester requirement includes ten hours a week of service as a teacher aide (i.e., performance of general tasks in the classroom), the second semester includes an assignment as a teacher assistant (i.e., assisting in conducting learning activities such as tutoring), and the third semester includes student-teaching on a four-person team with the regular teacher as well as an aide and an assistant. Throughout the sequence, on-site education courses are conducted, and emphasis is placed on providing opportunities (such as immersion assignments) to gain firsthand knowledge of urban neighborhoods. A program of this kind begins to approach the ideal described earlier.

Cooperative Program in Urban Teacher Education—
University of Illinois at Chicago Circle

In the fall of 1969, a pilot program at the Chicago Circle campus of the University of Illinois was expanded to establish the Cooperative Program in Urban Teacher Education (CPUTE). Conducted in cooperation with schools in District 19 of the Chicago Public Schools, the program provides a year of experience in an inner city school for future student-teachers followed by an additional year in a specialized teaching role to satisfy student-teaching requirements. Some of the most important characteristics of CPUTE include the following:

—"Learning Centers" were established by current and future teachers within schools to serve as sites for teacher training and development. A learning center team included four or five prospective student-teachers (interns); three to five regular classroom teachers, one of whom served as team leader; two high school students on a work-study assignment as teacher aides; and a group advisor (i.e., "facilitator" for the interns) who had previous intern experience in a learning center and had worked under the guidance of a clinical professor while satisfying student-teaching requirements.

—Two education courses (primarily for the interns) were taught in seminar style by teams of faculty from the College of Education. Interns committed five half-days per week to the two courses (two half-days in a learning center, two half-days in the campus seminar, and one half-day in independent study).

—Planning and decision-making for the program were a joint function of the College of Education, the Chicago public schools, and representatives from groups and agencies in the communities served by the participating schools.

Several aspects of the CPUTE program make it a particularly noteworthy venture in preparing teachers to work in big city schools.

First, because trainees can participate for two years in a setting that allows for sequential development, beginning with assignments as a teacher's aide and ending with meaningful participation on a team of established professionals, the program comes close to fitting the outline for an ideal described earlier.

Second, the program provides for a considerable amount of coordination with nonuniversity resources, including public school officials and community representatives, and also with Teacher Corps projects conducted in conjunction with the program during the past two years.

Third, several of the educational methods courses provided for participants in CPUTE were more closely tied to their field assignments (i.e., as interns and group advisors) than is usually true in teacher training institutions.

Fourth, and probably most important, results of the program during the first two years were judged so encouraging that the University of Illinois at Chicago Circle has now moved to make CPUTE's major components available in the basic training of all future teachers. As one would expect, problems are being encountered in this regard, particularly with respect to finding enough suitable school sites for a large number of participants and to maintaining sufficiently close and continuing interaction between trainees and faculty. This experience at Chicago Circle should help educators elsewhere learn something about how to face the problems of institutionalizing promising concepts in urban teacher training on a fairly large scale.

Conclusion

A limited number of colleges and universities have initiated superior short-term programs for improving the preparation of future urban teachers; less have established two- or three-year programs of the kind that might result in a great improvement in the quality of teaching in urban classrooms; still fewer have changed their basic programs to give future teachers the skills and understanding they will need to function successfully.

It is true that many colleges and universities sponsored Teacher Corps projects and other federally funded programs that usually provided two years of training with emphasis on preparation for teaching disadvantaged students. Unfortunately, these programs compressed too much professional material into the first year, more often than not were plagued by internal problems such as deep-seated philosophic conflict among trainees, and in any case, have been mostly phased out because of federal cut-backs and interorganizational disagreement in their administration.

Even if a large number of promising long-term programs had been initiated, however, a number of additional changes would still be necessary to achieve impact on improving instruction in urban classrooms. Under existing conditions, for example, graduates of even the best training programs ultimately have little impact in the schools because they are placed singly or in small groups into existing social systems where their efforts are dissipated and they are unable to implement the ideas they studied as trainees. In the end, most either adjust to the status quo or resign.

In a few cases, efforts have been made to overcome this problem by tying urban teacher training to systematic plans for reform in the schools. Queens College in New York, for example, is working with selected public schools, which serve as training centers embracing preservice training, induction into first-year teaching, in-service training, and instructional change in the classroom. A promising attempt was made in Kansas City in 1971–72 to place CUTE graduates in one elementary school where they constituted most of the faculty and worked under the guidance of several outstanding teachers, while trying to develop new instructional aproaches for the school; unfortunately, the school board allowed the program to be gutted after one year. And in Louisville, Kentucky, a serious effort was made to recruit and capitalize on the talents of Teacher Corps interns and other new teachers in systematically improving instruction in inner city schools, but for various reasons this effort fell short of both its teacher training and instructional reform goals.

What, then, can be concluded about the current status of urban teacher training in teacher preparation institutions in general or in urban universities in particular?

A few institutions have made significant adjustments in order to provide more realistic training for future urban teachers, usually by expanding or modifying the student-teacher segment of the traditional program. A handful of colleges and universities have gone beyond this to initiate longer programs that attempt sequential development of the skills needed for successful teaching in complex urban society. By and large, however, the typical preservice program at most teacher training institutions—wherever their location—is still largely the same as it was ten or twenty years ago.

In the meantime, it has become abundantly clear that a large proportion of graduates are not adequately prepared to teach in such difficult urban situations as an inner city neighborhood, a conflict-ridden desegregated high school, or a middle-class suburban school with large numbers of alienated students. No wonder that many urban educators are searching for ways to shift teacher training responsibilities over to other institutions such as local public schools or the federal government.

NOTES

1. For a detailed and multidimensional definition of "structure," see Russell C. Doll and Daniel U. Levine, "Toward a Definition of Structure in the Education of Disadvantaged Students," in A. H. Passow, ed., *Opening Opportunities for Disadvantaged Learners* (New York: Teachers College, 1972), pp. 128–161.

2. David E. Hunt, *Matching Models in Education: The Coordination of Teaching Methods with Student Characteristics* (Toronto: Ontario Institute for Studies in Education, 1970).

3. Robert S. Soar, "Teacher-Pupil Interaction," in James R. Squire, ed., *A New Look at Progressive Education* (Washington, D.C.: Association for Supervision and Curriculum Development, 1972), pp. 198–200.

4. The overall sequence described in this section resembles the program suggested by L. O. Andrews of the Ohio State University. See L. O. Andrews, "A Curriculum to Produce Career Teachers for the 1980s," *Theory Into Practice,* 6, no. 5 (December 1967), pp. 236–245.

5. B. O. Smith, *Teachers for the Real World* (Washington, D.C.: American Association of Colleges for Teacher Education, 1969), p. 71. The view I am presenting here is held by many leading teacher educators who believe that the teacher must possess and practice a variety of skills even though team teaching or "differentiated staffing" may somewhat reduce the range needed by any one person. However, it should be noted that there are other viewpoints. For example, Carl Bereiter believes that few persons can adequately combine the *instructor* or *communicator of knowledge* role with the *child nurturer* role; hence these tasks should be kept systematically distinct between separate staffs. See Carl Bereiter, "Schools Without Education," *Harvard Educational Review,* vol. 42, no. 3 (August 1972), pp. 390–413.

6. Smith, *Teachers for the Real World,* p. 57.

7. *Ibid.,* p. 71.

8. Adapted from Frances F. Fuller, "Concerns of Teachers: A Developmental Conceptualization," *American Educational Research Journal,* vol. 6, no. 2 (March 1969), pp. 207–226.

9. For a favorable view on such teacher training centers, see Stephen K. Bailey, "Teachers' Centers: A British First," *Phi Delta Kappan,* vol. 51, no. 3 (November 1971), pp. 146–149. For a skeptical response in a U.S. context, see Paul S. Pilcher, "Teacher Centers: Can They Work Here?" *Phi Delta Kappan,* vol. 52, no. 5 (January 1973), pp. 340–343.

10. Howard Getz et al., "From Traditional to Competency Based Teacher Education," *Phi Delta Kappan,* vol. 54, no. 5 (January 1973), pp. 300–302; W. Robert Houston and Robert B. Howsam, eds., *Competency-Based Teacher Education: Progress, Problems, and Prospects* (Chicago: Science Research Associates, 1972).

11. Even so, New York State education officials recently decided that all new programs for training teachers and administrators must be performance-based.

12. Not all innovative programs to train teachers for inner

city schools, however, have reported results this encouraging. The Camden Opportunity Professional Experience (COPE) conducted by Glassboro (N.J.) State College in 1966 and 1968, for example, reported that only 51 of 147 graduates had taught disadvantaged students at some time in the three-to-five year period following participation in the program.

13. For a good description of a "live-in" training assignment, see Julia Boleratz and Marjorie East, "A Cross-Cultural and Cross-Class Experience for Preteachers," *Journal of Teacher Education,* vol. 20, no. 4 (Winter 1969), pp 435–437.

PART FOUR

Internal Dynamics and the Future of Urban Higher Education

14

UNIVERSITY BUREAUCRACY AND THE URBAN THRUST

Thomas P. Murphy

Many a college or university has mistakenly undertaken the task of creating or expanding an urban program with the notion that a strong statement of intent is the key to success. Such an approach overlooks certain crucial internal and external realities. Chief among these are the internal realities of resource distribution within a bureaucracy. Educational bureaucracies in particular—because they are not called upon to react as quickly as those that must deal with fast-changing business and operational conditions—tend to place greater emphasis upon resource allocation. These expenditure patterns are relatively stable, so that changes are quickly noticed. Conversely, programs with long histories of healthy budgets have both precedent and a budget base in their favor.

External realities may also serve to override even the best and most sincere urban policy statements. The constituencies served by the educational bureaucracy influence the kind of urban program that can be developed. An approach appropriate for a community college will not fill the needs of a major state university. Further, one state university may have a widely diverse urban constituency, whereas another may serve a relatively homogeneous constituency. The special goals, needs, and opportunities of each should be reflected in the way such different institutions organize their urban response.

No mere policy directive can by itself nullify a galaxy of unfavorable internal and external influences. Framing an organizational structure to facilitate the development of action programs, academic degrees, research, and a continuing education program for the particular urban environment is not an easy task. Because the level of development for each aspect of the total urban program differs in each institution and even within different departments of the same institution, there is no universal formula to follow in designing the urban thrust.

Even if an ideal design existed, it would probably be difficult to implement. Many barriers and constraints may befall the reorganization of an urban university to meet future urban needs. While the constraints can be classified under the headings of financial resources and the number and quality of urban faculty specializations, the barriers defy exact classification. This does not lessen the importance of constraints; if the resources cannot be made available, then the discussion is moot. Even if resources are available, many a president or chancellor desiring to establish an urban program has discovered that there are institutional barriers which can thwart his plans. Such barriers may be categorized as financial, political, and organizational.

Financial Barriers and Conflicts of Interest

The need for financial resources to mount an effective urban program is both a constraint and a barrier. Financing an urban program involving academic, research, and action components is expensive—more expensive than many who have pressed for such programs ever believed. Urban programs can be funded either from "hard" internal funds over which the university has a certain amount of control, or through "soft" grant and contract money derived from outside sources. Most strong programs involve a combination of these funds. When either or both sources are reduced or unavailable, the program is in trouble.

If an urban program must be built with soft money, one

of the barriers is that faculty committees and administrators will raise questions about launching a program on an insecure financial foundation. The argument will also be made that because support from soft money is often reduced as a program gains stability, the university will eventually be called upon to provide all operating funds with its hard money, making it difficult to support programs in other important areas.

The problem with using internal funds is that virtually all institutions of higher education, especially urban universities, are financially pressed and are likely to remain so for a long time. In many cases, the annual increases through the budget process amount to less than the inflation factor superimposed upon last year's budget. At the same time, enrollments are mounting and many items in the budget are increasing much faster than the rate of inflation. As a consequence, few institutions have enough uncommitted money to launch or bail out an urban program.

Thus, in the long run, the program's growth will be funded either by spasmodic outside funding or through some reallocation of internal funds. But reallocation is a dirty word in academic circles because it means that some other programs must be cut back to free funds for the growth of the urban program. Until sufficient internal funds are available for both traditional and innovative programs, funding will be a serious problem.

Certain vested interests on the campus, generally the social science departments, will see the growth of urban programs as a means of supplementing the growth of their own departments. This would be of no significance if urban programs were independent of these interests. However, university decisions on establishing the urban program and setting its budget will be made through its committee structure; such committees necessarily involve a variety of campus schools, colleges, and departments. This means that the very departments most likely to be pared back will be represented on the committees charged with providing the necessary resources and with approving organizational changes.

Take the case of a campus where foreign language requirements for graduate and undergraduate students are being made optional. A sudden change in such a requirement would probably create a surplus of faculty in some foreign language departments. Wholesale firings would not be required, but no new recruiting could be done in this area, and many persons lacking tenure could not be reappointed. How will the chairman of such a foreign language department react when asked to approve a new urban program? Conflicts of interest are unfortunate but endemic in the university governance system.

Problems in achieving organizational balance are common to many organizations, yet few bureaucracies are as decentralized as a university. Most top administrators in nonuniversity organizations have considerably more power than university administrators over their committees and work groups. Few chancellors or presidents are willing to tell a faculty committee that it *must* approve a new urban program or *must* reallocate X dollars from existing budgets to fund it. At best, university management can hope for a vote authorizing the establishment of the program with a minimal level of funding, provided that it can find money through some additional funding source. Most university administrators must settle for a compromise and then face allocating their meager new resources to the expansion of the emerging program. Thus, even where a barrier has been avoided, a constraint is present to influence the outcome.

The Politics of Delay

Apart from the inherent conflicts of interest involved in running a university through a committee system of faculty members from diverse areas, the committee system has other weaknesses that make it difficult to establish new programs. One of these is the inaccessibility of committees, most of which are appointed on an annual basis with the understanding that real work sessions will be restricted to a few months of spring and fall. Then, because so many faculty members are on a variety of committees, the average committee is likely to meet once a month. A new program seeking committee approval can anticipate, at the most, access to six meetings in the course of an academic year. This assumes that the committee has no other business before it and that there is no carryover of old business that must be considered first. Such is not often the case. This situation is made-to-order for those members of a commitee who have a vested interest in killing the new urban program: The politics of delay becomes a very convenient strategy.

The process of implementation may be greatly facilitated if some members on the committees have vested interests in the operation of the urban program or have close allies among the sponsoring group. This relationship shows up most clearly in those situations where the urban program is to be run by a committee and must draw upon courses from various departments. One of the first questions that arises in formulating such a program is whether there should be a program of core courses. If the group decides "yes," it must then agree on core courses. Indeed, it must be decided if *new* courses should be organized and taught by an interdisciplinary faculty. If the group decides that courses on urban politics should be part of the core, the representative from the sociology department, whose course was not included in the core, may sulk. Later, he may try to induce a member of the curriculum committee to raise the question of balance in the core courses and suggest that the sponsoring committee recast its proposal. When this occurs, there will have to be additional meetings and gamesmanship within the urban committee before the matter can even come back to the curriculum committee. This may take up one or two curriculum committee meetings and thus jeopardize chances of securing action for the next academic year. The combined pressure of the curriculum committee members who are requesting changes in the course proposal and of the passage of time will generally bring about some accommodation within the urban committee for the sake of "getting on with the program"—which may leave its scars for future sessions.

If the curriculum committee should fail to complete its action on the proposal before the end of the academic year, the whole program will be held over for the next curriculum committee, which may not even be appointed until after the summer recess. Then the whole process begins anew and there may be substantial politicking on campus to determine who the new members of the curriculum committee should be because they may hold the key to passage or defeat of the proposal.

Similarly, personnel changes in the sponsoring group may occur. The political science representative may accept an offer at a new university, or the geography department, left out of the core in the first proposal for lack of an urban geographer, may recruit one and request that he be used. These changes may require rebalancing the core. If the students are to have sufficient electives, the required core cannot be too large. However, adding a course in urban geography to the core may require deleting another core course. Because this will undoubtedly be in a discipline other than geography, all the other disclipines will be thrown into competition. Unless several members on the committee want the urban program more than they want to defend some of their own parochial departmental interests, that dispute may not be resolved for months.

Some urban academic programs involve a combination of graduate and undergraduate courses and even degrees. This factor may further complicate the process of new program approval because many institutions have separate committees for graduate and undergraduate degrees. In a particular academic year, the sponsoring committee may succeed in shepherding its proposal through the undergraduate committee but fail to make it through the graduate committee or vice versa. One or the other committee may impose special requirements on the sponsors; in some cases, the two separate committees might impose contradictory requirements. Graduate curriculum committees, for example, show more concern with the quality and scope of library holdings and with the core courses established for urban degrees. Undergraduate curriculum committees may press for inclusion of an internship in the program. Some graduate committees will flounder on questions relating to the administration of the degree program. For example, who will be responsible for providing comprehensive examinations and supervising theses? What minimum Graduate Record Examination scores will be acceptable for admission to the program? What specific undergraduate grade point average must be met?

Setting such requirements can impede urban programs that seek to provide administrative skills to governmental employees already in the public service or those in mid-career or just returning from military service. These potential students may pose special problems. Arbitrary rating systems do not allow for the intensity of motivation often present in older students and ignore the need to stretch admission standards for minority students from inferior secondary schools.

Legitimacy of Sponsorship

The reaction of faculty budget and curriculum committees to the proposal for establishing a new urban program may depend in part upon the source of the proposal. In many institutions urban programs were initiated as a consequence of leadership from the office of the president or chancellor. Sometimes this has been a two-pronged pressure with the other support for the program coming from students in search of "relevance."

Frequently, community leaders also pressure the administration to "respond" to community needs. Few of these are the same persons from whom the university is seeking financial contributions, so that university administrators feel constrained to show positive action. This does not ensure that the university bureaucracy will respond. Many chancellors and presidents have attempted to cut red tape by directing that there be an urban center or program free from the established teaching or research arms of the school. Unfortunately, this has generally resulted in slowing up the process of approval, or in setting up an urban thrust that exists without the roots necessary to perform the function effectively.

Professors with tenure can be annoyingly oblivious to the pressures faced by top administrators and even to the demands of students. They often view administrators as subject to unreasonable outside pressures and students as temporary denizens of the campus. Their self-image is that of the true protectors of the academic environment and of the standards that permit academicians to hold their heads high at annual professional meetings. The top administrators in the university have relatively little power over such faculty when they are organized as a curriculum or budget committee. Governance by faculty committees can tie the hands of university management merely over the issue of legitimacy of leadership.

For this reason, the nature of sponsorship of the proposal for an urban program is crucial. Approval can be a relatively smooth process if the proposal is initiated by a cooperative faculty group and satisfies external pressures. If, however, top management must drag the faculty into the program, it is unlikely to succeed even if the effort to establish it should be successful. On the other side, even if faculty support is strong and the proposal is developed in a collaborative manner, top management may not share the concern with responding to urban problems. In this case, the program is unlikely to be funded at a sufficient level.

Regardless of the impetus for planning an urban program, the process of securing such a program does not vary much from case to case. A new program needs a strong recommendation from an appropriate group to the curriculum committees if it is to be taken seriously. Because by definition a new urban program has no fixed sponsorship, some kind of interdepartmental faculty group must first study the needs and then propose alternatives. One of the more popular approaches is to have the chancellor or the president appoint a task force on urban affairs, membership in which will not be set until several or all of the deans have been consulted. This group's membership should include most of the major interests concerned with the urban curriculum. If blessed with appropriate leadership, the group may be able to eliminate the otherwise competitive aspects of the proposal. Key questions are whether there shall be core courses, who shall teach them, what existing courses from the departments shall be appropriate electives, how the director or coordinator is to be selected, and where the program is to be housed. Some broader questions concerning the nature of the program—the relative mix and emphasis on degrees, research, and action programs—must also be resolved. A well-balanced group should be able to compromise on its differences.

Appointment of a monolithic group intent on rubber-stamping the chancellor's concept of the program will produce a proposal more quickly, but will probably incur the wrath of faculty members and departments whose interests are excluded from the early deliberations. This is likely to trigger the delaying mechanisms so easy to employ in the committee process. Therefore, the question of the legitimacy of the sponsoring group is a key matter.

In addition to curriculum committees, whose interest is generally limited to academic questions, an urban program proposal must be considered by a group representing total faculty interest. This has generally taken the form of a campus senate, which sometimes includes student and staff representatives as well as faculty and administrators. At this stage of consideration, the program is still far from approval. Convincing the curriculum committee that an academic program is possible within the framework of the campus is one matter. Convincing the more freewheeling senate that the new program is in the best interests of the institution and its various constituencies is another. For one thing, the senate is likely to have a committee on educational policy, which may be dedicated to reducing the number of degrees and specializations in the interests of preventing university resources from being spread even more thinly than they already are. Ideological opponents of urban studies may range from a conservative professor who wants to build models "uncontaminated by problem-solving" to a radical who has "learned" that anything the university touches becomes a "tool" of the "establishment." This committee may present an extremely formidable barrier.

All the opposing elements that have been unable to win their point throughout consideration of the curriculum questions can at this stage convert those arguments into financial, policy, and program priority questions for the total university. Sometimes the senate will give the appearance of accepting the rhetoric of the urban crisis and the need to be relevant by endorsing the proposal "in principle" without giving the administration a clear signal as to the relative priority of the new program. This can be a sophisticated tactic; it leaves the administrators to grapple with the financial questions while giving the new senate a convenient rationale for delaying program implementation. Here again, the origin of urban program initiatives and the legitimacy of their sponsorship may be more important to the overall success of the program than the very elements of the program.

The Multicampus University and Its Special Problems

In a multicampus university, establishing a new urban program has the added dimensions of intercampus competition and intercampus committees, which meet even less frequently than campus committees. Often there is even competition among members of the statwide board of regents, curators, or trustees.

Virtually all multicampus universities are state- or city-supported institutions that began with a primary campus and added others as the need arose. Thus, the large systems in California, New York, and Georgia grew up over a long period of time. In more recent years, the state systems in Wisconsin, Missouri, and Maryland added campuses at Milwaukee, Kansas City, St. Louis, and Baltimore to those already located at Madison, Columbia, and College Park. The shift in emphasis from rural to urban is obvious.

The administration established to direct and coordinate the activities of the various campuses has a university-wide role. However, as many of these systems have been initiated, the president of the "mother" campus has often been promoted to the position of university-wide president, with new chancellors selected to serve at the various campuses. This is a reflection of the importance of the mother campus. No matter how many institutions are in the state system, the original campus will still have most of the students and graduate programs, and the largest physical plant. Its former administrative leaders are necessarily the leaders of the new system, and the administrative heads of the other campuses feel some degree of discrimination whenever their requests are turned down on the basis of "system-wide priorities" or the nonavailability of funding. Not many urban universities share the good fortune of Georgia State, which is a separate institution from the University of Georgia, in having had no trouble convincing the legislators of the reality of urban problems.

In Maryland, Wisconsin, and Missouri the headquarters of the new systems were established at the mother campus. The system hierarchy tends to favor that campus when decisions are made on the location of programs that can be assigned to only one campus or that should be intercampus programs under the direction of a lead campus. This problem can become especially acute with the creation of an urban program. Increasing urbanization has led to pressures to establish new campuses in the city. Graduate faculty at the mother campus find that although they control the doctoral programs, the new urban institutions are located at the field laboratory. Tensions develop if the rural-based institution and its faculty attempt to work in the city. When professors from sociology departments in three different campuses of the state start working with the same city council and for the same community action groups, competition for the favor and resources of those groups can become intense.

Whenever one campus in a multicampus system attempts to secure approval of an urban program, questions arise at the other campuses. Even if the program is needed at the campus requesting it, other campuses do not want to have their own options for beginning similar programs reduced. Yet the system administrators and the state board may believe that the university system cannot support independent urban programs at each of the campuses. As a result, an alternative often proposed is for an integrated intercampus program with a lead institution.

Such a program often is not geographically feasible. The part-time graduate student, for example, may not be able to travel two or three hours round-trip for a two-hour class several times a week. Similarly, interchange of faculty among campuses would also be difficult, although not impossible, to schedule. The City University of New York, for example, has graduate programs staffed by faculty from the separate colleges in the city system; the subway system makes this feasible. Obviously there would be problems of control in an intercampus program based on a mythical interchange of students and faculty.

A specific basis for competition is that urban programs involve research and opportunities for outside financing as well as for teaching. No campus wants to be cut off from these possibilities. Programs such as English, history, and education are by tradition available at all campuses and the apparent "duplication" is never questioned. Urban programs, however, give the appearance of being a larger plum; therefore the competition is more intense, and the keepers of the budget are more concerned about the apparent proliferation of programs.

Running a multicampus program directly from the system headquarters is a second alternative. Yet the academic climate tends to work against such an arrangement. Campus faculty (and even chancellors) work to gain control over programs in which they participate, and these competitions are so intense that coordination requires especially effective academic and research management. Few university systems have been able or willing to attract highly capable academic managers to their staffs, a first priority in managing a multicampus graduate program.

A further difficulty in a multicampus university is that the state board generally contains representatives from various competing geographic and power interests within the state. A trustee from a large city with a new state university feels constrained to support his constituency in its desire to have an urban program, whereas board members with ties to other areas of the state, especially the home area of the mother campus will usually question these new priorities for resources and oppose urban programs on the basis that they are inefficient resource consumers. In the end, the city institution will probably be permitted to have the urban program, but with too small a budget to be effective.

City representation on university boards is deceiving. Although board members may be natives of the city, most are likely to be alumni of the mother campus because the city campuses did not exist at the time the board members went to school. Mother campus support is reenforced by such trappings as the only football team in the system. This situation exists at Wisconsin, Missouri, and Maryland, as examples. In short, the multicampus university does not consist of equal parts or partners. Ultimately, financing the state university is subject to the decisions of a state legislature where urban representation may also be weak. The appropriation committees of the legislature know there are tremendous fixed investments at the mother campus, which must be protected and maintained. In a tight budget, therefore, there is little room for discretionary funding to be funneled to the urban campuses—certainly not at a rate fast enough to enable them to overtake the mother institution in facilities and programs.

If the board and administration did not already have tendencies to induce specialization among the campuses, they would develop them as a result of the emergence of another barrier to the growth of new programs—the state commission on higher education. The growth of higher education has been so great that many states have not only a multicampus state university but also a state college system and perhaps a rapidly growing community college system. In addition, there is increasing interest in providing supplementary appropriations for private institutions from the same sources of revenue that support public institutions.

The state commission on higher education represents an attempt to provide an ultimate coordinating body to oversee the development of competing institutions, prevent unnecessary duplication, and insure the availability of adequate programs throughout the state. State universities are, therefore, being faced with the need to justify their new programs, not only in terms of the offerings of state institutions, but also in competition with private institutions, which may be adequately serving statewide needs for a particular specialization. Under such heavy competition, urban programs must be particularly well represented to survive the review process.

Organizational Structures

After an appropriate ad hoc group has been appointed to develop an urban program, the next step is to consider the options available for organizing and structuring the program. The possibilities range from establishing a special assistant to the chancellor for urban affairs to establishing a total urban university. Obviously, not all options are available to some universities. The total urban university involves the most resources and the greatest faculty commitment. The most developed urban programs also require full commitment from the administration. Opportunity costs to other program areas are the price of such decisions. A small program or an assistant to the chancellor may be a token move representing all that can be afforded under the circumstances.

Table 14–1 shows how potential modes of organization relate to the functional components of urban programs. The "assistant to the chancellor" model is heavily involved in the chancellor's urban public relations function but is unlikely to be involved in academic programs. This model in particular can be an important buffer for the chancellor who, whenever challenged by the community leaders, can point to his organization chart as evidence of his concern for urban affairs. A more sophisticated level of organization involves the use of a

Table 14–1

Modes of Organization of Urban Programs

program elements	Asst. to chancel- lor	Pro- gram coordi- nation	Inter- dept. comm.	Institute or center	College of urban affairs	Total urban univ.
Chancellor's urban public relations	H	L	L	L	L	H
Clearinghouse for urban research and urban programs	L	L	H	H	H	H
Urban courses	L	L	H	H	H	H
Urban degree	UN	UN	O	O	H	H
Urban research	UN	L	H	H	H	H
Urban action and service programs	O	O	O	H	H	H

Key:

UN = high level of responsibility for this program element
H = low involvement in this program element
O = very unlikely to be involved
L = may or may not be involved

program coordinator who may be located in the chancellor's office, in the college of arts and sciences, or in a professional school. This person will probably be involved in all the categories of urban programs listed in Table 14–1, but it is unlikely that the academic program will involve a degree. If the coordinator is located outside the chancellor's office, involvement in the chancellor's urban public relations will be less extensive, since some of those functions must be performed by someone physically present in the chancellor's office.

If the interdepartmental committee mode of organization is selected, academic programs as well as research programs will be given more attention. There will be even less involvement in the chancellor's public relations function, unless the committee chairman is given substantial released time for this purpose, or unless the committee has a professional staff member. Both the coordinator and committee models include the possibility of involvement in action programs, though this is not likely; if the university's commitment to urban programs and action is that extensive, a more aggressive organizational design is usually created. The interdepartmental committee model has numerous complications, one of which is the question of whether or not there should be a lead department. This question involves many of the same complications as the selection of a lead campus in a multicampus degree program. However, programs which have a degree will invariably provide released time for a director, who in turn will report to and perhaps be a member of the interdepartmental committee. This gives the program the kind of continuity and student access which is essential for interdisciplinary programs.

The establishment of an institute or center is clear evidence that there is high support—or at least expectation—on the part of the administration. The budgetary implications of having an institute or center are such that it would be extremely easy for the administration to block the establishment of such a program if it did not believe in it. The academic requirements for offering a graduate and/or undergraduate degree can be met through the committee system. The great advantage of the institute-center approach is that it implies a greater commitment to research and action programs as an integral part of the education program. This is sometimes helpful in approaching funding sources. Institutes are also much more likely to have internship programs and to involve graduate students in sponsored research.

Some institutes and centers appoint faculty directly and attempt to operate as if they were an independent department or discipline. Others are based on the assumption that there is no urban discipline as such, but that an interdisciplinary program draws upon all the traditional disciplines and requires their willing participation to be effective. Under this approach, faculty have joint appointments in which they increase or decrease the percentage of their time spent with the institute depending upon the research and action programs in progress. This is a very flexible device, which permits a continuous turnover of personnel yet maintains a certain continuity essential to effective academic programs. Like the less sophisticated approaches, the institute will be involved in the chancellor's public relations function, but not exclusively so; the chancellor's office will continue to handle many of the public relations projects.

In some cases, the urban involvement of a university may be sufficiently extensive to justify the establishment of a department or college of urban affairs. This was attempted at the University of Wisconsin-Milwaukee. Faculty members from a variety of disciplines were hired specifically for the new department and were assigned offices in one location. The effect was to give the students a more visible home for their academic work and to emphasize the many advantages of group academic and research identity. One of the disadvantages lay in the fact that urban involvement is so extensive in these circumstances that there are few departments on campus which are totally unrelated to it. Aside from forcing contested decisions about boundaries, the establishment of a college of urban affairs may tend to lock out some persons who would otherwise have at least occasional involvement in urban research, action, or teaching. At the departmental level, many of the universities which have attempted this model have done it within a social science realm, so that the involvement of engineering and physical science departments has been extremely limited. When this occurs, the loss to the program in terms of scope and substance is often substantial.

A related approach is the "college of public affairs," known in many schools as a "college of public and international affairs." This involves combining a variety of government-oriented academic programs such as international relations, foreign aid research, public administration, planning, political science, and urban affairs. New schools on this model have recently been established at the universities of Colorado and Indiana and have existed for some time at the universities of Pittsburgh and Washington.

The most extensive form of urban commitment is exemplified by the urban university that concludes that it is impossible to separate its urban programs from the rest of its educational program. Wayne State University in Detroit is one of these. Each department there relates its basic discipline to urban problems in virtually all curricula. This has tremendous advantages for the urban student, but its success has been limited by the fact that the university academic program must still encompass all disciplines, however esoteric. Some faculty in the peripheral disciplines, as well as some in the related disciplines, do not accept this focus wholeheartedly and are more interested in theoretical aspects of their discipline than in applications to urban problems.

Still, universities adopting an extensive and all-encompassing urban focus are more likely to succeed in making their mark upon urban problems than those attempting to get by cheaply. Whatever form of organization is adopted, it is essential to relate expectations to available resources.

Whether or not there is a formal urban program, a variety of responsibilities which might be classified as "chancellor's urban public relations" will require attention in every urban university. Examples of this public relations function are as varied as the program options which the urban university may choose to undertake. The chancellor is continuously called upon to make speeches to urban-related groups in the community and to relate to community political leadership. This is an "umbrella" function of value to all programs. The social and economic development committees which exist in the community often request university representation; this function relies upon business school or economics expertise. Legislators and businessmen request information concerning environmental and manpower problems, and so a strong service research arm in addition to the academic research arm is valuable. The local newspaper may place demands upon the chancellor to justify his urban involvement and concern with action programs in low-income areas. Potential donors often want to know what is being done in support of urban problem-solving, and numerous governmental and community leaders feel that there ought to be a focal point in the university they can contact to gain access to the various capabilities of the university. Good liaison with community leadership is invaluable to building good public relations. In the absence of an urban program these functions are handled by the chancellor himself or by a provost or dean whose academic area is closely related to urban problems.

Just beyond the urban public relations function is the role of providing a clearinghouse of information for those inside the university. This may take the form of a newsletter from the graduate school summarizing urban-related dissertations and research findings. It may involve publicity for the

HUD urban fellowships, urban volunteer opportunities for students, and circulation of research and personnel interests of urban-related federal agencies. From a research standpoint, clearinghouse functions are often performed by the campus research office or by the graduate school. Several clearinghouse substructures may coexist simultaneously.

A third major functional area is academic work. Though most campuses have some courses that contain urban subject matter, these offerings are often not clearly identifiable. There may be no planned sequence a student may follow to gain general knowledge, a certificate, or an academic degree in urban studies. From the student's standpoint, organizational substructures are the primary determinant of academic orientations.

Urban research programs are a fourth important area. Often they are merely the cumulative efforts of a variety of faculty acting independently; at their best they constitute carefully coordinated research designs. In some cases these programs exist on university money, but generally research is carried out under grants and contracts some federal agencies, foundations, and private contributors. Most urban universities use the local metropolitan area as their laboratory, but the larger and better funded programs may work nationally or even internationally. Programs such as the Joint Center for Urban Studies at MIT and Harvard can do all of these things and are prestigious enough to attract considerable grant and contract funding.

A fifth category of activity may be designated as action programs. These are related to the public relations functions covered earlier, but are more substantive and can involve working with existing or experimental and ad hoc groups in the community on a range of urban problems. In some cases, they are even more extensive and involve large-scale demonstration programs under university management. Since these programs do not involve student fees and can be quite expensive, they too are generally based on grant or contract funds.

The organization pattern selected and the number of program options chosen is an indicator of the level of commitment to urban study. This is especially true in the more powerful programs where heavy resource allocations are made and where as a consequence more alternatives are available. It is difficult to read much into the mere presence or absence of any of these aspects of the urban program. Each one must be examined in terms of its faculty involvement, contribution to teaching, research output, action programs, and relation to the rest of the university organizational structure.

Implementation Pitfalls

Securing official approval of urban program organization does not conclude bureaucratic problems. If anything, the emphasis will then shift to developing sufficient resources to do an effective job. Obviously, the support of the administration of the university is crucial, as is the support of departments and their chairmen related to the program.

One of the first issues to arise under a full-time coordinator or executive director approach is the selection of an individual to fill the position. Often the competing departments—and competition is ever-present because of the interdisciplinary nature of urban programs—make certain trade-offs in agreeing to the structure of the program. But trade-offs become more difficult when personnel must be chosen because the top position is of fundamental importance. What discipline should the leader represent? The director of the institute will have opportunities to pass graduate assistantships and direct research funds and contracts to his associates. Frequently the only recourse to avoiding a departmental standoff is to bring in a mutually acceptable candidate from the outside.

Faculty committees will also be essential to the implementation and operation of the urban program. If there is an institute or center, the executive director must have a faculty advisory board or board of directors. Because of the interdisciplinary nature of so many urban programs, they will generally report either to the dean of a nonprofessional college or of the arts and science college, or to a provost or vice-chancellor for academic affairs. The support of this administrative official is very important in securing resources for an urban program, for he will of course be especially active in administrative matters, whereas the faculty group will stress curricular and research matters. On the other hand, at some institutions a general call has been issued to the faculty and students to join an "urban assembly" which serves as the general watchdog of the institute and may even be accorded the power to select the board of directors, subject to a few ex officio appointments by the dean, provost, or vice-chancellor.

These faculty involvements are important because one of the next problems of the growing urban program is to decide who is to teach the courses that are agreed upon as the core. When recruitment of new faculty is at stake, the competitive spirit will again rear its head. Should a joint appointment be made with sociology, political science, economics, history, or geography? A director should be careful to balance these decisions on the basis of what is best for the institute or center rather than upon the more parochial interests of the department in which he holds a joint appointment.

One of the stumbling blocks to establishing new urban programs in a period of tight money and budgets is that only a small growth increment is available to university management to pass on to such programs. Conversely, in a situation where a campus is expanding very rapidly, administrators will have many options. For example, they can strengthen the new program by insuring that departments use new positions to hire urban geographers, urban historians, urban economists, and urban politics faculty rather than persons representing other specializations in those departments.

The budget cycle itself constitutes a problem in that it involves built-in delay. Universities work on the basis of a fiscal year and, in the case of state universities, this is tied to action by a legislature which much approve the university budget. Budgets are generally submitted by the university to its board of trustees or regents in the early fall and then are passed on to the governor for presentation to the legislature in January. The money voted during the spring session of the legislature is for use during the fiscal year beginning the following July. However, hiring for the next school year beginning in September must be done in the spring, often before the legislature has finished action on the budget. This means that the university is frequently in the dark as to the number of new positions it may have. Moreover, a new institute just attempting to expand is at a special disadvantage because more established programs and departments will have vacancies from the previous year or will have persons taking leave, and with their established status they can hire the better candidates on the market.

Similarly, the budget lag means that a new institute or center may not have hard dollars with which to work until the following school year. Frequently one of the assumptions of the program is that the cooperating departments will provide volunteered support. This can be very soft money indeed. Even a department that wishes to be cooperative is not likely to volunteer the teaching time of one of its faculty members before it has its own final budget from the administration and knows precisely where it stands in terms of its own teaching load. This is most understandable, but it means that the new program must settle for leftovers and benefit only on a contingency basis from departmental funds. It also means that if the urban program derives any voluntary support, it will learn of it rather late in the year and may have some difficulty in adjusting its program to make the best use of these resources. In the interim period before the approval of the first budget containing the urban program, a workable strategy may be the reallocation of campus funds to the institute. Unfortunately, university management generally does not hold back enough money to be able to do this in a substantial way.

A further hindrance is that the use of research funds as a source for developing the institute program is impractical during the first year. Foundations and government agencies are notorious for postponing their responses to proposals. It may take several months to put together a proposal under the auspices of the new institute, and then it will certainly take at least six months to get a response. Even if the response is affirmative, it will generally be geared to the beginning of a school year or a semester; it is rarely possible to start a new research program in the middle of a semester when faculty members are already committed to a teaching load. Few institutes start with the assumption that they will have full-time research faculty who could be hired at any time of the year, and many are opposed on principle to the use of research professorships.

The recruitment of the appropriate faculty is crucial to the program. Where volunteered faculty from the participating departments is the source of manpower, departments may make available those professors for whom they really have no use, possibly because of their poor teaching styles or because

of student disatisfaction. The department may be tied be contract for another year or two and so be happy to meet its
obligation to the institute by releasing this faculty member to
teach a course for free. But attempting to develop a new program through the use of an academic "foreign legion" is
extremely difficult. It leads to an unintegrated curriculum,
which is unfair to the students, and throws a wet blanket on
initial interest in a promising academic and research area.
Therefore, the new institute should be in a position to pay for
the faculty time it negotiates from the participating departments. In this way it is possible to select faculty members
who are good teachers and who are more honestly committed
to the urban program.

A further pitfall to selecting faculty is that, whether
volunteer or paid faculty are used, a new program will generally have difficulty with turnover. A faculty member available to teach core courses one semester may not be available
the next; multiple turnover may make it difficult to develop
a consistent and integrated curriculum.

Third, when faculty members must be hired jointly between the urban programs and one of the participating departments, there is often difficulty in agreeing on an acceptable
candidate. In a sense the two hiring agents have different
objectives. A person who is ideal for the institute because he
may be action-oriented or may have considerable experience in
urban management may not have the research credentials a
department desires.

Even when exceptional candidates are mutually agreed
upon, problems will inevitably arise because of intradepart-
mental competition for promotions, tenure, and pay raises.
What happens when the institute desires to reward the professor on joint appointment with tenure or a larger pay raise than
the department is prepared to accept? The institution may of
course be dealing with a small number of faculty members and
may not have many problems of comparability. The department, however, may be making decisions relating to a larger
number of faculty where comparability is extremely important.
All such problems may in time be worked out, but not easily.

Using joint appointment faculty can create significant
curriculum problems. When faculty are selected from different
departments they often do not know each other and have little

opportunity for contact. This means that the informal exchange which occurs within a department and contributes to the development of boundary lines between related courses does not take place. Even where some kind of arrangement is worked out between two cooperating professors, it is possible that neither one of them may be teaching the course the next semester, thus imposing a heavy obligation on the program director. He must insure that he is aware of arrangements made by the faculty and that a bilateral treaty between two professors is not in any way counter to what some other professors in the program may be doing.

The Student Constituency

New urban programs attract a variety of students. The student in search of relevance inevitably asks questions such as whether he can get credit for working with a street gang in the central city. Students in search of flexibility ask about the number of electives and "problems" courses available. Programs that are highly social-science oriented, and especially those governed by a committee, are not as likely to be receptive to these students as the more broadly based interdisciplinary programs represented by institutes and centers. It would not be an exaggeration to say that most of the students attracted to new urban programs may be labeled as "seekers." Some are seeking relevance, and others are seeking to run away from what they consider to be the tunnel vision of the specialized departments within which they are working.

Unfortunately, the sample of new students will also include weak students hoping to find an easy program with few requirements and few term papers. In undergraduate programs it is generally difficult to screen out these weaker students. In fact, in a pragmatic sense they may be needed to help provide the sheer numbers necessary to offer the courses essential to operating the program. At the graduate level much more control can be exercised over student selection. Fewer graduate students tend to switch departments; those who do generally have relatively good academic backgrounds which enabled them to be accepted by the other department in the first place. Obviously, a new program will attract a whole range of students having a variety of motives, some helpful and some harmful to its image. If the program quickly develops a reputation of being "easy" there will be great difficulty in recruiting the effective faculty needed to raise standards and provide a good teaching program.

Administrative problems for the faculty participating in this program will also have an impact on the students. For example, joint appointment faculty may operate with two offices, or more likely with a pooled desk in the area of the urban program and a permanent desk in their traditional department. This imposes unnecessary inconvenience on students, who bounce from department to department without finding anyone available to advise them. It is important that the program director insure that teaching faculty in the program schedule hours to meet with students. Understandably this is sometimes difficult, since the urban program faculty member has a primary commitment to his department—where decisions on his raises, promotions, and tenure will be made. Student advisement is also an administrative problem because departmental advisors often do not fully understand the purposes and methods of the urban program and may not permit students to take full benefit of its electives. A certain flow of these students is essential to enable the institute to gain the proper student load in elective courses.

Even getting exposure within the university catalogue can hamper a new program. It may take as long as two years to get into the official catalogue because of printing cutoff dates and biannual printing policies. The sole alternative is for the urban program to develop an ad hoc handout, but it may not be possible to get this information into the hands of all advisors. Even if it does, they may misinterpret it. A full-time office with a knowledgeable coordinator or director is therefore essential to the success of such an academic program. Only this kind of backup office can overcome the deficiencies of an "instant" faculty drawn from diverse places and representing different disciplines.

Further pitfalls lie in the tendency of so many urban programs to limit themselves to the social sciences. Clearly, urban problem areas such as transportation, air and water pollution, fire protection, urban law, health, and planning require some access to courses in civil engineering, law, pharmacy, health sciences, chemistry, and meteorology. Few universities have sufficient strength, however, to provide courses in the urban-related specializations in these fields. The large state universities have such programs but often are unable to develop a mechanism flexible enough to involve the science, engineering, and professional schools in the urban program. Academic tradition and professional inflexibility are as much a part of this problem as administrative difficulties. The result is that many programs are extremely limited in their scope and effectiveness.

Even where there is a sensitivity to the need to involve science, engineering, and professional schools in the urban program, other problems remain. What prerequisites should students from the urban program have to be able to take courses in these specialized areas? If waivers are granted to permit them to take these courses, will it work against their grade-point average and make it difficult for them to gain admission to graduate schools or doctoral programs? The prerequisites dilemma exists even within the social science areas. A student who will major and receive a degree in urban studies may have only four to six electives. If he wishes to take an advanced sociology course but does not have the prerequisites, it may be impossible for him to obtain the background he desires. Part of the problem is that the traditional departments have insufficient knowledge with which to evaluate the content of the urban core courses. They may, in fact, have already provided the student with a suitable knowledge of the literature to enable him to do very well in advanced elective courses. Bureaucratic advising processes and inflexible departmental sequences can frustrate the advantageous and innovative development of student programs. This is especially true in the case of sophisticated students who can anticipate the value of this background to their later education.

The Promise and the Reality

Many urban programs have been initiated as a result of the growth of urban tensions, often race-oriented. Feelings of guilt and of an institutional duty to "do something" have been triggered by endless demonstrations and civil disorders. Creation of an urban program helps salve the conscience and convince outsiders that something is being done to correct oversights.

However, universities have not been in the forefront of
institutions contributing the most to positive change in the
cities. The educational and research goals of a university are
long-term, both in process and in effect. Yet urban problems
cry out for immediate solution. Byt the time a new urban program is ready to move toward its objectives, more serious
problems may have superseded the initial disturbances that led
to the program's creation. Thus the program may labor under
the handicap of immature as well as obsolete goals. Faculty
members, even those in urban universities, do not necessarily
share the same commitment to solving these problems as
administrators. The director of the urban program may have
great difficulty "delivering" the urban faculty for research or
action programs as long as these faculty find their primary
reward through the departmental structure. All of this makes
justification of university budgets a difficult problem.

The university's involvement may in fact be viewed as
counterproductive. Students may organize rent strikes among
the poor, pressure for drug clinics throughout the city, or
disrupt the efforts of the United Fund because it is allocating
funds to the Boy Scouts instead of to the Twelfth Street
Community Action Program. This is not to say that the students are wrong in these approaches or that the city might
not profit by their challenge to older priorities. Nonetheless,
many action programs are counterproductive in terms of providing satisfying responses to the same benefactors who have
previously complained about the university's noninvolvement.

The administration's expectations may also be unrealistic.
Its support may therefore fade before research grant proposals
have been given a proper chance to develop a funding base for
the program, and before the sometimes ersatz collection of
urban courses has been refined into a comprehensive program.
Then too, they may succumb to the pressures of other governmental financial opportunities such as expanded funding for
the environmental area. Thus, faculty and administration attention may be diverted to a new thrust for an environmental
institute before the urban institute has every really had a
chance to succeed.

The first years of an urban program require substantial
support from the administration and from the faculty. If the
university is unable to guarantee this support from the begin-

ning, it would do better not to start the program. Where this kind of support exists, the program has a chance, provided it is able to attract effective leadership. A director must be able to secure support from the competing interests necessarily involved. The very structure and bureaucracy of the university is a tremendous stumbling block to the success of any interdisciplinary program. The continual threat of a turnover in top management may also work against development and success of the urban program.

Those associated with urban programs must be reconciled to the fact that they *may* in fact be just a passing fancy. On the other hand a program may, if very successful, lead to the establishment of an institute or a center with a more permanent structure. Likewise, a very successful institute or center might trigger the establishment of a school of public affairs or a college of urban affairs. Either way, those associated must be flexible. Ideally, many urban universities ought to be total urban universities where urban emphasis and efforts to apply disciplinary theory to urban problems are present throughout the curriculum, rather than in any circumscribed area or structure within the university. This option is unrealistic in the short run in many areas of the country.

Most universities will be lucky indeed to establish effectively functioning degree programs, whether led by a committee, a coordinator, or a center or institute director. Obviously, some will do a better job of this than others, and the existence of crisis may make it more likely that someone will eventually take the time to look at the serious questions of relating the academic programs to research and action. In all of these attempts the politics of university bureaucracy will be a constant companion.

15

LEADERSHIP, LEGITIMACY, AND ACADEMIC GOVERNANCE*

Homer D. Babbidge, Jr.

My interest is in the teaching-learning process *as it is institutionalized*. It may well be that the process goes on better in noninstitutionalized settings, but society has, by and large, chosen to carry out its work through institutions—church, hospital, college. Education, particularly institutionalized education, is not simply teaching and learning, however central these may be. Education is *not* a spontaneous happening. Teaching and learning, in contrast, can and do go on in every conceivable setting and in countless patterns. Education, however, is the means by which we impose on the teaching-learning process a degree of restraint, purpose, and pattern that *someone* thinks is an improvement over a random process of learning. This is basic to any discussion of academic governance, for the central issue in governance is, "who is the 'someone' who establishes purpose, pattern, and its concomitant restraints?"

*Taken from an address by Dr. Babbidge to the 1970 National Associate Conference of the Danforth Foundation.

Perhaps the first thought on governance I should offer is that it may be a highly academic—perhaps even idle—exercise to discuss academic governance, given the current mood of many of today's students. Having taken at face value the demand of students for reform in university governance, I have devoted a large part of my time and energies to encouraging a basic rethinking of the system of governance in one university. The positive response of students has been negligible. What response I have had has ranged from simple disinterest (by far the majority response) to cynical hostility to governance in any form. For whatever reason, students do not seem to want to take the subject seriously.

Simple disinterest in governance is comprehensible to me; it is something we have lived with a long time. Most students view the campus much like a hotel: They are interested in its management only when something goes wrong with room service. This widespread disinterest inspired the suggestion by Kingman Brewster that we borrow from the corporate model the practice of the management proxy. This would at least have the virtue of giving voice to the disinterested or satisfied majority.

What I find vastly more difficult to comprehend is the activist notion that institutions can be operated without a system of governance. Activists have become advocates of what someone has called "adhocracy"—the governmental dimension of "doing your own thing"—a nonsystem in which any community action is a kind of creative response to circumstance. This is an appealing but illusory notion.

Young people seem unaware of the elaborate systems required to undergird their "things" and the doing thereof—the highly formalized and elaborate systems required to produce the Volkswagen bus, the fuel that propels it, the highways over which it travels to Woodstock, the amplifying equipment without which the music would hardly qualify as a thing worth doing. And for those who do not favor Woodstock, what of the systems required to produce those seemingly essential ingredients of revolution: the mimeograph machine and the bull horn?

I would hope that students would appreciate that some system—hopefully less formal and elaborate—is required to deliver those educational resources prerequisite even to doing your own educational thing. My point is this: Even given the monumental disinterest and/or hostility that one encounters among students, some of us have a responsibility to reflect upon the problems of institutional governance. Such reflection may be more worthy of consideration than would appear at first blush. The crisis in governance that confronts our institutions of higher education may be only a foretaste of a crisis that soon will confront society at large—if it does not already. We are concerned, in our collegiate institutions, with governing free societies, knowing that the freer they are, the more difficult they may be to govern; and knowing too that if they cannot be governed, they cannot be free.

This last point deserves some elaboration, however obvious it may be to most of us. Noah Webster said in 1787:

> Many people seem to entertain an idea that liberty consists in a power to act without any control. This is more liberty than even the savages enjoy. In a free government every man binds himself to obey the public voice (or the opinions of a majority) and the whole society engages to protect each individual. In such a government a man is free and safe. But reverse the case; suppose every man to act without control or fear of punishment—every man would be free, but no man would be sure of his freedom one moment. Each would have the power of taking his neighbor's life, liberty, or property, and no man would command more than his own strength to repel the invasion.[1]

Whether or not one agrees that our larger system of governance has been called into question, few will disagree with the assertion that collegiate government faces a crisis of confidence. And it may just be that our response to the crisis we recognize might avert one we do not yet perceive.

But even if our problems do not have the significance I am hinting at, those of us in the academic world recognize that we must face our crisis on its merits. There are at least two crises wrapped up in one. The first of these is the crisis of the credibility of those who govern. The second is the crisis of the legitimacy of the system within which they govern. President Brewster of Yale has observed that we frequently confuse these; we have a regrettable tendency to place blame on men who govern rather than on the system that produces them or within which they must govern.

The two crises certainly are related. We know that weak or evil men can cause a good system of governance to fail; and we know that a bad system can frustrate the efforts of the fairest and finest of men. But the two crises deserve separate attention. What to do about them? Where to turn for solutions or, more realistically, ways to alleviate them? My inclination, for some time, has been to look to political models—in the absence of original ideas— for the possible solution to some of our institutional problems.

Modern colleges and universities (and those who populate them), rival the most comprehensive and complicated of human communities in their far-reaching involvements. You name it, and we've got it. This comes to be very important when we consider what's to be done about the governance of higher education. It is nice to say and to think that our universities cannot be all things to all people, but enough people reasonably expect enough different things of us that we may not have a choice. The appeal of Jacques Barzun strikes a sympathetic chord in all of us: Strip the universities of their involvement in nonacademic matters and return to the notion that a university is, in fact, a special or specialized institution. But, as appealing a notion as this is, I think it is unrealistic. How, in the face of human needs—to say nothing of social demands—does the college or university turn back? Which of our other institutions could or would shoulder the shifted burden of responsibility?

The higher education community, broadly defined, is so comprehensive, its goals and values so largely intangible, the measure of its successes so largely subjective, that it seems to me to require a form of governance analogous, at least in some respects, to political government. The business enterprise and its president have a profit and loss statement to gauge their success; the network and the comedian have their Nielsen ratings; and the manager of his baseball team have a won and lost record. No such indices exist for their counterparts in the academic world. We are a strangely mixed community that has great difficulty in agreeing on its goals, its values, and its priorities. It has great difficulty in agreeing even that it is a community.

But this is true of every political entity I know of, and I therefore believe that a system of governance can be devised to reconcile conflicts to the satisfaction of all but zealots. Assuming that my notion of looking to the political model has some merit, what can we learn that might be helpful with the two crises of confidence I've identified: the credibility of governors and the legitimacy of the system of governance?

The first is, in my judgment, the easier of the two to cope with. Let me say a word or two about the university presidency by way of suggesting a "political" device for establishing credibility. From the president's point of view— to say nothing for the moment of the interests of the institution—it becomes increasingly important to know whether or not he enjoys some degree of general support for his continuation in office. He will know quickly enough, of course, if his board of trustees desire him to leave. But I am thinking of those major constituencies without whose general approval he obviously cannot lead, and which do not enjoy the straightforward relationship with him that the governing board does.

Two basic political approaches to this problem can be identified at once. The first—what might be called the American approach—would be the election or appointment for terms in office. Depending on how one resolves the contending claims of stability and continuity on the one hand, and responsiveness and popularity on the other, these terms could be for two, four, six, or even ten years. But given the nature and rate of change in our society, some argument could be made for a term of four years or even less. One has only to recall the shift in popular support for a recent U.S. President to realize that the last four years in office can be the most difficult.

But more intriguing to me is the other obvious major political analogy—the parliamentary approach. It seems to me inherently more congenial to the academic community, and I am reasonably confident that its major shortcoming— the danger of a lack of continuity in leadership—would be to some extent self-controlling in an academic community. Most important to me, however, is the recognition that crisis can occur suddenly and frequently in the modern university, and a crisis of confidence can arise with only a moment's notice. And I see great advantages to both institution and president in being able to make the assessment reflected in a vote of confidence.

The essential points seem to be these: The modern university president must have more authority than he now has if he is to lead in any real sense; this authority cannot effectively be bestowed upon him solely by a traditional governing board (in the manner of the colonial governor), nor can it be extracted from those who now share authority with him; he can only earn it or win it, and he can only hold it and exercise it so long as he enjoys the confidence of those to be led or their representatives, and he can enjoy that authority only if he is ready to put it on the line. In this context, a single legislative body would help too, rather than separate student and faculty senates. It would take the chief executive out of the tie-breaking, referee role. It would force the community itself to reconcile differences.

The second crisis of confidence that centers on the legitimacy of our systems of institutional governance is of a greater order of magnitude. The problem, of course, is how to devise a system of governance the decisions and policies of which will be respected.

We hear much talk these days about more student involvement in government, about greater representation in policy councils, and about redistribution of power. Our campus communities are not seamless wholes, as it turns out, but fragmented communities populated by factions and characterized by contention for power.

I would remind you, looking to political history, that this is not a unique situation in American life. James Madison wrote in 1787 that "the most common and durable source of factions has been the various and unequal distribution of property [or in twentieth-century terms, power]. Those who hold and those who are without property have formed distinct interests in society. . . . The causes of faction," he concluded, "cannot be removed and relief is only to be sought in the means of controlling its effects."[2]

Factionalism in our institutions of higher education cannot be eliminated. It is probably a normal, even inevitable condition. But responsible leadership in higher education will seek, as Madison did, "a well constructed union" to "break and control the violence of faction."

And it is partly because I see our situation in higher educational institutions as approximately analogous to the confusion and contention that characterized American political life in 1787 that I have flirted with the notion of the Constitutional Convention as a device for acting out the frustrations and hostilities, for airing the contending views of factions within our institution. The Constitutional Convention, as I see it, is a full-scale, fundamental reassessment of basic goals and needs of our institutions, and the construction of a charter and structure of government designed to command respect and establish authority.

A colleague of mine has phrased the question as follows:

> The problem is: how to create a machinery of governance that commands the respect of the members of the university community so that the decisions produced by the workings of that machinery are recognized as legitimate, authoritative, and deserving of compliance, even if one does not agree that those are the right decisions. The point is fundamental. In a pluralistic community it is futile to expect that there will be consensus on the quality of the decisions that are made; it is to be taken for granted and indeed it is to be hoped that people will disagree on what should be done or on what should have been done. It is hard to imagine a democratic society, especially in time of radical change, that will be free of disagreement and disputation. The condition for the functioning of a free society is not the existence of consensus but a willingness on the part of people to accept as binding on them the outcome of the decision-making process. The question then becomes: what sort of decision-making process, what sort of system of governance can elicit this kind of consent and compliance?[3]

It is my contention that an issue of the magnitude that confronts us will not be resolved simply by adding a student to the board of trustees or—as James Perkins has observed—by changing the table of organization. A truly fundamental reappraisal, a "constitutional convention," is called for—a new Mayflower Compact, if you will.

Some institutions have been forced to this kind of reappraisal under extreme pressures; others—like Toronto—have

repaired the roof before the rain came. More of us should try
it. The alternative might be a university so embroiled in conflict that it ceases to be a university at all, or possibly a coercive
and repressive regime, imposed from above, in which all segments of the university community, unable to compose their
differences, must live by the edicts of what is, in effect, an
occupying power.

I find from experience that proposing such a reappraisal
can have a distinctly unsettling effect upon many people, and
not just those with a clear, vested interest in things as they are.
The idea of defining goals and purpose—perhaps especially
in a comprehensive, public institution—is mind-boggling. We
come face-to-face with John Gardner's observation:

> Sometimes institutions are simply the sum of the histori-
> cal accidents that have happened to them. Like the sand
> dunes in the desert, they are shaped by influences but
> not by purposes. Or, to put the matter more accurately,
> like our sprawling and ugly metropolitan centers, they
> are the unintended consequences of millions of frag-
> mented purposes.[4]

But I have to say to our university community that if
we cannot agree on a constitution for the University of Connecticut, we will be conceding that we do not know what it
is we are or seek to be; and that if the kind of constitution we
would write would be unacceptable to the people of the state,
then we are currently taking their money under false pre-
tenses.

Such a reassessment is troubling, too, because it forces
us to come to grips with unpleasant realities. Who, after all,
owns the institution? Who is entitled to participate in formulating its goals and values? We come quickly to a realization
that the campus is an incomplete community if only because
it doesn't raise its own revenues; that has profound significance
in talk of self-government. An hour's reflection requires that
we dispel the notion that the college is for the students and
therefore belongs to them. We find we have some unstated
purposes, the articulation of which would invite dispute; and
we have some purposes, now unfashionable, that require new
jurisdictions.

All this is made infinitely more trying because of the

atmosphere in which these matters must be debated. There are even those who want to change the goals and purposes of educational institutions so radically that they would no longer fit what I would regard as a reasonable definition of education. Levels of trust are low. The healthy skepticism we have tried to develop in the young has soured to cynicism. Adults are reacting as though reading from a student-written scenario.

Professor Leslie Lipson has listed seven deadly sins of our time. There is not one on which I would anticipate serious disagreement between the young and old in a college or university setting. I do not know a professor or administrator who is not against those sins. So what are we fighting over, the young and old of the educational world? Pace, tempo, style, method, credit? Certainly these should not divide an enlightened community to the brink of hostility and violence. Indeed, they should not keep us from creating a suitable form of government. But they may. And it may be that the biggest hurdle to sound university governance is the need for common readiness to recognize our need for one another.

It is not a clash of virtue and vice that besets our campuses and our society today. Basically good people are at the throats of other basically good people. People are pressing their separate visions of truth to the exclusion of all others. And until we come to our senses and decide that if we are to be a community, if we are to be parties to a new educational compact, we are going to have to rid ourselves of the sin of moral and intellectual arrogance—until that time, the resolution of issues of governance is going to be next to impossible. My political model, or anybody else's model, will be worthless without a widespread desire to resolve, rather than accentuate, the differences that divide men.

One is reminded of a notion that emerged from medieval rabbinical scholarship and later caught the fancy of St. Bonaventure in a famous Easter Day sermon: the notion of the four daughters of God. The four daughters of God were, of course, all virtues: Righteousness, Peace, Mercy, and Truth. They should, in all probability, have regarded themselves as equals, but in fact they fell to quarreling and squabbling, each asserting her primacy. Who, short of God Himself, could resolve the competing claims of Righteousness and Peace and Mercy and Truth?

And these virtues are, today, in fact making competing claims upon us. Shall righteousness take precedence over peace? Shall peace and mercy be sought at the price of truth and righteousness? These, it seems to me, are precisely the quarrels that test our society today and frustrate our sense of common purpose. In the Judeo-Christian tradition, of course, the introduction of a Savior is required to resolve the squabbling among the virtues. But I would submit that for those who believe that such a Savior has arrived, for those who believe He is yet to come, and for those who believe He will never come, there is a fifth virtue, the introduction of which we mortals can effect and which holds promise of reconciling the others. That virtue is humility. I mean by humility simply the readiness to acknowledge in the face of an awesome and mysterious universe, in which "a dead, blind wall butts all inquiring heads at last," the possibility of error and the possibility that virtue may reside in a truth other than our own and in persons other than ourselves. With a little such humility scattered around, we might just find the common cause so necessary to governance in a free society. We might yet see the day when, in the words of Psalm 22:

> Mercy and Truth are met together;
> Righteousness and Peace have kissed each other.

NOTES

1. Noah Webster, "An Examination into the Leading Principles of the Federal Constitution Proposed by the Late Convention Held at Philadelphia," 1787.

2. James Madison, *The Federalist* (New York: The Heritage Press, 1945), p. 57.

3. Albert Cohen, Chairman, Commission on University Governance, University of Connecticut, in a letter to Homer D. Babbidge, Jr., 1970.

4. John Gardner at inauguration of James Perkins as president of Cornell University, October 4, 1963.

16

MINORITY FACULTY RECRUITMENT

Thomas P. Murphy

The problems of establishing an urban university commitment can be categorized in terms of the varying degrees of lead time needed to realize the objectives implicit in such a major decision. Some objectives, such as the establishment of urban committees to prepare the way for future action, may be achieved fairly swiftly. Such short-term objectives are often characterized by relatively few decision points, modest demands upon finances, and a high ratio of positive to negative returns for affected faculty and administrators. Other objectives may take longer to achieve because of the greater difficulties involved.

Colleges and universities are finding numerous obstacles to the recruitment of minority staff members. These obstacles are difficult to overcome because even though present laws do not leave many decisions to the academic hierarchy, great problems still remain in the budgetary and "affirmative action" areas. Discrimination may be practiced only as in pre-civil rights times, or according to a more subtle "institutional" pattern. Either way, minorities often find themselves on the

losing side of a competition with candidates from the "old
school" channels of advancement. The acceptability of a person viewed as a potential colleague is perhaps the key to the
concern presently circulating in academic bastions over so-
called hiring quotas.

Most hiring quotas are actually hiring consideration
quotas, which seek to propel universities in the direction of
affirmative action. Nevertheless, older faculty members often
see their security threatened by moves to "blanket in" new
members. Tenure protects jobs, but not the folkways of conducting the business of higher education. Therefore, as yes-
terday's moderately opprobrious multi-discipline departments
are being followed by today's emphasis upon equal opportunity hiring, many tradition-bound academicians have fallen
into a state of shock. And, as many have learned in recent
times, change-induced shock is usually alleviated through
individual and collective resistance.

In fact, a 1972 survey of 471 college professors by Seymour Martin Lipset and Everett Ladd, Jr., revealed that a
majority did not believe that "a large share of future vacancies" should be set aside for "blacks, Chicanos, and women
. . . until they are proportionately represented."[1] Even the
intensity-of-belief indications are somewhat surprising:

strongly agree	3.3%
agree, with reservations	26.0
agree, no indication	16.8
uncertain	3.9
disagree, no indication	42.9
disagree, with reservations	7.2
strongly disagree	6.8

Part of the difficulty inherent in retooling higher education to meet the challenges of the cities, including the new
equal opportunity standards, is the incomparable strength of
tradition underlying university life. The historic origins of the
university in German scholarship and Yankee theologic and
philosophic education for children of the rich are important
to a full understanding of faculty concern that "high academic standards" not be lost in the scramble to integrate
minorities into the campus community. It is also important

to realize that the success of women's colleges in providing quality education to the largest minority and teaching employment to many graduates is a factor in the late-blooming rebellion for women's rights on campuses across the country.

Had the major universities begun their days as service institutions dedicated to the application of knowledge to societal problems, there would now be little point in discussing adaptations to urban populations and urban needs. Such an orientation would be an integral part of university culture. This is the paradox of American education: The constant dedication to scholarship that has made our citizenry second to none in educational level has at the same time led to an institutional inflexibility in universities in the most future-oriented of all nations. Thus, in addition to the burden of faculty resistance to change, minority hiring must also withstand the weight of critics' charges that equal opportunity in hiring must, by virtue of the disadvantaged nature of many minority backgrounds, necessarily be a threat to university scholarship.

Discrimination as Institutional Neurosis

In a very real way, hiring discrimination is a deeply ingrained dysfunction of the university's "nervous system." No stated policy of exclusion may exist, but the communications network will invariably receive and deliver messages according to a biased perception of the immediate needs of the system. The result—hiring discrimination—will, in fact, prove harmful to institutional needs, whether legal and financial as in the need to adhere to civil rights legislation and federal grant specifications, or based upon internal direction as with the decision to be an urban university.

The hallmark of institutionalized discrimination is the absence of *personal* blame and, hence, the futility of setting up sanctions directed at individuals. The institution and the applicant are placed in jeopardy by the actions or omissions of committee members. No one person at the departmental level is responsible for ensuring that just action is taken. Consequently, equal opportunity is often provided *after* the fact of discrimination rather than before. There are problems even when there is no overt and deliberate discrimination by any

of the administrators or faculty involved in the hiring process. Departmental procedures, the sources of information, the
low level of minority involvement on the appropriate committees, the word-of-mouth advertising of vacancies, the frequent
absence of clear criteria for hiring, and even the overemphasis
on what is termed merit and quality in hiring can all serve to
work against minority applicants just as effectively as a deliberate policy of discrimination.

In addition, conscious discrimination continues against
minority applicants by clusters of faculty members. In the
recruiting process for college and university jobs, the departments have the primary responsibility. Yet a department
usually consists of from only three to thirty faculty members;
thus, a small group is making a decision with institution-wide
implications. Within the department, the process is dominated by the senior faculty, generally white males, who already have tenure. Since few minority faculty members have
this status, the equity of the process is dependent upon the
values of these senior members. Although dramatic strides
have been made in reducing the number of cases of discrimination, this practice still continues in some departments of
some colleges and universities.

But consider the standard recruiting process, and the
opportunities it offers for institutional discrimination. Generally, the chairman in a small department (or a committee
in a large department) will be assigned the job of finding and
screening applicants for a faculty vacancy. This involves a
number of procedures. First, there is a file of applicants who
have already sent their vitae for consideration. These persons
often do so on the advice of their dissertation advisors or other
faculty members at the institution where they are securing
their doctorate. More than any other group, it is the faculty
at similarly ranked schools who have connections with members of the department seeking applicants. This is not unique
to faculty hiring; in most professional fields there is a serious
concern for the quality of the person being hired and for the
values that the profession and its subgroups wish to maintain.
Yet the vitae and the two-day recruiting interview do not
always provide sufficient data. Much reliance is therefore
placed on letters of reference and phone conversations, where

faculty members who know the student can say what they really think.

Because of the sensitivity of the hiring process, this procedure also works in reverse. The committee members or the department chairman with a position to fill will call or write faculty members of other institutions and ask them to refer qualified applicants. Even when unsolicited vitae are received, the natural reflex of the recruiting committee is to analyze the reference list and the applicant's school in an effort to determine which colleague may know the applicant. This again is used as a screening mechanism to find out whether a candidate is likely to meet the standards of the professional group and, therefore, be worth an interview.

All of these procedures seem quite reasonable, but the problem is that until very recently they have represented a closed recruitment system. This is more true for blacks than for women. Until recently, most black graduate students were attending black schools. If their professors had no personal contacts with a university's faculty, then reference checks would probably not be made by that school. Likewise, few of the black faculty members at the black colleges were regular members of the referral system, which was generally built around the alma mater of key faculty members at major universities. Faculty obsession with taking a known quantity over an unknown quantity has meant that the black applicant just would not be invited for an interview, if there were qualified white candidates sponsored by prestigious colleagues.

To some extent, this process has involved an exchange economy. Senior professors at major institutions owe part of their reputations to having produced outstanding students, yet these students gain their reputations by being placed in those institutions where they receive good professional exposure and command a good letterhead when sending out articles and books for publication. This placement affects even the chances of younger faculty being selected to give papers at the annual meetings of their professional associations. Such a channeling process can work by design only if the accepting institution receives a quid pro quo from benefiting faculty at the home institution. With the exception of Howard University, black institutions have not played the same game; as a result, most black students have been unfairly excluded from participation in this kind of system. Women have at least benefited from a larger exposure to faculty at prestige schools, and may often have better "pedigrees" than men.[2]

The only effective way to counter this type of institutional racism is with institutional approaches. Merely establishing a special assistant to the chancellor or president for equal employment opportunity is not sufficient. Most universities have already taken this approach, and it is not a pervasive enough commitment to reverse institutional racism.

Top management influence can speed up the development of counterprocedures. If, for example, tradition-bound departments are told that preference in filling faculty vacancies will be given those departments that hire minority specialists who can also be used in the urban program, then the number of black, Chicano, and female urban geographers, urban economists, and urban sociologists hired will progressively increase. This is a way of distributing positions to the traditional departments in a purposeful manner, one based upon an "effort" standard, while at the same time using these positions to strengthen the developing urban involvement and minority recruitment programs.

If, on the other hand, minority positions were given outright to the university's urban program, the departments would collectively react by using their considerable political acumen and strategic committee positions to reduce that program's budget and slow up promotion of its faculty. They could, in fact, limit the kind of sociologists, geographers, and economists the university could hire because the most qualified people in interdisciplinary fields tend to insist upon a regular faculty appointment along with their center or institute appointment.

When some top administrators have pressed the case for expanding the number of minority faculty members, they have met resistance on the basis of what have been termed arguments of quality. Those resisting have taken the position that they are being asked to hire minority faculty members who are unqualified just to meet an artificial quota. They argue that in the long run this will reduce the quality of education being received by all the students, including minority students.

There are some legitimate problems in this regard. If persons are hired who cannot meet existing quality standards, bad feelings will later ensue when such persons come due for promotion or tenure. Some universities have taken this problem very seriously and, in hiring minority faculty members who may not have had the publication record of some other applicants, have arranged for reduced teaching loads to assist them in demonstrating during a trial period their ability to do responsible research and write for publication. This kind of top management commitment is essential if any real breakthroughs are to be made in conservative-minded institutions.

In some cases, all that is necessary is to break the word-of-mouth system and make it possible for more minority members to learn about the vacancies. This can be done through such simple expedients as placing notices in the journal of the American Association of University Professors and in the professional journal of the discipline involved. Some prestige universities have in the past looked down on this process as advertising—an activity beneath their dignity. Now several professions (such as sociology) have passed resolutions at their annual conferences calling upon all departments to cooperate in opening up the hiring process by advertising vacancies in the association newsletter. A number of leading universities have adopted this as general policy to demonstrate their support for new modes of faculty recruitment. As a result, the lesser-known institutions have lost all reason to avoid advertising on the basis that it would tend to demean their less prestigious institutions and make it more difficult to raise their relative ranking.

The Need for Minority Faculty

Dramatic changes occurred in the 1960s in the racial composition of the student body of most major universities. According to a report of the Carnegie Commission, from 1964 to 1970 alone "the number of black students enrolled in institutions of higher education more than doubled, rising from 234,000 to 522,000."[3] This fantastic increase coincided with the adoption of major civil rights legislation, successful demonstrations led by Martin Luther King and others, and the traumatic urban riots.

As Table 16–1 shows, these increases were not in primarily black colleges for the 1964–68 period. In fact, while the black colleges had a relatively moderate increase in stu-

Table 16-1
Growth in Black Higher Education Student Body by
Type of Institution 1964-68

	1964 (fall)	1968 (fall)	Change, 1964-68 number	Change, 1964-68 percent
Total enrollment	4,643	6,801	2,158 ·	46
total black enrollment	234	434	200	85
percent of total enrollment	5	6	N/A	N/A
Enrollment in predominantly black colleges	120	156	36	30
percent of all blacks in college	51	36	N/A	N/A
Enrollment in other colleges	114	278	164	144
percent of all blacks in college	49	64	N/A	N/A

N/A—not applicable

SOURCE: U.S. Department of Labor, Bureau of Labor Statistics; U.S. Department of Commerce, Bureau of the Census; U.S. Department of Health, Education, and Welfare, Office of Education, as quoted in Carnegie Commission on Higher Education, *From Isolation to Mainstream*, February 1971, p. 14.

dents, there was a substantial shift away from dependence on black colleges. In 1964, black colleges enrolled 52 percent of black college students; by 1970, this figure had dropped to 28 percent. Clearly the predominantly white institutions of higher learning were recruiting black students and, through a variety of liberalized admissions policies, were making it possible for more blacks to attend college. Similar but less striking gains were made by Mexican-Americans and Puerto Ricans. Despite these great gains, there is room for improvement. In 1970, the 522,000 black students attending institutions of higher education represented 21 percent of the black population aged 18 to 21, whereas 46 percent of whites in that age category were attending college.[4]

Increased student enrollment led to substantial increases

in the size of college and university faculties as well. However, the gains scored by minority students in increasing their percentage of the student body were not matched by the hiring of increased percentages of minority faculty members. An urban university must make higher education opportunities available to its young people regardless of racial, cultural, or socioeconomic background; and, no less important, special efforts must be made to increase the number of minority faculty members at the institutions providing the education.

The case of increased participation of black and other minority faculty members should be self-evident. An institution attempting to provide comprehensive education could not presume to do so without faculty representatives from all kinds of sociocultural backgrounds. Philosophy notwithstanding, there are even more pressing reasons to increase minority faculty participation. Increasing the number of minority students attending college is an advance for society, but it will be a pyrrhic victory if it is not accompanied by awareness of and sensitivity to the special problems these students have.

The dropout rate of minority college students is extremely high. Numerous studies have attributed this to inferior secondary school backgrounds, a problem not confined to the rural South. The fact is that in any rising socioeconomic group there will be cultural disadvantages. Because parents have not experienced college or the benefits of middle-class living, their children have not had the same kind of intellectual support and motivating environments available to students from families already in the mainstream. Such students have a special need for faculty understanding and counsel and for access to persons in authority with whom they can identify. Experience has shown that this is best accomplished where faculty members are available who can identify with the student and convey to him a feeling that someone cares how well he does. Lack of such identity may explain in part why white counselors working with minority students often report cultural barriers. The sociologists' concept of role models is also important. Seeing minority faculty members treated as equals by their white colleagues helps encourage the students to pursue their work. On the other hand, if minority students feel that they will be discriminated against in school or that having a dgree will not make any difference in job opportunities, then, obviously, the student will not be motivated to achieve a quality education.

Admitting larger numbers of minority students while sustaining an extraordinarily high percentage of dropouts or academic suspensions can create a good deal of campus unrest, and has already caused faculty and administrators to recognize the inadequacy of their assumptions concerning the similarity of students' social and intellectual objectives as well as cultural values. Asa Knowles, the president of Northeastern University, commented in 1971:

> The demands of minority groups over the past five or six years racially have altered what has been called the "single environment" campus. Where there are members of minority-group students—black, Mexican-American, Puerto Rican, etc., the lines usually are drawn distinctively. Most black students serve as a good example of this trend. . . . They want courses in black art, history and culture as well as separate physical facilities on the campus. They want more blacks in each freshman class and more black teachers, counselors and administrators.[5]

Discrimination against racial minorities other than blacks presents a rather mixed picture. Orientals, for example, are represented on faculties at slightly higher percentages than their proportion of the general or college student populations would suggest. Indians, Puerto Ricans, Cubans, and Mexican-Americans are under-represented. Yet all of these groups tend to be concentrated in certain geographic areas: Cubans are a substantial proportion of the Miami area population, as are Puerto Ricans in New York, and both Indians and Mexican-Americans in the southwest, with pockets of these groups in other areas. These concentrations are such that national statistics on Ph.D. supply would be misleading. Obviously, special efforts should be made in areas where such minorities congregate and constitute a significant proportion of the college student body.

In the early years, few schools anticipated the development of racial demands, and, thus, schools are now finding that they are unprepared to raise the percentage of minority faculty or to know how best to respond to the separatist pro-

posals of the students. As suggested in Chapter 11, the long-
term interests of minority students may not be scored by yield-
ing to all these demands.

Supply Barriers to Recruiting Minority Faculty

Some substantial barriers exist to increasing the numbers of
minority faculty members. Data on the distribution of
degrees and students by minority group are not as systematic
and complete as desired. However, there are some helpful
data inputs. Table 16–2 reflects the 1969 racial distribution
of American college faculty. The "other" category includes
Spanish-surnamed, American Indian, Eskimo, and other
minority group faculty.

Table 16-2
American College Faculty by Race and Sex—1969

	All institutions			*In two-year colleges*		
	men	*women*	*total*	*men*	*women*	*total*
White	96.6%	94.7%	96.3%	99.1%	96.7%	98.4%
Black	1.8	3.9	2.2	0.5	1.4	0.7
Oriental	1.3	1.1	1.3	0.2	1.4	0.5
Other	0.3	0.3	0.3	0.2	0.5	0.3

	In four-year colleges			*In universities*		
	men	*women*	*total*	*men*	*women*	*total*
White	94.2%	91.3%	93.5%	97.7%	97.7%	97.2%
Black	4.2	7.4	5.0	0.4	1.0	0.5
Oriental	1.2	0.9	1.2	1.6	1.0	1.6
Other	0.4	0.3	0.4	0.3	0.2	0.3

SOURCE: Alan E. Bayer, *College and University Faculty: A Statistical
Description,* American Council on Education, Research Report, November
5, 1970, p. 12.

In a survey taken for a Ford Foundation project dedicated to increasing the number of black Ph.D.s, it was concluded that 1 percent of Ph.D.s earned in America are held
by blacks. Table 16–3 indicates the way in which a sample
of 1,096 was employed:

Table 16-3
Employment of Black Doctorates

Employment	Male no.	Male percent	Female no.	Female percent	Total no.	Total percent
College and university	729	84.8	208	88.9	937	85.4
Government	47	5.4	11	4.7	58	5.3
Social agencies	42	4.9	11	4.7	53	4.8
Industry	28	3.2	1	0.4	29	2.7
Other*	16	1.8	3	1.2	19	1.8
Total	862	100.0	234	99.9	1,096	100.0

*Includes retired and self-employed persons.
SOURCE: James W. Bryant, "A Survey of Black American Doctorates," Ford Foundation, Division of Education and Research, September 5, 1969, p. 8.

Of the black Ph.D.s sampled, 28.6 percent had received their Ph.D. in education and 26.3 percent in the social sciences. This survey also indicated that 80 percent of the black Ph.D.s were male. Comparing that data with a HEW statistical summary of doctorates earned between 1960 and 1971, the over-concentration of education degrees becomes apparent. During the ten-year period black and white women accounted for 13.8 percent of all Ph.D.s in the biological sciences and 19.8 percent of all those in education. Seventeen percent of all men and 29 percent of all women receiving doctorates in this time period took them in education. The comparable numbers for blacks alone as reported in the Ford survey (which covered a longer period of time) were 26.4 for males and 36.3 percent for females.[6]

After allowing for the heavy emphasis on black doctorates in education, as well as the intense competition from government, the difficulty of finding large numbers of qualified blacks for colleges is apparent. One of the best sources of such candidates is the black college. But even recruiting black faculty from black colleges may not be as easy as it sounds. As Table 16-4 indicates, only 26.8 percent of the faculty at the major black four-year colleges have a doctoral degree. Obviously, however, this is where the greatest number of currently active black faculty members are located. It is conceivably possible for major universities and a few other schools to offer raises substantial enough to lure such faculty members away, thereby weakening the black colleges. But this would seem to undermine the broader social objectives of improving education for all black students. Nevertheless, the marketplace being what it is, resisting these pressures is exceedingly difficult.

Table 16–4
Characteristics of Faculty at 67 Black Four-Year Colleges

	Number	Average percent per institution
Sex		
men*	4,590	63.7
women*	2,619	36.7
Status		
full-time	6,296	85.9
part-time	1,035	14.1
Highest degree earned		
doctorate	1,903	26.8
master's	4,284	60.3
bachelor's	563	7.9
professional	351	4.9

*For 66 institutions. One institution did not classify by sex, so total by sex is 7,209 and total faculty is 7,321.
SOURCE: Compiled by the staff of the Carnegie Commission on Higher Education from Otis H. Singletary, ed., *American Universities and Colleges,* 10th ed. (Washington, D.C.: American Council on Education, 1968), and presented in Carnegie Commission on Higher Education, *From Isolation to Mainstream,* February 1971, p. 62.

Some of the young blacks coming up through the doctorate channels will fill in behind those retiring, and the net effect will be an increase in the number of black faculty members. A 1971 survey indicated that between 1947 and 1969 the number of black doctorates increased from less than 381 to 2,280, which matches the sevenfold increase in black faculty at white schools during that period. The battle is not yet won, however, because the proportion of black doctorate-holders from 1964 to 1968 has remained stable at less than 1 percent of the total doctorates awarded.[7]

In 1971, David Rafky reported a survey involving 699 black faculty members working at 184 non-southern white colleges, which represented from 75 to 90 percent of such faculty. The survey used a comparison group of 399 whites from 300 colleges. Twenty-eight percent of the black faculty were women, compared to 18 percent of the white faculty. Rafky reached the following conclusions:

1. Seventy percent of the whites and 40 percent of the blacks had doctorates.

2. "Black doctorates are primarily employed by high-quality *public* colleges and universities."

3. "Low-quality schools apply different standards to whites and blacks. Of the blacks at these schools, 42 percent hold doctorates, compared to 68 percent of the whites. . . . This suggests that it is somewhat easier for blacks with limited credentials to obtain jobs at private high-quality schools than for whites and a great deal easier at low-quality schools. . . ."

4. "Although the whites are 'better' qualified than the blacks, the blacks are more likely to be at elite colleges and universities. Still, they remain in the lower ranks more often untenured. . . ."

5. "Older blacks are in better schools than their white counterparts. This is true even though blacks at all age levels publish less than whites. . . ."

6. "Of 554 black faculty members, 8 percent stated that difficulty in finding their present job was caused by racial discrimination. . . ."

7. "Blacks generally are not put at a disadvantage by the current methods used to obtain knowledge about positions. In fact, they (especially older blacks) seem to be sought out more than white faculty. But this tends to put at a disadvantage blacks who are not 'visible' and who do not participate in the academic grapevine. . . ."

8. "Blacks with the doctorate from high-quality schools who have published report jobs by invitation almost four times as often as whites with the same excellent credentials. . . ."

9. In terms of unsolicited job offers, whites reported 1.5 offers a year and blacks 3.1.[8]

All of these findings are consistent with the fact that most major institutions are aggressively recruiting black faculty, but that there is a shortage of black faculty in some specializations. The desire for quality means that those most in demand are already on the major campuses receiving their degree from prestige universities. The difficulty experienced by some blacks from the lower-quality schools is related to this concern for quality. Another inhibiting factor is the fact that an attempt to remove a black faculty member has such a high potential of becoming a cause célèbre that many faculty and administrators exercise extraordinary caution in hiring minority faculty.

Reviewing statistical reports that show an increase in minority faculty members can be misleading. A number of institutions have made dramatic percentage increases working from a very small base; on analysis, these increases have not turned out to indicate any drastic change in the procedures of the traditional departments. Many institutions have established Afro-American, or black studies, programs, and have thus created a number of faculty positions. Invariably, these have gone to black faculty members who have often been unable to secure joint appointments with the traditional departments. Likewise, numerous universities have been involved with the federal model cities and war-on-poverty programs and in the course of this involvement have used grant money to hire black professionals and semi-professionals. This practice has often led to misleading statistical reports. In their zeal to show progress, some administrators have listed grant-supported administrative positions with minority group incumbents as faculty positions.

Even some departments with a long record of hiring minority faculty members are not yet really open departments. For example, although the sociology department at one of the most prestigious universities in the nation has consistently had a number of black faculty members, this department has consistently used these faculty members only to teach courses on the sociology of race. This means that even a field as important to urban affairs and as popular in black colleges as sociology may, in fact, not have a large supply of qualified minority faculty members in other specializations in which potential growth may be the greatest. Further, the pigeon-holing of a faculty member in a narrow field generally leads to his publishing only in that field, thus when a vacancy occurs in a more general specialization he is unable to qualify either on the basis of teaching experience or of research publications in that field.

The U.S. Office of Civil Rights compiled data in the fall of 1970 on black enrollment in graduate and professional schools. The survey indicates that in comparison with a 1968 survey there had been an improvement from the "less than 2 percent of graduate enrollment at leading predominantly white institutions."[9] For example, the survey showed that the black proportions at Berkeley, Harvard, and Yale ranged in 1970 from 4.1 to 5.5 percent. These institutions had made special efforts to enroll blacks and because of their prestige were presumably more successful at this than were other institutions. This suggests that approximately 3 to 4 percent of present graduate and professional school students are black. More aggressive recruiting of minority doctoral candidates must be undertaken. Otherwise, it will be a long time before this production level will provide either an adequate supply of minority faculty to meet current quotas and goals or to meet the needs of the large number of black students now starting college.

Increased numbers of black graduate students represent a recent phenomenon. Because of the normal lag in securing a doctoral degree, few of these new minority students are yet qualified for major university faculties. From a proportionate standpoint, there are fewer qualified black than white faculty members available for any particular vacancy. This problem is especially acute in some fields, since black students are not equally distributed by discipline or geographic region in the nation.

Until only recently, most black students were in black colleges, where they have been hampered by the fact that the financial condition has been such that they have been unable to afford the facilities and graduate programs necessary in many specializations. The only comprehensive black university in the country has been Howard University, and it certainly could not carry alone the burden of producing all the black specialists needed, especially when so many educational, governmental, and business organizations have suddenly opened their doors and sought persons with such qualifications.

Sex Discrimination

Another reason that the pressures to hire minority faculty members have posed problems for some schools is that these pressures have become greatest at the very time when the same schools are being urged to increase the number of women on their faculties and when state universities are trying to hold down their budgets. As indicated earlier, just as there have been black colleges there have also been a large number of women's colleges. The difference, however, is that many of the women's colleges are prestigious, and in fact, their faculties have generally included men. In addition, whereas in some places their number was small and state universities admitted more, women were never locked out of major universities in the sense that blacks were. As a consequence, women have been part of major faculties for a longer period of time than blacks have, but were never hired in numbers anywhere proportionate to either the percentage of the student body that was female or the percentage of females holding degrees in the fields in question. The pressures for equal treatment of minorities have facilitated more aggressive demands by women's groups for similar affirmative action programs.

Dr. Alice Rossi points out that it would be erroneous to link the two movements as cause and effect. She argues that "the changed shape of the female labor force" (the change began in 1940) led to the women's movement and demands in the employment field.[10] Her reasoning is that while the work pattern of most women was *prior* to marriage or *until* children arrived, organized demands were not feasible. When women became a large and permanent portion of the work force, there was both an interest in and a basis for making organized demands.

These demands have, of course, dealt with the concerns

of senior women faculty who have the greatest investment in the profession. Therefore, attention has been paid to hiring as well as to other employment conditions. For example, whereas women earned only 11.6 percent of the Ph.D.s from 1960 to 1969, they constituted 23 percent of higher education faculties. This helps to account for the disproportionate number of women at the instructor and assistant professor levels. However, it does not explain the low proportions of women at the professor levels, especially in prestige universities. For example, in 1960, women constituted 9.9 percent of the faculty of 18 leading universities but 3.7 percent of the professors; 6.6 percent of the eight institutions with the largest endowments but 2.6 percent of the professors; and 11.1 percent at the 10 institutions with the largest enrollments but 4.3 percent of the professors.[11]

The new sensitivity to hiring under-represented groups has been developing at the same time as massive social and cultural changes leading to greater independence for women. For many years the assumption was that a woman who was teaching was either married and thus not the main support of a family, or was single and did not have the same family responsibilities as a man. The principle of equal pay for equal work was not applied to female faculty.

Most universities had nepotism regulations or policies so that a husband and wife were precluded from being on the same faculty. This often meant that while the husband was hired at the state university, the wife had to go to a nearby junior college or women's college, if either existed. Now, pressured by the HEW regulations, increasing numbers of institutions are relaxing their nepotism requirements.

Further, the change in life styles facilitating women's mobility to accept academic positions has made these considerations totally inappropriate. However, college and universities still discriminate against women not only in terms of the number hired, but also in the salaries they are paid, in the rank at which they are hired, in granting of tenure, and in promotions. All of these traditional practices must be changed.

With the new stress on interest group organization in our society, professional women have started to organize to increase their number on faculties, improve their level of participation in departmental matters and committee work, and demand equity in salary. At least three kinds of groups have developed. Some professional organizations such as the American Anthropological Association, the American Historical Association, American Physical Society, American Psychological Association, American Political Science Association, American Sociological Association, Association of American Law Schools, and the American Society for Public Administration have established official committees, subcommittees, and task forces on the status of women.

In addition, professional women in some disciplines, such as anthropology, history, psychology, political science, and sociology, have organized women's caucuses independent of the official organization. These groups collect data resumés on women in their profession and also hold panels at national meetings to discuss specific problems of women in their profession. The caucuses pressure for more openness in hiring women on the prestigious faculties, and more opportunity to participate in substantive panels of the national professional association, as well as more opportunity to publish in professional journals.

Cross-disciplinary groups have also emerged both on the campus and on a statewide basis. For example, there is a University of Michigan Commission for Women, a University of California-Berkeley League of Academic Women, and a University of Wisconsin Coordinating Council of Women in Higher Education. Rhode Island Women Educators is a statewide organization. National women's groups such as the Women's Equity Action League (WEAL) and the National Organization of Women (NOW) are also working to improve the status of women in academic life.

Until recently, a frequent administrative response to pressures for greater advancement for women has been that many of the women had family responsibilities, which precluded them being as career-committed as the men with whom they were competing. For this reason, they were not as likely to contribute articles to professional journals or write books. Also, when forced to take teaching positions in less prestigious colleges, women have generally had heavier teaching loads and little opportunity for research grants.

Because of this presumed difference in their professional approach and record, women have appeared less qualified for the most prestigious faculties or for administrative positions in their department, college, or university. Women's groups, however, argue that women are as career-committed but have been discriminated against in reviews of their articles and in the willingness of publishers to give them contracts. This argument is unlikely to be settled because facts are hard to gather. Virtually all professional journals circulate manuscripts anonymously so that the readers would not necessarily know articles had been written by women. It is true, however, that editors do not accept articles without the opinion of readers but are free to reject submissions on their own authority. Whatever the underlying reasons, until recently, few of the reviewers and readers were women, and women have published a disproportionately small percentage of the articles and books; now, however, more women are being appointed as reviewers and referees for professional journals and more are receiving book contracts.

The simultaneous pressures for hiring faculty members from several different minority groups have sometimes worked to the disadvantage of women or to the special advantage of black women because quota-conscious administrations see the possibility of counting such a faculty member in two quotas. Part of the difference is certainly attitudinal. John Kenneth Galbraith, evaluating the status of women in the economics profession, was quoted as saying, "People are uneasy and a bit frightened when it comes to discrimination against blacks, but with women it is a rather goodhumored thing that nobody really worries about. You can discriminate against women with a sense of security."[12]

A HEW survey of degrees awarded from 1960 to 1969 indicates that in certain fields it will be hard to find qualified women. For example, women earned only 4.5 percent of the Ph.D.s in city planning and 2.5 percent of all Ph.D.s in computer science and systems analysis; in engineering women earned 0.4 percent. Even in certain fields of the social sciences, women have received very few degrees: 5.6 percent of the doctorates in economics and 5.6 percent of those in geography went to women. In contrast, women earned 17 percent of the advanced degrees in sociology, 21 percent in anthropology, 20 percent in psychology, and 29 percent in foreign language and literature. In total, women earned 11.6 percent of all Ph.D.s between 1960 and 1969 and they were unevenly distributed in the various disciplines.[13]

Even within certain disciplines representation is disproportionate. For example, a report on primary fields of concentration for Ph.D.s in government and politics shows that women hold 4.2 percent of the degrees in public administration, 11.4 percent of those in political theory, 13.6 percent in international organization, 13.6 percent in American government, and a surprising 59.0 percent in comparative government and political development.[14]

Despite the problems that such figures suggest, the legal situation with regard to discrimination against women in college and university faculties is now clear: Title VI of the Civil Rights Act of 1964 relating to nondiscrimination in federally assisted programs applied to sex as well as race but excluded higher education and the professions. Title IX of the Education Amendments of 1972 prohibited sex discrimination in all education programs receiving federal assistance including those at universities and colleges. In combination with the Civil Rights Act of 1964, it provides women with the same legal protections provided minority faculty members. Nevertheless, some departments do not have much turnover and will continue to have specialized requirements making it difficult to respond to pressures for hiring both women and minority members. This means that pressures for the two constituencies will continue to be very closely linked.

On this point, Constance Holden has written that there does not seem to be any divisiveness with respect to black women and where their loyalties lie. She asserts that although black women have been only minimally involved in the anti-sex discrimination movement and "although some blacks have feared that the sex crusade would detract from racial progress, it is they who have been getting the promotions."[15]

Affirmative Action Programs

Many universities established human relations offices in the late 1960s to give substance to top management's policy statements on increasing the numbers of minority faculty members. Such offices have helped the administration investigate complaints of discrimination as well as to identify patterns of institutional racism and sexism.

One of the routine procedures for persuading departments reluctantly diversifying their faculty is to require that whenever a selection is made for a position the departments must document which minority members were considered and give some reason why they were not selected. The human relations offices can be useful in analyzing this documentation.

More positive approaches have also contributed to some improvements. The human relations offices have performed some function in maintaining data on various organizations willing to serve as referral points for minority applicants. While those in the disciplines generally know better than anyone else where to obtain applicants, some professors or chairmen had been so narrow in their approach that they have learned something about supply sources in their own discipline from the human relations office.

A variety of specialized sources of minority candidates have developed and are known to the human relations officers. For example, the Cabinet Committee on Opportunity for the Spanish-Speaking published a list of "Spanish-Surnamed American College Graduates" in 1970, which lists 3,000 such graduates, their fields of study, and degrees earned.

Gradually, the federal government has become more aggressive in applying the spirit of Title VII of the 1964 Civil Rights Act to colleges and universities. Education employees were exempted from that legislation, although Executive Order 11246, issued in 1965 by President Johnson, gave federal agencies a basis for pressuring higher education on this matter. Executive Order 11478, signed by President Nixon on August 8, 1969, required affirmative action programs in federal employment, and established federal complaint procedures. The Education Amendments of 1972 applied the discrimination provisions of Title VII of the Civil Rights Act to sex discrimination. Further, whereas Title VII had specifically exempted employment practices, the education amendments did not involve any exclusion.

Any college or university with a government contract, or a subcontract of at least $10,000 must now agree that it "will not discriminate against any employee or applicant for employment because of race, color, religion sex, or national origin" and that it "will take affirmative action to insure that all applicants are employed and that employees are treated during employment without regard to these factors."[16] Failure to comply with these requirements can lead to contract suspension, termination, or cancellation and, in fact, the university may be declared ineligible to receive any new federal contracts. These provisions also apply to grants for construction purposes. The provisions apply to all activities of the contractor and not just the federally funded departments.

Two different concepts are included in the federal regulations: nondiscrimination and affirmative action. The nondiscrimination requirement orders that any existing discriminatory conditions be eliminated. This provision applies to *all* persons and is not limited to members of minority groups. That is, the contractor must insure that employment and other benefits are not denied to any person on the basis of race, color, religion, sex, or national origin.

The affirmative action requirement is limited to women and minorities, defined as blacks, Spanish-surnamed persons, American Indians, and Orientals. This requirement goes far beyond guaranteeing neutrality with regard to race, color, religion, sex, and national origin in employment matters. As indicated in the *Higher Education Guidelines* for Executive Order 11246:

> Affirmative action requires the employer to make additional efforts to recruit, employ and promote qualified members of groups formerly excluded, even if that exclusion cannot be traced to particular discriminatory action on the part of the employer. The premise of the affirmative action concept of the Executive Order is that unless positive action is undertaken to overcome the effects of systematic institutional forms of exclusion and discrimination, a benign neutrality in employment practices will tend to perpetuate the *status quo ante* indefinitely.[17]

The guidelines carefully point out that an institution does not have to indulge in "reverse discrimination," select unqualified persons or overqualified ones, or to take any unfavorable personnel action against persons already on the payroll to create vacancies necessary to show affirmative action progress. Nevertheless, specific suggestions are included as to means of broadening the search for candidates so that women and minorities will have knowledge of and consideration for such vacancies as they develop.

Colleges and universities are required, therefore, to formulate written plans of affirmative action showing precisely what steps will be taken to more aggressively recruit women and minorities. Goals must be set related to potential opportunities over a particular period of time, and then reports must be made to indicate whether these goals were achieved. As the guidelines indicate, "goals are projected levels of achievement resulting from analysis by the contractor of its deficiencies, and of what it can reasonably do to remedy them, given the availability of qualified minorities and women and the expected turnover in its work force."[18] If, in fact, the anticipated vacancies do not develop or some change occurs in the labor market, or if qualified women and minorities are not available, the organization may not meet its goals. However, the federal government must analyze the reports and records of the organization and make a determination as to whether the university has made a good faith effort.

This two-pronged attack on the problem of discrimination and unequal opportunity has had substantial effects on some campuses. Where inadvertent discrimination had been practiced and the climate for change existed, drawing up a system of goals and procedures resulted in finding additional qualified minorities and women and hiring them. Putting teeth into the provisions regarding discrimination against women will lead some institutions to play the numbers game; special efforts will be made to find black women to show progress toward both goals.

HEW appears willing to take firm action against institutions not making a good faith effort to improve the fairness of their employment practices. In enforcing the equal employment provisions of the Civil Rights Act and of the Executive Order, HEW, in 1972, "temporarily suspended some 23 million dollars in federal research grants in 14 major universities, including Columbia and Michigan, for lack of cooperation."[19]

According to Timothy Ingram, "HEW's Office of Civil Rights appeared insensitive to the differences between universities and the construction industry and seemed to be applying wholesale to faculty members the same standards it used for hard-hats under the Philadelphia plan. Funds were withheld . . . not after a hearing and a finding of discrimination had been made but because colleges had failed to come up with adequate plans. When forced to clarify their hiring goals, the school found the distinction between 'goal' and 'imposed quota' a fine one."[20] He further notes that "HEW was trying to advance into new enforcement waters. Should, for example, schools be compelled to hire not single 'qualified' candidates, but those 'qualifiable'? Might they, for instance, hire a black biologist with a Masters rather than a white Ph.D. and train the black in a doctoral program as he teaches?"[21]

As a consequence, according to Ingram, university professors with ready access to the media started writing and complaining. The result was Nixon's August 17, 1972 announcement of a campaign to end quotas.[22] Quotas can be extremely unrealistic, but without them current conditions will not improve

In the end real progress will be contingent upon increasing the output of qualified women and minorities in specialized fields. Numerous federal programs, such as those of the Department of Housing and Urban Development and other departments, are helping to provide special fellowships for this purpose. There are also substantial government and foundation efforts to improve black colleges and over time these should improve the total work environment.

Of course, more is involved in effective recruitment than meets the eye. Sophisticated candidates learn that they must also look at the fairness of tenure and promotion procedures. We can expect to see increasing numbers of women and minorities on these committees. However, the seniority process and the era of tight education budgets will tend to slow up drastic changes in these policies and procedures.

NOTES

1. "Faculties Divided on Recruiting More Women, Blacks, Chicanos," *Chronicle of Higher Education,* November 13, 1972, p. 1.

2. There have been a number of studies of participation

at the professional meetings of the American Political Science Association. They are reported by Donald D. Barry and James G. Bommer, "Participation in ASPA Annual Meetings, 1964–1969," *Political Science,* Fall 1970, pp. 629–40; Joseph La Palombara, "Another View," *P.S.,* pp. 641–44; and Victoria Schuck, "Femina Studens Rei Publicae: Notes on Her Professional Achievements," *P.S.,* pp. 622–28.

3. Carnegie Commission on Higher Education, *New Students and New Places,* October 1971, p. 25.

4. *Ibid.* Also, page 26 of the report summarizes a 1969 survey of successful completion of one year of college by persons aged 25 to 34 which showed the following results: blacks 15 percent, Spanish-origin 15 percent, and whites 30 percent.

5. Asa S. Knowles, "Change in the Traditional Concepts of Higher Education," *School and Society,* November 1971, p. 406.

6. James W. Bryant, "A Survey of Black American Doctorates," Division of Education and Research, Ford Foundation, September 5, 1969, p. 8; and U.S. Department of Health, Education and Welfare, Bureau of Educational Research and Development, and the National Center for Educational Statistics, *Earned Degrees Conferred: Bachelor's and Higher Degrees, 1960–69* (Washington, D.C.: Government Printing Office, 1971).

7. David M. Rafky, "The Black Academic in the Marketplace," *Change,* October 1971, p. 65.

8. *Ibid.,* pp. 6, 65–66.

9. Carnegie Commission, *New Students and New Places,* p. 26.

10. Alice Rossi, "Women In the Seventies: Problems and Possibilities," a speech given at Barnard College Conference on Women, April 17, 1970, as reprinted by the U.S. House of Representatives, Committee on Education and Labor, testimony before the Special Subcommittee on Education on *Discrimination against women,* Part 2, 1970, pp. 1062–1077.

11. *U.S. House of Representatives, Ibid.,* pp. 1018–1019. See also Jessie S. Bernard, *Academic Women* (University Park, Penn.: Pennsylvania State University Press, 1964), who argues that the faculty rank of women is inferior to that of man

in all kinds of institutions and despite comparable qualifications and productivity.

12. Constance Holden, "Women in Michigan: Parlaying Rights into Power," *Science,* vol. 178, p. 964.

13. HEW, *Earned Degrees Conferred.*

14. Victoria Schuck, "Women in Political Science: Some Preliminary Observations," *P.S.,* Fall 1969, vol. II, no. 4, p. 645.

15. Holden, "Women in Michigan," p. 964.

16. President Lyndon B. Johnson, *Executive Order 11246,* September 24, 1965, as amended, Section 202 (1).

17. U.S. Department of Health, Education and Welfare, *Higher Education Guidelines for Executive Order 11246* (Washington, D.C.: Government Printing Office, 1972).

18. *Ibid.*

19. Timothy H. Ingram, "Fair Employment: The Machinery Continues to Rust," *Washington Monthly,* December 1972, p. 44.

20. *Ibid.*

21. *Ibid.*

22. *Ibid.*

17

THE FEDERAL GOVERNMENT AND URBAN HIGHER EDUCATION

Thomas P. Murphy and Elizabeth Knipe

It is most surprising that no federal policy exists for urban higher education. The fact that urban education receives daily public attention would suggest that someplace within the government leadership would be devoted to improving our urban education delivery system. Yet fragmentation is the only word that describes federal policy toward education. This is particularly true of federal policy toward urban universities and colleges.

The Federal Policy Vacuum on Urban Higher Education

Where in the federal government organization would it be reasonable to expect to find federal urban policy toward urban universities and colleges? One possibility is the U.S. Office of Education (OE). However, OE has its own fragmentation problems. It represents a variety of interest areas concerned with elementary, secondary, community college, four-year college, and university education. Within its organizational structure are also housed staff groups responsible for vocational education, education for the handicapped, adult education, and other specialized areas of education. Not surprisingly, a review of the entire OE organization chart does not uncover a single reference to the word urban, much less to urban *higher* education. The Bureau of Higher Education, which would be most likely to have such a unit, has five divisions with functional jurisdictions involving student financial aid, university programs, college support, student special services, and academic facilities. Urban concerns are difficult to crystallize in such an organization.

In short, therefore, no explicit urban university policy exists in OE; there is only an indirect policy influence through the impact of general federal higher education policy on urban universities. This is not surprising, as it reflects the organization of higher education pressure groups and their influence inside the government. These major interest groups are the American Council on Education, the American Association for Higher Education, the American Association of Colleges for Teacher Education, the American Association of Community and Junior Colleges, the National Association of State Universities and Land Grant Colleges, the American Association of State Colleges and Universities, and the National University Extension Association. The only higher education association having urban universities as its exclusive concern is the Association of Urban Universities and, unlike all the other organizations mentioned, it does not have a paid national headquarters staff housed in an impressive Washington office building.

Several of these organizations have subordinate committees which relate to urban universities. For example, the American Council on Education (ACE) has a Committee on Urban Affairs. However, the interests of urban universities must be subordinated to the general interests of the group. In January 1972, at the instigation of the ACE Office of Urban Affairs, twenty-two of these higher education associations participated in a conference to consider how they might promote urban involvement by colleges and universities. The group is now preparing policy statements for these organizations to consider which will endorse greater participation by colleges and universities in urban affairs.

More specialized organizations such as the National Association of Schools of Public Affairs and Administration also have urban affairs sections. This particular group, however, is an affiliate of the American Society for Public Administration and has less than one full-time professional employee in its national office. The Council of University Institutes of Urban Affairs represents an attempt to create a counterpart to the professional organizations which represent the various academic disciplines. However, this group also has little funding and falls far short of meeting the needs of urban universities which are fully involved in urban affairs to the extent that Georgia State College, Wayne State University, and the City University of New York purport to be.

It is strange that these groups have not been able to influence urban higher education policy in any major way. In a speech before the Educational Staff Seminar, Douglas Cater, former White House advisor under President Kennedy, indicated that he had been totally amazed at the power of education organizations to reverse presidential recommendations through lobbying activities.[1] This should *not* be surprising in view of the amount of federal and other money invested in education throughout the nation. It is estimated that the total annual expenditure for education approaches $85 billion. When the entire education establishment can agree on an item of legislation, it has the power to lobby it through Congress. But with respect to a policy for *urban* higher education the education lobby has never, unfortunately, been able to formulate any kind of policy or program that it wants enacted. A report prepared for the American Council of Education in 1972 concluded that higher education's leadership is politically naive and that as a consequence it has been unable to secure sufficient federal support for higher education. The report, funded by the Ford Foundation, recommended broadening the council and reducing its headquarters activity with the objective of making federal relationships its primary function.[2] Hopefully, the emerging coordination patterns of the national associations related to higher education may develop such a focus.

Another place to look for a federal urban university policy would be the National Science Foundation (NSF). Although concerned primarily with science and engineering, the role of the NSF has gradually been expanding. It has been taking a more flexible view of what constitutes "science," enabling the "social" sciences to participate more fully in its program of support for basic research. In addition, the scope of the NSF has been broadened to include applications in urban contexts through the relatively new Research Applied to National Needs (RANN) program. Nevertheless, the National Science Foundation is not in a position to offer general education aid to higher education; that would clearly be the role of the U.S. Office of Education. By law NSF must relate its funding activities directly to science or engineering. Of course, many urban universities are among those receiving NSF funding, but there is no *policy* concerning urban universities as such.

The functions of the National Endowment for the Humanities (NEH) and the National Endowment for the Arts (NEA) are similar in some respects to those of the National Science Foundation. All three provide indirect assistance to urban education while promoting specific educational policies. But, like NSF, the scope of the endowments is not sufficiently broad to justify expenditures to directly meet general education requirements of the universities. NSF, NEA, and NEH were created to meet specialized needs, whereas general education is the responsibility of the Office of Education.

It is certainly reasonable to expect to find an urban university policy in the Department of Housing and Urban Development. HUD funds urban fellowships and work-study programs which have been crucial for higher education. HUD also has a variety of sub-units such as research and technology, housing production, mortgage credit, metropolitan planning and development, urban renewal and housing management, community development, and international affairs. Many of these units have relationships with urban universities which enable them to perform research related to HUD functions.

Even the White House cannot be counted upon to integrate programs into a federal urban higher education policy. Its Office of Management and Budget (OMB) must analyze the budget proposals affecting education which are submitted by the Office of Education, the National Science Foundation, the National Endowments for the Arts and the Humanities, and the various mission agencies. Yet there is no single education budget supervisor in OMB. OMB monitors agency programs by assigning budget analysts to the various governmental organizations; that is, the organization of OMB reflects the organization of the federal agencies and departments. The amount of money spent on education must be coordinated by analysts assigned to the various agencies and departments. This does not take place in a manner that contributes to development of urban higher education policy.

When the federal budget has been presented in recent years, special analyses of major governmental programs such as education, science, space, and oceanography have been made to identify cross-departmental areas in which a variety of authorities spend money. The special analysis of education in the fiscal year 1974 budget (Table 17–1) showed the 1972 expenditures, 1973 estimates, and proposed 1974 expenditures broken down to reflect the various agencies involved with higher education.

A White House policy could exist even without OMB supervising education, but there is no education advisor reporting directly to the president, and both the dollar volume and the number of agencies involved present serious coordination problems. The Domestic Council, which was established in the Nixon Administration as a counterpart to the National Security Council, has had specialists on education. The Domestic Council's staff, numbering about sixty in 1972, con-

Table 17–1
Federal Outlays for Higher Education by Agency
(Dollars in millions)

Sublevel, agency, and program	1972 actual	1973 estimate	1974 estimate
Two-year institutions:			
National Institute of Health	24	61	55
Office of Education:			
Basic opportunity grants	—	—	137
Other student support	111	124	66
Occupational and vocational education	132	142	84
Other	54	40	45
Student grants (OASDI)	56	71	80
Veterans readjustment	535	733	696
Other	44	51	45
Subtotal, two-year institutions	956	1,222	1,208

Other undergraduate:

Military service academies	208	209	208
Reserve officers training corps	142	155	159
Health manpower (NIH)	49	77	65
Office of Education:			
Basic opportunity grants	—	—	485
Work-study and supplementary			
grants	326	370	199
Guaranteed student loans	207	263	320
Direct student loans	241	257	25
Construction loans and grants	169	109	93
Disadvantaged students and			
developing institutions	69	88	120
Other	50	65	44
Student grants (OASDI)	465	589	678
Special institutions	18	21	19
Bureau of Indian Affairs	14	22	21
Community development (HUD)	16	18	19
Veterans readjustment	712	950	896
National Foundation on the			
Arts and Humanities	9	15	25
National Science Foundation	31	17	13
Other	82	79	39
Subtotal, other undergraduate	2,807	3,304	3,428

Graduate and professional:

Health Services and Mental			
Health Administration	89	81	74
Health manpower (NIH)	358	396	439
Other National Institutes of Health	109	104	96
College teacher fellowships (OE)	54	27	20
Other Office of Education	50	59	43
Social and Rehabilitation Service	26	30	17
Howard University	26	40	42
Veterans readjustment	190	245	227
National Science Foundation	33	23	17
Other	27	29	16
Subtotal, graduate and			
professional	962	1,034	991

Postdoctoral:			
Health Services and Mental			
Health Administration	43	36	32
National Institutes of Health	70	65	57
Other	6	10	10
Subtotal, postdoctoral	119	110	99
Other:			
Health Services and Mental			
Health Administration	13	11	9
National Institutes of Health	23	46	48
Other	2	1	1
Subtotal, other	38	58	58
Total	4,883	5,728	5,784

Source: Executive Office of the President, Office of Management and Budget, *Special Analyses, The Federal Budget for Fiscal Year 1974* (Washington, D.C.: Government Printing Office, 1973), p. 116.

tained five specialists on education. However, as in the case of the Office of Education, their jurisdiction extends to all educational issues, and in recent years powerful and politically significant issues such as busing have occupied more of their time than the more specialized topic of urban higher education. More significant, perhaps, only one educational advisor remains on the Domestic Council staff after the post-1972 election cutbacks.

Although staff is important, the absence of a direct advisor on education does not mean that the world of higher education is isolated from the president. University presidents and well-known professors have in the past enjoyed ready access to the chief executive. The Kennedy Administration, for example, had McGeorge Bundy and Arthur Schlesinger of Harvard on the White House staff and boasted John Kenneth Galbraith as ambassador to India. The Johnson Administration had Meyer Goldman of Princeton in the White House. The Nixon Administration began with Henry Kissinger as a special counselor to the President and George Shultz of the University of Chicago as director of OMB. Since its creation in 1946, the Council of Economic Advisors has been directed by university-based economists. Scientists from MIT, Harvard, and

Princeton controlled the White House Office of Science and Technology under three of the last four presidents.

Even in urban affairs, university influence is evident. In the Kennedy and Johnson administrations, Dr. Robert Wood, former director of the Harvard-MIT Joint Center for Urban Studies, was Undersecretary of the Department of Housing and Urban Development. He launched the urban observatory program discussed in Chapter 2. Daniel Patrick Moynihan, another former director of the Joint Center, was a key urban and domestic policy advisor in the Nixon White House. In addition, professors were called upon to head important advisory committees. For example, Edward Banfield, then of Harvard, headed the model cities evaluation group. However, many of the university professors who have access to the White House as a result of their appointments to various advisory committees and councils have more on their agendas than the relatively narrow problem of urban universities. A large number of them head state systems or the major state university campuses which, for historical reasons, have been located in the rural areas; this greatly influences their priorities.

Congressional Nonpolicy on Urban Higher Education

On the congressional side, a similar problem exists in establishing a comprehensive policy toward urban universities and colleges. The House Committee on Education and Labor and the Senate Committee on Labor and Public Welfare oversee HEW education programs, and the same House and Senate committees supervise the programs of the National Endowments for the Arts and Humanities. These committees could generate pressure for an executive branch policy toward urban universities and colleges. However, their jurisdictions extend far beyond education. And, as in the case of the Office of Education itself, these committees also cover education at all levels. Yet because higher education constitutes only a portion of the total spending, it is easy to see why urban higher education is not given major attention.

Congress, like the Office of Management and Budget, is organized largely along the lines of the federal agencies and departments and therefore provides no focal point for comprehensive program review. Numerous congressional committees deal with education as it is financed through the mission agencies, the National Science Foundation, and the National Endowments for the Arts and Humanities. While the Senate Committee on Labor and Public Welfare supervises NSF, the House Education and Labor Committee does not. The National Science Foundation is subject to the House Committee on Science and Astronautics, which also monitors the National Aeronautics and Space Administration. NSF matters have been handled by the Science, Research, and Development subcommittee, one of the five subcommittees of the Science and Astronautics Committee, and the focus has been primarily on NSF's expenditures and investments with respect to research and development. Subcommittee staff indicate that in the ten years of the subcommittee's existence urban universities have never once been discussed as a special topic. As noted earlier, this does not mean that urban universities have not profited from some of the grants and contracts of the National Science Foundation; clearly they have. But there is no urban university policy from which new programs and formats might benefit. In fairness to Congress, the committee has shown serious interest in the application of science and technology to urban problems and has exerted a certain amount of pressure upon the National Science Foundation to expand programs such as RANN (Research Applied to National Needs), which in fiscal year 1972 received a budget of $54 million.

Other executive departments and agencies also receive reasonable program support but lack the same essential focus which could make the difference. The Department of Housing and Urban Development reports to the House Committee on Banking and Currency, which has a subcommittee on housing. The emphasis of this subcommittee has been on urban housing rather than on the broad problems of urban affairs. Although the parent committee has from time to time established ad hoc subcommittees on specific urban problems, this piecemeal approach has been inadequate. The urban affairs subcommittee of the Joint Economic Committee has covered some of the significant urban affairs questions. On the Senate side the name of the Banking and Currency Committee was changed to the Committee on Banking, Housing, and Urban Affairs and a subcommittee on Housing and Urban Affairs was established.

Still, none of these committees has paid any special attention to how HUD programs have affected urban higher education.

Other major agencies with education expenditures (the Departments of Defense, Commerce, and Transportation; the Atomic Energy Commission; and the Environmental Protection Agency) are supervised by a wide variety of congressional committees. It is not possible for these committees to propose independently or collaboratively a comprehensive urban university policy since they are considering total budgets of agencies in which general education may be a small part and in which urban education is usually not even an identifiable segment. This task was assigned to the Office of Economic Opportunity when it was created by the House Committee on Education and Labor, then chaired by Adam Clayton Powell of New York. This committee became involved in questions of urban higher education, but obviously it had to place first priority on education for poor people. There was a tendency to emphasize high school dropout problems, Head Start programs, and other issues at the elementary and secondary levels rather than those affecting higher education directly.

Even with regard to the innovative urban observatory concept put forth by HUD under Robert Wood's leadership, the HUD hearings in the 1960s and early 1970s show scant reference to the urban observatory program. When dealing with an agency with a budget of just over $4 billion (FY 1972), it is just not feasible to spend much time talking about a million-dollar item incorporated within the general research budget.

In addition, even if any of these committees had collaborated in putting together an urban higher education policy, they deal only with authorization legislation; that is, they approve programs and set ceilings on funding. The actual appropriation for any such program must come from the Senate and House Appropriations Committees, each of which have about fourteen subcommittees organized along agency lines. Design and coordination of a comprehensive urban higher education policy would thus have to be cleared through the appropriations committees as well. The path to ultimate coordination at the congressional level would be long and slippery; it is not surprising, then, that no such policy has evolved.

Defense and Science as a Basis for Federal Aid to Higher Education

Three categories of federal agencies have supportive relationships with urban universities. First, providing general support for higher education is restricted to the U.S. Office of Education, specifically its Bureau of Higher Education. A second category consists of agencies such as NSF, NEH, and NEA, which are not mission-oriented and operate under a broad group of disciplinary concerns. The third category consists of mission-oriented agencies which have relationships with universities because they need university inputs to their programs or because their field has a shortage of university-educated specialists. Many of these mission-oriented agencies support training programs in universities and, as in the case of some HUD programs, even support programs specifically designated for *urban* universities.

The important point is that money provided to urban universities by mission-oriented agencies can be characterized in two different ways. First, a large flow of money is channeled to such universities because their science, engineering, or other departments are related to the agencies' formal mission; in this respect, some of this money would flow to specific universities whether they were in the city or in a rural area. Other money, however, is urban-bound because of the nature of the programs involved.

As Table 17–2 demonstrates, the first source, despite its general focus, is crucial to the development of the urban university. Even though the money is not provided *because* the university is urban, it can still strengthen such a university in its attempt to be broadly involved in problems requiring the talents of the social and physical sciences as well as of the arts and humanities. Urban studies, as indicated in Chapter 14, involves all of these things, and any federal money which enables a university to strengthen its physics, chemistry, sociology, or economics departments will increase the opportunity for the university to apply a general discipline to urban problems as well. In this context, fellowships and research support from agencies such as the National Aeronautics and Space Administration, the Atomic Energy Commission, the Environmental Protection Agency, the Department of Health, Educa-

Table 17-2
Federal R&D Obligations to the Top 40 Universities and Colleges
Fiscal Year 1970
(dollars in thousands)

Institution (in order of R&D obligations)	State	Total obligations	Percent of U.S. total	USDA	AEC	Commerce	DOD	HEW	Interior	NASA	NSF	OEO
1. Massachusetts Institute of Technology	Mass.	91,048	6.52	—	7,563	109	44,086	7,275	656	26,014	5,345	—
2. Stanford University	Calif.	38,936	2.79	—	662	10	10,928	15,094	134	4,013	8,020	75
3. Harvard University	Mass.	36,149	2.59	—	1,785	—	2,998	19,576	55	6,003	5,231	501
4. University of Michigan	Mich.	33,561	2.40	46	2,458	—	7,710	12,659	250	5,504	4,934	—
5. University of California–San Diego	Calif.	33,364	2.39	—	2,027	49	10,663	7,728	—	3,369	9,528	—
6. University of California–Los Angeles	Calif.	32,916	2.36	—	4,496	5	6,216	15,593	328	2,369	3,909	—
7. Columbia University	N.Y.	32,444	2.32	20	4,639	46	7,274	13,408	120	1,866	5,071	—
8. University of Wisconsin–Madison	Wis.	31,765	2.28	1,598	2,983	—	1,010	14,652	340	1,603	4,833	4,746
9. University of Illinois–Urbana	Ill.	30,379	2.18	1,696	3,809	—	12,878	5,489	408	782	5,214	103
10. University of California–Berkeley	Calif.	27,829	199	—	556	—	4,875	11,235	628	6,297	3,604	634
11. University of Washington	Wash.	27,727	1.99	207	2,390	—	2,800	15,696	572	519	5,543	—
12. University of Chicago	Ill.	24,465	1.75	—	4,708	25	1,610	10,256	75	2,807	5,101	—
13. Cornell University	N.Y.	24,465	1.75	1,895	1,653	—	3,201	9,038	177	1,270	7,231	—
14. University of Minnesota	Minn.	24,191	1.73	1,675	1,658	—	2,508	13,576	828	1,475	2,261	210
15. New York University	N.Y.	21,454	1.54	25	1,658	37	2,434	14,724	64	702	1,260	550
16. Johns Hopkins University	Md.	21,150	1.52	28	953	32	2,366	15,466	65	486	1,754	—
17. University of Pennsylvania	Pa.	20,676	1.48	—	1,667	—	2,639	13,365	52	259	2,570	124
18. Yale University	Conn.	19,540	1.40	—	3,306	—	1,631	10,678	1	694	3,230	—
19. University of Maryland	Md.	16,530	1.18	943	2,158	—	2,819	4,550	229	3,183	2,544	104
20. Duke University	N.C.	15,458	1.11	2	797	15	3,283	10,083	19	149	1,110	—

Fiscal Year 1970
(dollars in thousands)

Institution (in order of R&D obligations)	State	Total obligations	Percent of U.S. total	USDA	AEC	Commerce	DOD	HEW	Interior	NASA	NSF	OEO
21. Ohio State University	Ohio	15,041	1.08	1,851	758	—	3,337	5,957	466	667	2,005	—
22. California Institute of Technology	Calif.	14,694	1.05	—	2,558	—	2,496	3,520	165	3,166	2,789	—
23. University of Rochester	N.Y.	14,591	1.05	—	4,603	—	884	6,966	—	233	1,905	—
24. Princeton University	N.J.	14,181	1.02	—	2,631	19	3,063	1,888	—	3,933	2,647	—
25. Washington University	Mo.	14,001	1.00	—	352	—	1,877	9,965	—	686	1,121	—
26. University of Colorado	Colo.	13,861	.99	—	880	458	1,832	7,341	95	1,503	1,752	—
27. Case Western Reserve University	Ohio	13,666	.98	—	991	—	2,523	7,935	110	697	1,410	—
28. University of California–San Francisco	Calif.	13,596	.97	—	659	—	324	12,500	—	113	—	—
29. Yeshiva University	N.Y.	13,331	.95	—	135	—	757	10,983	75	—	1,131	250
30. University of Texas–Austin	Tex.	13,053	.94	—	695	—	5,272	3,224	105	1,276	2,406	75
31. University of Utah	Utah	12,823	.92	—	1,057	4	2,898	6,339	864	161	1,480	20
32. University of Pittsburgh	Pa.	12,479	.89	—	453	—	1,150	8,314	212	664	1,686	—
33. Purdue University	Ind.	11,816	.85	2,700	1,589	—	2,222	2,229	260	711	2,105	—
34. University of Southern California	Calif.	11,561	.83	—	247	—	1,785	7,212	57	1,211	1,049	—
35. University of North Carolina–Chapel Hill	N.C.	11,246	.81	—	462	—	1,186	7,644	44	79	1,291	540
36. University of Miami	Fla.	11,117	.80	—	319	86	2,367	5,423	505	375	1,983	59
37. University of Florida	Fla.	11,082	.79	1,277	388	—	1,850	4,665	329	487	1,298	788
38. Pennsylvania State University	Pa.	10,522	.75	1,964	461	—	992	3,065	783	1,416	1,726	115
39. Michigan State University	Mich.	10,177	.73	1,598	1,957	—	382	2,999	220	47	2,974	—
40. University of Iowa	Iowa	9,765	.70	11	94	—	1,086	5,719	88	1,903	864	—
Total, 100 institutions	—	$1,202,029	86.11	$47,493	$93,094	$1,209	$233,021	$512,831	$19,588	$114,059	$169,354	$11,380

SOURCE: National Science Foundation, *Federal Funds for Academic Science* (Washington, D.C.: Government Printing Office, 1970), Table 11, p. 45.

tion and Welfare, the Department of Labor, the Office of Economic Opportunity, the Department of Commerce, and the Department of Defense can be very helpful.

Mission-oriented agency aid to universities can relate directly to urban projects which help urban universities improve their education programs and increase their impact on their own community as well as on national problems. Examples of projects which fall into this area include research or demonstration projects related to aging, air pollution, alcoholism, community action, community development, crime control, drug abuse, economic development, environmental education, Head Start, health services, juvenile delinquency, manpower development, mental health, minority business enterprise, model cities, rat control, social services, solid waste disposal, urban mass transit, and water pollution.

Even the National Aeronautics and Space Administration has made it possible for urban universities to propose projects with an urban focus as long as they also relate to the mission of the agency. For example, NASA has funded some important studies on the application of its technology to the development of special devices useful in firefighting and police communication. NASA's development of the space capsule as a closed ecological system led researchers to the possibility of applying what was learned in developing the capsule to the study and improvement of urban ecological systems. Numerous other agencies have funded research into pollution and transportation, two fields which have a direct relation to urban problems.

Notwithstanding fragmented funding, the willingness of government to become involved in problems of higher education has been increasing in recent years. In the beginning the federal government had little involvement in higher education, but the land-grant program developed under the Morrill Act after the Civil War was a major breakthrough, providing a substantial precedent for federal aid to universities. The next major breakthrough in federal involvement came following World War II when the G.I. Bill made possible tremendous increases in the number of young people able to attend college. Urban universities probably benefited disproportionately from the G.I. Bill: many veterans went to school on a part-time basis, an arrangement that was most convenient where jobs and the university were located close together.

The National Defense Education Act (NDEA) of 1958 extended federal involvement in higher education.[3] While today there is strong negative reaction to university involvement with the Department of Defense, the fact is that many of the breakthroughs in securing federal aid to higher education have followed attempts by the DOD and military agencies to aid universities for their own purposes. As part of the package, they have often provided extra money to be used at the university's discretion. For example, the NDEA fellowships were intended to influence the supply of trained people in areas critical to DOD needs so that recruitment problems would be eased in future years. In a ten-year period from 1959 to 1969 DOD provided 20,000 of these fellowships for a variety of graduate degrees, many of which may have had urban applications.

The National Aeronautics and Space Administration followed the same pattern of using graduate fellowships, especially in doctoral programs, to increase the manpower supply in specialties relevant to its mission.[4] In the 1960s, NASA provided 5,476 doctoral fellowships with no commitment on the part of the students to work for NASA or one of its contractors. NASA records indicate that 3,821 Ph.D.s were completed in the program. This policy of no commitment to agency employment was supported on the premise that any students completing degrees on these fellowships would increase the number of qualified persons available for NASA and its contractors. The Atomic Energy Commission has followed a similar pattern.

The Federal Council on Science and Technology, composed of the major science agencies in the federal government, developed in the sixties a plan to insure a sufficient flow of doctorates in science and engineering to meet the needs of all the federal science agencies as well as those of the civilian sector. Cooperating agencies agreed to fund specific quotas of science fellowships each year. If one agency's budget were cut so that it was unable to do this, often another agency—usually the Department of Defense—would move in to fill the void ensure a balanced national supply of doctorates.

When HUD was established in 1963, the pattern of using university fellowships to prime the supply of specialized people had already been established. HUD followed suit, and from its inception has made approximately 100 urban fellowships available annually at the master's and doctoral levels. Some model cities programs even used portions of their HUD money to help provide college educations for ghetto residents, thereby increasing the number of students attending universities under HUD's sponsorship. Also, some HUD planning and management money had been used for fellowships to increase the number of minority students in the planning field and to increase the total number of planners available to carry out urban programs.

Many agencies have provided money for research on problems of interest to them that have also had an impact on urban problems. Some mission-oriented agencies have also provided money to universities to build science and engineering laboratories. Thus, although urban universities were among those receiving fellowships, research, and construction funding, it was rarely *because* they were urban universities.

Priority for federal aid has been defense first and then science, the latter stimulated in part by the success of the Soviet sputnik in 1957. But all the while this federal support for higher education has created imbalances: research in science and engineering got a disproportionately large share of money mission agencies provided the universities; this money tended to cluster in limited areas of the nation. These were usually the coastal areas which had industries related to aeronautics, space, and electronics, three of the major fields important to federal research and development programs. By 1965 it became necessary to broaden support for higher education as people in regions being left out of the R&D explosion succeeded in pressuring the political leadership in congress, the state houses, and the cities to insure that similar funds would be provided to strengthen universities in their areas. In that year, President Lyndon B. Johnson issued a memorandum titled "Strengthening Academic Capability" which called upon agencies to distribute their money more widely.[5]

Thus an element of what might be termed "geopolitics" had entered into the distribution of federal R&D money. Although the federal government was not responsible for the location of the key university research centers such as Cambridge, Ann Arbor, and San Francisco, which were receiving the lion's share of mission agency research money, the government came under increasing pressure to help develop other areas of the country by making money available for fellow-ships and research.[6]

Table 17–3 illustrates the geographic distribution of federal R&D money and gives some indication of its concentration by agency. As can be seen, the major implication for urban universities is that most of the money has come from mission-oriented agencies rather than from the Office of Education, the National Science Foundation, or the National Endowments for the Arts and Humanities, all of which are authorized to expend money for the general strengthening of higher education.

Urban-Grant Universities

Developing the social science capabilities of the urban higher education institutions ought to have as high priority as developing national capabilities in science and engineering. Although many think colleges and universities are cloistered and introspective, most urban universities are highly involved in national, state, and local government and community affairs through the outreach of their professional schools, most of which emphasize research and/or service activities. Federal funds could be used appropriately to support these outreach activities and to strengthen the school at the same time.

The notion of university "activism" is not new. It stems from the involvement of the land-grant universities with agricultural problems following the passage of the Morrill Land Grant Act of 1862. This act was primarily responsible for promoting the growth of schools of agriculture and for changing the character of institutions of higher education during the last century. Land-grant universities have probably been the most successful service and professional institutions in the land. They have made American agriculture a showcase to the world through the combination of extension programs, teaching, and research activities.

The idea of an urban equivalent to the Agricultural Extension Service has not been lost upon the academic community. In 1958, Paul Ylvisaker, then with the Ford Foundation, called for an expansion of the Morrill Act to include statutory provisions for educational programs designed specifically for urban and suburban communities.[7] President

Table 17–3
Federal R&D Obligations and Colleges by Geographic Division,
Fiscal Year 1970 (in thousands)

Division	USDA	AEC	COMM.	DOD	HEW	Interior	NASA	NSF	OEO	Total
United States	67,412	101,413	1,611	265,485	594,368	26,943	126,783	193,388	18,520	1,395,000
New England	3,507	15,348	174	63,571	58,811	2,300	36,167	23,510	1,150	204,547
Middle Atlantic	4,949	23,030	137	35,503	130,834	3,732	14,687	37,602	2,641	253,122
East N. Central	9,560	22,175	25	44,900	91,536	2,398	15,065	36,050	5,416	227,127
West N. Central	9,259	3,048	5	9,526	45,190	3,276	5,106	9,087	613	85,110
South Atlantic	11,571	8,579	201	28,835	76,341	3,557	11,815	17,389	2,737	161,025
East S. Central	8,156	1,954	—	4,377	22,514	888	2,386	2,317	1,024	43,616
West S. Central	6,772	3,639	68	12,980	37,323	1,055	10,170	7,549	718	80,274
Mountain	6,000	3,122	839	16,748	20,236	5,636	7,230	12,366	1,552	73,729
Pacific	6,134	19,560	162	49,023	110,248	3,998	24,070	47,443	2,653	263,291
Outlying areas	1,502	958	—	22	1,335	103	87	75	—	4,082

SOURCE: National Science Foundation, *Federal Funds for Academic Science* (Washington, D.C.: Government Printing Office, 1972), derived from Table B9, p. 44.

Johnson echoed this sentiment at the opening of the University of California at Irvine in 1964.[8] Clark Kerr built upon these and other suggestions to propose the "urban-grant university" as a model of an aggressive approach to solving urban problems. He reasons that the precedent for generous federal grants has been set with the successful land-grant university experiment, and that the city and its problems should now become the "animating focus" of the modern society:

> The suggestion that the federal government should help with the land and with the money to build . . . new campuses or to change existing campuses is altogther reasonable. When the land-grant movement began, over 50 percent of the people in the United States lived on the land; today, only 10 percent do. The reasons for an urban-grant university now are at least as compelling as were those for the land-grant university in 1862.[9]

Certainly there are no philosophical barriers to the extension of land-grant university services to the cities. However, the present faculty rewards system could be a barrier. Many new institutes and centers have been set up within urban universities solely as a means of circumventing an encrusted university structure which refuses to respond to changing priorities.

Dr. Kerr also refers to the depression-era neighborhood youth assistance program to subsidize college students, government assistance to scientific research during World War II, and the G.I. Bill and National Defense Education Act money provided to a wide variety of students since World War II as fitting examples of federal financial intervention for societal purposes. He concludes, therefore, that the urban-grant university should receive federal funds and perhaps set up experimental stations much like those pioneered by the Agricultural Extension Service several decades ago.

The basis for the urban-grant university is likely to be a new kind of "urban agent" who will move into the inner core of metropolitan areas to bring the university and its services to persons who are unaware of or indifferent to the services of higher education. A coordinated approach using the skills of a multitude of disciplines would be employed to provide support to the new urban agents. In this respect, the agents might become the long-heralded "urban generalists." Given the precedent of the land-grant university, the concept of an urban-grant university is clearly within reach. As Daniel P. Moynihan put it: "The demand that the Ivy League universities somehow save the slums is no more than the nineteenth-century demand that cow colleges save the dirt farmers."[10]

In any case, if the university is to accept a role as either an urban-grant university or, as discussed in Chapter 2, an urban observatory, it must be willing to change. The assumption that the experience of the Agricultural Extension Service can be *directly* applied to the city is far too broad to be realistic. While it is valid to assume that certain techniques may apply from one situation to another, it is an erroneous assumption that the problems of urban and rural America are as similar as politicians and many educators believe them to be.

One of the major differences lies in the sophistication of the political process in urban society. The disadvantaged urban dweller is extremely suspicious of those who come to study and help him. Today's ghetto resident is not likely to accept unquestioningly any solutions or assistance presented without his participation or involvement. Cities have learned the importance of citizen participation, making it less likely they will commit blatant errors of the sort that occurred prior to 1964. Universities especially must be wary of paternalism. Until they learn that when they engage in service activities the needs of the client must come first, it is unlikely that a fully harmonious relationship between the city and the university will be achieved.

Turning Higher Education Policy to Urban Ends

Apart from the chartering in 1966 of Federal City College in Washington, D.C., as a land-grant college, the first new one in sixty years, no formal steps have been taken to adopt the urban-grant college concept. However, the evolving programs of general aid to higher education open up the possibility of deriving some of the benefits envisioned by the urban-grant university proposal. For example, a major breakthrough of interest to urban universities occurred with the passage of work-study provisions in the Higher Education Act of 1965 which now make it possible to provide federal money directly to students from low income families who are attempting to attend college. Further advances seem imminent.

In his 1970 Message on Education, President Nixon called for some far-reaching changes in the concept of aid to higher education. Briefly, the message stated that there must be equality of educational opportunity, increased aid for higher education institutions, support for research into educational problems, and encouragement for organizational innovation and efforts to reform the educational institutions from within. As explained by Sidney P. Marland, the U.S. Commissioner of Education, the equality of opportunity concept "would find reality in expanded student grants and loans. Establishment of a secondary market—the National Student Loan Association —would make possible a vastly expanded NDEA-type loan program."[11] The effect of Nixon's proposal would be to increase coverage of student aid programs from 1.5 million students in 1971 to 2.5 million students per year in the future.

The combination of granting such financial aid directly to students and of changing university policy, such as the introduction of open admissions, would obviously lead to continued increases in the number of students on campus. Some financially pressed institutions would have great difficulty providing the additional classrooms, dormitories, and other specialized facilities necessary to educate additional students. Thus, the second Nixon proposal involves "qualified cost-of-education allowances that would be tied to an institution's total federal student aid funds in recognition of the burden imposed on colleges and universities that seek to educate large numbers of economically, socially, and educationally disadvantaged."[12]

Increased encouragement and support for basic and applied research on higher education will be provided by the new National Institute of Education. Mr. Nixon proposed that it be established in the Education Amendments of 1972, and the Congress concurred.

The NIE mandate is to seek to improve education (including career education) through

  a. helping to solve or alleviate the problems of, and achieve the objectives of, American education.

  b. advancing the practice of education as an art, science, and profession;

    c. strengthening the scientific and technical foundations
       of education; and

    d. building an effective educational research and devel-
       opment system.[13]

NIE research programs would cover the teaching and learning process from the pre-primary through graduate school
levels. Of course, the impact of a more effective education process throughout the primary and secondary schools would have
tremendous implications for the colleges and universities, especially those in urban areas where a disproportionately large
share of the economic and culturally disadvantaged are located.
As Commissioner Marland stated, all levels of education would
be evaluated in terms of "improving the quality of education,
improving education of the disadvantaged, and effective use of
resources in education for greater productivity. . . . We will
want to examine the notion of a university not located in a
single spot but permeating the city, the suburbs and the country."[14]

    Establishment of a National Foundation for Higher Edu-
cation (NFHE) was also proposed but failed to pass. The
purpose of the NFHE would be to provide funds to encourage
innovation in higher education and to help meet the additional
cost of new experimental programs. In the words of Commissioner Marland:

> We feel this enterprise could go far toward helping to
> break the deplorable lockstep of post-secondary schooling
> and opening it up to new ideas, certainly, and to new
> people as well—individuals who are now excluded as too
> old or disqualified by reason of circumstance. . . . It
> would be up to you to make use of Foundation grants to
> examine the nature of your institutional purpose and to
> appraise how effectively you are carrying it out. The in-
> formation we have—on dropouts, surplus degrees, on
> generalized student disenchantment, on questions of eco-
> nomic solvency—suggests a pressing need for this kind
> of basic investigation.[15]

    A backdrop for the administration policy for higher edu-
cation is the work of the Carnegie Commission, various
studies of which have been quoted in the preceding chapters,

and the report of the Newman Task Force, which was funded by the Ford Foundation. This task force was formed at the suggestion of former Secretary of Health, Education and Welfare Robert Finch.

In addition, a summary study was prepared by Earl F. Cheit for the Carnegie Commission on Higher Education and the Ford Foundation. Cheit studied the financial condition of 41 selected colleges and universities and concluded that 17 of them had serious financial trouble. Eight of the institutions in this category were public universities and nine were private. Cheit's data indicated that "for the private institutions in this group federal funds represent the largest single source of operating income. In 1968–69, these private universities received 33 percent of their operating income from the United States. Tuition was the second largest source of funds at 31.5 percent."[16]

With regard to student aid, Cheit concluded that every institution studied had great difficulty providing sufficient student assistance. In 1968–69, his data indicated that "public research universities in this study were spending an average of $170 per enrolled student for student aid. For all the private universities in the study, the figure was an average of $428; for the subgroup of private research universities that we characterize as 'national,' the figure was an average per enrolled student of $632."[17]

The Newman Task Force Report concludes that there is a need for major reform and that the current experiments will not be sufficient to do the job:

> The probable success of these kinds of reforms is limited; they leave unaffected the institutionalized past decisions as to what higher education is all about. The system, with its massive inertia, resists fundamental change, rarely eliminates outmoded programs, ignores the differing needs of students, seldom questions its educational goals, and almost never creates new and different types of institutions.[18]

The Newman Report recommended, among many other reforms, that new educational approaches be supported by new federal and state funding programs; that colleges and universities be opened up for persons of all ages; that off-campus education be expanded; that consideration be given to establishing "examining universities" which could both provide proficiency examinations (in place of course work) for credit and confer degrees; that faculties be diversified and graduate schools reformed; and that there be a renewed commitment to achieving increased minority participation in higher education.

The Office of Education is supporting various experiments underway in programs such as the University Without Walls (see Chapter 12); the open university centers using educational television and testing, tutoring, and counseling capabilities as a basis for awarding course credit; a technical assistance consortium for improving services in black colleges; a civilian G.I. Bill program which would make educational benefits available to young persons who performed community service; and a reevaluation of providing fellowship funds to institutions rather than to students—a practice that tends to build good graduate programs and drive out weak ones.[19]

Clearly, all of these reforms and experiments involve urban universities and will have a major impact on them. Indeed a number of them, such as the student loan and institutional aid programs, will have their primary impact in immediate dollars on universities in urban areas which are serving the minority and poor populations. Likewise, the output of the National Institute for Education should on a long-term basis have its greatest effect on urban universities. The National Foundation for Higher Education would offer urban universities an opportunity to fund the more innovative programs which they need.

Although the higher education policy of the federal government is fragmented, and although there is no specific urban university policy, whatever federal funding develops will have as its greatest problem the urban centers where the greatest percentage of the disadvantaged potential students are located and where struggling urban universities and colleges are coming on the scene to attempt to meet the need. Community colleges, also expanding rapidly in urban areas, are performing a crucial role in higher education and presently enroll close to three million students, "at least 35 percent of the first-time college students."[20] These two-year institutions also present a challenge for federal urban higher education programs.

The federal government and foundation people have

studied the problem of developing a formula to provide funds to higher education institutions serving the disadvantaged. Specifically, the Carnegie Commission proposal was to "encourage colleges to participate more fully in the move toward equality in educational opportunities and to aid them in meeting increasing educational costs including those related to this effort." The commission recommended that "the federal government grant cost-of-education supplements to colleges and universities based on the number of students holding federal grants and enrolled in institutions." In terms of dollars, the Carnegie proposal involved a payment at 1970–71 levels of $500 per undergraduate students, $1,000 per master's level student, and $3,500 per doctoral student.[21]

In a 1969 report relating to federal support for higher education, an HEW task force proposed a more complex cost-of-education allowance of "$100 per student aided plus 25 percent of each individual grant in excess of $200. Thus, an institution's allotment for each term would be based upon the total amount of federal grants received by its students during that them."[22] The HEW group also recommended that doctoral fellowships carry a cost-of-education supplement of $5,000 and that each institution should be given a grant amounting to 25 percent of the federal funds it receives "under the NDEA loan program and the college work-study program to help offset the cost of educating federally induced enrollments."[23]

Clearly a policy of financial support for urban institutions of higher education is evolving. The trends increasing the number of students attempting to attend college in spite of the financial inability of their families to send them seem irreversible. Open admissions programs and the emphasis on equal educational opportunity and affirmative action programs directed at students are providing the opportunity for more admissions to colleges. The gap remaining is primarily financial—one the federal government is particularly qualified to fill. Meanwhile, although NIE and some other programs are concerned with substantive aspects of the problem, "muddling through" still seems to be part of our national policy.

NOTES

1. Douglas Cater, "Policy-Making in Education: A View from the White House Basement," report of a presentation to the educational staff seminar, March 1, 1971, p. 1.

2. Philip W. Semas, "Academic Leaders Politically Naive, Report Charges," *Chronicle of Higher Education,* November 13, 1972, p. 1.

3. U.S. Congress, Senate Committee on Labor and Public Welfare and House Committee on Education and Labor, *Compilation of Higher Education Laws,* November 1972, pp. 221, 245.

4. Thomas W. Adams and Thomas P. Murphy, "NASA's University Research Programs: Dilemmas and Problems on the Governmental-Academic Interface," *Public Administration Review,* March 1967, pp. 12–16.

5. Lyndon B. Johnson, "Memorandum on Strengthening Academic Capability for Science," *Weekly Compilation of Presidential Documents,* September 14, 1965.

6. Thomas P. Murphy, *Science, Geopolitics and Federal Spending* (Lexington, Mass.: D. C. Heath & Co., 1971), pp. 63–86, 111–50.

7. J. Martin Klotsche, ed., *The Urban University And the Future of Our Cities* (New York: Harper & Row, 1966), p. 51.

8. *Ibid.*

9. Clark Kerr, *The Urban-Grant University: A Model for the Future,* Number 8 of the City College Papers (New York: The City College, 1967), p. 7.

10. Daniel P. Moynihan, "Eliteland," *Psychology Today,* September 1970, p. 66.

11. Sidney P. Marland, "The Changing Role of Higher Education in America," speech given at American University, Washington, D.C., October 28, 1971.

12. Sidney P. Marland, "A Strengthening Alliance," speech given at the annual meeting of the American Council on Education, Washington, D.C., October 7, 1971.

13. *Education Amendments of 1972.* P.L. 92–318, 92d Congress, June 23, 1972, pp. 93–4.

14. Marland, "A Strengthening Alliance."

15. *Ibid.*

16. Earl F. Cheit, *The New Depression in Higher Education* (New York: McGraw-Hill, 1971), p. 131.

17. *Ibid.,* p. 132.

18. Sidney P. Marland, "Changing Role of Higher Education."

19. *Ibid.*

20. Sidney P. Marland, "Life, Work, and the Career Education Concept," speech given at the annual meeting of the American Association of Junior Colleges, Dallas, Texas, February 28, 1972.

21. Carnegie Commission on Higher Education, *The Capitol and the Campus* (New York: McGraw-Hill, 1971), p. 153.

22. U.S. Department of Health, Education, and Welfare, *Toward a Long-Range Plan for Federal Financial Support for Higher Education,* (Washington, D.C.: Government Printing Office, 1969), p. 31.

23. *Ibid.*

18

THE FUTURE URBAN UNIVERSITY

Thomas P. Murphy and M. Gordon Seyffert

Institutions of higher education have long thrived in urban areas, of course, and it is not new to suggest that education might profitably be located in major cities, where both people and educational resources are the most plentiful. And yet until recent years it has been, unfortunately, a novel suggestion to imply that metropolitan educational institutions should approach urban problems with anything more than the jaundiced eye of the impassive scholar and critic. For far too long it has been accepted practice to allow the metropolitan university or college to bask in its reputation of cosmopolitan wisdom without ever having to produce practical demonstrations of relevance to urban needs. Urban strains of the past decade have challenged the previous attitudes, so that it is now clear that "physical location is not in fact the major determinant of whether an institution qualifies as an urban university."[1] Those universities that choose to remain in the forefront of the educational field must become responsive to urban needs in the fullest sense, and one route to educational relevancy will be the provision of first-class education and professional training for the citizens and urban managers of tomorrow. This chapter explores the growing adoption of the urban university concept and some of the problems associated with that adoption.

Barriers to Change in the Educational System

For all the attention that has been focused upon urban problems, few successful solutions have yet been forthcoming from universities. Despite the oft-repeated belief that the universities have been highly concerned with the development of cures for urban ills, it appears that only palliatives have been made available so far, and that even the lowly "practitioners" have come to a quicker awareness of the problem, if not solutions. In 1969, George Arnstein noted that:

> The framers of the 1966 Model Cities program knew then what many Americans are only learning in 1969 that many of our established institutions are not tuned in to today's poor and their social needs. The welfare system is little more than a costly crutch; federally funded state employment services have produced an elaborate referral system which is not referring; schools may be serving suburban college-bound youth with upward aspirations, but they are not talking the language of urban youth in many central cities. Tax policies are not meshing with housing goals; hunger exists despite food stamps and school lunch programs, and public transportation is ensnarled by the private automobile. Worst of all, our representative political institutions are leaving too many citizens at the bottom unrepresented.[2]

Today the problems have become even more obvious, and our governmental and economic institutions have become progressively more committed to providing the managerial, legal, technological, and financial experimentation essential to progress in the struggle against urban ills. But despite the pressing need for urban involvement on the part of our large universities, many factors mitigate against their successful participation. In the first place, the university system is frequently burdened with the weight of years of passive response to change. Free of the tyranny of profit or representation objectives, universities have tended to drift, responsible only to the emphases of their inner community of scholars. To respond to the challenge of urban innovation, the university will necessarily have to develop a greater capability in planning and leadership areas than has been available under the traditional "teaching, research, and extension" models of American higher education.

The failure of the universities to plan has resulted from a long history of following rather than leading society along the path of change. Recent student disruptions and faculty restlessness have resulted in part from the refusal of universities to accept a role of leadership. Likewise, the very fact that institutions such as Columbia University and the University of Chicago should be caught unprepared for the urban crisis after decades of existence within the city suggests that universities are now, and have historically been, ill-prepared to meet urban challenges creatively.

Henry Heald describes the traditional state of mind of the university community in the urban setting as follows:

> Too often it is an attitude preoccupied with the darker elements in the situation; defensive, not infrequently apologetic; oriented more toward the avoidance of failure than the affirmative realization of large possibilities and high hopes.[3]

Perhaps it is this basic psychological flaw that accounts for an outdated faculty rewards system. In any case, it would be bad enough if the universities were hobbled only by their defensive behavior. Unfortunately such behavior generally leads to errors in judgment when responsibilities are accepted. In the current case of non-urban universities tackling urban problems, a common mishap hinges upon the failure to place the problems of the urban dweller within an urban frame of reference. Too frequently the university tries to adapt the disadvantaged person to the middle-class Protestant-ethic value structure of the suburban or small-town dweller. Similarly, after years of experience with what are called "adult education" programs, many universities still have not come around to recognizing that the needs of urban professional and disadvantaged persons are miles apart from the needs of the small-town person who desires to continue his high school education within the bounds of the standard undergraduate college program. Even urban universities have shown themselves to be unresponsive and even patronizing upon occasion, as attested by the inconsiderate use of the ghetto as a laboratory for hordes of enterprising social science graduate students. Is it any wonder that "the poor don't hate the university or even distrust it; they just ignore it, just as it ignores them"?[4]

A danger in adapting educational institutions to urban needs is that it is easy to overemphasize the service aspects of the university's mission, especially when federal funding is available for such service programs. When federal funding evaporates, however, the university is under pressure to continue responding to requests for services that do not pay their way and thus indirectly impinge upon teaching and research functions. Maintaining a balanced approach is, therefore, very difficult.

The problems are complex, and the universities are attempting to please without being sufficiently critical. Daniel P. Moynihan has described the necessary solutions to many social situations as being "counter-intuitive."[5] By this he implies that the common-sense solution proves all too often to be the incorrect solution. It used to be that half the battle came in determining the nature of the question to be asked; now it seems that the *answers* may be so complex as to be nearly impossible to derive without extremely sophisticated techniques. This is a shock to many social scientists. As Moynihan points out, the future role of the social scientist will be to "assert the *absence* of knowledge on many urgent issues of the turbulent and ambitious society we have created for ourselves."[6]

In counterpoint to the increasing complexity of problems, universities appear to be maintaining a somewhat primitive approach to service, one not even adequate to the needs of easier days of the past. The present irony is that although some of the universities may be accepting the urban challenge, either complete acceptance or complete rejection of the new role may result in equally unsatisfactory conclusions. Harold Syrett comments on the dilemma:

> In some respects, the modern college or university is viewed as a public utility into which anyone can be

plugged to obtain whatever services he or she desires. It seems that any college that subscribes to this view will permit itself to be nibbled to death. At the same time, any urban public college that fails to recognize that it has many important functions to perform in the community of which it is a part also will fail as a public institution.[7]

A final difficulty mitigating against involvement arises within the organization of the university campus itself. One of the first barriers on any campus where there is an interest in urban affairs derives from the fact that a campus is a decentralized institution. No one department or school has within its jurisdiction all of the disciplines and all of the people interested in urban affairs. Some institutions have attempted to cope with this problem by creating urban centers or schools, instituting them with a charter to become involved in urban affairs and with the opportunity for joint appointments with various departments especially interested in urban matters. This model has had some success, but it generally has proved too narrow an approach since it tends to exclude from urban involvement those whose interest and impact is spasmodic or peripheral. An alternative has been to establish a "coordinator" to help bring the diverse strengths of the university to bear on specific urban goals or programs. This approach generally provides a focal point with which to communicate with the urban community without excluding any sector of the campus. However, it fails to provide a strong enough power base for program, academic activities, or budgetary advocacy.

To date, no single ideal method of directing effectively the many talents of a university campus appears to have been found. If, as we may assume, a broad-based but coordinated effort will be the only credible candidate for success, a hybrid organizational model must soon be discovered. Even then, much of the solution necessarily will depend upon having the right people in key leadership positions.

The organizational challenge is to provide an approach that, in some way appropriate to the particular urban area, combines the advantage of a separate structure with the full opportunity for involvement of all academic departments. One criterion for evaluating the appropriateness of any organizational structure proposed will be whether it inhibits or encourages the involvement in urban affairs by all faculty members of whatever discipline who have an interest in becoming involved.

The Educational Goals Dilemma

In addition to the presence of organizational barriers, such as institutional immobility, misjudgment, insensitivity, and leadership vacuum, universities continue to be hampered in their quest for meaningful contribution by unresolved issues relating to educational goals. At variance are the opposing concepts of individual faculty autonomy and corporate responsibility.

Part of the difficulty of designating goals for the modern urban university is that the society at large still maintains ambivalent attitudes toward the role and function of the university. One group of scholars harks back to the ancient concept of the university as the medieval fortress of intellect, a separate and independent societal institution. Another encourages the involvement of universities in the most central challenges to the effective management and development of society. In between lies the great mass of the American populace, ignorant for the most part of the conflict in values. Let us now examine the two positions.

During the medieval era the university was often set apart from the town by walls or natural obstructions, and it is this physical separation that best depicts the scholarly detachment from economic and political life characteristic of those times. In this setting, the role of the university was to balance or mediate against those economic and social institutions that had become overbearing in their power and influence upon the contemporary society. Many persons in today's society would prefer to see the university resume this function of detached critic and mentor. In this concept of the university as a nurturing force behind ideas and ideals, any interaction between the university and society is viewed as potentially harmful to the independent status of the university. As Professor Irving Kristol puts it, "We want our social theorists to be bold and keen and unrestrained in the use they make of their imaginative and analytical powers. And it is precisely because we want this that we must look askance at the proposition that academic men ought, as a species, to get involved in the management of our society."[8] The objective, then, is to achieve a proper social distance between the university and surrounding elements in order that academic objectivity might be preserved and the accepted truisms of western culture be passed on to the young free from any bias imparted by conventional social problems.

But if the university as a separate and detached institution has always been a prominent concept among educators, "the free university," as ex-Senator Eugene McCarthy has said, "is more abstraction than reality."[9] Many of our colleges and universities, including particularly our oldest eastern schools, were established as religious institutions with limited purpose and have assumed their prominence and independence only through the evolution of new disciplines in non-religious fields of study. In turn, each of our newer academic institutions may be expected to attain an increasing degree of independence in academic status as new directions are charted and new capabilities are assumed. Meanwhile, the encourgement by universities of faculty collaboration with the "establishment" via everything from scholarly publications to Washington assignments has, in the opinions of men such as Senator McCarthy, corrupted the hard-earned institutional freedom of the universities. Under this doctrine the difficulties now being encountered by the universities are thought to be troubles of their own making, troubles which might have been avoided if universities had maintained their proper distance and objectivity.

Thus to the traditionalists the concept of an urban university contains unforeseen threats to the status of the university. The traditionalist proposes instead to improve the current output, rather than adopt new programs. Regarding this alternative McCarthy asserts:

> The real charge to the universities is to preserve and reconstitute the university as a center of normative, purposeful, and critical thought—free from pressures of factions, political, religious, and economic; and free, insofar as is possible, from identified errors of the past.[10]

Even if the university is not to be separated from society by the physical barriers of medieval times, a non-physical separation or detachment is still highly cherished in some quarters. According to the traditionalists, it is only in this fashion that the university might truly act as an agent of social change.

On the other side are those who seek "relevant" goals for universities. They see the educational system rapidly being outpaced by the complexities of modern life. Ten-year Asian wars, riots in the cities, environmental crises, unrest in organized religion—these and many other events are said to be the appropriate topics for university discussion. Black studies, for example, are said to be closer to the needs of the students of the seventies than would be the traditional fare of anthropology departments. Whether this is a valid claim or not has yet to be decided. In the meantime, however, the university is cast adrift in the turbulent waters of national disruptions, both on and off campus, while many widely respected persons view the prime function of the university in today's social turmoil as merely charting its path of survival. Under this view the universities are leaving the era in which they could afford the luxury of specialized high-status goals owing to the classification of higher education as a privilege reserved for the "better classes." But today, so the theory goes, university attendance has come to be recognized not as a privilege, but as a distinct right of persons who in our modern technological society must possess a college education in order to gain entry to job opportunity and social mobility.

Among those embracing the survival concept is Dr. Kenneth B. Clark, noted psychologist at the City College of New York. Dr. Clark has particularly scored the universities for their contempt of the underprivileged urban dweller in the light of our society's rapid urbanization. He, too, sees the American educational institution as maintaining the atmosphere of the medieval walled city, but does not find in this studied independence any praiseworthy traits or highly esteemed societal contributions. In fact, he portrays the American educational institution as reaping the harvest of a dangerous course of action which might have been foreseen by a more compassionate institution. He states:

> Given the persistence and deification of this detached definition of scholarship and the purposes of education, it is easy to understand how some insightful observers, both within and outside the academic community, could look upon colleges and universities as indifferent, insensitive, or even cruel as the institutions prided themselves and sought to make a virtue of their pursuit of truth and

beauty in the face of the flagrant injustices, ignorance and filth that afflicted the masses of their fellow human beings.[11]

Now the university must change in order to survive. Recent attacks upon the relevance of educational institutions may be translated as claims that the university no longer maintains a common purpose and that its educational philosophy and goals have become obsolescent in the face of problems which now threaten the very existence of the institution. Ironically, many young people see the earning of a college degree as becoming increasingly meaningless at the very time that others are clamoring for admittance to the institution. And, paradoxically, both may feel that the institution lacks a coherent statement of purpose. But whereas the first group seeks to withdraw from the influence of society, the latter finds in the very steadfastness of the educational institution a proven if somewhat imperfect path to social and economic advancement.

To insure their survival, Dr. Clark recommends that universities "must demonstrate their seriousness by resisting all temptations to engage in gimmickry, in superficial, flamboyant and 'public relations' types of programs."[12] He further states that "the chief test of the seriousness of the new programs will be the difficulty of implementing them and the amount of resistance from a variety of traditional and vested interest groups."[13]

Open Admissions

Many will judge the credibility of new programs on a theoretical basis: their success in democratizing American education. One of the educational advancements now being given highest priority by our colleges and universities is the open admissions program for educationally underprivileged students from urban areas. Although this program reaches out to satisfy immediate social needs, it, too, is a recommendation that returns us to the earliest traditions of European universities. Even though the universities then had the express purpose of training the social elites for service to the church and state, they also had the characteristic of being the foremost institutions of education in their society; in almost every case Euro-

pean universities sought to provide a liberal education for
people who had never known the luxury of effective primary
and secondary education. The problems confronted by urban
universities will be somewhat similar. Vast numbers of blacks,
Chicanos, and American Indians have not received educational opportunities commensurate with their citizenship status.
Whether this is the fault of racial discrimination or inadequate
educational services and financing is, or should be, a moot
issue for the purpose of setting national goals. In any case, it
has been determined that our future as a nation may rest upon
our ability to train and advance large numbers of underprivileged youngsters in the hopes of maintaining a stable and productive society—or, in other words, for society to survive.

The chief objection to an open admissions policy comes
from those scholars who fear that academic standards might
be lowered to oblige the needs of those whose academic qualifications are inadequate by traditional standards. There are
several rejoinders to this position. First, many years ago agricultural students were admitted to supposedly liberal-arts-
oriented colleges and universities for the purpose of upgrading
the agricultural "professions." The universities and colleges
did not break down, but distinguished themselves over a period
of 100 years for their service to the social and economic well-
being of the country. Second, universities and colleges have
a public responsibility as institutions receiving public funds to
work in support of the public welfare. Under current circumstances this would mean opening previously restricted institutions to those who most need educational opportunities. Entwined in this logic is the belief that many presently enrolled
in college are not deriving maximum benefit from their opportunity, but are remaining in college because of such factors as
prestige, parental approval, protection from the draft, and the
job safety which it promises in future years. A third basis for
refuting the allegation that disadvantaged students will lower
academic standards is the proven demonstration that such individuals, like persons everywhere, would strive to better
themselves if given adequate personal opportunities. Institutional factors may impede the progress of open admissions
programs, but no program has ever failed for lack of motivation of its students. One of the more successful examples of an
open admissions program is that of the City College of New

York, where many of the some 35,000 students presently attending this college are products of the highly-segregated black and Puerto Rican educational institutions of New York City. Most of these students make up in motivation what they lack in academic preparedness, and in many cases they also have much to offer the institution. For example, in cases where students are allowed to volunteer for tutorial programs, minority students who have offered to help their peers have often contributed more to the success of academic programs than has the institution through its traditional teaching methods.

A possible compromise in this disagreement might be offered by sharing responsibility for the equal provision of educational opportunity between universities and lesser academic institutions:

> We hear a lot of talk about open admissions these days. As is true of so much sloganeering, the talk does not include any very precise definitions. Whatever the term open admissions may mean—and it means different things to different people—it most certainly does not mean that all who apply to the university should be admitted. The old land-grant colleges tended to admit just about every high school graduate who came along and knocked at the door. They did this in part because there were no alternate opportunities. Today through the development of fairly elaborate junior college systems, we are providing alternate opportunities for the first two years of college work. If we think of the educational mission of the university as primarily one of providing liberal education and preparation for the professions (including business, government and education), we should concentrate our severely limited resources on pursuing that objective.[14]

Of course this solution offers no radical change from present policies, but rather an increasing emphasis upon the emerging needs of disadvantaged and minority citizens. Thus, while the above option may adequately serve certain areas of the country, other sections having more intense needs may employ different patterns of response.

The need for more potent open admissions programs has been amply demonstrated by comparisons of academic "productivity" in disparate sections of the country. In the mid-sixties more than 50 percent of our high school graduates continued their education in college. But in New York City, "Negro students earned only 3.7 percent of the 21,000 academic high school diplomas awarded in 1963 and Puerto Rican students earned only 1.6 percent of them," despite the fact that 32.8 percent and 24.2 percent of New York City public elementary school students are are Negro and Puerto Rican, respectively.[15] Under such conditions of gross disparity it becomes a question of social responsibility for universities to seek out students who do not seem to have an equal opportunity of receiving a college education. If universities do not serve society in this way, it is they who must bear the consequences of their decision.

Traditionally, colleges have first assumed a given academic capacity and then offered themselves and their resources to those students who were most capable of partaking of such opportunity. In today's society, however, it is suggested that a better approach would be "to identify the population that must be serviced and build a program for this group."[16] Leslie Berger has suggested that American colleges and universities might follow the prototype set forth by the SEEK (Search for Education, Elevation and Knowledge) program established in 1966 at the City University of New York, which enrolls students who do not meet the commonly accepted admittance requirements of higher education institutions in order that they might be given an opportunity to perform under favorable learning conditions.[17] The SEEK program has apparently traversed quite a distance in developing the potential of these students, "seeking" as it has to promote the integration of these persons into the university system on their merit as individuals rather than as accomplished students. For the traditionalist, a number of casualties have resulted from the change, one of which is found in the numerous curriculum revisions undertaken for the benefit of enhancing black and Puerto Rican culture. Undoubtedly, in some institutions the pendulum has swung too far.

One of the more publicized changes accepted in typical open admissions programs is the adoption of English as a second language for academic purposes. The reexamination of academic traditions necessitated by this program has prompted considerable faculty introspection, and this alone may be healthy insofar as it promotes continuing evaluation of educational objectives. The results of the open admissions program at City College have been encouraging. Berger reports that the retention rate of students who enrolled in one test group has shown that disadvantaged students can indeed succeed in classes with "regular" matriculated students.

The importance to the urban university is made obvious by the challenge to conventional standards. Dr. Berger states:

> The results of the program call into question certain notions that prevail in our educational system. The fact that most of the SEEK students were guided into general and vocational courses in high school, yet are still succeeding in college, would seem to indicate that some of the underlying assumptions of current educational philosophy and practices are in need of a thorough reassessment.
>
> It has been shown that these students can succeed academically. But that is not the only issue. The socio-political atmosphere of the United States is at a crucial stage, a crossroads. The success of this program depends perhaps upon whether the impact of the developing black consciousness on a predominantly white society results in constructive growth and action or, on the contrary, in despair.[18]

The preceding statement suggests some ideas which may transcend the more narrow notion of open admissions. The American university system is currently in need of drastic overhaul precisely because of the imbalance of services, but hopefully not to the exclusion of a more general reevaluation of the nature of educational needs. In attempting successful reform, the urban universities must account not only for the immediate needs of our nation's cities, but also for the greater societal needs of the future. Compromises between the past and the future must not be predicated solely upon immediate needs of the present, but must be so inherently sound as to withstand the test of time. Any successful reform, as John Fischer has observed, must be:

1. Founded on a single guiding concept—an idea capable of knotting together all strands of study, thus giving them both coherence and visible purpose.

2. Capable of equipping young people to do something about "what is going on in the world"—notably the things which bother them most, including war, injustice, racial conflict, and the quality of life.[19]

His conclusions will not let us rest easy. It may be that none of this is really possible. Perhaps the knowledge explosion has doomed our educational system to permanent incoherency; perhaps the only notion which will suitably unite us behind a single purpose is that of survival. We must hope that the answer is otherwise.

Whither Universities?

The role of the university in the solution of urban problems will undoubtedly expand in the future beyond the traditional roles of teaching, research, and extension. A new and fundamentally different function for the university will be to initiate dialogue between academicians and urban practitioners, acting as facilitator, coordinator, catalyst, or change agent. In part, this new task will be be accomplished through the fulfillment of traditional functions. For example, the training of many new specialists in urban problems will serve to strengthen ties between city and university. Universities located in urban areas will increasingly find it expedient to employ city administrators and other practitioners in furthering university activities, such as teaching of new urban specialists. Given the right questions, research activities of the new urban universities will also prove highly beneficial in solving urban ills.

The new emphasis will put additional strains on both the city and the university. Increasingly, both will find it necessary to justify their endeavors on the basis of the contribution rendered. Contributions from the university will increasingly consist, as Malcolm D. Talbott has indicated, of the suggestion of "alternative policy considerations."[20] This will serve to increase not only the efficiency of government but also, where participation of citizens is encouraged, its representativeness as well. Talbott points out that in helping to further the community's objectives, the university itself will be advanced.[21]

Equally as important as the promotion of new roles for the urban university will be reform of the academic rewards system to provide sufficient faculty support for urban projects. It has often been pointed out that universities give lip service to promoting promising urban endeavors but have difficulty producing action. "Publish or perish" is still heard, and many urban activists are hampered in their commitment to practical problems by the realities of faculty politics. Perhaps too little attention has been paid to the need of granting equal value to all university goals. Needless to say, adequate funding as well as adequate administrative support will be required to develop a more balanced attitude among faculty members. Only if these conditions are met will it be possible to determine which faculty members have been shackled by the existing rewards system and which ones have been using it as a convenient shield.

A lesson for universities in the 1970s is that they must lose a modicum of control in order to assert more influence. Presently, as Norton Long has said, "they serve the whole world in general and do not serve anyone in particular."[22] It appears that universities, like cities, have chosen over the years to add on program after questionable program without ever closing down those that prove unproductive or fully evaluating the impact of their decisions. Under the current financial crisis the universities are again crying for aid and comfort, but their condition is due not only to a lack of resources but also to an inability to face realistic cutbacks of ineffective or outmoded programs. As Professor Long observes, universities must now "be concerned with specific populations whose condition they hope to improve in specified ways."[23]

Several approaches are possible for the concerned administrator. He may become enamored with the notion of the university as urban citizen and partner and so strive, as the University of Chicago and Columbia have done, to become a good institutional neighbor in the local communities. Or he may choose, instead, to make a name for his school as a resource institution, providing professional consulting aid and other services. Yet assuming that universities are indeed slated to become more urban in their involvement, a fully successful commitment will be achieved not only by the "corporate citizen" or "institutional consultant" roles, but also by pursuing the primary historical function of the university—that of educator. This could be accomplished in several ways:

1. As an educator of different types of people —
primarily those who in the past have not met the normal
standards for admission.

2. By providing a different and more relevant type of
education to prepare people for life in cities and to deal
with urban problems. Here I [include] student volunteer
work in the community, the sending of students out into
the community for part of their educational experience
and black studies programs.

3. Education for public officials and technologists who
will work in cities.

4. Continuing or extension education.

5. The role of colleges in educating para-profession-
als, new careerists, and the hard-core unemployed.[24]

That the strictly educational avenue is the most probable
source of involvement is dictated by the fact that it is currently
the most popular. The newer concepts suggested by the urban-
grant university might best be examined within this context.
Hopefully, other innovations will follow the now developing
tentative gestures.

Indeed, the greatest change which has overcome the
American university in 40 years has been the immense expansion of college and university facilities made necessary by
an exploding population of college-age youths. Institutions
such as the City University of New York and the University of
California have burgeoned beyond the wildest expectations
of many older alumni. What has this expansion produced? In
the main, the result has been a critical attack by society at
large against the sin of "bigness." That such a condemnation
is patently unfair to the university is demonstrated by the in-
effectiveness of society in dealing with its own expectations.
As John Gardner has so aptly pointed out, the universities
have only responded to the grand expectations of middle-class
society; that all able-bodied youngsters should receive immediate higher education, whatever their capabilities or motivations. Facing an awesome postwar demand, universities had no
choice but to expand to meet the growth of the population,
so that "the institutions being scolded for largeness today are
the ones that have been most responsive to the American eager-

ness to broaden educational opportunities." According to Gardner, "we should have the grace to live with the consequences of our choices."[25]

The moral is clear: If the universities of today are to come to grips with the problems of tomorrow, an effort must be mounted to address questions of educational policy as well as matters of numerical significance. The problem may really be considered one of conflicting values in which opponents dispute the merits of rival approaches to change.

The concept of the urban university may be viewed in two ways. In one sense, it is simply a matter of "going where the ducks are." This view recognizes the intermediate and long-term effects of intra- and interstate migration. In a much broader sense, the urban university is a response to projected qualitative needs of the urban dweller of the future. Here the emphasis lies with the assumption that living patterns, and therefore educational needs, will be altered as the combined pressures of urban technology, employment qualifications, social interactions, and, hopefully, economic betterment impinge upon the educational values and attitudes of the individual.

And yet the history to date of the urban university appears to revolve around the quantitative, rather than the qualitative, approach to educational needs. Consider the prevailing views of the 1950s and early 1960s toward educational opportunity. The typical rationale for limiting educational opportunity to a middle-class elite follows a traditionalist logic:

> College is a privilege. Anyone who doesn't like it can leave it. Anyone who disrupts the educational process should be kicked out.

or

> I worked my way through college. I see no reason why we shouldn't raise fees. Those that are really motivated will find a way to get to college. I don't see why there should be a bigger state tax bite for public or private education or why the federal government should be using my hard-earned dollars to subsidize the education of disinterested low-ability kids from the inner city.[26]

Contrast the above logic—that educational opportunity

should be expanded only to meet the requests from the expanding middle-American community—with the qualitative approach of the "educational insurgents," who claim that "the opportunity to attend college is no longer a privilege; it's a right because so many areas of our society require a college education in order to gain entry. . . . A democratic society depends upon a well-educated public, and we must try to educate everyone to the maximum extent possible—even the disinterested, poorly equipped, low-ability inner city kids."[27]

Conflicting values are highly evident here, and the resolution of differences will be crucial to the successful marriage of university and metropolis. What few planners realize is that the designation of the university as the source of all training and knowledge is *not* an accomplished fact. Among those capable of perceiving the "threat" to the position of the university is William Birenbaum, who notes that:

> In most cities, public libraries, for example, are more extensive and accessible compendiums of knowledge than the universities. Many urban art museums possess both scholars and treasures far superior to those possessed by the universities. Practicing politicians sometimes display far greater wisdom and teaching talent than practicing political scientists. Throughout American urban society, many institutions other than the universities provide laboratories and workshops for some of the nation's keenest minds. Beyond the universities, one need only look to the Pentagon, Solidarity House, the Rand Corporation and other "think tanks," the Committee on Economic Development, the Twentieth Century Fund, or the General Motors Technical Center to grasp what is essentially a point about the competition for talent.[28]

The implication is clear. There is little question, as Samuel Gould has noted, "that national destiny is shaping today's universities, rather than the other way around."[29] Our present methods of responding to the urban crisis represent merely a patchwork approach, a solution which is really not a solution but instead a mere temporary "fix." As with our scientific and technological advancements, educational policies of the future will have to undergo a process of assessment to prove viable within the urban setting.

If directing the course of educational development today seems a difficult task, the educational planner may take heart in the fact that his job is no more difficult than that of forecasters everywhere. It would seem that behind most of the flowing speeches and glib articles seeking to examine the needs of future urban universities there exists a common erroneous assumption found throughout America today. All of our best projections and estimates of future need, the forecasters would have us believe, may be trustingly constructed upon simple extrapolations of present needs and educational parameters. Implicit in this assumption is the belief that we will grow in the future as we have grown in the past, that what is good for today will be good for tomorrow. The problem is that our present educational system was, in fact, built upon this very same assumption. Thus, our educational institutions are founded upon an outdated educational philosophy.

NOTES

1. C. Brice Ratchford, "The University's Role in Urban Problems," speech given at the University of Missouri Intercampus Urban Seminar, St. Louis, Missouri, March 25, 1971.

2. George Arnstein, 'Colleges Can Re"ach Out to Troubled Cities with Action, Assistance, Analysis," *College & University Business,* September 1969, p. 51.

3. Henry Heald, "The Universities' Role in Reshaping American Cities," in J. Martin Klotsche, ed., *The Urban University And the Future of Our Cities* (New York: Harper & Row, 1966), p. 21.

4. Arnstein "Colleges Can Reach Out," p. 59.

5. Daniel P. Moynihan, "Eliteland," *Psychology Today,* September 1970, p. 68.

6. *Ibid.*

7. Harold C. Syrett, "Challenges Facing Urban Universities," *School & Society,* February 1970, p. 90.

8. Irving Kristol, "Toward Universities for Education," *Current,* May 1970, p. 54.

9. Eugene J. McCarthy, "The Real Failing of Our Universities," *Harvard Alumni Bulletin,* September 15, 1969, p. 26.

10. *Ibid.,* p. 28.

11. Kenneth B. Clark, "The Governance of Universities in the Cities of Man," *American Scholar,* Autumn 1970, p. 566.

12. *Ibid.,* p. 568.

13. *Ibid.*

14. James C. Olson, "Urban Concerns and the Urban University," proceedings of the Inter-vampus seminar on urban problem-solving, Kansas City, Missouri, February 16–17, 1970, p. 29.

15. Leslie Burger, "University Programs for Urban Black and Puerto Rican Youth," *Educational Recrod,* Fall 1968, p. 382.

16. *Ibid.,* p. 383.

17. *Ibid.*

18. *Ibid.,* p. 388.

19. John Fischer, "Survival U: Prospectus for a Really Relevant University," *Harper's,* September 1969, p. 12.

20. Malcolm D. Talbott, "The Role of the University in the Solution of Urban Problems," speech given at the inter-campus seminar on urban problem-solving, Kansas City, Missouri, December 12, 1968.

21. *Ibid.*

22. Norton E. Long, "The University and Its Urban Constituency: The Land Grant Tradition in an Urban Setting," speech given at the University of Missouri-Inter-Campus Urban Seminar, St. Louis, Missouri, March 25, 1971.

23. *Ibid.*

24. George Nash, "The Role of the Title I Program in University Involvement in the Urban Crisis," speech given at the state Title I directors' meeting, Hot Springs, Arkansas, October 1969.

25. John W. Gardner, "Agenda for the Colleges and Universities," in Alvin C. Eurich, ed., *Campus 1980* (New York: Delacorte Press, 1968), p. 5.

26. E. Laurence Chalmers, Jr., "Reconciling the Value Conflict in the United States," speech given at the Kansas City Press Club, Kansas City, Missouri, February 20, 1971.

27. *Ibid.*

28. William Birenbaum, "Cities and Universities: Collision of Crises," in Eurich, ed., *Campus 1980,* p. 55.

29. Samuel B. Gould, "The Modern University: Concerns for the Future," *Science,* March 24, 1967, p. 1511.

Bibliography

BOOKS AND REPORTS

Abrahamson, Julia, *A Neighborhood Finds Itself* (New York: Harper & Brothers, 1959)

Brunsman, Howard G., "The 1970 Census of Population and Housing: Choices Made and to be Made," *Proceedings of the Third Annual Information Systems and Programs,* 1965.

——*Bulletin,* 1971, Walden University.

Carnegie Commission on Higher Education, *The Capitol and the Campus,* April 1971, p. 153.

Carnegie Commission on Higher Education, *New Students and New Places,* October 1971, p. 25.

Carter, Douglas, "Policy-Making in Education: A View From the White House Basement," a report of a presentation to the Educational Staff Seminar, March 1, 1971.

Cassella, William N., Jr., "An Urban Research for the New York Metropolitan Region, in *Urban Research and Education in the New York Metropolitan Region,* Vol. 11. A report to the Regional Plan Association.

————"Catalog of Courses, Fall 1966," Experimental College at San Francisco State.

Charlton, H. B., *Portrait of a University, 1851-1951s To Commemorate the Centenary of Manchester University* (Manchester, Eng.: University Press, 1951).

Cheit, Earl F., *The New Depression in Higher Education,* (New York: McGraw-Hill Book Co., 1971.)

Clinard, Marshal B., *Slums and Community Development: Experiments in Self-Help.* (New York: The Free Press, 1966).

————Communiversity, Fall '72, the course catalog, UMKC Communiversity.

Devonshire, the Duke of, President of Owens College, "The President's Speech," in *Record of the Jubilee Celebrations at Owens College* Manchester, for the Committee of the Owens College Union Magazine (Manchester, Eng.: Sheratt and Hughes, 1902).

Dickenson, Robert E., *The City Region in Western Europe* (London: Routledge and Kegan Paul, Ltd., 1967).

Doll, Russell C. and Levine, Daniel U., "Toward a Definition of Structure in the Education of Disadvantaged Students," in A. H. Passow, ed., *Opening Opportunities for Disadvantaged Learners* (New York: Teachers College, 1972).

DuBois, W.E.B., *The Souls of Black Folks,* (London: Longmans, Green and Co., 1965).

————*A Fact Book on Higher Education* (Washington, DC., American Council on Education, 1969).

Floud, Jean, "The Robbins Report and the Reform of Higher Education in Britain," George Z. Bereday and Joseph A. Lauwerys, eds., *The World Yearbook of Education 1967: Educational Planning,* (London: Evans Brothers Limited, 1967).

Geddes, Patrick, *Cities in Evolution,* New and Revised Edition, (New York: Howrad Fertig Inc., 1949).

Grattan, C. Hartley, *In Quest of Knowledge: A Historiacl Perspective on Adult Education,* (New York, Association Press, 1955).

Greenberger, Martin, ed., *Computers and the World of the Future,* (see especially part 4, "A Library for 2,000 A.D.), (the MIT Press, Cambridge, Mass., 1962).

Heald, Henry, "The Universities' Role in Reshaping American

Cities," in J. Martin Klotsche, ed., *The Urban University: And the Future of Our Cities,* (New York: Harper & Rowe, 1966).

Hennessy, Bernard, *Political Internships: Theory, Practice, Qualification,* (University Park: Penn State University Press, 1970).

Houston, Robert W. and Howsam, Robert B., eds., *Competency-Based Teacher Education: Progress, Problems, and Prospects* (Chicago: Science Research Associates, 1972).

Hunt, David E., *Matching Models in Education: The Coordination of Teaching Methods with Student Characteristics* (Ontario Institute for Studies in Education, 1970).

Jacobson, Elden E. and Palmer, Parker J., *Urban Curricula and the Liberal Arts College,* Washington Center for Metropolitan Studies—Department of Higher Education, National Councli of Churches, 1971.

Kerr, Clark, *The Urban-Grant University: A Model for the Future,* Number 8 of the City College Papers (New York: The City College, 1968).

Klotsche, J. Martin, ed., *The Urban University: And the Future of Our Cities* (New York: Harper & Row, 1966).

Knowles, Asa S., *Handbook of College and University Administration-General* (New York: McGraw-Hill Book Company, 1970).

Laidler, Josephine and Skemp, A.R., "Historical Sketch of the Owens College, 1851-1902," in *Record of the Jubilee Celebrations at Owens College Manchester,* for the Committee of the Owens College Union Magazine (Manchester, End.: Sherratt and Hughes, 1902).

Illich, Ivan, *Deschooling Society* (New York: Harper & Row, 1971).

Lauter, Paul and Howe, Florence, *The Conspiracy of the Young,* (New York and Cleveland, The World Publishing Co., 1970).

Lichtman, Jane, *The Free University Directory,* Washington, D.C. American Association for Higher Education, 1972.

Madison, James, *The Federalist,* (New York: The Heritage Press, 1945).

Magian, A. C., *An Outline of The History of Owens College* (Manchester: Pontefract Brothers, 1931).

Medhurst, Franklin, and Lewis J. Parry, *Urban Decay: An*

Analysis and a Policy (London: Macmillan and Company, Ltd., 1969).

Municipal Manpower Commission, *Governmental Manpower In Tomorrow's Cities,* (New York: McGraw-Hill, 1962).

Montague, Peter, "Civil and Mechanical Engineering," in John Knapp, Michael Swanton, and F. R. Jevons, eds., *University Perspectives,* (Manchester, Eng.: Manchester University Press and New York: Barnes and Noble, 1970).

Murphy, Thomas P., *Government Management Internships and Executive Development* (Boston: D. C. Heath and Co., 1971).

———*Operations Manual,* Campus Free College, July 1972.

Perloff, Harvey S., "University Urban Programs: An Overview," *Corporation Role with University and Community,* National Association of Manufacturers, Spring 1972.

Rossi, Peter and Dentler, Robert, *The Politics of Urban Renewal: The Chicago Findings* (New York: The Free Press of Glencoe, Inc., 1961).

Slayton, William L., "The University, The City, and Urban Renewal," in Charles G. Dobbins, ed., *The University, The City, and Urban Renewal* (Washington, D.C.: American Council on Education, 1964).

Soar, Robert S., "Teacher-Pupil Interaction," in James R. Squire, ed., *A New Look at Progressive Education* (Washington, D.C., Association for Supervision and Curriculum Development, 1972).

Simon, Lady Shena of Wythenshawe, "Manchester," in William A. Robson, ed., *Great Cities of the World: Their Government, Politics and Planning,* (London: George Allen and Unwin, Ltd., 1954), p. 326.

Snow, C. P. *The Masters* (New York: Charles Scribner's Sons, 1951).

Taylor, Ralph H., "Defining and Implementing the Urban Observatories Concept," in Steven B. Sweeney and James Charlesworth, eds., *Governing Urban Society: New Scientific Approaches,* The American Academy of Political and Social Science, Philadelphia, 1967.

———University Without Walls, February 1972, pp. 10–34, Union for Experimenting Colleges nad Universities.

Vermilye, Dychman W., *The Expanded Campus* (San Francisco, Calif.: Jossey-Bass Co., 1972).

Webster, Noah, "An Examination into the Leading Principles of the Federal Constitution Proposed by the Late Convention Held at Philadelphia," 1887.

Wood, Robert C. "Contributions of Political Science to Urban Form," in Werner Z. Hirsch, ed., *Urban Life and Form,* (New York: Holt Rinehart and Winston Inc., 1963).

GOVERNMENT PUBLICATIONS

Commission on Adult Basic Education, Adult Education Association of the U.S.A., *Newsletter,* Vol. 2, Fall, 1972).

Education Amendments of 1972. P. L. 92-318, 92d Congress, June 23, 1972.

President Lyndon B. Johnson, Executive Order 11246, September 24, 1965, as amended, Section 202 (1).

Intergovernmental Personnel Act of 1970, 84 Stat, 1969. This was S. 11, 91st Congress, signed by the President on January 5, 1971.

U.S. Civil Service Commission Bureau of Intergovernmental Personnel Programs, "Temporary Intergovernmental Assignments under the Intergovernmental Personnel Act," a Report to the President, September 1, 1972.

U.S. Congress, Senate Bill 2134, 92d Congress, Reprinted in the *Congressional Record* of February 8, 1972, Vol. 118, no. 16.

U.S. Congress, U.S. Senate Committee on Labor & Public Welfare, Conference Report No. 92-798, May 22, 1972.

U.S. Congress, Senate Committee on Labor and Public Welfare and House Committee on Education and Labor, *Compilation of Higher Education Laws,* November 1972.

U.S. Department of Health, Education and Welfare, Bureau of Educational Research and Development and the National Center for Educational Statistics, *Earned Degrees Conferred: Bachelor's and Higher Degrees, 1960-69* (Washington, D.C., U.S. Government Printing Office, 1971).

U.S. Department of Health, Education and Welfare, *Higher Education Guidelines for Executive Order 11246,* 1972.

U.S. Department of Health, Education and Welfare, Office of Education, *Program IMPACT Report,* Community Service and Continuing Education, Higher Education Act of 1965—Title I, 1972.

U.S. Department of Health, Education and Welfare, Office of Education, *Opening Fall Enrollment in Higher Education, 1967, Supplement A:* Undergraduate and Postbaccalaureate Students, by Marjorie O. Chandler and Mabel C. Rice (Washington, D.C.: U.S. Government Printing Office, 1968).

U.S. Department of Health, Education and Welfare, Organization for Social and Technical Innovation, *Urban Universities: Rhetoric, Reality, and Conflict,* June, 1970.

U.S. Department of Labor, *Manpower: Challenge of the* VTFJS (Washington, D.C.: U.S. Government Printing Office, 1960).

Lyndon B. Johnson, "Memorandum on Strengthening Academic Capability for Science," *Weekly Compilation of Presidential Documents,* September 14, 1965.

ARTICLES AND SPEECHES

Adams, Thomas W. and Murphy, Thomas P. "NASA's University Research Programs: Dilemmas & Problems on the Governmental-Academic Interface," *Public Administration Review,* March 1967.

Aleshire, Robert, "The Metropolitan Desk: A New Technique of Program Teamwork," *Public Administration Review,* June 1966.

Andrews, L. O., "A Curriculum to Produce Career Teachers for the 1980s"; *Theory Into Practice,* VI, 5 (December 1967).

Arnstein, George, "Colleges Can Reach Out to Troubled Cities With Action, Assistance, Analysis," *College & University Business,* September 1969.

Bailey, Stephen K., "Teachers' Centers: A British First," *Phi Delta Kappan,* v. 51, no. 3 (November 1971).

Bereiter, Carl, "Schools Without Education," *Harvard Educational Review* v. 42, no. 3 (August 1972).

Boleratz, Julia and East, Marjorie, "A Cross-Cultural and Cross-Class Experience for Preteachers," *The Journal of Teacher Education,* v. 20, no. 4 (Winter 1969).

Burchinal, Lee G and Haswell, Harold A., "How to Put Two and a Half Tons of Research Into One Handy Little Box," *American Education,* Volume 2, Number 2, February 1966.

Berger, Leslie, "University Programs for Urban Black and Puerto Rican Youth, *Educational Record,* Fall 1968.

Bryant, James W., "A Survey of Black American Doctorates," Division of Education and Research, Ford Foundation, Sept. 5, 1969.

Cohen, Albert, Chairman, Commission on University Governance, University of Connecticut, in a letter to Homer Babbidge, Jr., 1970.

Clark, Kenneth B., "The Governance of Universities in the Cities of Man," *The American Scholar,* Autumn, 1970.

Davey, Thomas J., "Determining Priorities and Developing Basic Research on Urban Problems," in Stephen B. Sweeney and James C. Charlesworth, eds., *Governing Urban Society: New Scientific Approaches,* The American Academy of Political and Social Science, Philadelphia, 1967.

————"Faculties Divided on Recruiting More Women, Blacks, Chicanos," *The Chronicle of Higher Education,* Nov. 13, 1972.

Fairfield, Roy P., "Quality Control and/or Health in Union

Graduate School," unpublished working paper, 1971.

Fischer, John, "Survival U: Prospectus for a Really Relevant University," *Harper's Magazine,* September 1969.

Fuller, Frances F., "Concerns of Teachers: A Developmental Conceptualization," *American Educational Research Journal,* v. 6, no. 2, (March 1969).

Gardner, John at inauguration of James Perkins at Cornell, October 4, 1963.

Getz, Howard, et al., "From Traditional to Competency-Based Teacher Education," *Phi Delta Kappan,* v. 54, no. 5 January 1973).

Gosling, David, "Appraisal: Precinct Centre, Manchester," *The Architects' Journal,* XLIX (December 6, 1972).

Gould, Samuel B., "The Modern University: Concerns for the Future," *Science,* March 24, 1967, p. 1511.

Hampton, Robert E., "Partners in Problem Solving: The Essence of the IPA," *Civil Service Journal,* April-June 1971, pp. 1-4.

Holden, Constance, "Women in Michigan: Parlaying Rights into Power," *Science,* vol. 178, p. 964.

Ingram, Timothy H. "Fair Employment: The Machinery Continues to Rust," *Washington Monthly,* December 1972, p. 44.

Jacob, Herbert and Lipsky, Michael, "Outputs, Structure, and Power: An Assessment of Changes in the Study of State and Local Politics," *Journal of Politics,* 30, No. 2 (May 1968).

Jenkins, Martin, "The Involvement of Colleges and Universities in Model Cities and Community Development Programs," unpublished report for Model Cities, Title 1— Comprehensive Planning Conference, Kansas City, Missouri, Jan. 27, 1972.

Jobling, R. G., "The Location and Siting of a New University," *Universities Quarterly,* XXIV (Spring, 1970).

Kalish, James A. "Flim-Flam, Double-Talk, and Hustle: The Urban Problems Industry," *The Washington Monthly,* November, 1969.

Keyes, Ralph, "The Free Universities," *The Nation,* October 2, 1967.

Knowles, Asa S., "Change in the Traditional Concepts of Higher Education," *School and Society,* November 1971.

Kristol, Irving, "Toward Universities for Education," *Current,* May 1970.

Lauter, Paul and Howe, Florence, "What Happened to the Free University," *Saturday Review,* June 20, 1970.

Lindsay, Leon, "Urban Corps Fights for Survival," *Christian Science Monitor,* August 26, 1964.

Long, Norton E., "The University and Its Urban Constituency: The Land Grant Tradition in an Urban Setting," Speech, University of Missouri Inter-campus Urban Seminar, St. Louis, Missouri, March 25, 1971.

McCarthy, Eugene J., "The Real Failing of Our Universities," *Harvard Alumni Bulletin,* September 15, 1969.

"College Students in Local Government," *Management Information Service,* ICMA, March 1972.

Marland, Sidney P., "A Strengthening Alliance," a speech to the annual meeting of the American Council on Education, Washington, D.C., October 7, 1971.

Marland, Sidney P., "The Changing Role of Higher Education in America," a speech at American University, Washington, D.C., October 28, 1971.

Marland, Sidney P., "Life, Work, and the Career Education Concept," speech to annual meeting of the American Association of Junior Colleges, Dallas, Texas, February 28, 1972.

Maund, Robert, City Planning Officer, the Corporation of Manchester, quoted in the Manchester *Guardian,* November 9, 1967.

Moten, Chauncey D., "A Study of Perceived Changes in Behavior, Attitudes and Outlooks as Related to Participation in a University—Conducted Four Year New Careers Program," The University of Michigan, August, 1972.

Moynihan, Daniel P., "Eliteland," *Psychology Today,* September, 1970.

Nasa, George, "The Role of the Title I Program in University Involvement In Urban Crisis," Speech, State Title I Directors Meeting, Hot Springs, Arkansas, October, 1969.

National Academy of Public Administration, *Evaluation of the Urban Observatory Program,* November 1, 1971.

National Associations of Schools of Public Affairs and Administration, *Public Affairs and Administration Programs, 1971–72 Survey Report* Washington, D.C., June 1972.

National University Extension Association *Newsletter,* Vol. IV, Number 26, December 31, 1971.

National Advisory Council on Extension and Continuing Education, Sixth Annual Report of the National Advisory Council on Extension and Continuing Education Pursuant to Public Law 89–329, 1972.

Netzer, Dick, "A Metropolitan Statistical Center: Purposes and Functions," in *Urban Research and Education in the New York Metropolitan Region* Vol. II. A Report to the Regional Plan Association 1966.

Olson, James C., "Urban Concerns and the Urban University," Proceedings Inter-campus Seminar on Urban Problem Solving, February 16–17, 1970, Kansas City, Missouri.

Pattison, Mark, "On Education," a speech before the Social Science Congress on 13, October 1876.

Pilcher, Paul S., "What We Must Do: A Mobilization of Scientists as in Wartime May Be the Only Way to Solve Our Crisis Problems, *Ekistics,* Vol. 28, No. 169, December 1969.

———"Public's Confidence in Educators Drops," *The Chronicle of Higher Education,* Vol. VII, Number 11, December 4, 1972.

Ratchford, Brice, "The University's Role in Urban Problems," Speech, the University of Missouri Inter-campus Urban Seminar, St. Louis, Missouri, March 25, 1971.

Rossi, Alice, Speech, at Barnard College Conference on Women, 1970.

Semas, Phillip W., "Academic Leaders Politically Naive, Report Charges," *Chronicle of Higher Education,* November 13, 1972.

Small, Hazel C., "Special Programs As Research," *Adult Leadership,* December 1972, Vol. 21, Number 6.

Smith, B. O., *Teachers for the Real World* (Washington, D.C.: American Association of Colleges for Teacher Education, 1969).

Somit, Albert and Tanenhaus, Joseph, "Trends in American

Political Science: Some Analytical Notes," *American Political Science Review,* LVII, No. 4 December 1963.

Syracuse University, *Memo From Syracuse,* Adult and Continuing Education Report, No. 1, August 1972.

Steggert, Frank X., "Urban Observatories: An Experiment in Institutional Building," Speech prepared for delivery at the 1969 National Conference of the American Society for Public Administration, Miami Beach, Florida, May 19, 1969.

Stone, Donald C., *The Response of Higher Education to the Administrative Needs of the Public Service* (Washington, D.C.: National Association of Schools of Public Affairs and Administration, April 1971).

Students for a Democratic Society, *The Port Huron Statement,* August 1963.

Syrett, Harold C., "Challenges Facing Urban Universities," *School and Society,* February 1970.

Taher, Grace M., ed., *University Urban Research Centers,* 2nd Edition, 1971-72 (Washington, D.C.: The Urban Institute, 1971).

Talbott, Malcolm D., "The Role of the University in the Solution of Urban Problems," Speech, Inter-campus Seminar on Urban Problems.

Trombley, William, "Role of Professors Cited by Lippmann," *The Washington Post,* Monday, May 9, 1966, (Quoting Walter Lippmann).

Trow, Martin, "The Democratization of Higher Education in America," European Journal of Sociology, Vol. 3, No. 2 (1962).

About the Editor

Thomas P. Murphy is Executive Director of the Institute for Urban Studies, and Professor of Government and Politics at the University of Maryland, College Park, Maryland. From 1966 to 1971, he was Assistant to the Chancellor for Urban Affairs, Director of Graduate Public Administration Programs, and Professor of Public Administration, at the University of Missouri, Kansas City. He was also Executive Director of the Commission on Organization of Jackson County, Missouri, 1967–1969, and County Manager of Jackson County for six months in 1969.

From 1961 to 1966, he was at the National Aeronautics and Space Administration as Staff Assistant to NASA Administrator, James E. Webb, Assistant to the Associate Deputy Administrator, Dr. George L. Simpson, Jr., and Deputy Assistant Administrator for Legislative Affairs. His earlier government experience includes work with the Federal Aviation Agency, the U.S. General Accounting Office, the U.S. Air Force, and the Internal Revenue Service.

Dr. Murphy received his Ph.D. in Political Science from St. John's University, New York, in 1963, his M.A. from Georgetown University in 1960, and his B.A. from Queens College in 1952. His articles on Congress, politics, urban affairs, budgeting, and organizational structure have appeared in *Trans-action, The Economist, Western Political Quarterly, Ethics, Public Administration Review, Administrative Science Quarterly, Contemporary Review, Review of Politics, Union Theological Quarterly, Natural Resources Journal, New Leader, and Polity.* His prior books include *Metropolitics and the Urban County* (1970), *Emerging Patterns in Urban Administration* (1970), *Science, Geopolitics and Federal Spending* (1971), *Pressures Upon Congress* (1972), and *Government Management Internships and Executive Development* (1973).

He has been active not only as a professor and an administrator but also as a citizen-participation, planning, management, organization, training, and budgetary consultant at the federal, state, and local levels. Primary involvements have been with the U.S. Department of Housing and Urban Development, the Office of Economic Opportunity, and state, city, and county governments in Alabama, California, Iowa, Kansas, Maryland, and Missouri.

About the Contributors

Homer D. Babbidge is Master of Timothy Dwight College at Yale University. He is also lecturer in American Studies and a Fellow of the Center for Educational Studies at Yale. From 1962 to 1972, Dr. Babbidge was President of the University of Connecticut. He was an assistant to the Secretary of the Department of Health, Education and Welfare (1957–58) and subsequently became Assistant U.S. Commissioner of Education and Director of the Division of Higher Education (1959-61). Dr. Babbidge is a member of the American Studies Association, the American Historical Association, the Council of Advisors, National Scholarship Fund for Negro Students, the National Board of Advisors, the National Association for Retarded Children, and a trustee of the Hazen Foundation. He is the author of *Noah Webster: On Being American,* published by Praeger in 1967, and is co-author (with Robert M. Rosenzweig) of *The Federal Interest in Higher Education,* published by McGraw-Hill in 1962. Dr. Babbidge received his B.A. (1945), M.A. (1947), and Ph.D. (1953) from Yale University.

Peter Spang Goodrich is a Ph.D. candidate in the Department of Government, University of Manchester, England. His interest in the relationship of the City of Manchester to its university stems in part from his previous experience as a research assistant at the Institute for Urban Studies, University of Maryland. He is also currently conducting research on British attitudes toward European integration after joining the European Community. This complements a previous longitudinal analysis of British opinion on Europe from 1952 to 1972, which he completed for his M.A. thesis at the University of Maryland. Mr. Goodrich also holds an M.B.A. in Management from Western New England College and an A.B. in American Government from Georgetown University.

Samuel C. Jackson, former General Assistant Secretary of the U.S. Department of Housing and Urban Development, recently became a member of the law firm of Stroock and Stroock and Lavan. While in the Department of Housing and Urban Development, Mr. Jackson had department-wide responsibilities for the development and implementation of basic policies for all HUD housing, planning, and development programs. He was one of the original commissioners of the U.S. Equal Employment Opportunity Commission, serving from June 1965 to June 1968. Mr. Jackson received his law degree from Washburn University in 1954.

Elizabeth A. Knipe is currently the Washington Research Representative for Chilton Research Services of Philadelphia. From 1969 to 1971, she was a research assistant for the National Academy of Public Administration. While at the Academy, Miss Knipe concentrated on education training programs in the federal (including the Federal Executive Institute) as well as state and local governments. From 1963 to 1967, she worked as a staff assistant to the director of the Senate Juvenile Delinquency Subcommittee for the U.S. Senate. Miss Knipe received a B.A. degree from Trinity College in Washington in 1959 and an M.P.A. from University of Missouri, Kansas City, in 1969.

Daniel U. Levine is Professor of Education and Director of the Center for the Study of Metropolitan Problems in Education at the University of Missouri, Kansas City. He joined the University of Missouri after teaching in the Chicago public schools and serving as an associate on the Chicago School

Survey in 1963. He has been a consultant on several experimental programs for training urban teachers, and is the co-author of *Education in Metropolitan Areas.*

Martin Mayer was graduated in 1947 from Harvard, where he majored in economics and also studied philosophy and music. After working as a reporter and editor for several publications, he became a free-lance writer in 1954.

Mr. Mayer is the author of two novels and three reportorial studies, including *Madison Avenue, U.S.A., The Schools,* and *The Lawyers.* His articles on education, business, television, music, law, and other subjects have appeared in *Esquire* (for which he writes a monthly column about music), *Harper's, Saturday Evening Post, TV Guide, Better Homes and Gardens, Life, The New York Times Magazine, Horizon, Musical America, The Reporter,* and *Commentary,* among others.

From 1961 to 1965, Mr. Mayer was a member of the Panel on Educational Research and Development in the Executive Office of the President, and from 1962 to 1967, he was chairman of a New York City local school board. His book *Social Studies in American Schools* is based on his work as a consultant to the American Council of Learned Societies in 1961–62. He was director of a study of international secondary education for the Twentieth Century Fund.

Gordon Seyffert is a recent graduate of the M.P.A. program of the University of Missouri, Kansas City. He is presently working for the Center for Management Development, the continuing education arm of the UMKC School of Administration. Previously Mr. Seyffert has served as a community development agent for the University of Missouri Extension Division, and as a research assistant in the Chancellor's Office for Urban Affairs at UMKC. He is currently interested in the impact of Congress and the state legislatures upon urban affairs, and the means by which urban "solutions" are tested and adopted by urban institutions

George E. Spear is Associate Dean, Continuing Education and Extension, and assistant professor of education at the University of Missouri, Kansas City. A former newsman and editor,

Dr. Spear has been involved with urban adult education since 1965. He was a Mott fellowship intern and received his Ph.D. in adult and community education from the University of Michigan.

He served on a four-member task force in 1972 that studied and made recommendations for developing a comprehensive urban thrust for UMKC and is a member of that institution's advisory council on urban affairs. A national research project on adult basic education teacher training was completed in 1972 under his direction, and he is director of the new Center for Resource Development in Adult Education, funded by the U.S. Office of Education. He has also served as a consultant on public school desegregation.

Warren W. Willingham is the executive director for Program Research, Educational Testing Service of Princeton, New Jersey. He is also the consulting editor for the *American Educational Research Journal* and the *Journal of Educational Measurement*. From 1968 to 1972, Dr. Willingham served as the senior psychologist and director of the College Entrance Examination Board (CEEB). He also was director of research for CEEB from 1964 to 1968. Dr. Willingham was a member for the National Council on Measurement in Education from 1968 to 1971. His books include *Free Access Higher Education* (1970) and *The Source Book for Higher Education: A Critical Guide to Literature and Information on Access to Higher Education* (1972). Dr. Willingham received his B.S. from the Georgia Institute of Technology in 1952 and his Ph.D. from the University of Tennessee in 1955.

James Zarnowiecki is currently serving as a Washington Intern in Education with the National Advisory Council on Vocational Education. His preparation as an educator ranges from junior high and secondary high school teaching to public administration in the Shawnee Mission Public Schools in Metropolitan Kansas City. His interest in citizen involvement and participation has involved him in internships. In this vein, his latest projects involve popular education at the Smithsonian and a Handbook for the School District Ombudsman. James Zarnowiecki received an A.B. from Loyola University of Chicago in 1966, and an M.Ed. from Xavier.